# Steward of a Living Tradition

"Few are as well positioned to write of stewarding a living tradition of Catholic education as John Sullivan. Sullivan brings a lifetime of reflection to bear on concrete questions of how educational practice can be a contemporary participation in the Gospel and engagement with a Christian conversation stretching back across the centuries. He ranges across matters of pedagogy, leadership, curriculum, learning, vocation, and more, bringing careful Christian engagement to each. There is much here worth pondering and working into our practices."

—DAVID I. SMITH,
Director, Kuyers Institute for Christian Teaching and Learning,
Calvin University

"Professor Sullivan's latest book, *Steward of a Living Tradition*, captures the delicate balancing-act of ensuring that the voices of tradition can continue to speak fluently to contemporary scholars. This collection of essays is essential reading for all with an interest in the relationship between liberal studies and education. It confirms the author's status as one of the most engaging, informative, and coherent thinkers in the world of Catholic educational studies."

—LEONARDO FRANCHI,
Lecturer of Pedagogy, Praxis, and Faith, University of Glasgow

"This book presents some of the key publications of over twenty-five years of scholarship devoted to research on Christian faith, theology, and Christian education. Topics range from medieval wisdom and monasticism to Blondel and Newman and a rich engagement with some major themes in Catholic education including leadership and vocation. These selected articles and book chapters are the product of the exemplary career of Professor John Sullivan, a leading thinker in Catholic theology and education."

—STEPHEN MCKINNEY,
Professor, School of Education, University of Glasgow

"This book is a collection of beautifully written, accessible, eminently readable and scholarly chapters. It is essential reading for those interested in how Christian faith and theological understanding relate to educational practice. The book is a testament to and a record of John Sullivan's exceptional lifetime's work as a Christian educator in secondary schools, universities and in the church."

—PATRICIA KIERAN,
Associate Professor, Mary Immaculate College

"Sullivan's skill lies in his ability to combine lived experience of Catholic education with the theological and human aspects needed to bring credibility to the sector in times of change, challenge, and mistrust. This book is an excellent road map for anyone who genuinely wants to become a 'living logo' and authentic leader in the Catholic educational sector these days. It will help them to strategically ground respect for people as the key linchpin around which everything else rotates. *Steward of a Living Tradition* is a must read for all involved across the Catholic sector these days!"

—ANN MARIE MEALEY,
Director of Catholic Mission, Leeds Trinity University

"In *Steward of a Living Tradition*, John Sullivan presents the choicest fruits of his distinguished career exploring what might constitute a truly Christian approach to education. Winsomely erudite, theologically rich, and at times deeply pastoral, this book will be treasured by generations of those seeking to advance the work of connecting the Christian faith with the task of education."

—KYLE R. HUGHES,
Lecturer in New Testament, Reformed Episcopal Seminary

# Steward of a Living Tradition

*Christian Scholarship and Educational Practice*

JOHN SULLIVAN

☙PICKWICK *Publications* · Eugene, Oregon

STEWARD OF A LIVING TRADITION
Christian Scholarship and Educational Practice

Copyright © 2025 John Sullivan. All rights reserved. Except for brief quotations in critical publications or reviews, no part of this book may be reproduced in any manner without prior written permission from the publisher. Write: Permissions, Wipf and Stock Publishers, 199 W. 8th Ave., Suite 3, Eugene, OR 97401.

Pickwick Publications
An Imprint of Wipf and Stock Publishers
199 W. 8th Ave., Suite 3
Eugene, OR 97401

www.wipfandstock.com

PAPERBACK ISBN: 979-8-3852-3555-1
HARDCOVER ISBN: 979-8-3852-3556-8
EBOOK ISBN: 979-8-3852-3557-5

*Cataloguing-in-Publication data:*

Names: Sullivan, John, 1949–, author.

Title: Steward of a living tradition : Christian scholarship and educational practice / John Sullivan.

Description: Eugene, OR: Pickwick Publications, 2025 | Includes bibliographical references and index.

Identifiers: ISBN 979-8-3852-3555-1 (paperback) | ISBN 979-8-3852-3556-8 (hardcover) | ISBN 979-8-3852-3557-5 (ebook)

Subjects: LCSH: Education (Christian theology). | Teaching—Religious aspects—Christianity. | Catholic Church—Education. | Learning and scholarship—Religious aspects—Christianity. | Catholic schools.

Classification: BV4501.3 S85 2025 (paperback) | BV4501.3 (ebook)

VERSION NUMBER 05/01/25

Scripture quotations are from the New Revised Standard Version, copyright © 1989, Division of Christian Education of the National Council of the Churches of Christ in the United States of America. Used by permission. All rights reserved.

Chapter 1, "Religious Faith in Education: Enemy or Asset?," is reprinted with kind permission from the publishers Taylor and Francis, and first appeared in *Journal of Beliefs & Values* 33 (2012) 183–93.

Chapter 2, "Learning from Medieval Monasticism," is reprinted with kind permission of the editor of the journal *Networking*. An earlier and shorter version of this was originally published in *Networking* 21 (2021) 19–21.

Chapter 4, "Blondel and a Living Tradition for Catholic Education," appears with kind permission of the managing editor of the *Journal of Catholic Education*. It was first published in *Catholic Education: A Journal of Inquiry and Practice* [now *Journal of Catholic Education*] 1 (1997) 67–76.

Chapter 5, "Hügel and Catholic Education," and chapter 3, "Hugh of St. Victor: Medieval Wisdom for Modern Educators," are reprinted with kind permission of the editor of *Downside Review*. These articles were originally published in that journal in vol. 117 (1999) 79–88; and vol. 139 (2021) 165–82, respectively.

Chapter 7, "Addressing Difference and Commonality in Leadership Preparation for Faith Schools," is reproduced with permission from *Journal of Education and Christian Belief* (now *International Journal of Christianity and Education*). It first appeared in vol. 10 (2006) 75–88.

Chapter 8, "The Dynamics of Ownership," is reproduced with permission from *Journal of Education and Christian Belief* (now *International Journal of Christianity and Education)* It first appeared in vol. 9 (2005) 21–33.

Chapter 9, "Leading Values and Casting Shadows in Church Schools," is reprinted with kind permission of the journal in which it first appeared: *Journal of Religious Education* 51 (2003) 44–49.

Chapter 11, "Succession Planning for School and Church," is reprinted with kind permission of the journal in which it first appeared: *Journal of Religious Education* 59 (2011) 44–49.

Chapter 12, "Pilgrims or Project Managers: Premodern Challenges for Contemporary Students," is reprinted with kind permission from the editor of *International Studies in Catholic Education*, where it was first published online on Sept. 19, 2024; https://doi.org/10.1080/19422539.2024.2399545.

Chapter 15, "Newman and Interconnectedness: Integration and University Education," is reprinted with kind permission of *Journal of Religious Education*, where it first appeared in vol. 60 (2012) 48–58.

Chapter 16, "Towards a Curriculum for Life in Christian Formation," was first published in the online journal *Journal of Religious Education and Theology* 1 (2021) 18–31, and appears with kind permission of the editor.

Chapter 17, "Christian Education and the Discernment of Vocation: From 'Whatever' to 'Amen,'" first appeared in *Re-Imagining Christian Education for the 21st Century*, edited by Andrew Morris, 87–98 (Chelmsford, UK: James, 2013).

Chapter 18, "Understanding and Overstanding: Religious Reading in Historical Perspective," is reproduced with permission from *Journal of Education and Christian Belief* (now *International Journal of Christianity and Education*). It first appeared in vol. 11 (2007) 25–38.

Chapter 19, "Living Tradition and Learning Agency: Interpreting the 'Score' and Personal Rendition," first appeared in *Christian Faith, Formation and Education*, edited by Ros Stuart-Buttle and John Shortt, 93–114 (London: Palgrave Macmillan, 2018). It is reprinted here with permission from Springer.

Chapter 20, "Catholic Pastoral and Prophetic Responses to a Secularizing Landscape," is reprinted with kind permission from the editors of *Verbum Vitae* 42 (2024) 55–76.

Chapter 21, in an earlier and shorter version, "Catholic Education as Ongoing Translation," was published in *International Studies in Catholic Education* 4 (2012) 200–207, and is reprinted with kind permission of the editor.

Chapter 22, "Communication, Media, and Inculturation," was first published in the online journal *Educa—International Catholic Journal of Education* 2 (2016) 9–28. It is published here with kind permission of the Association for Catholic Institutes for the Study of Education.

Chapter 23, "Being a Citizen in the Church," was first published in *Furrow* 63 (2013) 669–79, and is reprinted with kind permission of the editor.

This book is dedicated to Daniel/Donal O'Leary (1937–2019), in loving memory and with deep gratitude for his heartwarming life and witness as a personal soul-friend and as a steward who so faithfully represented and who so winsomely rejuvenated the living tradition of Christian faith.

# Contents

*Abbreviations* | xi

*Introduction* | xiii

## PART ONE: TRADITION AS A RESOURCE | 1

1. Religious Faith in Education: Enemy or Asset? | 4
2. Learning from Medieval Monasticism | 20
3. Hugh of St. Victor: Medieval Wisdom for Modern Educators | 27
4. Blondel and a Living Tradition for Catholic Education | 48
5. Hügel and Catholic Education | 58
6. Firmness and Openness in the Catholic University | 67

## PART TWO: LEADERSHIP | 76

7. Addressing Difference and Commonality in Leadership Preparation for Faith Schools | 80
8. The Dynamics of Ownership | 95
9. Leading Values and Casting Shadows in Church Schools | 111
10. Living Logos: Christian Leadership | 123
11. Succession Planning for School and Church | 132

## PART THREE: EDUCATION AS A SPIRITUAL ENDEAVOR | 142

12  Pilgrims or Project Managers: Premodern Challenges for Contemporary Students | 147

13  Towards the Real Presence of Teachers | 165

14  Vulnerability, Affectability, and Openness to the Divine | 176

## PART FOUR: CURRICULUM AND LEARNING | 192

15  Newman and Interconnectedness: Integration and University Education | 198

16  Towards a Curriculum for Life in Christian Formation | 215

17  Christian Education and the Discernment of Vocation: From "Whatever" to "Amen" | 229

18  Understanding and Overstanding: Religious Reading in Historical Perspective | 243

19  Living Tradition and Learning Agency: Interpreting the "Score" and Personal Rendition | 260

## PART FIVE: CONNECTING TRADITION TO CULTURE | 281

20  Catholic Pastoral and Prophetic Responses to a Secularizing Landscape | 286

21  Catholic Education as Ongoing Translation | 310

22  Communication, Media, and Inculturation | 327

23  Being a Citizen in the Church | 345

*Bibliography* | 357

*Index* | 379

# Abbreviations

| | |
|---|---|
| BETL | Bibliotheca Ephemeridum Theologicarum Lovaniensium |
| *Comm* | *Communio* |
| *HeyJ* | *Heythrop Journal* |
| *JEH* | *Journal of Ecclesiastical History* |
| LCL | Loeb Classical Library |
| *NV* | *Nova et Vetera* |
| *ProEccl* | *Pro Ecclesia* |
| *RelEd* | *Religious Education* |
| *TD* | *Theology Digest* |
| *TS* | *Theological Studies* |

# Introduction

I AM A STUDENT of souls and the spiritual, of minds and learning, of how principles influence practices, of how institutions bring together individuals and construct community, of how tradition engages modernity, and of how history illuminates the present and prepares us for the future. My special interest is in how Christian faith and theological understanding relate to educational practice. Reaching the age of seventy-five has been a prompt for me to look back on my career and to reflect on how I might describe my life's work as a Christian educator in secondary schools, universities, and the church. I hope it is fair for me to claim that I have tried to serve as a steward of a living tradition in the world of education.

Most commonly, the role of steward has been considered one that is accountable for the efficient running of a household, or piece of land, or of property, or of possessions. The notion of steward, however, can be and has been extended by some authors. For example, borrowing an expression from Lee S. Shulman, Chris Golde applies stewardship to the expectations of a successful PhD student, one who is trained to be a steward of an academic discipline or a profession, dedicated to the integrity of its work in the generation, critique, transformation, transmission, and use of its knowledge.[1] For Golde, "Stewardship encompasses, on the one hand, a set of roles and skills, and, on the other, a set of principles. The former ensure competence, and the latter provide the moral compass."[2] Furthermore, "a steward of the discipline thinks about the continuing health of the discipline and how to preserve the best of the past for those who will follow."[3] More recently, Sarah Irving-Stonebraker refers to the responsibility of Christians—as "priests of history" to steward the past, to ensure that the wisdom conveyed in Christian tradition, instead of being lost, is brought to bear in our current

---

1. Golde, "Preparing Stewards," 3.
2. Golde, "Preparing Stewards," 9.
3. Golde, "Preparing Stewards," 13.

circumstances.[4] St. Paul, in 1 Cor 4:1, refers to the faithful (including himself) as "stewards of the mysteries of God." That title seems to me to be one way of describing the role of Christian educators.

In this book, I describe the role I have tried to play as a Christian educator in secondary schools, in universities, in ongoing professional development, and in the church as striving to serve as a steward of a living tradition. The task of such a steward seems to me to have five components: first, to transmit and mediate the tradition faithfully; second, to question and critique it responsibly; third, to articulate, explain, and interpret it as clearly as possible in order to make it accessible; fourth, to deepen and transform the tradition, insofar as this lies within one's capacity, so that it remains vibrant and fertile; fifth, to apply the tradition to the world's needs. More succinctly, educators who serve as stewards of the living tradition of Christianity, seek to model in themselves and to enable in others a critical appreciation and creative appropriation of their tradition.

After summarizing how I envisage the role of a steward, in what follows I comment on the nature, scope, complexity and key features of Christianity as a living tradition insofar as these are pertinent for teachers and leaders in Christian schools and universities. Then

Many aspects of the role and task of serving as a steward are illustrated through these chapters: the steward

- is charged with caring for, looking after, tending, and serving what she or he is entrusted with;
- must oversee, coordinate, and facilitate the use of time, talents, treasures, and relationships within the organization;
- does not own or possess what he or she is mandated to preserve and promote;
- must be accountable for how their role has been carried out;
- is expected to be fruitful, add value, and leave in good condition that which they are responsible for, creating a climate of enhancement of the mission;
- should be closely familiar with and loyal and attentive to the owner's wishes;
- has a leadership role in equipping and empowering others to take on their roles and contribute to the flourishing of the owner's business;

---

4. Irving-Stonebraker, *Priests of History*.

INTRODUCTION

- is expected to honor the inheritance of the past (which has been temporarily handed over to her or him) but also to secure the future;
- has to be ready and willing to relinquish the role and hand it on to someone else.

Those who hope to serve as a faithful steward of the living tradition of the Christian faith need to be attentive to the Lord of the work, as well as the work of the Lord. Only if Christ is Lord of their own lives can they have a role in God's work in healing the world. If, however, they can proclaim "Jesus is Lord," not just with their lips, but with their lives, they can never underestimate the ways that God can work through them to bring to pass his purpose for the world. There are three tasks facing Christians, each of which applies to the one who is a steward. First to prepare the ground for the gospel. Second, to present the gospel. Third, to participate in the gospel ourselves. Without giving priority to the third of these tasks, neither the first nor the second can be effective. The quality of the work of the true steward depends greatly on that person's relationship with the one they seek to serve. This point is underlined in the reflection given by Sister Bernadita Dianzon on a gospel passage about a manager or steward:

> Dedication to one's duty is endowed with a deeper purpose when on focuses on the quality of one's relationship with the Master who has given the charge. One does not obey just because there is a corresponding remuneration for doing so, or one fears being reprimanded. Rather, one obeys because he/she makes the concerns of the master one's own and prioritizes them over one's personal interests. Faithfulness to duty becomes an opportunity to express one's faithfulness to the Master himself. And seeing the Master pleased with one's service is itself a reward. It gives meaning to one's existence and becomes a way of offering back to the divine Giver the fruit of his gifts.[5]

Christian educators who wish to serve as a steward of the faith tradition in the world of education need more than obedience, fidelity, and a commitment to cherishing its wisdom. They also require two further qualities. First, a willingness to question and interrogate the tradition for its sources, its foundational principles, its inner coherence, its implications for life, practices and decisions, and its continuing application to and relevance for today. Second, a willingness to take the risk of translating the tradition for a new context, to engage with it with invention and creativity. A living tradition cannot help being reshaped by the particular ways that

5. Dianzon, "October 23: Luke 12:39–48."

its adherents receive it, share it with others, and put it into practice in the specific circumstances in which they find themselves.

Traditions are communal conversations that involve beliefs and attitudes, feelings and actions, all of which are ways of reading and responding to the world. A tradition has roots and a connection to these roots has to be maintained if identity is not to be lost. But a tradition is always porous rather than hermetically sealed off from external influences. Continuity and renewal should not be seen as in opposition; they belong together. The experience of everyday life, as well as of professional practice, calls for improvisation; the rule book and established customs can never cover every eventuality that we encounter. Authentic living traditions themselves both permit and provide the resources for fresh interpretations, ones that are faithful as well as innovative. If this was not the case, they would become ossified, inert, an obstacle to growth and locked in the past. The chapters in this book bring out, in one way or another, the imperative in Christian education to pass on the wisdom to be found within the faith tradition, but also the need to engage with it both critically and creatively, so that it remains vibrant, dynamic, and life giving.

Christians find it hard to be generically Christian, that is, without attachment to particular expressions of the faith, ones that commit themselves to some traditions while not doing so for other traditions. They find themselves somewhere in between specificity and generality. To the extent that they embrace particular forms of worship, ways of (and contexts for) reading the Bible, modes of prayer, types of church organization and life, they find themselves less familiar and comfortable with alternative ones in each case. Commitment to particularity within the range of Christian traditions enables depth of penetration, gives access to long-term belonging, and opens up the riches made available through the various forms of engagement. At the same time, it keeps one at a distance from the insights, benefits and burdens of forms of Christian life which fall outside of these commitments. The very wide range of possible expressions of Christian faith preclude serious simultaneous commitment to them all; one has to choose. I leave open the question as to whether the rich variety of expressions of Christianity are due to human failure to detect and follow God's will or simply a manifestation of the mysterious fertility and diversity of creation and God's multiple ways of reaching and blessing God's people.

Christians find themselves wrapped up in particular patterns of worship, nurtured within specific ecclesial communities, nourished by certain kinds of teaching and learning activities, and pressed to take part in various types of outreach. Their belonging and their sense of mission have a particular flavor, one which gives them, to some degree at least, a sense of coherence and purpose. This positive sense can be weakened or even fractured either by personal doubts and feelings of guilt but also by a painful awareness of shortcomings within their tradition with regard to its relation to or treatment of those outside it. Opening themselves up to the different forms of worship, church organization and practice, self-understanding and signature style and tone of other Christians will inevitably bring into question the validity, adequacy, comprehensiveness, and fitness for purpose of what has been their previous experience of church life.

It must be acknowledged that each particular tradition is itself plural in nature, marked by an ongoing and lively internal argument about its central claims and practices; traditions are neither monolithic nor settled; differences between adherents of a tradition can be deep and neuralgic. Furthermore, there is substantial overlap between traditions, allowing much mutual appreciation and collaboration. Indeed, it often happens that one feels much closer to some people in Christian traditions different from one's own than one does to some people in one's own. In addition, there is a built-in imperative and mandate within Christian faith towards the evermore inclusive reaching out to others, both in terms of communicating the gospel and of serving others (with each of these being seen as integral to the other). It seems then that Christians are called to particularity as the route to accessing and deepening their faith, but also to universality in their aspirations for how they receive from and share with others who differ from them. As limited human beings, they necessarily pass through the way of particularity. As called to share God's life, they are called to reach out universally. This dual call applies as much to their relations with people of other faiths (including those who claim affiliation with no religious faith). It is appropriate for Christians both to preserve difference as they protect and develop their traditions and at the same to make every effort to ensure that these traditions, despite the limitations of their particularities, never lose their capacity to learn from and, where possible, to work together with other traditions (within and beyond Christian faith) in service of the common good and with universal concern.

Christian tradition is on the one hand given and received—something inherited and at the same time something reconstructed and renewed, which calls for agency and initiative on the part of its adherents. The handing over of a tradition does not rely on docility or passivity on the part of those who receive it. Two centuries ago, Goethe (1749–1832) warned, in his play *Faust*, that "that which is inherited must be earned anew by each generation in order to be possessed."[6] Christian tradition requires participa-

---

6. Goethe, *Faust*, lines 682–83.

tion and performance, but also questioning and critique. Fidelity and obedience to it needs to be accompanied by judgement and discernment about interpretation and implementation. Efforts need to be made with regard to both conservation and development. Conservation is not a matter of mere repetition, though it does entail being vigilant about ensuring that key aspects of the tradition are not watered down or lost. And development is not a jettisoning of, or an exercise of radical surgery on, what has been received, but an extension of this, building on the inheritance, unfolding what is inherent in what is being carried forward. Such development is necessarily a risk, in that it involves a going beyond, taking a new step or initiative that allows the tradition and its adherents to enter new horizons, to engage with new interlocutors, to face new challenges—and, in doing so, to understand the tradition in fresh ways. As Picasso is reputed to have said, tradition is having a baby, not wearing your grandfather's hat. Or, as Jorge Gracia claims, "It is of the essence of tradition to go beyond what has been handed down."[7] Gracia compares the way tradition operates to the description of old wine in new skins in the Gospels.[8] "Disregarding the new context in the understanding of the old is like putting new wine in old skins: The old skins burst and the wine is spilled and lost. But taking into account the new context in the consideration of the old is like putting old wine in new skins: The wine is modified while remaining the same in significant ways."[9]

Any tradition needs a degree of stability and continuity in order for it to become embedded in lives and practices, but as new questions, circumstances, contexts and challenges arise, there will always be an unstable equilibrium maintained between those components which are universal, enduring and invariant and those features which are particular, temporary and variant. It is not always easy to distinguish between what is central and necessary on the one hand, and what is accidental and contingent, on the other hand, within a tradition. One can misidentify signs of stability as indications of permanence, assuming that what is familiar has always been the case. Yet, as theologian John Thiel observes, "Historical study usually shows that the unity, stability, and concreteness of tradition emerged from a history of interpretive ambiguity, disagreement, and conflict."[10] It may be claimed that traditions have both a fixed and a mobile aspect. To neglect the aspect that is fixed is to run the risk of losing contact with what is essential

---

7. Gracia, *Old Wine in New Skins*, 29.
8. Matt 9:17; Mark 2:22; Luke 5:37.
9. Gracia, *Old Wine in New Skins*, 122.
10. Thiel, *Senses of Tradition*, 39.

to the faith; to neglect the aspect that is mobile runs the risk of stifling the faith. "Living traditions are neither perfectly rigid nor purely malleable."[11]

Two further features of the Christian tradition can be noted, both of which play a part in ensuring that it continues to be vibrant, fertile and dynamic. First, there is a reciprocal influence between Christian tradition and any culture that it encounters. Christians who live out their faith will inevitably, with varying degrees of efficacy, influence the culture within which they live. Correspondingly, they cannot help but be influenced by that culture. I say more about the relationship with culture in the section on inculturation (below). Second, Christian tradition, insofar as it genuinely comes from God as its author and vivifying force, is inexhaustible; it cannot be controlled or contained; it transcends all its expressions and all the terminology used to describe it. As John Thiel notes, "Tradition as the eventful transmission of the divine Word in history by its very nature resists every notion of permanence as closure, short of the *eschaton*."[12]

A brief comment on the subtitle of this book. Christian scholarship often takes place well away from, and without reference to, educational practice. In whatever particular academic discipline Christians are working, insofar as they explicitly draw on their Christian faith as inspiration and guide for their research and writing (and many academics who are Christian do not do this), their work is aimed primarily at fellow academics. Often against the grain of the professional contexts and cultures in which I have worked, I have tried to bring my Christian faith to bear on my scholarship, which has engaged with theology, philosophy, history, cultural analysis and leadership studies, in ways that are deliberate, explicit, and transparent. At the same time, believing that theory and practice develop organically, interactively, and cyclically, I have endeavored to allow my Christian faith and the scholarship that underpins it to motivate, direct and inform my efforts and decisions as a teacher and leader in schools, universities, and within the church. In other words, I have thought it important to ask myself constantly: What does my scholarship, as a Christian, have to say to me about my practice as an educator? What difference, if any, does my faith and scholarship make to how I act as a teacher? Yet this process of relating Christian scholarship educational practice is not one way. It is also necessary to ask oneself regularly: How is my experience as an educator influencing and developing my understanding of my Christian faith and the scholarship that seeks to penetrate and appreciate reality as the arena

---

11. Tilley, *Inventing Catholic Tradition*, 44.
12. Thiel, *Senses of Tradition*, 44.

of God's creation? What difference, if any, does my experience as a teacher (and as a learner) make to my relationship with Christian faith?

\* \* \*

The book brings together twenty-three pieces (mostly previously published articles of mine from several different journals, written between 1997 and 2024), each of which exposes some aspect of what is entailed in serving as a steward of the living tradition of the Christian faith in the world of education. The book is divided into five headings: tradition as a resource; leadership; education as a spiritual endeavor; curriculum and Christian learning; connecting tradition to culture. It engages both with historical perspectives and with contemporary professional and cultural realities; it addresses intellectual and spiritual dimensions of Christian education; and the aim which drives each of the chapters is a concern to make tradition both accessible and meaningful to those for whom it is unfamiliar. Themes pervading the book include fostering a critical appreciation for and a creative appropriation of the living tradition of Christianity, fluency and flexibility in sharing that tradition, vocation and vulnerability, and a striving for interconnectedness and integration. Each of the five parts will have a short introduction that gives an overview of the chapters in that section and how they relate to that part's overall theme.

I am grateful to the countless number of authors, teachers, students, colleagues and friends from whom I have learned whatever is worthwhile in what follows. A special debt of gratitude is due to my wife Jean, who has been a model steward of our household; and also to our son Paul, who has readily offered computer assistance to his technophobic father. The staff at Wipf & Stock, who have helped to bring the book to publication, have all been unfailingly kind, patient, and helpful throughout the whole process. Thank you to Robin Parry, Rebecca Abbott, Karlie Tedrick, George Callihan, Matthew Wimer, and any others behind the scenes whose names I did not get to know. You have all been a pleasure to work with and your contributions have improved the outcome in all kinds of ways. Any shortcomings that remain are simply down to me.

# PART ONE
# Tradition as a Resource

## INTRODUCTION

Christian educators should ensure that they have a sound and deep familiarity with the resources available to them from the long history of Christian education, the intellectual and spiritual "treasures" and the well-tried practices of the past. But it is also likely that, though necessary, this will not be enough. There needs to be a willingness to indwell and to deploy the tradition but also to see where something new is called for, if we are to be true to that tradition in changing contexts (just as previous contributors to the tradition themselves combined fidelity with improvisation). As will be argued later (in ch. 20), there is a place for improvisation in the Christian life, but before one can improvise on a score, to use a musical analogy, one must first be familiar with that score and able to do justice to it.

There is a constant state of flux, of development in the composition of a faithful life. Yet at the same time there needs to be stability, a recognizable and enduring pattern and core. Thus, the closely connected questions of what should remain the same and what needs to change in our understanding of our faith must continually be asked. Our answers can at best only be provisional; they are neither insulated from nor secure against any future cultural changes and new challenges for the faithful. It follows from this that Christian education needs to provide both formation (with connotations of stable habits, convictions and practices) and the capacity for flexibility, displayed in discerning responsiveness to changing circumstances. Teachers should help students to create new maps as well as use old ones. In other words, there is always a need for a creative rereading of tradition. "Every new generation is given the noble task of adding its own new chapter to the book [of the Christian faith tradition] . . . while re-reading and processing

## PART ONE | TRADITION AS A RESOURCE

what has been written by our ancestors, in the light of a new historical context. Our calling is not merely to re-read and repeat the past, but to re-imagine the salvific Gospel message for new times and new people."[1]

Teaching is one of the ways that tradition is communicated, although not the only one. This makes tradition a privileged context for the study of tradition, since the faithful teacher always works both to preserve and to renew tradition. A tradition does not continue if it is not taught. But good teachers seek to go beyond mere repetition and preservation; they hope to contribute to making that tradition vibrant, relevant and able to speak powerfully and winsomely in the language to the concerns of their own day. Through teaching the past is interpreted and made available in and for the present and at the same time the present is understood and interpreted in the light of the past.

The first essay in part 1 faces head-on the assumption held in some quarters that religious faith is inimical to educational endeavors. In response, I cast some light on the relationship between religious faith and education by a preliminary mapping of the field. There are three parts to the chapter. First, I lay out the assumptions from which the rest of the chapter builds. Second, I seek to identify possible links between religion and education. As a subset of this, I explore a range of ways that theology might relate to education. Third, as a step towards a more healthy relationship between education and religious faith, I offer reasons why the church needs the academy and the academy needs the church. In the light of a convergence of the concerns that I show are shared by religious believers and educators, it is suggested that religious faith in the context of education should be considered an asset rather than an enemy.

Each of the other essays in part 1 demonstrates how a Christian educator, whether working in a school or in higher education, can draw on the Christian intellectual and spiritual tradition and deploy it as a resource which provides inspiration, illumination, challenge and guidance for their role in fostering learning. Thus, chapters 2 and 3 look back at central features of medieval Christianity and suggest that teachers today can find salutary wisdom for their work with students. Chapter 2 seeks to learn from some of the assumptions and practices of medieval monasticism, while Chapter 3 offers a critical retrieval of the writings of the twelfth-century Christian educator Hugh of St. Victor. Chapters 4 and 5 move to the early years of the twentieth century to engage with the thought, first, of the French philosopher Maurice Blondel and then of Friedrich von Hügel, both faithful lay Catholics who took great pains to engage constructively with the

---

1. Bouwens, "Recontextualizing Catholic School Identity," 150.

PART ONE | TRADITION AS A RESOURCE

philosophic and scientific ideas of their era. In both cases, I seek to show first, that they model how Christians can combine intelligence, fidelity and openness, and second, that they can contribute to a healthy Catholic philosophy of education. Blondel's contribution is given through his nuanced appreciation of the nature, components and operation of a living tradition, and how this relates to the tasks of Catholic educators. Hügel's contribution is shown in the way he demonstrated that an embrace of the distinctive claims and commitments of a particular denomination could be combined with a generous openness and inclusivity with regard to those with different affiliations and commitments. He also offers insights that help to resolve the potential tensions that might arise between three key themes within Catholic educational theory: the integral development of the human person, the autonomy of the disciplines, and the synthesis of faith, life, and culture.

In the final chapter of part 1 I explore the apparent tension between two commitments that seem central to Christian education: fidelity to what has been revealed and handed on to us via the tradition, and openness to others and to what has not yet been revealed to us—assuming that God not only has spoken, but still speaks, and does so often through those who are different than us. Pope John Paul II, in *Ex Corde Ecclesiae*, calls upon Catholic universities to combine the ongoing and unending search for the truth with the certainty of already knowing the truth (in Christ).[2] Surely this applies also to other Christian universities. This call seems to require both firmness and openness on the part of those working in Catholic universities. Can these qualities be held together? How do firmness and openness relate to one another? In this chapter I explore some aspects of the perplexing challenge of receiving what has already been given while remaining open to what has not yet been revealed to us via our encounters with various kinds of otherness. I argue that being open to others (and to various kinds of otherness) depends on firmness of conviction, but also that, in holding our convictions, we must, if we are to remain open to the transcendence to which God is calling us, allow the boundaries of these convictions to be porous, broken open and reconfigured. If the capacity to remain open to others and to new truths relies upon firm and enduring foundations, such openness is also linked to humility, interdependence, generosity, and love— all of which are likely to unsettle our foundations on the road to conversion and all of which can be channels for grace.

---

2. John Paul II, *On Catholic Universities*.

# I

# Religious Faith in Education
## *Enemy or Asset?*

IN THE LATE NINETEENTH and early twentieth centuries, relations between religious groups and the state over education—its nature and purpose, its content and its control—were often neuralgic, as the liberal democratic state sought first to complement and gradually to reduce the influence of the churches, in order to establish its own provision. In the early years of the twenty-first century we have witnessed a renewed salience of tensions over religious issues in education. Religion remains an area around which educational controversy revolves. Concerns for parental rights to bring up their children according to their own philosophy of life jostle with the needs of a pluralistic liberal democratic society to promote key values such as tolerance, equality, liberty and respect for different beliefs and ways of life. A desire to ensure that children are not trapped by educational decisions made by their parents and the expectation that critical and independent thinking will be fostered in school might appear to be in tension with the provision of a secure and stable foundational worldview and set of values, which can later, with growing maturity, be reflected upon and if desired, revised or rejected. One has to believe and value something in order to begin to make judgments about other beliefs and values; critical assessment of what comes our way does not occur in a neutral personal vacuum where we start with no affiliations or commitments. Pluralism seems to require respect for different ways of life (both religious and nonreligious ways of life), while the flourishing of democracy seems to require that society (through education) promotes the values (and types of reasoning) that facilitate the operations of democracy. Yet, as philosopher of education Walter Feinberg so acutely puts it: "Once a child is placed in one religious tradition rather than a different one, or for that matter in a nonreligious tradition, perspectives are set, horizons shaped, understanding circumscribed, boundaries constructed, roles marked off, and a collective identity stamped."[1] No wonder that the educational space seems such a sensitive one. Religious faith, in the context of education, can, according to one's perspective, seem either an enemy to be kept at bay or an asset to be warmly welcomed.

In this chapter I hope to cast some light on the relationship between religious faith and education by a preliminary mapping of the field. There are four parts to the chapter. First, I lay out the assumptions from which the rest of the chapter builds. Second, I seek to identify possible links between religion and education. As a subset of this, I explore a range of ways that theology might relate to education. Third, I analyze two contrasting—and unsatisfactory—ways of relating education and religious faith, which I call the ways of domination and of divorce, pointing out their respective defects. Fourth, as a step towards a more healthy relationship between education and religious faith, I offer reasons why the church needs the academy and the academy needs the church. In the light of a convergence of the concerns that I show are shared by religious believers and educators, it is suggested that religious faith in the context of education should be considered an asset rather than an enemy.

## SEVEN ASSUMPTIONS

Before exploring immediately the possible relationships between religion and education, let me begin by being transparent about seven preliminary assumptions that I do not have space to argue for here. Although not all of these assumptions are universally held to be true in our society, I trust that many of them will be uncontentious.

The first of these is that education (in any culture and context) is about the capacities of human nature: energy, emotions, intelligence, memory, will, conscience, wonder, imagination and hope—and how these are developed, oriented, ordered and integrated in service of what is conceived to be the good life for individuals and for society. I acknowledge that there will be deep disagreements between different groups, both as to which particular configurations of human capacities are promoted and as to the ends that are pursued in education.

Second, I take it that the practice of education will inevitably be influenced by one's view of oneself, the world or reality, truth, society, children, the kinds of knowledge one thinks worth passing on, how people learn, the

---

1. Feinberg, *For Goodness Sake*, 18.

needs of this time and place, of the worthwhile life, and of threats to such a life.

Third, our worldview plays a central role in both education and in religious faith. Our worldview influences what we take in, accept and notice, how we perceive messages being sent to us by various individuals and groups, what we care about, where and how we fit incoming lessons or messages into what we already hold, know and are committed to and what we do with it afterwards.

Fourth, from a faith perspective, there is the danger of cultural captivity. This can occur when there is too ready an assimilation to contemporary cultural norms and too little regard for the distinctive light cast by faith. For example, the salience of belief in progress, human autonomy, scientific reason, technology and social planning, together with the relegation of faith to the private realm, can quite obscure insights offered by religious faith and revelation. Only too easily can believers find themselves seduced by some of the gods of our time, for example, academic success, sport, technology, league table positions, tolerance, feeling good, self-creation, shopping, constant connectivity and celebrity status. Education can protect people from forms of cultural captivity, including of course, religiously formed cultural captivity. It can serve, among other roles, to expose ideologies, where interests and power are covertly protected and promoted under the cloak of apparent rationality. Of course, education can also reinforce such ideologies. Religious faith can easily slip into forms of ideological captivity that distort or contradict its message. When this happens, religion can become blind to its own pathologies and irrational tendencies; it can be self-serving, abusive and concerned with institutional survival above all other considerations. As Simon Blackburn wrote, in a recent review, "The militant wing of secularism talks freely of superstition, ignorance, bigotry, self-deception, stupidity, tribalism and rank hypocrisy."[2] Here education, not only in the faith itself, but also an education that is strongly buttressed in its independence and offering in secular institutions contrasting perspectives, can play a valuable part in exposing, challenging and calling to account religious ideologies.

Fifth, schools, colleges and universities are intermediate organizations. They provide a space between the nation-state on the one hand and individuals and families on the other hand. They can serve as a countervailing force between different types of pressures that might undermine human flourishing. Particular groups might be inward-looking and have narrow horizons; they have the potential to resist wider loyalties and shy away from a sense of commitment to the equality, dignity and liberty of all. Universal

2. Blackburn, Review of *Dishonest to God*.

imperatives from the state (and from multinational companies) can erode local identities and practices, undermining in the process the building blocks of a wider sense of belonging. I simply assume here that educational institutions, as intermediary bodies in the way I have described, should be places with a degree of independence from both particular and universalizing pressures, even if accountable to both; without some degree of independence, they cannot function properly *as* educational spaces.

Sixth, I assume there is a multiplicity of legitimate ways that one might understand the relationship between religious faith and education. I am not here advocating any one particular model.

Seventh, I assume that there is bound to be some tension between educational imperatives and imperatives that focus more on promoting religious fidelity, though I do not believe that this tension is doomed to be destructive, even if this has happened in some cases in the past. The conversion, commitment, participation, belonging, surrender and dedication required by religious faith do not have to be embraced at the cost of neglecting the capacity for questioning, critique, detachment, testing, individual authenticity and appropriation expected of the educated person. Anthony Blair (who teaches leadership studies at Eastern University, Philadelphia) says that the "twenty-first century is characterized by the intersection of two driving forces—a theocratic impulse, . . . and . . . an anti-religion posture that exceeds the theoretical neutrality of mere secularity."[3] But, in my view, the choice we face is neither theocracy nor secularism. Strong religious convictions do not make toleration, inclusiveness and fair treatment for all impossible. As life guiding, religious faith provides a source of values and hopes, a basic orientation to community, a story and a tradition within which one can learn how to develop one's gifts and character, and within which one is supported in rehearsing how to share one's life projects with and for others, inside and outside the faith community. Of course, it is not part of my case that one cannot learn how to do these things outside religious faith. Nor am I claiming that religious people do these things or develop these qualities, better than others. Perhaps this seventh assumption of mine, that there is an alternative to both theocracy and secularism and that we do not have to choose between them (because religious convictions can be combined with many of the qualities required for the flourishing of liberal plural democracies), is more contentious than some of the others.

---

3. Blair, *Church and Academy*, 23.

## LINKS BETWEEN RELIGION, THEOLOGY, AND EDUCATION

Any attempt to suggest that religious faith and education can have a positive relationship might face a number of objections. Education is about liberating the person from his or her present and particular cultural location and human inheritance. It is about equipping them to make their own decisions about worldview, lifestyle and affiliation. It is about developing critical thinking skills. It should provide each person with a capacity to question and to distrust, inexorably, all authorities, religious, social, political, cultural, (including, of course, their own). It should make people open-minded, always ready to treat truth as provisional at best and ready to jettison such provisional "truths" in light of new evidence. It must avoid, at all costs, closing down questions, doubts and issues, or implying in any way that some issues are beyond discussion, that they have already been decided in any irreversible way. Rather than embedding people in particular positions and affiliations, education should develop an appreciation of diversity and a capacity to enter with ease into multiple perspectives. It should give people the confidence to be creative in their selection from the cultures around them, and it should privilege individual ownership, authenticity, originality, innovation over communal belonging and its associated disciplines (and the benefits claimed for such communal belonging). It should maximize tolerance of and respect for alternative lifestyles in service of greater freedom for all. While promoting individuality, self-expression and a strong sense of self-worth, it should, at the same time, induce a proper caution and humility about our grasp of any truth, if such a truth is tenable within the relativity of cultures and the flux of time.[4]

If education is conceived of in this way, then attempts to convert, evangelize, catechize or form others in faith can appear as a threat. Such attempts may come across as seeking a premature commitment. They may seem too confident in the truth being advocated. Religious believers may appear too judgmental about those who do not accept this truth. The faithful may seem to want to embed people in particularity, in particular practices and communities, in such a way as to trap them, to disable them from a more appropriate universality. Formation in faith may ask for a surrender of self that is demeaning of human dignity. It may attribute far too much importance to authority (biblical, ecclesial), thereby undermining individual freedom and inviting oppression. It may so prioritize fidelity to tradition that it fails to address contemporary needs and renders itself irrelevant. It

---

4. This and the following two paragraphs draw from Sullivan, "Education and Evangelization."

may pay insufficient attention to the diversity of views (and situations) and to objections to its teaching, leading to narrow vision, tribalism, sheeplike acceptance, complacency, self-righteous attitudes, condemnation of those who differ and exclusive practices that do not promote human flourishing.

While all this *can*, sadly, be true in some, perhaps in many, cases, it certainly does not have to be so. It is possible to try to communicate religious faith without slipping into coercion, threats, harassment, psychological bullying, manipulation and invading freedom; one can propose a faith perspective in ways that are respectful, transparent, honest and gentle, just as one can do so without these qualities. Neither education nor religions have lived up to the best they can be. It *can* be the case that education and the communication of religious faith come across as radically different activities, deeply opposed, in spirit and in practice, to one another. Yet, they can also be mutually reinforcing rather than incompatible, and mutually beneficial rather than hostile to one another. Despite the fear that to allow faith into educational arenas might "open the door to all sorts of educational viruses that congregate under the heading of indoctrination,"[5] this does not have to happen; nor does religious belief inevitably act as "irrelevant, toxic clutter."[6] Instead, it can serve both as a resource provoking insight into the depths of the human condition and as offering an alternative to many contemporary assumptions that should not too automatically be taken for granted, especially if we wish to stimulate critical thinking.

One can seek to understand the relationship between education and religious faith in different ways. These will include historical, philosophical, theological, psychological, political, social/cultural, and pedagogical dimensions. Let me briefly refer to the first four of these, as examples of possible ways of reflecting on how religious faith and education relate to one another. A historian could explore the record of how in the past religious groups have influenced the provision of education more generally and how they have educated their people in matters of faith in particular and also assess to what extent the legacy of past influence still operates and with what effects. Here one could trace the influence of religious faith on the curriculum of educational institutions, on tools and techniques for learning, and on the formation of teachers. A philosopher might analyze the key concepts that map out the relationship between education and religious faith, for example, in considering such topics as the nature and sources of knowledge, the purposes of education, the role of teachers, instruction, authority, freedom, indoctrination, the rights of children, parents, teachers

---

5. Nick Spencer, in Cooling, *Doing God in Education*, 8.
6. Cooling, *Doing God in Education*, 14.

and the state, and so forth. A theologian might focus on the nature of revelation, the central educational messages of the gospel, or the (educative) mission of the church. Alternatively, he or she might articulate the basic grammar of the Christian faith, a Christian anthropology that influences how we envisage learners (and teachers), develop a sacramental perspective that illuminates the curriculum or suggest elements in a spirituality that should inform educational practice. A psychologist might turn our attention to the springs of motivation, to the unfolding of human development at its various stages, or to the factors that encourage learners to be open to or resistant to learning. Alternatively, she or he might investigate the coping strategies employed by children, young people and adults in their mutual interaction in educational activity.

I do not intend to go down any of these routes. Instead I want to do something much more limited. My aim here is to offer, very sketchily and schematically, merely a preliminary outline of possible connections between religion and education.

Links between religion and education may lie in the content of what is taught, the values that are transmitted, the fundamental purposes that undergird and that orient the educational enterprise, the personnel who play key roles as teachers or via the structures and agencies set up to ensure delivery—most likely, through a combination of several of these. More particularly, in the case of Christianity—still the religion that has most influenced education in the UK, in Europe, in the USA, and in Australia—links between the church and education also include content, goals, personnel and institutions, as well as both the methods of teaching and the media being deployed.

Although religious faith goes beyond its theology, theology, in the case of Christianity, is the form that intellectual reflection on the faith takes: reflection on the sources of the faith, its coherence, its self-understanding, its defense against criticisms, its rules of interpretation, and its interface with other forms of thought. Inevitably, for Christians, theology and education should be related; otherwise incoherence would be built into how the endeavors of theology and education were envisaged and carried out. Here I summarize three different ways of mapping out the range of possible relationships that pertain between theology and education.

One useful classification of the relationship between theology and education has been provided by Sara Little. Here I draw upon a summary of her analysis, as given by James Riley Estep.[7] Little offers five ways of relating

7. Estep, "What Makes Education Christian?," 29–30. Little's analysis is to be found in her entry "Theology and Education," in Cully and Cully, *Harper's Encyclopedia of Religious Education*, 649–51.

these two activities. First, theology might be treated as a source, providing the content of what is taught in education. Second, theology might be drawn upon as a resource in a situation where education as a social science has implicit goals and learning theories that are determinative of both structure and content, but where theology could play a supportive role by helping meet goals or to provide a broader perspective or to assist in interpreting experience. Third, theology might act as a norm. If this is the case, various subject areas are selected and interpreted in relation to theological formulations. Here theology is the filter through which other subjects are taught. Fourth, education, as a practice, might be interpreted as a way of doing theology (as compared with other theological "languages" such as liturgy or service). According to this view, when one engages in critical reflection on the meaning of experience (conscious of God's presence), one is theologizing. Here theology is the product of education. Fifth, theology and education can operate in a dialogue. Here they are viewed as separate but related disciplines, each with its own special contribution and functions; each draws on a cluster of related disciplines from which it utilizes appropriate contributions. Mutual interaction and interdependence would be signs of such dialogue. Estep adds a sixth possible type of relationship between theology and education. This would be a negative relationship, where theology is considered irrelevant to education.

In a different classification exercise, Professor John Hull presents five possible links between theology and education.[8] First, theology might be both necessary and sufficient for an understanding of education; in this case there is no need for the social sciences. Second, theology might provide a necessary but not sufficient understanding of education; in this case, the social sciences are also necessary. Third, theology might provide a sufficient but not a necessary understanding of education; other belief systems might also offer sufficient accounts of education; in this case, theology is not necessary, but provides an optional extra perspective. Fourth, theology might provide a possible and legitimate understanding of education, but one which is neither sufficient nor necessary; in this case, the presence of theology should be minimal. Fifth, and here there is a parallel with Estep's mention of a possibly negative relationship: theology might be thought of as an impossible and illegitimate way of understanding education; in this case, it should have no contribution to offer.

The relationship between faith (and theology) and learning has thus been interpreted in various ways. My third typology comes from Anthony Blair, who offers a slightly different analysis from those of either Sara Little

---

8. Hull, "Christian Theology and Educational Theory," 128–29.

or of John Hull.[9] Blair refers to four models: convergence, triumphalism, values added (sometimes called "separate spheres"), and integration. "The 'convergence model' in the nineteenth century perceived no distinction or conflict between knowledge received through revelation and that received through other epistemologies."[10] This model assumed that the knowledge that is gained via revelation and that gained via one or other scientific discipline were mutually confirming."[11] In contrast to this expected harmony between faith and learning, some adopted a triumphalist stance. This triumphalism "took both secular and Christian forms, as proponents on both sides of the divide sought to discredit the truth claims of the other."[12] Such triumphalism is reflected in each of the two unsatisfactory ways of relating faith to education that are discussed in section 3, below. The third model as described by Blair has two labels, and is known either as "values added" or as a "separate spheres" model. The "values added" label is used when it is assumed that learning is "a neutral activity that is indistinguishable from one environment to another, and one's faith commitment is played out in "sacred" activities, such as chapel services, missions or service projects, personal relationships, and other non-academic activities, which are regarded as supplements to the core academic mission."[13] Here value is added to learning by extra-curriculum activities, but the actual learning itself remains untouched (in any direct sense) by faith considerations. When the term "separate spheres" is used, it is assumed that there cannot be a conflict between secular and sacred knowledge "because they occupy different spheres. The two kinds of knowledge do not change each other in fundamental ways, but they can enrich each other."[14] Here there is a radical distinction between different types of knowledge, one that entails a real separation between them, with no interaction taking place "across the boundaries" of one discipline and another. In contrast, with the "integration model" "one's faith is expected to inform both the theory and practice of one's discipline."[15] Here significant influence by religious perspectives is

9. Blair, *Church and Academy*, 56–57.

10. Blair, *Church and Academy*, 56.

11. Blair, *Church and Academy*, 57, quoting Hamilton and Mathisen, "Faith and Learning at Wheaton," 268.

12. Blair, *Church and Academy*, 57.

13. Blair, *Church and Academy*, 58.

14. Blair, *Church and Academy*, 57, quoting Hamilton and Mathisen, "Faith and Learning at Wheaton," 270.

15. Blair, *Church and Academy*, 58. Blair has in mind Arthur Holmes and Nicholas Wolterstorff as examples of integrationist approaches, but there is a large body of literature on integration of faith and learning. As examples, see Harris, *Integration of Faith*

expected to be exerted on how knowledge is approached in the mainstream curriculum. There are various versions of how such integration might be understood, stemming from different theological emphases. Not least among these are differences arising from Protestant and Catholic interpretations of Christian faith, though in reality the picture is more nuanced than this oversimplified binary divide.

## DOMINATION AND DIVORCE

In this section I compare two contrasting ways of relating education and religious faith, finding both of them unsatisfactory. The first of these, which I shall call the way of domination, takes two different forms: one allows educational considerations to dominate when religious faith is the focus of study; the other privileges faith considerations over educational ones. Domination in any relationship is to the detriment of each party or element. In this instance both education and faith suffer. The second way of relating education and religious faith, often developed in response to strife caused by one or other form of domination, I will call the way of separation or divorce. If religious faith and education are divorced, in order to keep the peace between them, both, I contend, can be distorted and diminished.[16]

Before the rise of the historical perspective, critical questioning, awareness of alternative worldviews (an essential aspect of pluralism) and the development of a hermeneutics of suspicion, it was natural that religious faith should be taught as if automatically true, as part and parcel of belonging to society and as authoritative over one's life. It was quite acceptable that such faith was reinforced by diverse agencies which jointly provided a comprehensive, inexorable and demanding plausibility structure. In some quarters religious faith is still taught in this way, but much less frequently. In the traditional model, faith was taught unilaterally, from above to below, and was to be received without question or modification. Curriculum, pedagogy, modes of assessment, institutional and community ethos, together with shared and regular worship provided a habitus or ecology in which what was taught, how it was taught, and the goals of such teaching would all be directed by the church. Only what fitted under the church's umbrella could be included. Where candidates for new knowledge that contradicted

---

*and Learning*; Jacobsen and Jacobsen, *Scholarship & Christian Faith*; Litfin, *Conceiving the Christian College*; Downey and Porter, *Christian Worldview and Academic Disciplines*; Van Brummelen, *Stepping Stones to Curriculum*.

16. The following four paragraphs are drawn from Sullivan, "Education and Religious Faith."

revelation, or what was accepted as orthodox teaching derived from revelation, surfaced, these were filtered out, ignored, or suppressed.

Whenever received religious orthodoxy is rigidly protected, not allowed to be interrogated, isolated from alternative perspectives and only permitted to be interpreted in strictly prescribed ways, there is the danger that its assimilation will be shallow and that the faith of adherents will be precarious in the face of unforeseen difficulties. On the one hand, they will be anxious to avoid serious questioning. On the other, the faith community will be inflexible when it comes up against those who differ from them. Such faith might be inadequately appropriated. Its special features, through ignorance of alternatives, might be unappreciated. Its capacity to respond creatively, when called upon to apply itself to new frontiers of knowledge or experience, might be strangled at worst or at least stunted and inhibited. In this situation religious faith dominates the process of education to the detriment of both education and faith. This kind of domination is unhelpful, for individuals and for society and it does not work for either. It certainly does not equip faith effectively and it also invites a damaging counterattack.

Domination, whether of one person by another or of one group by another, does not assist in the development of maturity, of coming to a responsible and confident autonomy, where one chooses a way of life for oneself rather than have this imposed on one by others. It does not enable the emergence of the capacity for independent judgment or for "owning" who one has become. Such domination can exert a real influence, even when it is covert, indirect, unintentional or "sweetened" by "soft pressures," such as acceptance, favorable treatment or rewards.[17] If parity of esteem for people with differing worldviews, respect for the dignity of each person, and liberty of conscience for all are to be social realities rather than merely pious aspirations, then there are implications for how educational decisions are reached and for how priorities are managed and coordinated in schools, colleges, and universities—at the micro-level of the classroom, at the macro-level of the whole institution, and at a systemic level that embraces all educational institutions.

Instead of religious faith dominating—and undermining—education, in a self-defeating way, the opposite stance can be taken. Here educational considerations, according to some educational orthodoxies,

---

17. Elmer Thiessen provides ethical criteria to distinguish between ethical and unethical proselytizing in *Ethics of Evangelism*, chs. 7–8. Unethical behavior might include hidden agendas, disguised identities, lying, deception, failure to reveal or address uncomfortable truths, and exploiting vulnerability (physical, psychological, emotional, or social). All of these strategies can be employed on behalf of both religious and anti-religious positions.

filter out religious concerns, prevent religious ways of "reading" the world, downgrade religious knowledge as unworthy of study and remove religious practice from educational environments. Faith must be kept on hold in a school or university context, retained for the private sphere of life, but has no currency in the public domain. Church and state, faith and the public life of society, are kept strictly separate. *Laïcité* is the term the French use for this state of affairs. The school becomes the milieu in which citizenship in a plural, secular society is prepared for, a milieu that is uncontaminated by religious prejudice and unsullied by any deference towards faith. As a political and educational policy that remains highly influential and hotly contested.[18]

Even where *laïcité* is not operative, the climate in many publicly funded schools and universities can be highly suspicious of religious faith, resistant to its claims to truth, desirous of avoiding the questions it poses and uncomfortable with the sentiments it seems to want to advocate. Often the official stance is not hostility to religion, but neutrality between all worldviews. For religious believers, of different persuasions, however, it can seem as if the so-called neutral referee functions really like a player in disguise, forcing them to suppress important aspects of who they are. When, in the process of education, the "rules of the game" prevent adequate space for and treatment of religious ways of living, seeing, thinking and acting, another form of damaging domination is at work, undermining religious faith but also diminishing education.

Philosopher of education Elmer Thiessen argues that, in the concern, shared by many in a post-secular society, to avoid putting people under inappropriate pressure and to avoid intrusion in what should be a private decision in matters of worldview or morality, there has been a failure to distinguish adequately between ethical and unethical forms of persuasion, in the process blurring the difference between, on the one hand, having convictions about what is true and valuable and wishing to share these convictions, and, on the other hand, being dogmatic, arrogant, condescending about one's claims.[19] Education in a post-secular society needs to facilitate the capacity to engage with pluralism in ways that are both critical and constructive. Currently there is a high degree of sensitivity as to where to draw the lines between witnessing to a position (expressing one's own identity) and "pushing" this position (threatening someone else's identity). Much depends on the context and relationship between the parties involved. There

---

18. See, for example, Pena-Ruiz, *Dieu et Marianne*; Poulat, *Notre laïcité publique*; Bauberot, *Laïcité 1905–2005*; Coq, *Laïcité*; Foray, *Laïcité scolaire*.

19. Thiessen, *Ethics of Evangelism*, 196.

is a danger that truth and tolerance might be treated as mutually exclusive, so that having strong convictions about truth and wishing to convey these to others is seen as opening the door to denying the truths held to by others and aiming inappropriately to change people's minds, thereby undermining their freedom of conscience. Here "freedom of conscience has been transformed into a moral imperative not to influence anyone's conscience on worldview matters" and tolerance has changed its meaning, from restraint as to how one responds to views of which one disapproves, to "mutual acceptance of each other's views as equally valid."[20]

I have described two kinds of domination—by religion, of the process of education—and of religion, by the principles and procedures governing education. Sometimes this second type of domination is presented as a divorce between, or as a keeping apart of religious and secular education. Either way, fundamental assumptions are unduly protected from critique, alternative perspectives are ignored or, even worse, distorted and what is passed on is too tightly prescribed and too limiting in its scope and reach. Both education in general and educating people in religious faith in particular need a breadth of material to be examined in the course of study, a breadth of methods employed in the engagement with those materials, a breadth of viewpoints to be encountered and a breadth of languages for communication to be tried out in investigations and explorations.

Such breadth prevents educational "scripts" from being too tightly laid down and it ensures that assumptions already embedded in our culture are exposed for evaluation. There are assumptions within our wider culture that should be resisted. For example, common assumptions about knowledge that might be encountered include the following.

First, there can be an unwarranted confidence in our capacity to know; this can slip into arrogance. Second, some assume the dispensability of all authority other than our own, mistaking overstanding for understanding, as if we should not expect to stand in the light of, or submit to the requirements of some "external" authority. Third, others expect a high degree of individualism in the learning process, forgetful of our radical interdependence. Fourth, it can be taken as read that the occasion in which we learn the truth has merely an incidental character, as if it did not matter who we are learning with, the company we keep, what else we are learning at the time and how we are conducting our lives. Fifth, these assumptions are frequently linked with the expectation that increased, open-ended, and constantly revisable choice is the goal or the fruit of education. This leads to a shying away from the notion that education might prepare us for long-term

20. Thiessen, *Ethics of Evangelism*, 36, 107.

commitments, for decisions that bind us, and a recognition that, as we open some doors or embark on some paths or become one kind of person, other doors, other paths and other ways of being become closed to us.

Stanley Hauerwas vividly expresses this danger when he says: "Students are inscribed into capitalist practices in which they are taught that choosing between ideas is like choosing between a Sony and a Panasonic."[21] Making individual choice and autonomy absolute or fundamental values can have unfortunate side effects. It can prolong indecision and the right to drift among students, undermining the capacity for commitment. It can, through lack of appreciation for the role played in life by limits, create insecurity and anxiety rather than increase a sense of freedom.[22] It can also end up by destabilizing institutions and threatening democracy itself.[23] Such concerns about educational assumptions remain contentious in a post-secular society and deserve more substantial exploration than is possible here.

## CHURCH-ACADEMY COLLABORATION

Religious faith is promoted by the church and education's highest standards are promoted in the academy. The church and the academy might sometimes seem to be enemies, but they need each other. There are potential shortcomings on both sides if either works in isolation from the other. Collaboration benefits both.

Why does the church need the academy? How might a positive relationship with the academy help the church? I suggest nine ways in which the church can benefit from such a positive relationship. First, the academy can help the church find out how to become relevant to the questions of the day and current ways of thinking. Second, it can help the church to develop a greater clarity about her message. Third, it can prompt (even demand) greater honesty and humility, pressing critique and awkward questioning and evaluation of the gaps between claim and reality. Fourth, the academy can teach the church about learning, how the processes of learning work, what influences learning, what enhances it, or what damages and inhibits it. Fifth, the academy can help the church in the task of developing connectedness and depth across different areas of knowledge and the multiple dimensions of life. Sixth, without educational input into the life of faith, Christians can develop in an imbalanced way, so that academic maturity takes place while faith remains relatively static and immature. This is often

---

21. Stanley Hauerwas, quoted in Rengger, "Idea of Politics," 236.
22. Coq, "Quels sont les enjeux," 38–39.
23. Coq, "Quels sont les enjeux," 43.

revealed in the way interview questions are answered by many candidates for teaching and school leadership posts. They can display considerable and sophisticated grasp of many professional issues related to teaching and to leadership, but often then slip into making superficial and simplistic comments when their understanding of the bearing of faith is probed. Seventh, the church needs the academy to assist it in avoiding the offering of poor arguments and weak presentations on behalf of faith. Eighth, the church needs the academy in order to be challenged to appreciate the wisdom of those outside its borders, thereby being willing to learn from them and to reach out more inclusively to those who are different in any way. Finally, the church needs the academy's contribution to ministerial formation and education, as well as in the school and university sector, if it is to provide formation appropriate for professional service in a complex world.

Does the academy need the church? I believe that there are four reasons for claiming that it does. First, the academy needs the church in order to increase the range of its debating partners—and therefore to extend its capacity for communication. Second, the academy needs the church to ensure it addresses fundamental questions about life and death and human flourishing—to ensure it engages with existential seriousness. Third, the academy needs dialogue with the church (and faith communities more generally) to ensure that it encounters comprehensive mega-narratives that offer alternatives to current secularism. Fourth, the academy needs dialogue with the church as one of the ways to avoid forgetting the past and the potential sources of human wisdom made available via living traditions.

Although the picture I have painted might at first sight seem to show that the church needs the academy more than the academy needs the church, it does also suggest that there is real mutual gain when they collaborate. There are many areas where cooperation may be advantageous and serve human flourishing, provided that each "partner" takes the other one seriously and recognizes in the other expertise it does not possess itself. For instance, plural societies seeking to promote respect for diversity could learn something from the painful and not always productive experience of ecumenical endeavors carried out within the churches at the same time as the churches could learn from the many secular initiatives to promote a more inclusive society. In addition, the concern, both of the churches and of secular educators, to reach out more effectively to the communities they serve and to secure widening participation (in responding to the message of the gospel and in accessing learning opportunities respectively) might be more effectively pursued by cooperation rather than by mutual denigration. Furthermore, lifelong learning has more chance of becoming a reality if a multiplicity of settings and types of learning, formal and informal, are provided, and if these are related to the key moments and major challenges of life; the church has long experience of being close to people from cradle to grave.

Another area where there might be congruence of aim, even if differences of emphasis and approach, might be in promoting the development of a critical-prophetic capacity in believers and learners. It follows from the gospel, but also from secular critical pedagogy, that a prophetic, unmasking or prophetic role should be part of the armory of the educated and the faith informed. Here hypocrisy, ideology, and idols should all be exposed. Yet another factor is that complex real-world problems require multiple perspectives and approaches; if the churches and educators in general are to promote the common good, partnership rather than hostility between them would help.

Then there are two other considerations that might encourage at least occasional collaboration rather than constant mutual opposition between religious believers and educators. First, as intermediate institutions, placed between state control and atomistic individualism, churches (and, of course, the organizing bodies of other faith communities) and schools, colleges and universities have similar interests, both in preserving a space for their own sphere of influence, free from too much intrusion from government, and in fostering a sense of belonging and in mobilizing commitment. Second, religious believers and educators have it in common that they care about truth. It is unlikely that any one person or social agency can claim with any credibility today to possess the fullness of truth. It is incumbent on all the faithful and on all educators that their search for truth is relentless and unending, patient and resilient, inclusive, open and unrestricted in the range of epistemologies being relied upon—going beyond a simple reliance on authority, rationality, empiricism or intuition. Since both secular educators and religious believers are in the "truth-seeking business," here there is surely scope for mutual learning and cooperation.

In some of the areas outlined in the last few paragraphs, the need for collaboration might be felt more strongly on one side rather than on the other; in some cases the need might be felt on both sides; in some cases the need for cooperation might be interpreted differently. But cumulatively, I hope I have offered a host of reasons why collaboration, rather than separation, isolation, or hostility, might seem desirable. Although it would be wise for religious believers and for secular educators to continue to exercise caution about the assumptions, goals and approaches of their partners in any collaboration, such reservations should not prevent them from working prudentially together for the common good, each being, at least potentially, an asset rather than an enemy for the other.

# 2

# Learning from Medieval Monasticism

Despite significant differences of context and vocation for the layperson and the monk, important lessons about Christian formation and education can be learned from the Benedictine tradition. André Gushurst-Moore has recently provided a very fine retrieval of St. Benedict, effectively showing what Christian educators today can learn from Benedict's teaching.[1] And Ronald Rolheiser has, in simple and down-to-earth ways, demonstrated how the home can realistically be thought of as a domestic monastery.[2] Here I review the ways that, historically, Christian formation has taken place in the church, referring specifically to some features of the Benedictine tradition. Key features that should be present in Christian formation today, ones that were fostered by Benedictines, include being multidimensional and holistic, hospitable, listening and inclusive, liturgical, communal, and lifelong.

Over generations, people have been instructed in their Christian faith in a wide range of ways: from their mothers by the hearth at home, from sermons in and outside of church, from the liturgy, from hymns, from the work and worship of confraternities and guilds, from stained glass windows, paintings, tapestries, religious plays on festive occasions, through hearing stories from the Bible and the lives of the saints, through pilgrimages, processions and devotions at sacred shrines, and from the their experience of pastoral care. At its best, Christian formation displays an interrelation of the moral, physical, mental and spiritual, a combination of the inner and outer. The linguistic, affective, cognitive, and embodied dimensions of learning are all linked.

---

1. Gushurst-Moore, *Glory in All Things*.
2. Rolheiser, *Domestic Monastery*.

Education has always been a vital and central priority for Christians. Indeed the great historian of Christianity, Jaroslav Pelikan, once commented that "the church is always more than a school. But the church cannot be less than a school."[3] Such education, for centuries, rarely took place in what we would recognize as schools. "Rather this process takes place through and within practices—some of them deliberately and intentionally educational, but most pursuing other goods, such as communion with God or love of neighbor."[4]

During the first millennium—and for centuries afterwards—the Benedictines made a major contribution to the promotion of learning. Ten hallmarks of Benedictine education were picked out by the Association of Benedictine Colleges and Universities in 2007: love of Christ and neighbor; prayer: a life marked by liturgy, *lectio*, and mindfulness; stability: commitment to the daily life of this place, its heritage and tradition; conversation: the way of formation and transformation; obedience: a commitment to listening and consequent action; discipline: a way toward learning and freedom; humility: knowledge of self in relation to God, others, and creation; stewardship: responsible use of creation, culture, and the arts; hospitality: openness to the other; community: call to serve the common good.[5]

Interestingly, the Rule of St. Benedict recognized that each monk's formation had to adapt to their individual rate of development, even though the shape and ordering of community life, accompanied by discipline, *lectio divina* and prayer, would apply to all. The notion of differentiation, of adapting teaching to the capacities and needs of learners, is not a modern invention. The formation to be provided would be ongoing and lifelong. Bernard of Clairvaux confirmed the twin purposes of the Cistercian formation program (which built upon a Benedictine foundation): becoming equipped in order to be able to edify others—a charitable service—and in order to be edified oneself. Without this one would lack prudence and wisdom. Such formation, for Bernard, should address, engage and develop reason, memory, and will.

The daily life of monks was framed and governed by the Divine Office, accompanied by discipline, good works, and regular gatherings of their community in the chapter house. "A regime of fasting, of interrupted sleep and of a total denial of sexuality knitted together the days and the years in the abbey."[6] They spent time together (even if in silence) during meals, as

3. Jaroslav Pelikan, quoted in Bass, "Foreword," ix.
4. Bass, "Foreword," x.
5. Association of Benedictine Colleges and Universities, "Education."
6. Milis, *Angelic Monks and Earthly Men*, 146.

well as having in common the vows they had each taken—of obedience, chastity, poverty and stability. Rozanne Elder refers to the expectation that novices should learn "the manners of God's city."[7] This might be paralleled today by the notions of socialization and acculturation, that is, learning "how we do things here," a process adopted by any community aiming to induct people into its way of life. An important part of training the will, so that it could operate in service of living the truth, was physical discipline. William of Saint Thierry expected that novices "must learn to guard their speech and their eyes, control their gait and their hands, temper their laughter and their curiosity, honor the seniors, love the juniors, and obey the superiors."[8] It is frequently assumed today that the exercise of authority is more likely to be corrosive of freedom, rather than constitutive of it.

Monks were expected to adopt—and adapt themselves to—a habit, or habitus. Stephen Jaeger describes this habitus as including, not only clothing, but also attitude, inner posture, frame of mind, stance, position.[9] It also included posture understood as both

> the position taken on an issue and the position in which the body is held. . . . The education in manners aims precisely at the governance of impulse. . . . The body is meant to be "read"; the well-composed body is itself a text-book of virtue. Like a musical instrument, the inner world can be "tuned" through adjusting the outer.[10]

"Tuning" the body has repercussions on character development. If the student walks and gestures gracefully, speaks confidently and persuasively, and holds his head and eyes in a moderated and controlled way, then the inner world will be held to the laws of grace, restraint, and moderation that are in force in the outer. "Dress, gesture, speech, tone of voice, table manners, posture and gait are the point of departure for the cultivation of virtue."[11]

Perhaps what most marks out the medieval from a modern approach to education and formation, is its stress on the will. Far from being blind to and cruelly suppressive of the drives of our nature, monastic writers evidently displayed a shrewd insight into how our choices have consequences that change us and which can thereby reduce our freedom. Self-expression

---

7. Elder, "Formation for Wisdom," 199.
8. Elder, "Formation for Wisdom," 199–200.
9. Jaeger, *Envy of Angels*, 9–10.
10. Jaeger, *Envy of Angels*, 13.
11. Jaeger, *Envy of Angels*, 106.

and radical autonomy, so often lauded in our day, can lead to self-imprisonment and to the erosion of true freedom. Too many of us today assume that we can exercise and reverse our choices easily and without consequences for our psychological make-up.

Formational purposes and practices depended upon a strong emphasis on the role of affections, the will and the body, on liturgy and community life, on a range of closely connected disciplines related to food, clothing, posture and gesture, and on a richer and more complex understanding of both memory and of reading than is customary today. We should note that learning about God did not take place separately from learning about life in general. Many purposes guided religious formational practices: "spiritual salvation, social liberation, personal well-being (moral or social), ethical action, inner contemplation, community solidarity."[12] These were all seen as mutually implicating and reinforcing one another. Example, participation, observation, imitation, habituation, celebration—all played a part in Christian formation, for monks, but also for laypeople. Cumulatively these were intended to prepare the self to hand itself over to the Creator and to open the way to transformation by God into our true identity.

Attitudes to food and to eating were treated as having spiritual significance. As Blake Leyerle points out, "Every monastic tradition lavishes attention on [food and fasting]. What kinds of foods one can eat, when, how, and with whom, are all matters of . . . consuming interest."[13] Leyerle quotes a monk: "How can we guard our hearts when our mouths and our stomachs are open?"[14] Similar concerns arise today about diet and health, although they are usually expressed differently. Whatever we voluntarily take into ourselves has the capacity to modify our character. This applies also to the images we gaze upon, for example, on the internet. As with the intake of food, the images that engage our attention steadily and inexorably change who we are becoming, usually without our realizing this internal transformation.

Monks considered the intake of words as similar to the intake of food. "Like food, written words only become useful once they have been metabolized, that is to say, memorized. In antiquity memorization meant more than a simple facility in retrieval, but an active ability to rearrange and adapt the material learned."[15] This capacity to adapt and deploy creatively what is learned is quite different than the regurgitation often asked

---

12. Van Engen, *Educating People of Faith*, 22.
13. Leyerle, "Monastic Formation and Christian Practice," 87.
14. Leyerle, "Monastic Formation and Christian Practice," 97.
15. Leyerle, "Monastic Formation and Christian Practice," 108.

for in examinations. Another medieval monastic insight we might learn from today is their expectation that, instead of their reading being a process of establishing mastery over a text, so that its assimilation was governed by their needs, priorities and worldview, rather reading was a process in which they stood under the text, allowed themselves to be changed by it, and eventually to be assimilated into its purview. The word that is received, if accepted appropriately, effects a change in the monk, assimilating him to the word, bringing him into closer conformity with it. Not only were readers of Scripture "read" by what they read; they were consumed by it. This was a truer appreciation of what is entailed by understanding, as compared with our contemporary tendency to mistake understanding for "overstanding" or as establishing mastery over something, rather than opening oneself up to what it has to offer.[16]

Reading was viewed in a more comprehensive way than it is today; it involved the body, the mind, the will, the emotions, and the memory. Its purpose was to facilitate transformation. The goal of transformation is the effective realization of human freedom in loving response to our Creator. Such transformation occurs when our humanization opens up into our divinization. The deep reading promoted by *lectio* offers a powerful alternative to the more superficial, undisciplined and instrumental modes of reading prevalent today among many students. Formation carried out in a Benedictine ethos provides an educational vision that integrates the multiple dimensions of our nature—physical, emotional, social, moral, intellectual and spiritual. Rather than education being colonized by technological, materialistic, therapeutic, and worldly success-oriented aims, it is guided by the priority of the spiritual, with the goal of preparing us for heaven.

Two further points are pertinent here: first, to stress the role played in the monastic tradition by liturgy as an integral, indeed, central element in Christian formation; second, how Christian educators were to view the relationship between Christian and non-Christian culture.

Evelyn Vitz claims that "the Catholic liturgy was the major source of education about their faith for laymen and-women of the Middle Ages."[17] It is easy to underestimate the power of liturgy to influence the outlook and imagination of congregations. In an interview with Peter Stanford in *The Tablet*, Marina Warner refers to "the sensory wrap-around effect of incense, candles, music, procession and assembly."[18] Such an effect occurs indirectly and implicitly. "What the faithful learned from the liturgy came in

---

16. See ch. 19 for a development of this point.
17. Vitz, "Liturgy as Education," 20.
18. Stanford, "Exile Returns," 9.

essentially by osmosis: by the mere fact of being in church and attending services through the different seasons, over many years."[19] Vitz continues:

> The liturgy trained not just minds but also bodies.... The faithful stood, they bowed, they knelt and genuflected, they crossed themselves.... They may well have been awake all night in vigil before Mass; during Lent, and at certain other times, they came fasting or having abstained from sexual intercourse.... Their knowledge of the liturgy was in their bodies as much as in their brains.... Men and women received a substantial amount of religious information through the senses. They heard the music of the liturgy; they smelled the incense; they saw the candles. They watched the clergy process through the church to the altar and repeatedly kiss the altar.[20]

And, of course, they experienced all this, not in isolation from others, but accompanied by a very strong sense of community, the same community to which they belonged outside the church. For most people, there was no notion of being "outside" the church. Many activities we might consider as secular took place within church buildings, including entertainment and dancing as well as community decision-making events.

As for how Christian educators were to treat non-Christian culture, the best elements of pagan culture were not to be dispensed with; but they had to be brought into proper harmony with thinking and practices that were impregnated by Christian faith. If we adapted this tension for our own time, we might refer to the need (in Christian education and formation) to treat the passing on our of religious tradition in its wholeness and integrity as a task that is both essential and life giving, but, at the same time to acknowledge that this tradition needs to be supplemented by and brought into dialogue with contemporary forms of secular knowledge. Such an encounter with contemporary thinking and culture would inevitably require modifications within our understanding and implementation of the faith tradition we have received from the past. However, the assumptions, norms and priorities of contemporary culture need to be carefully sifted and prayerfully discerned in the light of the Christian tradition; not everything can be accepted as legitimate or assimilated into a reformulated faith. Some aspects of contemporary culture—in any age—are in need of purification before acceptance, others are open to reshaping and elevation, while yet others must be judged to be contradictory to and undermining of the faith.

---

19. Vitz, "Liturgy as Education," 21.
20. Vitz, "Liturgy as Education," 24.

We may not be able to reinstate the conditions, assumptions, and practices of medieval monks, but there remains much of great value that we can still learn from them.

# 3

# Hugh of St. Victor

*Medieval Wisdom for Modern Educators*

WHILE DISPUTATION AND DIALOGUE have always been at the heart of university teaching and learning, other features of medieval education can strike a discordant note in the modern university. Among such features might be included the bearing of the virtues and affections on the development of rationality and wisdom, the importance given to the integration (rather than the separation) of the intellectual and the spiritual dimensions of our being, and the notion that university teachers should act, not just as exponents of knowledge and facilitators of learning, but also as exemplars and models of the right living out of that knowledge. There was also the expectation that, in addition to the labors of teachers and students, our minds might be both illuminated and empowered by a divine source.

Furthermore, it was firmly believed that this divine source provided the foundation for the ultimate unity of all knowledge. Attempts to import any of these aspects of education—once considered normal and necessary in the early years of the medieval university and by scholars more generally (whether Christian, Jewish or Muslim)—into contemporary universities (with the possible exception of a few faith-based ones which adopt a more explicitly countercultural stance) would be interpreted as provocative. They would be felt by many to fall into one of the following errors: intruding into the private realm, undermining autonomy, unduly moralistic, culturally imperialistic, demeaning to the professional status of academics, far too accommodating to and gullible about claims made by religious communities,

PART ONE | TRADITION AS A RESOURCE

and corrosive of that specialization and differentiation in scholarly disciplines that has led to a never-ending expansion of knowledge.[1]

While not wishing to lament the loss of a former age, nor to denigrate the genuine strengths of contemporary universities, in this article I revisit the aforementioned, once commonplace, features of medieval education in order to make explicit the challenge they pose for the assumptions that appear to govern university teaching and learning today. As a way into commenting on these features I will draw from the writings of a preeminent medieval scholar who lived in the era not long before the rise of universities, Hugh of St. Victor (1096–1141). In particular, I will focus on what he had to say about the nature of and preconditions for learning and how these relate to moral and spiritual development. My hope is that such an encounter might present alternative and enriching approaches to teaching and learning today, expand the options open to students and their teachers and, in the process, help to reduce the gaps that often appear between the worlds of academe and everyday life.

After a few introductory remarks, the chapter engages with Hugh's educational thinking in four steps, leading to a brief final section. First, both Hugh and his abbey are put in their historical context and an initial summary of his view of education is provided. Second, I focus on his major educational treatise, the *Didascalicon* and draw key themes from that work; these relate to his understanding of the arts, reading, memory and restoration. In the third step, I turn to Hugh's guidebook on the formation of novices, examining three topics with implications for learning: the discipline of the body, the role of example and imitation, and the influence of horizontal and peer learning. Fourth, there is a comparison of the ethos of the university today with Hugh's educational outlook, with a view to bringing out more explicitly both similarities and differences of assumptions and priorities. Finally, I raise the question: Is there a need and an opportunity today to retrieve key aspects of Hugh's thought; is it time for a contemplative turn in education?

What was the spirit that animated many medieval educators, of whom Hugh of St. Victor was a leading example? What larger project did they believe they were embarked upon? Why did they think their efforts mattered? What were the underlying assumptions and ideals that inspired, governed and guided their work? The art of reading and the art of living are parallel works, to be taken together as representing Hugh's understanding of education and formation. The basic orientation, fundamental assumptions,

---

1. For examples of the suspicion of, hostility to, and discrimination against those holding or seeking to express religious perspectives in the academy today, see Kanpol and Poplin, *Christianity and Secular Border Control*.

dominant practices, most urgent problems, common aspirations and expectations, leading priorities, framing concepts, underlying commitments and aversions, pervasive sensibilities and wider shared horizons—all these comprise what we mean when we refer to a community's outlook, mental milieu or worldview. Educational and academic practices, such as reading and following a prescribed methodology, that on the surface might appear similar in both medieval and modern times, in reality functioned quite differently for exponents of both reading and scholarship. This is not to suggest that either medieval or modern societies are homogeneous. People of all historical eras respond to the norms of their time with varying degrees of acceptance, resistance and of consistency, depending on context, upbringing, experience, accident, opportunity, resources, and intentionality.[2]

## HUGH AND HIS ABBEY

The Abbey of Saint Victor was a center of higher learning, just outside Paris, which attracted many creative scholars and teachers, especially in its early days and for much of the twelfth century. Its residents were canons regular, priests living in community under the Rule of St. Augustine. Neither secular clergy nor monks, they combined religious devotion, academic studies and attention to developing moral virtue; their ethos exuded a distinct blend of emphasis on letters, manners and spirituality. Apart from stressing the value of learning, virtue, and the path of personal holiness, their goal was to provide a haven of communal harmony internally and a ministry to the wider community externally. Their daily lives were regulated by precise rules governing their behavior, movement and modes of communication; these rules laid down guidance about speech, dress, diet, who should be imitated and which virtues should be pursued.

The historian Ian Wei sets Hugh of St. Victor in an intermediate position between that of the monks and that of the teachers in the schools—the early scholastics. While many monks, such as Bernard of Clairvaux, thought that it was necessary to reject the world and its values (including secular knowledge) in order to arrive at religious knowledge, and criticized the teachers of the Parisian schools, first, for having dishonorable motives for study, such as greed, desire for fame, or self-indulgent delving in an unbridled curiosity; and second, for not providing the appropriate conditions

---

2. For a brief overview of medieval understandings of teachers and scholars, of *scientia* and *sapientia*; the inextricable links between intellectual, moral, and spiritual virtues; and similarities and differences between the ethos of medieval and modern universities, see Sullivan, *Christian Academic in Higher Education*, 55–60.

for fostering true knowing,³ the Victorines stood out among religious communities for the way they held together, on the one hand, the traditional pathways of communal prayer and ascetic discipline, and, on the other hand, intellectual inquiry and involvement in the world beyond the abbey. James Halverson points out that "Hugh did not demand that his students become scholars, pastors, or ascetic mystics, though some did. The school of St. Victor taught students who would go on to 'good jobs' in royal and ecclesiastical courts or noble and merchant households. These influential knowledge workers were ideally placed to apply their restored minds to restoring the human community."⁴

Hugh came to St. Victor around 1115, first to learn, but by 1120 he was teaching there, eventually elected as abbot in 1133, a post he held until his death in 1141. The various schools of Paris in the twelfth century, including that at St. Victor, attracted in large numbers many of the best and most influential scholars in Europe. Not long after his death his reputation was such that he was considered to be a second Augustine, a title for which there could be no greater accolade among medieval scholars. In the thirteenth century, Bonaventure, a major figure who combined university teaching and writing advanced works of theology with leadership of the rapidly growing Franciscan order and the provision of important spiritual guidance for his spiritual brothers, praised Hugh for displaying the qualities of Augustine, Gregory the Great, and Dionysius and for excelling three of Hugh's contemporaries who developed the thought of these masters, Anselm, Bernard of Clairvaux, and Richard of St. Victor.⁵

Hugh left a large body of writing that was immensely influential, being read throughout France, Germany, and Eastern Europe, mostly by Benedictines, Cistercians, Augustinians, and Carthusians.⁶ This work included the *Didascalicon*, on the right way to approach learning, *De institutione novitiorum*, a practical guide for novices (which also includes much of educational relevance), many works on meditation and prayer, plus other works of scriptural exegesis, together with his magisterial study of the sacraments. In all of these he maintained a focus on the formation of the person and how to read rightly, the close connection between knowledge, discipline, and virtue and the necessity of establishing harmony between external behavior and the inner self. Hence one is struck by the importance he attached to aspects

---

3. Wei, *Intellectual Culture in Medieval Paris*, 85.
4. Halverson, "Restored Through Learning," 50.
5. Bonaventure, *Reduction of the Arts*, 45.
6. Illich, *In Vineyard of Text*, 85n43.

of life rarely thought to have educational significance today, for example, clothing, gestures, manner of talking, and etiquette at table.

For Hugh, the first step on the path to God is taken when one learns how to govern one's body, for without such mastery the inner life will remain at the mercy of physical needs and drives. Similarly, the path to truth also depends on self-discipline, for scholarship has its own forms of asceticism. Hugh stresses the importance of imitating the good example given by others, both within and beyond the community of Saint Victor, and allowing oneself to be deeply influenced by such example. Self-discipline was to be joined by sociability, humility, courtesy and spirituality, all founded on and enlightened by sacred Scripture and secular learning. These qualities were conducive to study because they helped to detach a person from self-importance, possessiveness, pride, distractions and noise. He even went so far as recommend exile, or being on foreign soil, as a factor likely to enhance the conditions for studying, because the discipline of leaving transitory things behind and being on unfamiliar territory helped one to be more detached from comforts and more open to receive and to learn.

Underlying Hugh's vision for formation and education was a positive anthropology, a strong belief in human dignity, based on humanity's status as made in the image of God, a conviction that each person is *capax dei*—able to receive the divinizing grace of God and capable of being perfected despite current shortcomings. He laid out a curriculum and program of formation that was carefully constructed to develop the rationality, emotions, will, imagination, spirituality, character and moral life and sense of community of students. This added up to a comprehensive, coherent and integrated worldview. The path that led to this included the removal of obstacles to right seeing and living, training in the habits of attention, openness to truth and wisdom, followed by engagement with, loving relationship with and performance of the truth encountered. Truth and virtue were intimately connected for Hugh; one could not reach either without the support of the other.

## THE *DIDASCALICON*

Composed in late 1120s, written for those embarking on higher education (although at a younger age than is the case today), highly influential, both immediately and for several centuries afterwards, the *Didascalicon*, Hugh's most famous work, was intended to show how education can contribute to the restoration of divine wisdom in human persons who had lost their capacity to receive this wisdom because of sin. Such restoration required, for Hugh, the contemplation of truth and the practice of virtue. Salzmann says of the *Didascalicon*, "It is celebrated, along with John of Salisbury's later *Metalogicon* (1159), as the most important work on human learning from the 12th century renaissance."[7]

The program of studies outlined and explained by Hugh was simultaneously noetic (concerned with our cognitive capacities), ethical (with implications for our behavior) and spiritual (bearing upon our relationship with God). Hugh divided up the arts into four categories: theoretical ("which strives for the contemplation of truth"), practical ("which considers the regulation of morals"), mechanical ("which supervises the occupations of this life"), and logical ("which provides the knowledge necessary for correct speaking and clear argumentation").[8] The theoretical arts included theology, physics and mathematics (usually known as the quadrivium, which embraced arithmetic, music, geometry and astronomy). The practical arts covered ethics, economics and politics. The logical arts, or trivium, included grammar, rhetoric, and logic (or dialectic). His inclusion of the mechanical arts (fabric making, armament, commerce, agriculture, hunting, medicine, and theatrics) was a significant innovation, indicating a concern for everyday life that displayed a more outward-looking perspective than that usually held in monasteries. As Paul Rorem notes, "Hugh shows a robust pleasure in the rich variety of our created world, the world of weaving and saddles, swords and trowels, commerce and orchards, fishing and porridge and mead."[9] Contrary to what one might expect of a medieval member of a religious community, as Halverson underlines, "Hugh has an unequivocally positive view of commerce."[10] "The pursuit of commerce reconciles nations, calms wars, strengthens peace, and commutes the private good of individuals into the common benefit of all."[11]

Taken together, this cluster of four types of arts is intended by Hugh to bring about a wide range of benefits. First, it contributes to the apprehension of truth (both secular and sacred). Second, it facilitates the capacity for abstract thinking and decision-making (without which moral deliberation is not possible). Third, it enhances our capacity to make our way in the world. Fourth, it enables us to communicate clearly, honestly, rationally and persuasively. Fifth, it provides the right conditions for the development of wisdom. Sixth, it puts in place the building blocks and essential skills and habits which equip us to continue learning thereafter, without the direction

---

7. Salzmann, "Soul's Reformation," 142.
8. Hugh, *Didascalicon*, 60.
9. Rorem, *Hugh of Saint Victor*, 39. See Hugh, *Didascalicon*, 75–79.
10. Halverson, "Restored Through Learning," 49.
11. Hugh, *Didascalicon*, 77.

of teachers and on our own initiative: it makes lifelong learning possible. Finally, it cooperates with God's grace in restoring us to our authentic nature as beings made in the image of God and called to express that likeness in our relationship with the rest of creation. This spiritual significance of learning from the arts applies, for Hugh, not just to the learning of theology, but to *all* of the arts. Hugh's program for the arts is to be considered as a whole; each of the arts depends on all the others for its proper and optimal functioning. They are essentially interconnected: "These so hang together and so depend upon one another in their ideas that if only one of the arts be lacking, all the rest cannot make a man into a philosopher."[12]

The arts were seen by Hugh as second-order activities, building upon activities normally carried out unreflectively in everyday life. Thus,

> All sciences were matters of use before they became matters of art. . . . Before there was grammar, men both wrote and spoke; before there was dialectic, they distinguished the true from the false by reasoning; before there was rhetoric, they discoursed upon civil laws; before there was arithmetic, there was knowledge of counting; before there was an art of music, they sang; before there was astronomy, they marked off periods of time from the courses of the stars.[13]

He quotes with approval Hugh's advice about the prerequisite conditions for and key factors underpinning study, advice attributed to Bernard of Chartres: "A humble mind, eagerness to inquire, a quiet life, silent scrutiny, poverty, a foreign soil."[14] These qualities indicate a more deliberately ascetic understanding of the nature of study than is commonly held today. While eagerness to learn, a quiet life and silent scrutiny seem obviously conducive to learning, being supportive of the necessary effort and concentrated focus, it is likely that humility, poverty and the sensibility of being a foreigner would come less readily to mind for twenty-first-century students. On humility, he claims that the student, first, should "hold no knowledge in contempt"; second, "that he blush to learn from no man; and third, that when he has attained learning himself, he not look down upon everyone else."[15] On poverty, Hugh quotes Jerome: "A fat belly does not produce a fine perception," meaning that self-indulgence, luxury, and giving too much attention to satisfying the desires of the flesh are likely to act as impediments to the discipline required for fostering a yearning for learning.

12. Hugh, *Didascalicon*, 89.
13. Hugh, *Didascalicon*, 59–60.
14. Hugh, *Didascalicon*, 94.
15. Hugh, *Didascalicon*, 95.

And, for those who aspire to become, in due course, a citizen of heaven, no land here should benefit from our ultimate loyalty: "The man who finds his homeland sweet is still a tender beginner; he to whom every soil is as his native one is already strong; but he is perfect to whom the entire world is as a foreign land."[16] In all these cases, commitment to the truth, which calls for dedication to virtue, requires a high degree of detachment from anything that might distract one from these goals.

In the *Didascalicon* Hugh deals with four steps which trace out the path towards perfecting the human person, all of which depend for their efficacy on the workings of divine grace: study or instruction, meditation, prayer, and performance. The fifth step he mentions, contemplation, is addressed in a separate work. "The first, study, gives understanding; the second, meditation, provides counsel; the third, prayer, makes petition; the fourth, performance, goes seeking; the fifth, contemplation, finds."[17]

His view of reading was more expansive than our own. For him, reading mediated between the world outside us (the macrocosm) and the world within us (the microcosm). All knowledge, if used properly, can play a part in cooperating with God in restoring in us our true nature and in restoring a fallen creation to right relation with its Creator. The desire for truth is legitimate because it can orient us to find the divine source of all truths. The pursuit of learning was, for Hugh, an intrinsically noble vocation, one that turns students away from false goals, such as wealth and fame, and that orients them instead towards the contemplation of higher things. Gillian Evans notes the fear among many medieval thinkers that the pursuit of learning also has its shadow side, "because it could lead into the realms of trivial inquisitiveness, obsessive preoccupation, greed, unbridled desire, the playing with the fire of magic and superstition, where lay various kinds of profound danger to the soul."[18] His view of reading was also more expansive than ours in another way: beyond being a means to access and accumulate knowledge, reading had a soul-forming role; what was read was to be impressed on the reader's character, reflected on, in the sense of being the object of meditation (focused scrutiny), and so internalized that it would be reflected (or expressed) in the reader's consequent activity, self-presentation, and communication.

The cultural commentator, Ivan Illich, wrote an extended reflection on the *Didascalicon* called *In the Vineyard of the Text*. Here I pick out two of his observations about differences between Hugh's age and our own, the first on

16. Hugh, *Didascalicon*, 101.
17. Hugh, *Didascalicon*, 132.
18. G. Evans, *Getting It Wrong*, ix.

the notion of there being a final cause and the second about the nature of reading as a bodily activity. Medieval scholars accepted the notion that there is a final cause behind all phenomena and actions; this final cause is their ultimate purpose, that for the sake of which a thing is done. This final cause, from our perspective, lies ahead of us as an invitation tugging us towards it, although from Hugh's perspective, as a typical medieval thinker, this final cause is embedded already in reality. One of the reasons this teleological view is resisted today is that it seems to undermine our autonomy and our capacity to impose our purpose on the world, rather than, as premoderns saw it, accommodating ourselves to fit into a preordained order (as created by God). For Hugh there is a given structure and order to the universe; everything is interconnected, because all things are bound together in the design of the Creator. Illich notes that

> The thought of an ultimate goal of all readings is not meaningful to us. Even less is there any idea that such a goal could motivate or "cause" our action whenever we open a book. We are steeped in the spirit of engineering and think of the trigger as the cause of a process. We do not think of the heart as the cause of the bullet's trajectory.[19]

We tend to think of reading as an activity that is silent, carried out by individuals in isolation from one another (rather than corporately, alongside others), and as something that goes on "in our heads," rather than as a physical activity. In contrast, as Illich points out, reading is experienced by Hugh as

> a bodily motor activity.... The lines [on the page] are a sound track picked up by the mouth and voiced by the reader for his own ear. By reading, the page is literally embodied, incorporated. The modern reader conceives of the page as a plate that inks the mind, and of the mind as a screen onto which the page is projected and from which, at a flip, it can fade.... For the monastic reader... the reader understands the lines by moving to their beat, remembers them by recapturing their rhythm, and thinks of them in terms of putting them into his mouth and chewing.[20]

Two further points about Hugh's educational philosophy, as exhibited in the *Didascalicon*, should be made here: first, his understanding of memory and, second, the concept of restoration. Both mark out clear differences

19. Illich, *In Vineyard of Text*, 13.
20. Illich, *In Vineyard of Text*, 54.

between medieval and modern conceptions of the mind and of the purpose of education.

*Memoria*, according to Hugh's use of the term, might be described as an internally imagined and structured representation of the elements of the culture that was being imbibed by the student, a kind of mental map, or perhaps a floor plan of the house of knowledge. This inner representation of what was being learned was gradually built up by a docile acceptance of instruction and explanation, willingness to engage in the disciplines laid down by teachers, imitation of the example given by teachers, other model members of the community and the lives of the saints, constant repetition, patient attention to the prescribed texts and practices and adoption of the key images, metaphors and symbols that were deployed by Hugh and other Victorine teachers in order to organize and structure knowledge and feed the imagination so that this knowledge could be readily envisaged and brought to mind by students. For example, Hugh often made great play with such symbolic images as ark, building tree, house and book. One finds an extended deployment of the metaphor of tree in book 2, chapter 15, of his first treatise on Noah's ark:

> The tree of life, the word of the wisdom of God, is sown in fear, watered by grace, dies through grief, takes root by faith, buds by devotion, shoots up through compunction, grows by longing, is strengthened by charity, grows green by hope, puts down its leaves and spreads its branches through caution, flowers through discipline, bears fruit through virtue, ripens through patience, is harvested by death, and feeds by contemplation.[21]

"The ultimate aim of *memoria* was to make a particular text part of oneself, to allow it to be inscribed on one's heart in order to build character, promote citizenship, instill prudence, engender piety, and ultimately to attain perfect happiness."[22] Harkins quotes Jean Leclercq's landmark study of monastic culture, *The Love of Learning and the Desire for God*:

> For the ancients, to meditate is to read a text and to learn it "by heart" in the fullest sense of this expression, that is, with one's whole being: with the body, since the mouth pronounced it, with the memory which fixes it, with the intelligence which understands its meaning, and with the will which desires to put it into practice.[23]

---

21. Hugh, *Selected Spiritual Writings*, 93.
22. Harkins, *Reading and Work of Restoration*, 35.
23. Leclercq, *Love of Learning*, 21–22.

In contrast, the modern view of memory tends to limit its scope to that of a "data repository, which can be 'out-sourced' to external substitutes (i.e., reference books or electronic media)."[24] The very idea of training the memory, especially for students in higher education, seems outmoded and unnecessary, a quaint echo from a former age which did not benefit from modern technological aids for accessing information. However, despite contemporary neglect of, or even suspicion of the use of memory in education, Pope John Paul II laments the suppression of memorization as an educational tool and argues that it continues to play a necessary and valuable part in any sound engagement with a living tradition.[25]

As for restoration, when Hugh uses this term to describe how the arts in his curriculum operate as aids to bringing a person back into line with God's original intention for humanity, he is suggesting a complex amalgam of notions, including to reform a person from their errant ways, to reshape the pattern of their lives, to liberate them from those proclivities that distort, weaken, or even destroy their essential nature, to reconcile them with God and neighbor and to reorder their cognitive, moral, and spiritual capacities so that these function properly. The arts should operate as remedies which address specific ailments to which humanity is prone. For Hugh, the theoretical, the practical, and the mechanical arts address respectively wisdom, virtue, and the needs of daily life; these arts are "remedies against three evils to which human life is subject: wisdom against ignorance, virtue against vice, and need against life's weaknesses."[26] Since Christ is, for Hugh, the Wisdom from whom we have to learn how we can live rightly in relation to God, and since following Christ is our way to union with God, and since the way we learn who Christ is passes through Scripture, which is received from the church, then the process of restoration and reformation, to which the arts contribute, might simultaneously be called one of "Christo-formation," "churchification," and "scripturalization,"[27] as well as of humanization.

## THE FORMATION OF NOVICES

For Hugh, the world is a book written by the finger of God and the human person's life, as expressed in words and actions, is also a book, from which her nature and character can be read. In his guide book for the instruction of novices he quotes Prov 6:12–14: "A scoundrel, a villain, wears deceit on

24. Coolman, *Theology of Hugh*, 156.
25. John Paul II, *Catechesi Tradendae*, §55.
26. Hugonis de Sancto Victore, *Didascalicon* 6.14 (not included in Taylor's edition).
27. Coolman, *Theology of Hugh*, 22.

the lips, looking askance, shifty of foot, wagging the finger" to indicate that the body mirrors the internal state of a person and that it can be deployed to express as well as to hide malign as well as benign purposes. A major aspect of education, not addressed directly in the *Didascalicon*, was the ordering of the body as an essential component in the process of restoring human beings to their true position as images of God. Thus, his *De institutione novitiorum* should be considered as a counterpart to and completion of his broader work on learning in the *Didascalicon*. Falque, in a significant article on *De institutione novitiorum*, views this work as transcending traditional teaching on the formation of novices by developing a philosophy of gesture and speech that exposes a rare harmony between the internal and external dimensions of our being. The path towards knowledge, discipline, and goodness includes attention to our bearing and gestures, imitation of the saints (to bring us to reflect the divine likeness more closely), discernment of how to conduct ourselves in words and actions, orchestrating these (in church, cloister, refectory, chapter house, dormitory, or private cell), so that they fit harmoniously into the symphony of the community. Falque points out that attention to bearing, gesture and speech applies to teachers as well as to novices and students, by noting, in a striking play on words, that "il convient donc d'être en *chair* pour être en *chaire*" (it is necessary to incarnate, to model in the flesh [one's teaching] if one is to speak from the teacher's desk [or, by implication, from the pulpit]). He then goes on to quote Hugh: "The word of God comes to us each day under cover of a human voice"; the implication is that we are called to be that voice for each other.[28]

Mirko Breitenstein traces the enduring influence of *De institutione novitiorum* across the next few centuries, not only in the formation of members of religious orders, but also in the education of laypeople, especially at the courts of rulers.[29] Hugh's guidebook blends teaching about conduct, virtue, the relationship between the individual and his community, personal and communal salvation and heightening consciousness about the effects of actions on the human environment in which they occur. Its structuring principle is the integral relationship between knowledge, discipline and goodness, each being a precondition for the others.

Two ideas that seem countercultural in our contemporary university context pervade this treatise: first, the important role played in education and formation by the discipline of the body; and second, the strong emphasis put on example and imitation. After commenting on these two themes, I will draw out, as an implication of the second theme, a feature of monastic

---

28. Falque, "Geste et parole," 410.
29. Breitenstein, "Success of Discipline."

life that raises a challenge for contemporary universities in their dealings with students: the degree to which they promote learning from the example of their peers.

With regard to the first of these themes, Hugh believed that there is a close connection between the discipline of the body, moral maturity and correcting disorders of the mind. "Discipline is a shackle for cupidity, a prison for evil desires, a bridle for wantonness, a yoke for pride, a chain for anger; it subdues intemperance, binds light-mindedness, and stifles all the disorderly motions and illicit appetites of the mind."[30] Our movements, gestures and speech reveal our character, but if these are regulated, our character can be modified for the better. This will, in turn, enhance our capacity to seek, to welcome and to embrace truth. Mastering our outward behavior has the additional benefit, for Hugh, of promoting harmony in the community of the abbey to which the novices seek to belong.

As for the second theme, Hugh constantly stresses the importance of learning from the example of others. This requires humility, deliberately setting out to imitate such examples, most especially of the saints. Such imitation depends upon a bending of the will and the subjection of pride, followed by a commitment to so act and speak that one's actions and words can serve as an example and encouragement to others, inside and beyond the abbey. In advocating the need to imitate good example, Hugh was careful to distinguish seniority of rank from the worthiness of the exemplar; anyone could serve as a model, if their behavior called out for this. "Monks followed saintly models, written guides, 'scripts.' They did not write their own script, as modern man is supposed to do."[31] They did not prize originality or desire to stand out from their brethren; conformity to a rule and to a saintly model did not leave much room for self-expression, diverging from others, or claiming a special identity for oneself. Following the example of the saints (who themselves have most closely imitated the example of Christ), in Hugh's perspective, will improve and enhance our personhood, not suppress it. He warns the novices, "if I neglect to imitate the good I know, then I can say that my thought is right, but unprofitable.... It profits me nothing if I do not take it to myself as a pattern for living. For another person's virtue is of no profit to me, if I neglect to copy it as far as I am able."[32] He draws upon an image commonly deployed among medieval writers, of a seal pressed into wax: "Just as the wax into which a seal is pressed must be made soft in order to receive the form or image of the seal, so too must the

30. Porwoll, "Parisian Pedagogies," 140, quoting Hugh, *De institutione novitiorum*.
31. Van 't Spijker, *Fictions of the Inner Life*, 10–11.
32. Hugh, *Selected Spiritual Writings*, 81.

hardness of human pride be softened by humility in order for the student to be re-formed into God's image through the impression of the lives of the saints."[33]

Hugh expected his students not only to be ready to imitate the saints and those of their elders who gave good example, but also their peers if these displayed qualities that merited emulation. In some respects, imitation of peers was easier because these fellow students were not so far in advance, in terms of virtue and studiousness, that their standards were unattainable. As Porwoll notes, "Peers offer models for imitation because their lives have admirable qualities still within our reach."[34] In fact, every member of the community at St. Victor should be considered a fellow disciple; even in a hierarchical society such as that which pertained in the twelfth century, learning could be as much horizontal (between equals) as vertical (received from one's teachers and superiors).

Horizontal learning occurs naturally when people associate with each other in community life and when they work together in some common endeavor. Mutual influence, imitation, modeling, and observation lead them into a shared repertoire of practices, knowledge, and beliefs. Long, Snijders, and Vanderputten describe horizontal learning as "knowledge transmitted and acquired in a context of informal interactions, to which traditional categories such as 'teachers' and 'disciples' do not necessarily apply."[35] In these circumstances, "many skills and a great deal of knowledge—from cooking to singing, from adopting behavioral patterns to acquiring certain mindsets—were transmitted and acquired in a context of intense 'horizontal' interactions."[36] This is particularly the case in a close-knit community such as a monastery, where "horizontal learning can be understood as the process of gaining increased familiarity with the performances, rituals, and conventions that together formed the community's repertoire."[37]

Horizontal learning still has a part to play today, not only in the context of classroom group learning and via peer-to-peer and "study buddy" support systems, where there is physical presence, but also in blended learning which uses online learning systems (such as Moodle) which offer regular built-in opportunities for students to engage with their tutor and with fellow students in raising questions and in sharing insights. These methods,

---

33. Harkins, *Reading and Work of Restoration*, 283, quoting Hugh, *De institutione novitiorum*.
34. Porwoll, "Parisian Pedagogies," 147.
35. Long et al., *Horizontal Learning*, 9.
36. Long et al., *Horizontal Learning*, 10.
37. Snijders, "Communal Learning," 46.

however, in contrast to Hugh's conception of community learning, often tend to omit consideration of moral and spiritual issues.

Hugh held to the notion of co-discipleship, where all acknowledge that they are subject to a divine teacher and master and where they are expected to serve as guardians of each other's soul, offering mutual support, example and correction. Many factors influence how far horizontal or peer-to-peer learning takes place. These include the context in which a community is set, the purposes and priorities of participants in that community, their roles and relative status, the nature and quality of their relationships, their respective experiences and expertise, the degree of institutional support for collaboration and fostering friendships, and the presence or absence of agencies and demands that work against cooperation and reciprocal learning. Steckel notes of medieval religious communities, that, despite being strongly marked by hierarchical structure, horizontal learning was remarkably prominent, and also that their very functioning *as* a community of faith itself constituted a didactic space.[38] One might draw parallels here between the communal nature and horizontal learning that took place in religious communities such as that at St. Victor and that which took place in medieval guilds for a variety of different professions and crafts. These guilds addressed in a holistic manner the practical, social, spiritual, emotional, economic, and political concerns of their members.[39] In both settings hierarchy and order were salient and strongly embedded, yet, at the same time, mutual learning and support were also evident.

In the nineteenth century, John Henry Newman put great weight on the central part played in learning by living in community and he was convinced that conversations between students outside of class can be expected to contribute significantly to their education and to the development of their thinking and values.[40] The company kept by students can have a real impact on whether their learning is integrated, owned, and acted upon. Community living can also play an ethical role, exemplifying and promoting courage, self-control, truthfulness, friendliness, and an environment of trust. Contemporary concerns for students focus less on fostering example, imitation and moral development and more on providing learning support for individuals, supplying material comforts, sporting facilities and entertainment and suggesting strategies for alleviating anxiety. The emphasis put on service learning, in many universities, goes some way to counter this trend of stepping away from seeking to promote moral development.

---

38. Steckel, "Concluding Observations."
39. See Rosser, *Art of Solidarity*.
40. Newman, *Idea of a University*, 146.

PART ONE | TRADITION AS A RESOURCE

## THE UNIVERSITY TODAY COMPARED TO HUGH'S EDUCATIONAL OUTLOOK

In the university today, there is an emphasis on individual choice rather than prescription in what is studied, how and in what order it is investigated. There is much less emphasis than in Hugh's abbey or in the medieval university on providing a common educational experience or insisting on a mandatory curriculum that all students should follow. In pedagogy, there is a heavy reliance on technology and fewer face-to-face encounters between faculty and students. The diversity among both faculty and students is much more salient than was the case in Hugh's abbey or in the medieval universities; this includes with regard to gender, class, race, background, expectations, lifestyles and aspirations. Georgedes points out several differences between medieval and modern higher education.[41] She refers to the salience of relativism in the modern university as compared with an assumption that there is an objective truth to be found; a focus on materialism rather than openness to the transcendent; scientific knowledge holds sway as the yardstick by which other forms of knowledge should be judged; neuralgia about religious, particularly Christian claims, is pervasive; learning is usually not based on prescribed texts; there is strong "pressure to respond to demands of business and government" and less emphasis placed on the humanities.[42]

By comparison with medieval teachers and students, and the wider society to which they belonged, today there is a marked lack of moral consensus. The notion of providing a haven from the demands of the world beyond the university—a safe space for self-cultivation and reflection on fundamental questions—rather than a focus on how to address immediate problems facing the world—for many today seems elitist. We witness today the downgrading of the humanities and the hegemony of science and business. The powerful influence of marketing in contemporary universities—with its emphasis on branding, keeping staff on message, highly conscious of how the university presents itself and protects its public image with regard to potential students, funders, accrediting bodies and the general public—often seems excessive, distorting, incongruous, and corrosive of an ethos of free inquiry, radical questioning, independent thinking, and creativity. There is a tendency to reduce the ethical dimension of education to compliance with legislation and the protection of human rights, steering clear of any substantive attempt at moral formation.

---

41. Georgedes, "Religion, Education," 93.
42. Georgedes, "Religion, Education," 94.

In contrast to the practice at St. Victor—of deep and regular immersion in the thought of a limited number of authors (most notably, Augustine of Hippo), of reaching up to the mind of an exemplar, upon which to model oneself—in modern universities, students and their teachers engage with a huge range of authors, but rarely (except in the case of some research studies) in depth and over a protracted period of time, nor in the company of others (other students and colleagues having exercised their individual choice as to topics and sources). The composing of the inner self, as advocated by Hugh, is a strikingly different notion from the constant self-advertising carried out on social media today. The modern self often seems distracted, always being reassembled, apparently lacking a center or core or locus of stability or source of coherence. He or she seems concerned with reputation and "being liked" and needing the continuing affirmation and reinforcement of that sense of being accepted and approved of by the virtual community or "friends," if their well-being is not to feel threatened. The only revelation of interest to medieval thinkers was divine revelation, given to us for our salvation, not self-revelation in order to demonstrate our achievements and preferences. In their unself-conscious use of language and in their social interactions, medieval people seem to have been far more oriented towards transcendence and nurturing an awareness of the presence of God than is the case with many men and women, for whom the default position is that faith is a private and optional matter, to be spoken about with great caution in company, lest one appears "preachy" or unduly dogmatic.

In many respects, Hugh's educational prescriptions differ from those in our own day: his emphasis on memory, on both the moral and the spiritual dimensions of learning, the role played by divine illumination, the importance attached to the community, the centrality of the notion of restoration, the crucial role played by sacred Scripture, and the importance of self-knowledge. To these can be added the need for discipline of the body, the powerful influence of example and imitation, and the integrative nature of education. Hugh believed that there is an ordering in reality, to which we have to adjust and accommodate ourselves. Such restoration or reordering can also be described as a process of conversion, which Hugh considered a necessary step towards, and as a prerequisite for, accessing truth and wisdom. This is in contrast to the notion that a sound use of different disciplinary methods imposes a kind of man-made order on an aspect of reality—an aspect that is not connected to what is disclosed by other disciplines (or, at least, in no obvious way). The fragmentation of the curriculum brought about by a high degree of specialization, leads to a lack of the sense of the whole. Hugh emphasized the importance of a well-ordered and stable foundation on which further study can reliably be built. Today there seems to be little agreement about what is foundational and thus what must constitute a necessary starting point and an appropriate learning pathway for students to follow. In contrast to contemporary higher education, Hugh's vision was more holistic and integrated, and it stressed formation rather than information. It relied on a much more directed route through the curriculum, rather than one which was individually chosen by students or their teachers. Most obviously different was the Hugh's assumption, one he shared with most of his peers, that our studies have a salvific significance for us. The process of learning remained incomplete until the content of study was so internalized that it could be lived out in knowledge and love of God and neighbor. By reading and responding to Scripture, students would become able to participate in the ongoing story of salvation, which would bring about a restoration of right relationship with God, and thus with the world that God has created.

According to Hugh's worldview, we can understand the whole history of the world as a linked process in two parts: first the creation of everything by God; then the gradual "winning back" or restoration of right relationship with God. For Hugh the human body resembles the physical universe: both come from God, who has established an order which promotes the right conditions of flourishing for all beings; human beings have a privileged role as images of God and stewards of creation but have strayed from that order, disrupting and distorting both themselves and the world around them; they are called, through a properly ordered formation and education, to learn how to read and respond to the world rightly as coming from God and so to restore harmony within themselves and within creation as all are returned to God. Such right reading and then appropriate response rested on two capacities flowing from being made in the image and likeness of God: first, from the image, the capacity to recognize truth; second, from the likeness, the capacity for love and goodness. Human beings are called to serve as priests of creation, mediating between God and creation, their bodies joining them to the material world, their spirits to the heavenly world. Furthermore, Hugh taught that, in order for us to exercise the role given to us by God, each of us has three "eyes": the eye of the flesh, by which we can see the visible world and all the things in it; the eye of reason, by which we can see within ourselves and detect our own nature; the eye of contemplation, by which we come to a vision of God and of everything else in God's light. Education, within this mindset, or horizon of expectation, was intended to train these "eyes" to operate effectively, for the sake of our earthly and supernatural flourishing. Both sacred and secular literature have a positive part to play as constitutive elements in any sound educational program.

For Hugh, the reading of Holy Scripture introduces us to the story of what God has done, what his will and purpose for us is, and it has the power to turn us away from our sinful ways and towards God's mercy and to the path of returning to our true nature and role in creation. Our reading in Scripture of the figures who have been touched by God should inspire us to imitate their example. Hugh lived in a world where one's assumptions and outlook were soaked in biblical imagery, to a degree that is almost impossible for us to recapture. A very high proportion of his writings focused on the Scriptures, either expounding their meaning or teaching his readers how to equip themselves to approach them appropriately. He drew upon the traditional triple pathway into Scripture of history, allegory, and tropology: learning what has been done in the history of salvation, what should be believed and, in light of these two, how one should live. However, given the lack of salience of these Scriptures in the worldview of most people, and the highly secularized nature of contemporary Western society, this aspect of his thought will seem alien and beyond retrieval in most universities.

After referring to different goals for modern universities, such as producing future citizens to contribute to liberal democracies, equip academic disciplinary specialists who can advance the pursuit of new knowledge, or prepare workers to sustain or create wealth in the market economy, Williams makes a case for "didascalic Christian humanism" along lines laid down by Hugh.[43] This refers to "the perennial concern for human and humane knowledge and culture, the integrated formation of students, the comprehensive flourishing of individuals and communities, and the worship of the God" from whom everyone comes and to whom we return. Central to the notion of didascalic Christian humanism is the training and formation of our intellectual appetites, carefully integrated with the ordering of our moral and spiritual nature. Such Christian humanism—and its relevance for both education and cultural renewal—has been cogently advocated in recent years by Jens Zimmermann.[44] Apart from wonder at the world and the desire to understand it, our intellectual appetite can be distorted by wrong means of, and motives and goals for, pursuing knowledge (for example, the story of Dr. Faustus). In contrast, in the tradition of didascalic Christian humanism, properly ordered intellectual inquiry adopts a grateful, humble and respectful approach to knowledge and seeks to promote the well-being of all. It frames learning as a way to look after our fellow humans and our world and it draws from and culminates in worship of God, as

---

43. B. Williams, "To Wonder, Learn."

44. Klassen and Zimmermann, *Passionate Intellect*; Zimmermann, *Incarnational Humanism*; Zimmermann, *Re-Envisioning Christian Humanism*.

known in and through Christ, both the source of our being and as the Way, the Truth, and the Life. Williams's advocacy is unlikely to be persuasive outside of faith-based institutions and even there will encounter suspicion and resistance.

## A CONTEMPLATIVE TURN?

For Hugh, education is a process of person building, developing perceptions, affections, habits, skills, and virtues that lead to integrity, harmony, and beauty. The educated person becomes capable of, and is fitted for, receiving divine wisdom and his learning is so oriented that it should culminate in contemplative intimacy with God. The acquisition of knowledge, in his view, should lead to wisdom, virtue, self-knowledge, and harmony between the inner and outer life of a person. *Memoria, meditatio,* and *moralia* were at the center of his thought. The first two contributed to reforming the intellect, while the third contributed to reforming the will, initially by following discipline imposed externally, and then via the internal development of virtues and affections. I say "contributed to," because the primary agent for Hugh was always the grace of God's Holy Spirit, working within both our intellect and our will.

There have been attempts in recent years to retrieve some of the insights of a more contemplative, spiritual, and wisdom-oriented approach to education, one that is consonant with that proposed by Hugh.[45] Despite the disparities between Hugh's educational outlook and modern assumptions, if we appreciate what we are learning properly, according to its real depth and potential significance—what it has to teach us in its own right and from its own nature, not according our needs or uses—it can at the same time reveal to us something important about ourselves and of our place in the world and how we should respond. To come to such an appreciation requires us to foster the capacity to receive the world and others as gift rather than as an opportunity to grasp. This calls for a contemplative stance that informs and grounds our activity. Scientific knowledge and technical application, while valuable and necessary for survival, physical health and material comfort, cannot supply meaning, purpose, and value in our lives. These come primarily from our relationships.

At the time of writing this chapter, many countries are suffering from the global pandemic COVID-19. This has led to a massive reduction in the

---

45. E.g., Keator, *Lectio Divina*; Lichtmann, *Teacher's Way*; Powers, "Catholic Education and Formation," 85–89; Sullivan, "Teaching as Contemplative"; Sullivan, *Christian Academic in Higher Education*; Summit and Vermeule, *Action Versus Contemplation*.

frenetic daily cycle of production, consumption, travel, and activity. Millions of people are facing, not only an economic and health emergency, but also an unprecedented widely enforced time of lockdown, constraint of movement, and social isolation in order to prevent the spread of the disease. While it is too soon to know what changes, if any, in individual and social behavior will emerge when this crisis is over, it is to be hoped that it might prompt, not only a more robust awareness of the need to protect the vulnerable and to devise imaginative innovations in the way we manage our collective lives (for example, in business, manufacturing, and education), but also a heightened concern for the common good and the desire to collaborate in mutual support, accompanied by a deeper sense of the need for personal restraint and self-discipline if all are to flourish, and a form of public discourse that is more kind and respectful. In such a context Hugh of St. Victor, despite the many differences between his worldview and that of our own society, still has some salutary lessons from which we can learn.

# 4

# Blondel and a Living Tradition for Catholic Education

NEIL POSTMAN HAS ADVOCATED a return to and a reexpression of the "metaphysical" rather than the "engineering" aspects of education, that is, answers to the question why as having priority over how.[1] He argues that education flourishes best when it is sustained by an overarching narrative, a story that "tells of origins and envisions a future, a story that constructs ideals, prescribes rules of conduct, provides a source of authority, and, above all, gives a sense of continuity and purpose."[2] This kind of narrative must have "sufficient credibility, complexity, and symbolic power" to enable those who rely on it to organize their lives around it.[3] Such a story will "give point to our labors, exalt our history, elucidate the present, and give direction to our future."[4] The kind of story that Postman says is necessary will be "foundational," that is, it will provide key concepts, goals, metaphors, and values for the conduct of education, but it is not to be held uncritically, nor is it unrevisable; indeed, the best of stories will have the capacity to cope with criticism, revision, and constant adaptation to changing circumstances.

It can justifiably be claimed that Catholic education has just such a "story." It operates out of a substantive, comprehensive, and integrated worldview. In communicating that worldview to surrounding cultures, the Catholic Church has demonstrated the capacity without denying the past or its central *principles*, to adapt and to develop its own self-understanding. Both the Catholic worldview and its story about education are highly

---

1. Postman, *End of Education*, 3.
2. Postman, *End of Education*, 5–6.
3. Postman, *End of Education*, 6.
4. Postman, *End of Education*, 7.

contestable in our society. Even within its own terms, however, Catholic education runs the risk of deifying the past, exalting authority, neglecting the critical faculties of pupils, and rendering them passive recipients rather than active collaborators in their own learning. One way of preventing this risk from being realized is for Catholic educators to draw out more fully the implications of the notion of "living tradition." A thoroughgoing appreciation of this notion and an engagement with its implications for education would simultaneously meet at least some of the educational objections to the existence of separate Catholic schools (for example, those relating to the passivity of learners and the danger of indoctrination), and minimize the possibility that what is communicated is a tradition that is frozen or ossified, one which, to use the language of faith, thereby fails to advert to the continuing and creative operation of the Holy Spirit in believers. At the same time a deeper appreciation and appropriation of living tradition would give scope for the operation of that "metaphysical" narrative asked for by Postman as a necessary foundation for any healthy form of education.

## BLONDEL ON "LIVING TRADITION"

Probably no one has contributed more importantly and effectively to the notion of living tradition in the Catholic Church than the French philosopher Maurice Blondel (1861–1949). He pointed the way to a notion of tradition which serves not only to conserve but also to discover. It is possible to detect his influence on the thinking of key twentieth-century Catholic theologians and thereby to trace his imprint on the Second Vatican Council, an imprint which was indirect since it passed through the intermediary work of others. Drawing upon a range of Blondel's work, I shall first summarize his key insights and illustrate his contributions to Catholic thinking on the notion of living tradition and then briefly indicate some of the educational implications which follow.

The essay which provides several of Blondel's seminal ideas on living tradition is "History and Dogma." This originated in a number of articles which appeared in 1904 as a contribution to the controversy about the role of historical criticism in the church's life. Blondel claimed to point a way forward which both avoided the pitfalls of those who fixed the church in a restricting and narrow immobilism, and also escaped the dangers stemming from those who yielded too much to contemporary scholarship. Blondel's view might be summarized in the following way. God's last word has not been spoken. Christ is still communicating as he promised he would: "I still have many things to say to you but they would be too much for you now. But when the Spirit of truth comes, he will lead you to the complete truth" (John 16:12). But truth cannot be contained in a purely intellectual manner, for such an approach would bypass those who find this difficult. Furthermore, the truth that comes from God lies always beyond mere human formulations and cannot be captured in them. "There can be no given moment of history when the mind of man has exhausted the mind of God."[5]

The only way we can enjoy the truth is by drawing upon the collective experience derived from faithful action by the church's members. Tradition makes it possible for something to pass from the implicitly lived to the explicitly known. In the overall lifestyle of the church, more riches are carried than can be unpacked and passed into currency at any one particular epoch of its existence. Tradition is a "living synthesis of all the speculative and ascetic, historic and theological forces. . . . It embraces the data of history, the efforts of reason, and the experiences of faithful action."[6] In this synthesis we all have a contribution to make, for tradition has to do with the whole body of the church, not just any particular privileged section of it. "Without the Church, the faithful could not detect the true hand of God in the Bible and souls; but, unless each believer brought his little contribution to the common life, the organism would not be fully alive and spiritual."[7]

Blondel feared that some scholars had exaggerated the power of historical investigation, while other scholars had overrated the efficacy of philosophical reasoning. In accessing the truth about God's ways and purposes, these two forms of human inquiry are inadequate. Despite the need for both, something more is required: "the mediation of collective life and the slow progressive labor of the Christian tradition."[8] There is a certain light shed by the orderly and repeated performances of Christian practices: "Faithful action is the Ark of the Covenant where the confidences of God are found, the Tabernacle where he perpetuates his presence and his teaching."[9]

There is, for Blondel, a kind of meaning and verification carried in our action which goes beyond the competence of our powers of reasoning. As he says, "A man can carry out completely what he cannot entirely understand, and in doing it he keeps alive within him the consciousness of a reality which is still half hidden from him. To "keep" the word of God means in the first place to do it, to put it into practice."[10] A dialectic between

---

5. Blondel, "Histoire et dogme," 213.
6. Blondel, *Letter on Apologetics*, 215.
7. Blondel, *Letter on Apologetics*, 277.
8. Blondel, *Letter on Apologetics*, 269.
9. Blondel, *Letter on Apologetics*, 274.
10. Blondel, *Letter on Apologetics*, 273-74.

devotions and truth operates in such a way that the humble faithful can benefit from a profound intuition more penetrating than that enjoyed by the most erudite of intellectuals.[11]

Together, dogmas and the practices enjoined on us by the church make one body and it would be "murderous vivisection" to try to separate them.[12] The constant theme echoing throughout Blondel's writings comes from St. John: He who does the truth comes to the light. In "History and Dogma" he puts it thus: "The miracle of the Christian life is that from acts at first difficult, obscure, and enforced, one rises to the light through a practical verification of speculative truths."[13]

Following this presentation of faithful action as the focus of tradition, we are reminded by Blondel that there can be no doctrinal unity without a prior common discipline and a conformity of lifestyle.[14] Joint action (and, even more, shared suffering) would open the way for greater unity than could ever be achieved by a theological vanguard or pioneer elite group. To pay attention to tradition as a whole, rather than giving emphasis only to part of it, would enable us not only to preserve what is valuable from the past (this much at least about tradition is commonly appreciated), but to move forward, for "its powers of conservation are equaled by its powers of conquest. [Tradition] discovers and formulates truths on which the past lived, though unable as yet to evaluate or define them explicitly."[15] We should, therefore, be wary of shedding too quickly or casually those aspects of the Christian tradition which do not easily "make sense" to us, those features which jar on our understanding or sensibilities. It may be that through an uncomfortable confrontation between the expectations of a living tradition and the individuality of our own experience there is an opportunity to avoid illusion and to widen our horizons.

## THE LEARNING CHURCH

Blondel did not advocate an uncritical acceptance of all features of the church. He was well aware of many defects in the church he loved, and he realized that purification was necessary as part of the process of building a new synthesis for his time. He could be scathing about some aspects of church life and especially a distorted view of authority then operative in the

11. Blondel, *Carnets intimes*, 1:339–40.
12. Blondel, *Carnets intimes*, 2:279.
13. Blondel, *Letter on Apologetics*, 274.
14. Blondel, *Action*, 413.
15. Blondel, *Letter on Apologetics*, 267.

higher echelons of the clergy. Coming from such a man, from the center, these criticisms have all the more force.

The predominant party in the church was wrong to exercise a power that was political, rather than spiritual in style, for this was incompatible with the gospel. The church was supposed to serve, not tyrannize over souls. It seemed to Blondel that the face of the church too often presented to the world was a serious aberration from the ideal: "a Catholicism without Christ, religion without a soul, authority without a heart."[16] It was wrong to think that God could be served by making him reign in society without preparing souls to receive him. The emphasis on imperialism and prestige was a far cry from the strength that comes from weakness; the former smacked of paganism, whereas the latter came closer to Christianity, Blondel insisted that authority was assisted but not inspired and such authority needed to consult and to be clarified and joined by the prayer and study of the faithful; it should not flow just one way, from above to below. Authority was an organ of tradition, not a replacement for it.[17] Though he did not minimize the principle of authority, Blondel certainly rejected authoritarianism in the church, because it exalted a part of tradition above the whole in a most unhealthy manner for the body which shared Christ's life.

Nothing illustrated the misuse of authority more than the dangerous distortion of clericalism. This was endemic in the church at the beginning of the twentieth century, inherent in the one-way thinking which saw everything in terms of from above to below, an over-hierarchical conception of the church. Rule by clergy was a kind of guardianship over minors who were never allowed to grow up, take risks, or show any initiative. "Clericalism," said Blondel, "was founded on an objectivism which identified the human container with the divine content"; it was behind the immobile mentality prevalent within the church and also responsible for much of its fanaticism and lack of humanity. He considered it "the most dangerous of traitors, the most false-hearted and deadly of the enemies of Catholicism, since it contradicted the essence of the Church and made of it a sect, something unilateral, formal, intellectual, neither good, loving, nor lovable."[18] The stress given by Blondel to the contribution of the whole body of the faithful in his treatment of living tradition differed greatly from the distinction which was too sharply made earlier this century between the teaching and the learning church, the clergy and laity. Indeed, if the laity were always treated like children, how could the candidates for the teaching church ever

---

16. Blondel, *Carnets intimes*, 2:158.
17. Blondel, *Exigences philosophiques*.
18. Blondel and Wehrlé, *Correspondance*, 2:288.

be recruited; from such juvenile and inexperienced sheep, how could wise pastors be found?[19]

Toward the end of his life, at the age of eighty-five, Blondel returned again to the topic of tradition and the need to balance the risks of growth with the need to safeguard the church against specious novelties. He continued to emphasize that the transmission of truths, functions, and powers involved in tradition required more than a simple acceptance from the faithful. He remained supremely confident about the "unquenchable power of enriching invention" which resided within tradition.[20] It was not a chain which had to be dragged along, weighing us down; rather, it should be thought of as an umbilical cord, providing lifeblood and nourishment.[21] In these last comments on tradition he reiterated his earlier themes: Tradition and innovation are not opposed to one another; responding to the promptings of the Spirit and submission to authority are not incompatible; revelation is inexhaustible; the church lives through growth; each generation has its trials, its mission, and its effective fruitfulness in adapting what is permanent and what is moving in the church to one another.[22]

## EDUCATIONAL IMPLICATIONS

At the beginning of this chapter I suggested that an appreciation and application of the notion of living tradition would help in addressing some concerns about Catholic education. I have taken Blondel as an influential thinker within Catholicism, one who contributed greatly to that church's understanding of living tradition. Let me now draw out eight implications of his comments for schools.

First, undue weight is not to be given to the past. Rather than being backward-looking, seeking always to preserve, to hand on, to transmit, church schools should, in the light of a rich appreciation that tradition is living, respond to the changing circumstances and new questions facing pupils and staff. What kind of balance is struck, in the course of each year's work, to ensure that students are invited, not only to enter into the educational and ecclesial heritage from the past, but also to respond to the concerns and questions thrown up by new circumstances through their own contributions and projects?

---

19. Blondel and Laberthonnière, *Correspondance philosophique*, 181, 188.
20. Blondel, *Philosophie et esprit chrétien*, 2:81.
21. Blondel, *Philosophie et esprit chrétien*, 2:82.
22. Blondel, *Philosophie et esprit chrétien*, 2:83.

Second, Blondel reminds us that, if tradition is to flourish and to be welcomed, there must be due emphasis given to the experience, insights, problems, and questions of the particular members of the school community, both pupils and staff. Furthermore, each person should be able to feel that his or her contribution is both needed and valued by the school community. How hard do our schools try to communicate to each and every student that his or her questions are taken seriously and that he or she has particular talents and abilities which both the school and the wider society (including the parish) is in need of?

This leads into the third implication of Blondel's analysis of living tradition which is that the church's representatives cannot be credible or effective teachers if they are not simultaneously still learners. They must not give the impression of having "arrived" or of being "complete" and therefore of having stopped developing. They should be models, not only of lifelong learning in academic terms, but also of lifelong growth in faith and an ever deepening appreciation of the mysteries of God's world and ways. If one side of this coin is that Blondel believed that the church could not claim to teach if she was not prepared to go on learning, the other aspect of this is that the church cannot expect her members to receive what she has to offer if at the same time she does not allow the learners themselves to give, to make a contribution, so that there is a certain reciprocity or mutuality about the teaching and learning process. It follows from this that teachers will elicit and respond positively to feedback from their students about the helpfulness of their endeavors; that they will model commitment to devotional practices; and that they will demonstrate to these students a familiarity with the discipline, lifestyle, and feelings associated with being a student (for example, excitement in finding new ideas and a desire for feedback on their own progress).

Fourth, Blondel's comments warn against the church school adopting an overbearing attitude in its efforts to convey the truth, even salvific truth. Its tutelary role should never slip into tyranny. There must be room for questioning, for growth, for disagreement, for learning by mistakes, for exploration, even when this appears to stray from orthodoxy. The church school should seek to serve its pupils, not keep them in a state of servility. This will require an atmosphere which facilitates discussion and debate, which encourages the expression of tentative and provisional views, which invites students to exercise responsibility and initiative in a variety of forms and contexts, and which also allows them to withdraw (without reprimand) from these if they choose.

If in this point Blondel warns against prematurely closing the argument, this is related to a fifth implication of his thought, namely that church schools should take care to avoid an excessive reliance on rationality as the only means to arrive at truth. His comments about moving slowly from the implicitly lived to the explicitly known, about attending to the multiple dimensions or many-sidedness of life, and about the integral development of the human person should guard us against any over-intellectual emphasis or any compartmentalization of knowledge or separation of the curriculum from the devotions, problems, and practices experienced by members of the school community. An excessive overreliance on rationality will be avoided if the curriculum is broad and balanced; if pedagogy allows for student input, as well as reception; if it responds sensitively to student feedback; if many forms of achievement are praised; if all students are encouraged to experiment, to cooperate, to offer, and to receive help; and if the school community shares its sorrows, highlights its concerns, values, and priorities, and celebrates its achievements through sacred and secular rituals.

This brings us to a sixth implication. If there is to be no sharp separation of academic from more "existential" concerns within a school, the school should expect to display, offer, and train its members in faithful action, both in its devotional expression and in social action. There would be formation in spirituality and in community service and these would be seen as mutually supportive strands. Associated with these practices the school should be prepared to retain those aspects of the tradition which might appear at first to be uncomfortable or to be demanding for its members, for example, the call to self-denial, to ongoing and ever-deepening conversion, to loyalty to and engagement with the whole liturgical cycle and its constitutive elements, not just to those which readily appeal or those which are easily understandable.

Seventh, not only did Blondel display in his own teaching all the qualities of inclusiveness, in his writing he urged a sensitivity to the differing spiritual, intellectual, and personal needs of learners. His comments about the need for adaptability on the part of the teacher, whether religious or other teachers, echo contemporary calls for attention to differentiation in approaches to (and readiness for) learning. Part of this sensitivity which Blondel asks for expresses itself in the patience he advocated in the face of misunderstanding, confusion, error, or shortcomings. In avoiding an overbearing atmosphere the school will not seek too quickly to uproot the weed growing alongside the wheat (Matt 13:24–30). Blondel always displayed a high degree of both patience and precision in pointing out mistakes and distortions, but he also advocated that searchers needed a friendly space in which to develop and to try out their ideas. Teachers in Catholic schools should be noted for this form of "hospitality."

Such patience did not imply an undiscriminating tolerance. The eighth implication of Blondel's understanding of living tradition is that a degree of vigilance is required in order to safeguard the church, and, by extension, the school, against the corrosive effects of ideas or practices which either directly or more subtly contradict and undermine the mission and purpose of the church school. Some emphases and priorities offered in the educational world will appear in the light of such vigilance to damage the carefully nurtured "wine" of Catholic education, either by "watering it down" or by mixing it with "acid." Threatening elements might be forms of competitiveness, within and between schools; unbalanced kinds of curriculum, pedagogy, or policies for assessment and behavior; distorted expressions of egalitarianism; or concessions to pluralism or to a liberal view of education. If our openness to the continuing unfolding of truth made accessible to us by the Holy Spirit entails remaining in communion with the wider church (and therefore not acting as if the school were an island, operating in isolation from the rest of the church), so too our vigilance or safeguarding role must be carried out in harmony with that wider ecclesial communion. Our nurturing of living tradition is not for the sake of ourselves alone, but is to be exercised both together with and on behalf of the whole church. In this light, a Catholic school will welcome and engage positively with, rather than resent or reject, the oversight and inspection which is carried out on behalf of the church, whether the trustees are from a diocese or from a religious order.

## CONCLUSION

I have shown how Blondel demonstrates in his treatment of living tradition the possibility of combining fidelity and creativity in the context of a Catholic school. If real contact with active minds is to be made, then new intellectual creations are necessary, Blondel would say, not because former ways of expressing the faith are easily dispensable but because further explorations of the riches of the faith are essential for effective communication with outsiders, indeed often extremely helpful for promoting deeper understanding of the legacy of faith for insiders too.[23]

If we adopt a Blondelian perspective, there are limits to the extent to which we are able to clarify or mark the boundaries of the distinctiveness of the church or of the church school, because no definition of pure Christianity is possible since it is a living reality, not a concept or theory, and introducing someone to the faith is bringing them into a way of life, not to

---

23. Blondel, *Carnets intimes*, 2:41.

a mere acceptance of a formula.[24] Ossification and immobility are incompatible with living tradition, a notion which implies a church on the move Blondel considered that the capacity for movement is both essential for and integral to the church's nature and mission. His view was that if we wish to win souls and to spread the good news of Christ (as opposed to defending institutions), this is best done from a moving vehicle, not from a fortress.[25]

In order to pass on a faith in the context of living tradition, according to Blondel, a blend of docility and initiative is required: docility to tradition and also to the needs of others, initiative to adapt the life of tradition to the needs of individuals. Blondel employed the imagery of music and text to bring out this blend. Faith as docility on its own is like music that is written but remains on the page unplayed; faith as confidence and trust and initiative is like music that is played, but without the text is in danger of rambling away pointlessly and getting lost.[26] An appreciation of living tradition provides several pointers as to how a Catholic school might attempt to promote in its pupils an active receptivity, a critical solidarity, and a discerning openness. An appropriation of living tradition, along the lines suggested by Blondel, makes it possible for Catholic schools to maintain their distinctiveness while displaying an openness to the insights and questions of pupils and to the changing needs of the times.

Blondel was, of course, not the only major exponent of living tradition to have influenced modern Catholic thought. Both Möhler and Newman in the nineteenth century highlighted key aspects which contributed to later thinking on living tradition; Möhler stressed the role of the Holy Spirit in the experience of the faithful, while Newman significantly advanced our understanding of the development of doctrine.[27] But by bringing together reason, experience, and faith, by giving emphasis to the collective experience of the faithful, by showing the relationship between devotion and arriving at the truth, by describing a more healthy role for authority than prevailed in the church of his time, and by showing how tradition can facilitate a meeting place for what is permanent and what is changing in the life of the church, Blondel powerfully enhanced the Catholic Church's ability to appreciate and to apply the notion of living tradition to its own self-understanding. In doing so he has bequeathed a legacy which can assist Catholic educators in guarding against at least some of the risks to which any substantive worldview and any associated "strong" school ethos are prone.

24. Blondel, *Carnets intimes*, 2:282, 290.
25. Blondel, *Carnets intimes*, 2:273.
26. Saint-Jean, *Apologetique philosophique*, 298.
27. Möhler, *Unity in the Church*; Newman, *Development of Christian Doctrine*.

# 5

# Hügel and Catholic Education

IN CONTEMPORARY CATHOLIC EDUCATIONAL theory three key themes coexist in a tension which is not always creative: the integral development of the human person, the autonomy of the disciplines and the synthesis of faith, life, and culture.[1] It is not easy to see how these three can be held together, since they emphasize different priorities: the first emphasizing the individual, the second focusing on the academic subjects of study while the third underlines the importance of religion in the conduct and interpretation of life.

Furthermore, the Catholic claim to have a distinctive approach to education can appear to sit very awkwardly alongside the parallel claim that such education seeks to be "catholic" in the sense of inclusive. On the one hand, too strong an emphasis on distinctiveness might lead to an exclusiveness about who is admitted and what is permitted. On the other hand, too great a concern to display inclusiveness might leave Catholic schools open to the criticism that they merely duplicate "secular" schools and therefore that they do not warrant special support, funding, legal protection or self-sacrifice on the part of the faith community.

Yet any attempt to articulate the distinctiveness of Catholic education is likely to entail identifying in that very process of articulation at least a partial rejection of alternative approaches to education as either pernicious or inadequate. To define anything is to establish edges or borders beyond which the focus of attention ceases to be itself. As Spinoza said, "Omnis determinatio est negatio."[2] Every determination of what a thing is inevitably involves clarifying what it is not. The purpose of this chapter is to

1. Congregation for Catholic Education, *Religious Dimension of Education*.
2. Norton, *Imagination, Understanding, and Virtue*, 16.

demonstrate, through a retrieval of the insights and example of a writer whose work is rarely referred to in philosophical reflection about education, that the Catholic attempt to combine distinctiveness with inclusiveness is both possible and fruitful and that the key themes of integral human development, autonomous disciplines and a synthesis of faith, life, and culture can be interpreted and understood in such a way that they mutually support and illuminate one another.

## BARON VON HÜGEL

Baron Friedrich von Hügel (1852–1925) has been almost completely neglected in the literature on Catholic education. Yet within his writings there are many insights which are relevant to the difficulties alluded to above.[3] This well-connected, devout, but independent layman participated significantly in the debates which took place in the early years of the twentieth century about how the church should respond to the insights of modern thinking. He combined several roles in his wide range of contacts and through his many interests and extended span of correspondence: he was a biblical critic, religious historian, philosopher of religion, spiritual director, and ecumenist. Despite the great respect with which he was held, especially among Christians beyond his own communion, it is only fair to record that he failed in his own lifetime to convince many of his fellow Catholics to attend carefully to his version of an integrated and well-rounded Catholicism.

Throughout his writings we find a picture of what might be meant by an integral human formation, though this was not a phrase he used himself. The synthesis of faith, culture and life that he hints at is one which displays a dynamic and deep equilibrium. He shows how wholeness, holiness and humanity can be held together, indeed, how they need each other. The themes of richness, fullness, growth, infinite expansion, abundance, balance, and inclusiveness pervade his works. By demonstrating in his own life and writings the importance of balancing the institutional, intellectual and mystical elements of religion, allowing each of these to supplement, stimulate, and purify the other two, and not allowing one element to dominate, he managed to inject warmth, vitality, depth, and genuine openness into the picture of what an educated Catholic could be like.

---

3. See Kelly, *Hügel's Philosophy of Religion*, for a concise summary of his life and thought.

PART ONE | TRADITION AS A RESOURCE

## OUR NEED OF THE NONRELIGIOUS DIMENSIONS

One of the most important and pervading themes in Hügel's works is the need, for the sake of our religious health, as much as for the health of the rest of our personality, for the proper development of all the other, nonreligious dimensions of our being, our physical, emotional, aesthetic, social and intellectual growth. The multiplicity of our inner life provides the necessary materials, stimulants, interactions, and obstacles from which richness, balance, and harmony can emerge.[4] The body and the senses have a crucial role here for Hügel. In his view epistemology and psychology combine in showing us that we need the stimulation of the senses for the awakening of our spiritual awareness.[5] If God is only apprehended only in, with and on occasion of, yet also in contrast to, other realities (a fact, Hügel believes, that obtains in knowledge of any kind that we claim to have) then we must fill our lives with a wide range of interests, for their own sake and for our spiritual development.[6] The body is not the enemy of the spirit, but "the stimulator and spring-board, the material and training ground" for it, and through its agency we must "strive to awaken and utilize" every aspect of life, with its special characteristics, "in its right place and degree, for the calling into full action of all the rest."[7]

By taking the incarnation of Christ as a model for our appreciation of how the human and the divine can coexist, rather than be seen as opponents, Hügel underlines the Catholic belief that nature is not driven out or destroyed by grace; it is built on and transformed. "Typical growth in religious depth and fruitfulness is *not* a growth away from the stimulations, occasions, concomitants, vehicles and expressions of sense."[8]

The different spheres of life all have their part to play. It is right and proper to encourage people to cultivate, rather than to deflect their attention away from, an interest in politics, economics, language, history, science, and philosophy.[9] These various levels in life contribute to each other. Therefore we should study religion both together with and apart from them,

---

4. Hügel, *Mystical Element of Religion*, 2,:281, 283, 371, 393, 395.
5. Hügel, *Selected Letters*, 349.
6. Hügel, *Selected Letters*, 260.
7. Hügel, *Essays and Addresses* (1921), 238.
8. Hügel, *Essays and Addresses* (1921), 230; emphasis in original.
9. Hügel, *Essays and Addresses* (1926), 38, 229.

since the presence of God "underlies, environs, protects and perfects all the lesser realities."[10]

Presumably Hügel wished to preserve two values here: the mutual illumination and stimulus offered when subjects are studied together or in each other's light and yet also the necessity to protect the separate identity or relative autonomy of each, so that it can be truly itself rather than merely the handservant of or subservient to another discipline. He jealously defended the rights of historians and scientists to operate freely and according to their own methodology, with a right to their own sphere of jurisdiction, and without interference from theologians or church authorities. "Religion is not directly either Ethics, or Philosophy, Economics or Art, yet at the peril of emptiness and sterility, it has to move out into, to learn from, to criticize, and to teach, all these other apprehensions and activities."[11] Theology may well be the crowning discipline but this does not entail crippling or distorting the others; rather it means adopting an open and inclusive attitude towards them. Such openness, while recognizing the genuine insights, values and truths contained in other disciplines, does not disallow theology the right to indicate their limitations or where they might need complementing. Similarly theologians will benefit from the perspectives and insights gained through deep immersion in other disciplines. In Hügel's view we should neither "sacrifice religion to these activities or these activities to religion. . . . God is the God of the body as he is of the soul; of science as he is of faith; of criticism and theory as of fact and reality."[12]

As Hügel is keen to remind us, "Man is not a mere sum-total of water-tight compartments."[13] For, although the various areas of knowledge "have to be discovered and treated according to the principles and methods immanent and special to that department," their insights must be brought to bear upon each other.[14] For example, "Science will help to discipline, humble, purify the natural eagerness and willfulness, the cruder forms of anthropomorphism, of the human mind and heart. . . . [It] will help to give depth and mystery, drama and pathos, a rich spirituality, to the whole experience and conception of the soul and of life, of the world and of God. . . . Crush out, or in any way mutilate or de-autonomize this part, and all the rest will suffer."[15] There will be similar gains which flow from serious study

10. Hügel, *Reality of God*, 33, 36.
11. Hügel, *Eternal Life*, 330.
12. Hügel, *Eternal Life*, 332.
13. Hügel, *Mystical Element of Religion*, 1:xxvi.
14. Hügel, *Mystical Element of Religion*, 1:44.
15. Hügel, *Mystical Element of Religion*, 1:45.

of all the disciplines, since they offer insights into real and essential aspects of our nature and our world. "However much man may be supremely and finally a religious animal, he is not *only* that; but he is a physical and sexual, a fighting and an artistic, a domestic and social, a political and philosophical animal as well."[16]

## FRICTION

Hügel was well aware that it would be no easy task to bring all these different parts of our personality into some kind of harmony. Integral human development could not happen without much friction, cost, and pain.[17] He was convinced, to a degree that puzzled his closest friends, that to experience our nature as internally discordant was both normal and necessary for our human and spiritual growth.[18] The different energies and needs within us and the various opportunities and environments pressing upon us were bound to conflict with one another, to cause friction, tension and to co-exist in an uneasy rivalry.[19]

The theme of friction and its place in our development recurs frequently throughout all of Hügel's writings. The friction within us which is caused by the mutual chafing of the different parts of our personality serves several functions. Sometimes it prevents religion from overstraining us by forcing us to develop another part of ourselves, perhaps a part that had been neglected in our attempts to meet religious requirements.[20] Sometimes the sheer "non-fit," the "otherness" of, for example, science or religion, one to another, forces us to make room within us for a perception which transcends our previous categories or exceeds the bounds of inadequate language.[21] At other times, the purpose of the inner friction which we experience stems from the fact that "the primary function of religion is not the *consoling* of the natural man as it finds him, but the *purification* of this man, by effecting an ever-growing cleavage and contrast between his bad false self, and . . . his true good self."[22]

Clearly Hügel has a rich understanding of the complexity of our inner lives and of our need for guidance which will ensure that we do not become

16. Hügel, *Mystical Element of Religion*, 1:47; emphasis in original.
17. Hügel, *Eternal Life*, 357.
18. McGrath, *Baron Friedrich von Hügel*, 157–8.
19. Hügel, *Essays and Addresses* (1921), xii.
20. Hügel, *Essays and Addresses* (1926), 219.
21. Hügel, *Selected Letters*, 94.
22. Hügel, *Selected Letters*, 72; emphasis added.

unbalanced by particular enthusiasms of our own or by the demands of others. Among the various possible avenues we could travel in life we must be prevented from pursuing any path, including the religious one, too far or too soon, lest we be ill-equipped or unready for the journey and its eventual rigors. Some of the tensions and frictions from which we suffer will be experienced as the conflicting calls of the senses versus the spirit, or of the past versus the present, or of the institutional versus the individual.[23] No matter, for we need all of these tensions to enter into us, to recognize the call, which comes from beyond our own little worlds, through these experiences, to wake up and to allow ourselves to be enlarged in consciousness and character.

One of the ways that Hügel's perspective reflects an emphasis more prevalent in his own era than in ours is the notion of life as a testing ground for the growth of personality, as a seedbed for the emergence of spirit, as a training school of sanctity.[24] In the scheme of things heroism is called for and this only comes through facing real struggle. "Real temptation, true piercing conflict, heavy darkness, and bewildering perplexity . . . risks of failing and falling: all this forms an essential part of this painful-joyous probation and virile, because necessarily costing and largely gradual, self-constitution of man's free-willing spirit."[25] Hügel acknowledges the dark side of life and recognizes that there is a role for asceticism as a valid and, indeed, essential and constituent part of the Christian outlook, despite the apparent hardness of this viewpoint and despite the combat and concentration it requires of us to follow this way.[26]

Finally, there is another, perhaps surprising, dimension to the role of friction in our lives. Part of its value lies in the challenge it throws out to the religious dimension in us. Our very church allegiance will find itself checked, purified, steadied and sobered—and therefore made more wholesome—by the struggles faith has with the institution of the church.[27] For the church needs to learn from and to be enriched by our tussle with it, just as we will benefit enormously by being ready to receive the wisdom and training it offers to us. And this is where those other, nonreligious, elements of life come into their own. For "religion will have to come to see that it

---

23. Hügel, *Essays and Addresses* (1926), 62, 24–47.
24. Hügel and Smith, *Letters*, 162.
25. Hügel, *Mystical Element of Religion*, 1:369.
26. Hügel, *Selected Letters*, 275.
27. Hügel, *Selected Letters*, 201.

cannot attain to its own depth, it cannot become the *chief thing*, if it does not continually renounce to aspiring after being *everything*."[28]

## CHURCH AFFILIATION AND INCLUSIVENESS

Hügel has shown us—although he does not use these terms—some of the depths of what might be meant by integral human development and also the contributory role played in this development by both the autonomy of the different subjects or disciplines and the synthesis of faith and culture. He also exemplifies how one can combine a firm commitment to a church with a genuine openness to people with different convictions and institutional affiliations.

The first mistake to avoid, he would claim, is any attempt at complete identification of the visible with the invisible church. This would be incompatible with Catholicism.[29] Only God can read men's hearts; no earthly institution, even the church, has yet reached perfection; and God's Spirit may dwell in, but it also transcends his church.

A second mistake would be to have an unbalanced or excessive veneration for the authority of the church. Hügel is convinced that such authority is an absolutely essential factor assisting in the soul's growth, but, even so, it still only constitutes part, not the whole, of our religious life. We must also be realistic, open and honest about the shortcomings of that authority.[30]

The recognition of shortcomings does not seem to have undermined Hügel's loyalty to his church in any way. In his view, with the combination of features which co-exist within the church there will be value for our spiritual lives in both the prudent and the daring sides of her character, when she is being conservative and when she is being creative, even if we are not able to appreciate one or other of these features at the time we experience them. And, of course we must acknowledge, Hügel points out, that "church officials are no more the whole church . . . than Scotland Yard or the War Office or the House of Lords, though admittedly necessary parts of the national life, are the whole, or average samples, of the life and fruitfulness of the English nation."[31]

If Hügel's commitment to the church was firm and unwavering, both alert to the riches she offered and ready to accept the discipline she imposed, he remained, nevertheless, open eyed as regards her limitations. He

28. Hügel, *Selected Letters*, 95; emphasis in original.
29. Hügel, *Essays and Addresses* (1921), 230.
30. Hügel, *Essays and Addresses* (1926), 10, 12, 23.
31. Hügel, *Essays and Addresses* (1921), 17.

was also open-minded about and ready to learn from other faiths which he recognized and appreciated as having elements of truth and light in them even though he could not accept that they were all equally true.[32] The Catholic Church's claim to universality should in no way lead to intolerance.[33]

Hügel's openness and sensitive approach to those of other Christian denominations led him, when they asked his advice, to take great care not to pressurize them to become Catholics, lest they did so when they were not ready and, in doing so, disturbed their own equilibrium and ended up in a worse state than they were in before leaving behind their former religious affiliation. Souls outside the church were not lost; they were safe with God, wherever they were. Instead of an excessive urge to win converts as rapidly and in as large numbers as possible, rather he sought to strengthen and deepen whatever beliefs (however tentative) and whatever religious practice (however tenuous a hold in their lives) they already had.[34] Part of his caution against too zealous an attempt to proselytize others stemmed from the harm he felt he had done, the confusion he had sown and the disturbance he had caused for some of his friends and even to members of his own family by sharing too readily and forcefully his own religious position and convictions.

This caution led him to adopt a balanced approach to others who were seeking religious guidance. He advocated a way that was "fervent without fanaticism," one that combined an encouraging and a sympathetic approach without displaying an indifference to the claims of his own faith.[35] In this openness to people who were not fellow Catholics, Hügel was out of step with the prevailing ethos of his church. It can justifiably be claimed that he was a forerunner of that more positive and ecumenical attitude towards other Christians and to adherents of other faiths which emerged at Vatican II. A fortress Catholicism, with its temptation to exert a military discipline over its members and to display a closed and defensive mentality in the face of criticism, was uncongenial to him.

## CONCLUSION

Hügel did not use either of the expressions which are central to the current Catholic understanding of the goal of education, namely "integral development of the human person" and "synthesis of faith, culture, and life."

32. Hügel, *Reality of God*, 13, 21.
33. Hügel, *Reality of God*, 151.
34. Hügel, *Letters to a Niece*, x.
35. Hügel, *Eternal Life*, 352.

Nevertheless, it will be apparent, from this presentation of his thought, that he had a rich and nuanced appreciation of their meaning and the reality to which these phrases refer. In his own work it is clear that both integral development and the desired synthesis depend upon those other features to which he gave such emphasis: openness to the truth wherever it was to be found, respect for the autonomy of the disciplines and a nurturing of the critical faculties of both the already committed faithful and those who still sought a religious home. If we are open to the differences between people and ourselves, if we welcome their "otherness" and the particularity they present to us, if we are genuinely inclusive, we will adapt ourselves to their needs. Such inclusiveness and openness, together with the freedom of maneuver, flexibility, and responsiveness that follow from them, are built upon the confidence, the inner sense of security and stability and the settled conviction of one who stands on firm ground. Hügel demonstrates in his work that it is possible, within the parameters of a Catholic perspective, to combine distinctiveness and inclusiveness. These two qualities are not mutually exclusive, but maintaining a creative tension between them will be a complex and costly exercise.

# 6

# Firmness and Openness in the Catholic University

## INTRODUCTION

John Paul II calls upon Catholic universities to combine the unending search for the truth with the certainty of already knowing the truth (in Christ).[1] This call seems to imply both a distinction and yet also a fundamental unity between searching and possessing. Ruth Barcan, with reference to contrasting expectations of the contemporary university, points out the tension between being "the bastion of tradition and culture" and "an engine of innovation and discovery."[2] In this chapter I explore some aspects of the challenge of receiving what has already been given while remaining open to what has not yet been revealed to us via our encounters with various kinds of otherness. What does being open-minded require of us? How does a tenacious holding onto truth and the kind of firmness of conviction that serves as a foundation for consistent values and coherent decision-making relate to responsiveness to what is newly made possible in our personal circumstances and cultural context, in the questions that arise through our experiences and conversation partners? How does commitment relate to non-possessive presence to and participation in God's creation? Does the sense of interconnectedness that is integral to holding a fixed conviction, faith and identity, from which we view the world and engage in it, allow space for experiment, flexibility, new learning, and development? I will argue that being open to others depends on firmness of conviction but also that, in holding our convictions, we must, if we are to remain open to the

1. John Paul II, *On Catholic Universities.*
2. Barcan, "I Shouldn't Really Be Here," 39.

transcendence to which God is calling us, allow the boundaries of these convictions to be porous, broken open, and reconfigured. If the capacity to remain open to others and to new truths rests on firm and enduring foundations, such openness is also linked to grace, humility, and generosity—all of which are likely to unsettle our foundations on the road to deeper conversion.

One might claim that this chapter brings out some of the creative tension necessary between two scriptural imperatives. First, and with regard to being firm, there is the injunction in Col 1:23: "You must persevere in the faith, firmly grounded, stable, and not shifting from the hope of the Gospel that you heard." Second, with regard to flexibility and openness, there is also the injunction in 1 Cor 9:22: "Make yourself all things to all types of people in order to reach them with the good news." A thermostatic role is required, enabling us to move appropriately between these two imperatives of being firm and being open. A thermostat is sensitive to temperature, enabling the heating to come on when the temperature drops below a certain level, or to go off when it reaches a certain level. When I am in a room full of people who seem to me to be overdosing on firmness, authority, and the importance of following tradition, I feel the need to make the case for greater openness, freedom, and flexibility. When I am in a room full of people who seem to me to be overdosing on freedom and the need for space for innovation, I feel the need to make the case for the gifts made available to us through our living tradition and for firm adherence to this tradition.

As a final introductory point, I believe that holding firmness and openness in a creative and dynamic tension has implications for practice in several areas of the life and work of a Catholic university. These include how the relationship between faith and scholarship is envisaged, student admissions, faculty appointments (and promotion), curriculum provision, and internal ethos, by which I mean the language employed, relationships, modes and tone of communication, leadership styles, decision-making processes, priorities, and the distribution of resources. It also has implications for governance, for evaluation (what is evaluated, by whom, how and according to what criteria) and for external relations. However, I won't be addressing these practical implications here as my focus is a more philosophical unpacking of the nature of the tension between firmness and openness.

## EMBRACING BOTH POLARITIES

Some commentators have lamented the damaging effects on the identity and ethos of Catholic universities caused by internal secularization, too ready an assimilation of postmodern ideas and a careless appropriation of pervasive cultural ideals about inclusivity, pluralism, and relativism.[3] According to such views, any attempt to promote a distinctive Catholic worldview runs the risk of being interpreted as discriminatory and insufficiently open to others. Masson alerts readers to a double paradox pointed out by Bertrand Binoche: "We can only live in peace by accepting once and for all that we must give up seeking agreement on what is essential. What we surrender because it is open to disagreement becomes automatically unessential."[4] In other words, by embracing too readily currently acceptable cultural norms, Catholic universities might soon find themselves at first unwilling and then eventually quite unable to articulate and live out what is at the very heart of their raison d'être. Yet it is central to the task of a university to raise and to address critical questions, to explore new areas of knowledge and fresh perspectives, and in doing so, reinterpret what has been received from the past. The university is an institution dedicated to developing and teaching various types of knowledge in order to go beyond what it has inherited; its preservation role must not stifle its need to transcend the limits of what is currently known.[5] Gillis shrewdly puts his finger on the extremes to avoid when he observes that "sometimes those who are deeply invested in the institution's Catholic identity can become provincial in their protectionism. Sometimes, those who favor enfranchising persons from all traditions and none, want to do so at the cost of core Catholic beliefs and practices."[6] "Traditionally, Catholicism has emphasized the *already* element of what it knows, to the detriment of the *not yet* of what it has yet to learn."[7]

Teachers and leaders in all kinds of educational institutions know that firmness is necessary. One needs to be show firmness of resolve to pursue a particular path, if one is to avoid being sidetracked by temptations, setbacks, and alternative goals that are likely to deflect attention and energy from one's intended destination. One needs to show firmness in order to protect the weaker (among students and colleagues) from being manipulated or mistreated by the stronger. One needs firmness in proclaiming the

---

3. Ricard, "Ouverture du colloque," 95; Fforde, "Crise de l'Occident," 128.
4. Masson, "Université catholique de Lille," 150.
5. Lafforgue, "Recherché fondamentale," 31.
6. Gillis, "Welcoming the Religiously Other," 12.
7. Haughey, *Where Is Knowing Going*, 37; emphasis in original.

mission of the institution unambiguously, courageously, and persistently—in the face of opposition, unpopularity, and factional interests. Firmness helps to reduce confusion and to enhance clarity with regard to aims and the steps needed to achieve these aims. Teachers need firmness to focus and to maintain the attention of their students on the central purposes and tasks of their classes, alert to potential distractions. Such firmness is a sign that one knows where one is going and is aware of what is needed to get there, and that one has the resilience to withstand difficulties and obstacles that might undermine progress.

At the same time, teachers and educational leaders know that openness is necessary. Without openness, expressed as sensitivity, flexibility and willingness to try approaches that are creative, teachers who pursue their lesson plans inexorably might be responsible for classroom experiences that are wooden, unduly predictable, unexciting, and insufficiently related to students' interests and questions. They are likely to make it harder for students to maintain attention, to feel included and to connect what is offered in the curriculum to their own experience and perspective. Classroom rules and institutional procedures that are enforced too rigorously can create resentment, stifle initiative, crush the spirit; they can press for compliance while undermining the conditions that elicit and nurture authentic ownership and commitment. Without an appropriate degree of openness at both the level of teaching-learning encounters and at the level of the whole institution, important questions will not be faced, possible criticisms of current practice will not be allowed to surface, formality will reign, and personhood will suffer.

These requirements for both firmness and openness apply to Catholic schools, colleges, and universities as much as to other educational communities. Firmness supports, promotes and defends what is essential and distinctive in the mission. Openness ensures that, in pursuing essentials, sight is not lost of new possibilities in the tradition, because of inflexible commitment to past innovations that no longer serve their purpose; openness also helps to ensure that reinforcing distinctiveness is not carried out at the cost of slipping into one or more kinds of exclusiveness. Those who work in Catholic universities are recipients of a rich intellectual and spiritual tradition. This is not be received passively. We need to assimilate, internalize, own, and incorporate it into our lives; we need to interrogate, more deeply understand, and better appreciate, implement, and communicate what has been handed on to us. We need to allow it to transform us as we gradually grow into it. Encounters with others and with otherness both challenge and facilitate these various aspects of personal growth.

The stretching and growth that occur (or which are at least made possible) by engaging with otherness can be uncomfortable, disorienting, even disturbing. The questioning of our assumptions, the alternative perspectives considered, the pressure to take into account factors we had previously ignored or of which we had been unaware, the placing of our commitments in a wider context, the different interpretations of values we espouse, the contrasting values we are confronted with, the misunderstanding of what we thought was obvious—all this undermines complacency and changes our sense of identity; it reconfigures elements in our worldview, expands our sympathies, offers new ways to read and respond to life by sharpening our listening and provides us with new lenses for seeing the world.

Collins distinguishes between an objective, transcendent truth to be known and a subjective, immanent truth that is already known.[8] In commenting on John Paul II's thinking on truth, Collins points out that believing in the reality of eternal truths is quite compatible with holding that the expressions of these truths agreed by the church are not themselves eternal.[9] Furthermore, "what is known can be wholly true without being the whole truth." It seems then that both firmness and openness are required. Firmness in the sense of taking the tradition seriously, allowing the truth that is known to be held onto, submitted to and lived out, and in the sense of maintaining a vigilant awareness of and a readiness to confront what contradicts or undermines such truth; yet also openness in the sense of a constant awareness that there is much more still to know, that our grasp on truth is both incomplete and precarious, in need of purification and correction (of our motives and our expressions), requiring constant amplification and an endless deepening of our appreciation of its implications for our personal and institutional practices—combined with a reaching out that is simultaneously confident, humble, welcoming and generous to other people, perspectives, disciplines, concerns and expressions.

The notion of truth illustrates some features of the dialectic between firmness and openness. Truth serves as a steadying, stabilizing and steering force. It offers a foundation, a protective framework, an orientation and stimulant to search further, to go beyond where we arrived so far. It provides a propulsive force for the pilgrimage of life. There is a necessary rhythmic relationship between knowing the truth and its application and implementation; we cannot do the right thing if we do not know the truth; but only if we are living the right way can we come to the truth; here there is an endless cycle of interaction. Furthermore, there is some degree of tension when we

---

8. Collins, "Philosophy in Blessed John Paul II," 122.
9. Collins, "Philosophy in Blessed John Paul II," 123.

consider the scope of truth. Truth is eternal and universal in its significance and scope; but it has to be realized in specific and particular circumstances and actions that are both enabled and constrained by our temporal nature.[10] The truth of Christ, as offered to us via the church, serves as a yardstick or criterion or source of illumination for weighing other claims to truth; but our appreciation of the nature, demands and reach of truth in Christ can be assisted and enhanced by our openness to other forms of truth.

The relationship between firmness and openness can be viewed as one of the many forms of polarity we experience in our lives. Other examples of such polarities include those between subjective faith and objective truth, freedom and authority, the inner and outer life, identity and otherness, the individual and the community, body and spirit, attachment and separation, silence and speech. Learning takes place via the polarity of receiving a preexisting schema and then critiquing, correcting and modifying it. I have been arguing that the Catholic university dwells within the polarity of holding onto and letting go, in the sense of robust adherence to what is true and valuable in the tradition while at the same time remaining open to what comes to us from beyond our tradition and being ready to discern which elements, practices and expressions of tradition no longer serve their purpose. All of our commitments and loves, if they are to be healthy and life giving, find themselves being incarnated within a matrix characterized by polarities. Love for others needs both firmness and openness, for example, love for wife or husband, for children, for students, for parishioners. Commitment to the mission of Catholic universities needs a similar combination of firmness and openness. Each pole only makes sense in the context of the other, interacts with it and is influenced by it; one might say each co-creates the other in a reciprocal, dynamic, and ongoing encounter, opposition, and eventual (if incomplete) harmonizing.

The philosopher Louis Norris, almost seventy years ago, developed a fertile theory of polarity. I begin my reference to his book by picking out just two of his many helpful observations, first on the purpose of deploying the notion of polarity and second on understanding the workings of polarities as a process of "contrapletion." "Polar thinking provides a means of assessing the tensions among the values and thus of weighing 'the things that matter most.' . . . The concept of 'contrapletion' implies that two poles of thought, while they stand over against one another [*contra*], at the same time fulfil one another [*plere*]. 'Contrapletion' expresses and conserves both poles of a relationship. It suggests juxtaposition and yet supplementary

---

10. Norris, *Polarity*, 130, 138.

diversity."[11] While there is value in both firmness and openness, neither pole, on its own, is sufficient. For, on the one hand, as Norris points out, "stagnation in religion or thought comes from too circumscribed concern with the past and with the commonly accepted view of things. But a frenzied trial and error search for every possible outlet for religious interest or for philosophic novelty also ends in fatigue, frustration, and superficiality."[12] The former gives too much weight to firmness as a virtue; the latter, too much reliance on openness as a good. The art, we might say, is in holding the two in dynamic tension. Norris suggests that, when a pole is combined with its opposite, we have what he calls "polar augmentation." "Here each pole grows in significance as its connection with its opposite is sought."[13]

Norris provides a further insight into the working of polarity, one especially relevant for Catholic universities which seek to bring together to their mutual advantage, instead of keeping apart, secular and spiritual knowledge, virtues and values. "Though spiritual values may give meaning and unity of perspective to the whole of experience, they always do so in terms understandable through the factors they illuminate. . . . Spiritual values stand not only in contact with secular and temporal things, but they also come to their full nature in and through these other values. . . . Man must be informed about and attached to the rich variety of values within his world in order for the unifying of his perspective in religious insight to mean anything."[14]

In the search for the whole that is integral to the task of Catholic universities, then openness, as one of these polarities, is a prerequisite. Only a minority among supporters of Catholic universities would reject Anthony's argument that "instead of sheltering Catholic intellectual discourse from disruptive or disturbing voices, we should be nourishing and cultivating a lively intellectual, moral, and spiritual life that has no fear of engagement with any dialogue partner who seeks a genuine exchange of ideas"[15] or her proposal that "we must welcome scholars of different worldviews, both for their acknowledged gifts and for the challenges they pose, because these challenges may be gifts not yet recognized."[16]

Acknowledgment of our ignorance should be another motivator for being open to others. There is much that we do not know. To start with,

11. Norris, *Polarity*, x, 8.
12. Norris, *Polarity*, 25.
13. Norris, *Polarity*, 29.
14. Norris, *Polarity*, 126, 128, 132.
15. C. Anthony, "Newman's Idea of a University," 36.
16. C. Anthony, "Newman's Idea of a University," 37.

God will always remain beyond our ken; we never have our understanding of God sorted or settled. Then, we remain a mystery to ourselves, despite rare moments of insight, often granted to us by others who shock us by their observations of who are and what we are like. As for other people, no matter how well we think we know them, they too escape our grasp; they have depths that we cannot reach. If we think of the church, she too seems to be full of surprises for us, some welcome, others quite unwelcome. If we were not open to surprise, we would be closed to grace.

Open-mindedness, like other intellectual virtues, is a quality that needs to be held onto with firmness (which does not mean rigidity); it needs to be stable, enduring, robust in the face of temptation, resilient in withstanding difficulties—if its possibilities are to be enjoyed, if its demands are to be experienced, if its genuineness is to be tested and confirmed and thus made evident to others; and if its relationship to and dependence on other intellectual virtues is to be appreciated. Open-mindedness not only suspends (at least temporarily) our prejudices, and offers a space for serious consideration of views; it not only creates a space for the other person or persons; it also creates a space within oneself, a space in which a creative interpretation of a situation or issue can be generated. Finding flaws in one's thinking through critical encounters with those who differ from one makes possible growth in our understanding.

Yet such openness needs to be founded on firm commitments if it is to be more than fleeting and arbitrary. With regard to our intellectual commitments, Roberts and Wood observe "Not to be at all conservative about them would be not to believe, not to understand, not to have ways of perceiving. . . . Insofar as we participate in the intellectual life at all, we are perforce and naturally both conservative and open."[17] They point out that "to be the most advancing of knowers, people need to be willing to think outside the presuppositions of their communities, to doubt authorities, and to imagine unheard-of possibilities."[18] Thus, it is no surprise that, in a recent book on Catholic universities, Orji claims that "Catholics can and do understand their own tradition better when they engage with others in dialogue."[19] While engaging with others needs both humility and generosity, it also requires caution and discernment. In a footnote, Orji draws attention to the concern that "the pull of mainstream culture is so powerful that a minority

---

17. Roberts and Wood, *Intellectual Virtues*, 84.
18. Roberts and Wood, *Intellectual Virtues*, 255.
19. Orji, *Catholic University*, 21.

institution that integrates many of its features risks relinquishing its own distinguishing traits."[20]

## CONCLUSION

Pope Leo XIII, when calling the church (in 1879) to rely more consistently and comprehensively on the thought of Thomas Aquinas, set out to revitalize tradition through a process of *vetera novis augere et perficere*—to augment and complete the old with the new. I take this to mean four things: first, hold onto what is good from the past; second, do so with an awareness of its historicity, its contingent features, its limitations and shortcomings; third, be open (with discernment) to what is good in what emerges in our present time; fourth, make sure to integrate the new with the old, so that fidelity can enable both continuity and creativity. The outcome to be hoped for from a healthy combination of both firmness in upholding and maintaining the tradition, on the one hand, and openness to expanding and refiguring it through openness, on the other hand, is a critical appreciation and a creative appropriation of that tradition. Too much firmness leaves the way open to the false security of conveying unexamined beliefs; too little firmness, through conceding too easily to skepticism about the reliability or relevance of tradition, can leave the way open to the false security of a solitary self-reliance.[21] Dogmatists close down the exploration too quickly by assuming their judgments are firm and unassailable; relativists permanently postpone making any judgment about truth and thereby prevent themselves from learning by acting upon it. Being open to an encounter with those with whom we think we differ might lead us to find more in common than we anticipated. It should also widen our horizons and in the process deepen our appreciation for the mystery of the great Other, God, and for God's creation.

---

20. Orji, *Catholic University*, 83; see also, on features of contemporary culture that are corrosive of Catholic education, McKinney and Sullivan, *Education in a Catholic Perspective*, 209–13.

21. Orji, *Catholic University*, 212.

## PART TWO
# Leadership

### INTRODUCTION

A steward usually has to direct the work of others, ensuring that the contributions of individuals serve the interests of the whole. A steward's leadership role will influence the use of time, talents and resources; it entails bringing the efforts of many into harmony. We can distinguish leadership and management, although often being a steward entails a combination of both. Leadership links principles, purposes, and people. It uses the currency of vision, trades in ideas, mobilizes energies, and seeks coherence, or a match between ethos and practice. It strives to reach a perspective that allows one a proper confidence in the judgments being made about direction and priorities. It relies on releasing the talents of others in service of a bigger picture, an ideal and attractive scenario. Commitment is its goal, one that cannot be attained without voluntary and internal consent. Management works in narrower parameters, tends to accept from others overarching purposes and ends, while being focused on finding ways ever more effectively and efficiently to carry out the means necessary. It deploys the levers that are to hand and concentrates on good use of them. Too often motivation is based on externals, systems and structures, bypasses the intrapersonal sources of commitment, ignores the power of ethos, and ends up in compliance. Management works in the system. Leadership works on the system.

The leader needs to know the nature and purpose of the business she or he is responsible for, how its various components work together, and the threats that need to be guarded against. In the context of educational leadership there needs to be both technical competence and the application of emotional literacy, with regard to both self-management and the management of others. Relational skills are paramount in all authentic leadership, but especially so in education. This is increasingly being recognized in the literature on leadership, where there is an emphasis on interpersonal skills, communication, the fostering of teamwork and trust, encouraging cooperation, participation, initiative, and flexibility. An influential writer on leadership points out:

> In this chaotic world, we need leaders. But we do not need bosses. We need leaders to help us develop a clear identity that lights the dark moments of confusion. We need leaders to support us as we learn how to live by our values. We need leaders to understand that we are best controlled by concepts that invite participation, not policies and procedures that curtail our contribution. . . . We all have to learn how to support the workings of each other, to realize that intelligence is distributed and that it is our role to nourish others with truthful, meaningful information.[1]

Knowing how to encourage, to listen, to affirm, and to be responsive—these qualities are more likely to elicit commitment than being technically accomplished, especially if they are allied to integrity, intelligence, articulateness, and shrewd judgment.

Educational leaders have to hold together an understanding of the wider environment, the internal dynamics of their school or university, and their own deeper self. They have three areas which need constant attention: meaning, community, and excellence. The first requires of them a clear and coherent philosophy; the second depends on the quality of relationships that are nurtured; the third has its focus on standards that are being achieved. In both schools and universities, leaders need to promote an agreed story about their institution's aims, mission, priorities, and roles. The need to possess a realistic picture of their staff at their disposal—their age, gender, length of experience, expertise, interests, and currently untapped potential. At the same time they need where people are currently at, with regard to their levels of performance, their expectations, their hopes, and their fears. It will also be expected of leaders that they are aware of external requirements that impinge on the organization, for example, legislation, social and political forces, bodies that evaluate (academically or professionally) or mandate the work being carried out.

The church historian Eamon Duffy makes a helpful observation in connection with Christian leadership: "The Church needs structure and order if it is to survive; it needs fire, ardour, heart if it is not to become a

---

1. Wheatley, *Leadership and New Science*, 131.

prison for the spirit; it needs intellectual rigour and commitment to the truth if it is to have a gospel to preach."[2] None of these elements should dominate the others, and all need to be present and operative to ensure that there is a healthy balance (often a creative tension) between them.

Irving and Strauss, in their analysis of what leadership requires from a Christian perspective, identify three main tasks, each of which has three components. First, authentic and purposeful leaders should model what matters, engage in honest self-evaluation, and foster collaboration. Second, understanding the priority of people should involve attention to valuing and appreciating staff, creating a place for individuality, and both understanding and promoting relational skills. Third, navigating toward effectiveness entails communicating with clarity, providing accountability, and supporting and resourcing colleagues and projects.[3]

Chapter 7 has its focus on leadership preparation for faith-based schools. It seeks to identify to what extent such preparation can be carried out in common with other schools and to what extent there needs to be separate or additional components, if justice is to be done to the Christian character of the school. In chapter 8 I explore the nature of and the interaction between three types of ownership that Christian educational leaders need to promote: proprietary ownership, professional ownership and participatory ownership. Chapter 9 concentrates on the moral dimension of leadership within church schools. First, it explores how values are upheld and promoted by leaders, then it deploys the notion of "shadows" to identify unintended side effects of current practice and internal conflicts of ethos and roles; third, it suggests that a retrieval of Aristotelian insights on rhetoric can assist school leaders in their moral leadership role. Chapter 10 comments on key dimensions of educational leadership, including holding together the ethical, political and spiritual. Then it describes what I believe should be particularly evident features of any leadership that claims to be Christian, brings out the importance of ideas-based leadership, before exploring the modeling or example-giving role of leaders, using the metaphor of "living logos." Chapter 11 ends the section on leadership by explaining why succession planning is a key feature of effective leadership and why it is needed for the healthy flourishing of Catholic parishes and schools. In the second part of the chapter I outline twelve elements that, when combined, would help to create the conditions in which succession planning has a chance to take root. In this way parishes and schools would move closer to

---

2. Duffy, "Who Leads the Church," s.vv. "Three forms of leadership."
3. Irving and Strauss, *Leadership in Christian Perspective*.

being the kind of learning communities required by the gospel and thus live out their mission more appropriately.

# 7

# Addressing Difference and Commonality in Leadership Preparation for Faith Schools

FAITH SCHOOLS CURRENTLY FORM a legitimate part of state supported educational provision in the UK. Once their essential distinctiveness is granted, then it follows logically that a distinctive form of leadership will be required for these schools. It would seem odd to claim that exactly the same preparation for leadership is required for significantly different educational communities. If the state allows, even encourages, the maintenance of faith schools, as an element in diversity of provision and out of respect for parental choice, then it follows that allowance should also be made for separate provision of training and development opportunities for leaders in such schools. Such separate provision is a potential source of conflict between government, faith communities and the teaching profession.

In this chapter I argue first that leadership is essentially connected to purposes. Then I bring out some of the ways that leadership of faith schools, and more particularly, leadership of church schools, requires priorities and capacities additional to and different than those required in mainstream schools. Third, as an example of the type of separate and specific provision for church school leadership that is needed, there is a brief description of an MA program which I directed between 1997 and 2002. Fourth, there is an analysis of some of the tensions and conflicts brought about by the desire of churches to have separate provision of leadership preparation opportunities. Finally, it is suggested that, although there are difficulties that arise when faith schools emphasize their distinctiveness too much, so too there are dangers when insufficient attention is paid to this distinctiveness and when other professional and educational orthodoxies are imposed.

## LEADERSHIP AND PURPOSE

Despite the plethora of studies on leadership, about its provenance and sources, its expression and modes of operation, and the diverse contexts in which it is exercised, it is not an activity that can easily be separated from its raison d'être or from the particular purposes it seeks to promote. Thus, though we may well ask such questions as "*Who* is doing the leading? *How* are they doing this? *Where* is it happening?," we get nowhere near an in-depth understanding without taking into account what it is there *for*, *why* does it exist, what are the *ends* that direct the means, what are the permeating intentions or overarching purposes that govern the methods employed. While we can acknowledge and accept that there will be many generic features of effective leadership, and therefore many transferable qualities and skills, nevertheless the specific purposes of an institution, company or community will significantly color or shape the kinds of leadership required. Such purposes may dictate, to greater or lesser degree, which reference groups are dominant, which constituencies are considered to have priority, what styles or methods may be prescribed, permitted or forbidden, and the criteria that are employed for evaluating failure and success.

This focus on purposes links with Sergiovanni's emphasis on the allegiance that stems from shared commitment to ideas, in contrast to leadership that relies either on status in an institution or on position in a bureaucracy on the one hand, or, on the other hand, leadership that relies on the use of motivational sticks and carrots to secure a personal following.[1] These ideas should serve as "compasses," rather than as "scripts," Sergiovanni rightly points out, since they should not determine for us every step on our way.[2] They give us a sense of direction, while leaving us scope and space to decide particular routes.

Of course, the purposes or ideas that provide a warrant for leadership are not merely disembodied, abstract notions, for they are intimately and inextricably interlinked with a particular way of life, one that is both personal and part of a living tradition. The purposes emerge from a community that authorizes the leaders, grants them a mandate, establishes parameters within which to channel their efforts and provides yardsticks for assessing progress. In this sense the purposes belong to believers, that is, they are held as dear, as worthy of commitment and sacrifice. They have grown out of a pattern of living (one that for Christians includes proclamation of the gospel, building community, worshipping God, and serving those in need) and

---

1. Sergiovanni, *Leadership*, 6, 8, 29, 30.
2. Sergiovanni, *Leadership*, 62.

they are directed towards maintaining and enhancing that way of living. The purposes we espouse are not simply the fruit of some neutral, detached, logical analysis. They are the result of choice, positive and negative, and of a common life lived in accordance with that choice. That common life is the soil in which the ideas and purposes flourish and find their meaning and significance. This first aspect of my assertion, that the purposes that underpin leadership are not disembodied or abstract, relates to their social origins and to the relevance we feel they have for our commitments and convictions.

This is not the whole story, however, for these purposes, while expressing what we are hoping to achieve, also remain always subject to the contingency of circumstances, shortcomings, accident, charisms, and serendipity. They do not work out in practice quite in the way we meant them to in our intentions. There are unforeseen helping and hindering factors, side effects and consequences. Purposes are open to diverse interpretations, controversy, a spectrum of responses, and alternative mixtures of their constitutive elements. There is nothing automatic, necessary, or eternal in any particular "packaging" or presentation of a set of ideas. In the light of this feature, leaders always find that, in order to be faithful to their goals, they have to balance continuity and innovation and draw upon both memory and imagination.

## LEADERSHIP OF FAITH SCHOOLS

How does this relate to the leadership of faith schools? Two implications follow from my preliminary comments. First, faith schools have some, perhaps many, purposes in common with other schools. Therefore there will be at least some generic qualities and skills that prospective leaders for faith schools can usefully learn alongside of other potential school leaders. Second, leaders of faith schools have some purposes that differ in significant ways from those espoused in mainstream schools. The kinds of different purposes indicated briefly here imply additional specific leadership dimensions for faith schools, dimensions that cannot be addressed in the absence of joint affiliation to the faith community that sponsors such schools and from which they derive an important part of their identity.

With regard to the first point, all school leaders should ensure that the promotion of student learning is central to the deployment of resources and to all decision-making. Whatever subordinate purposes or additional goals leaders might have pressed upon them, for example, in meeting government requirements for economic efficiency, for producing future contributors to the economy and pliant and well-behaved citizens, in the school context their leadership must be in service of education; it must create optimal conditions for learning. In the UK such promotion of learning must address the requirements of the national curriculum and its associated assessment arrangements, even if these are considered inadequate as a basis for education, and therefore need supplementing. School leaders must comply with legislation, for instance, regarding health and safety, child protection, data protection, and equal opportunities. They are accountable, in different ways, for the results achieved by pupils and for the effective use of resources, to various bodies, for instance, to government inspectors, to local education authorities, to parents, and to school governors. Many aspects relating to the legal framework, to the local context, to support services, to curriculum, assessment, inspection, governance and management and personnel matters should be learned in common by school leaders, regardless of the kind of school in which they intend to work.

As for my second point, some of the purposes pursued in faith schools differ radically from those pursued in mainstream or common schools. I give just a few examples of different emphases. Thus, if all education imports, consciously or unconsciously, some idea of what it is to be human and some conception of human flourishing, then education based on a religious faith perspective, for example, Christian education, relates an understanding of humanity to its understanding of divinity. I should respect my pupils and colleagues, not only because of commitment to the principles of liberty, equality, and fraternity, though this is a perfectly sound and adequate reason, but also because they, like me, are made in the image and likeness of God, are the recipients of God's love and the forgiveness and redemption offered in Christ, and are called by the Holy Spirit to grow ever more fully into the stature required for sharing in the divine life. Cumulatively these Christian understandings have the effect, not simply of adding to the leader's task, but of transforming it, including in those aspects and purposes of leadership held in common with mainstream schools and as described in the paragraph above. Thus, if educational leadership more generally supports teaching and serves learning, then Christian educational leadership in particular should support Christian teaching and promote Christian learning.

Christian education will aim for the holistic development of students, as do other types of education, but it will envisage this development as best happening in the context of discipleship. In promoting the all-round, or integral, development of persons, Christian educators will support and encourage, as other educators do, the intellectual, emotional, aesthetic, physical, moral, social, and spiritual dimensions, but they will conceive of these as elements ordered in the light of their understanding of Christ as the Way, the Truth, and the Life.

In aiming for a broad and balanced curriculum Christian educators will wish to see interconnectedness and coherence, rather than isolation and fragmentation, brought out. For them, God is our ultimate environment, the reason for everything that exists, the source, sustainer, and goal of its life, and therefore in the various subjects of the curriculum we are learning about God's world, God's purposes, and God's people and creatures, whether we advert to this explicitly or not. Drawing from a sacramental perspective, education should alert and sensitize pupils to God's presence in all experiences. Furthermore, in the expansion of our powers and in the development of our capacities that education promotes, there is also necessary an ongoing conversion of the will, a turning away from sin, a disciplining of self.

From a religious perspective there are close connections between our metaphysics, our view of reality, our mysticism, that is our response to and relationship with that reality and our morality, that is, our behavior, priorities, and decision-making in the light of these first two. God, as known in Christ, makes all the difference; this difference is utterly hidden, misunderstood, or distorted if the faith perspective is restricted to a slot on the timetable or relegated to the realm of the private option, on a par with a hobby.

I have written at considerable length elsewhere about some of the intellectual, political, and spiritual qualities and skills required by leaders in church schools; and I don't want to retread that ground here.[3] However, I hope it will be clear from the points I have just made here that if there are significant differences (from common schools) in the purposes being pursued in church schools, then there will also be important differences in the expectations of the leadership of such schools. Intellectually, effective church school leaders need a confident and articulate theological literacy. Politically, they must have the capacity to operate out of and to address the ecclesial community and its key stakeholders and gatekeepers. Spiritually, they should be mature in their own spiritual development, sufficiently steeped in the faith community to be trusted as an elder and familiar with its liturgical "repertoire" and style. The very terminology which best describes what is needed as preparation for church school leadership, formation for ministry, immediately shows that leadership for such schools requires opportunities for training, education, and development that go well beyond what is offered and needed for common schools.

---

3. Sullivan: "Wrestling with Managerialism"; *Catholic Schools in Contention*; "Living Logos"; "Leadership and Management"; "Dynamics of Ownership."

## ADDRESSING DIFFERENCE AND COMMONALITY

Formation implies an assimilation and an integration of four dimensions. First, there is initiation into a way of thinking and understanding, the operationalizing of a coherent conceptual "tool kit" and "story." Second, there is a way of behaving, a set of practices into which we are inducted. Third, there is a way of belonging, affiliation to a particular community, with associated sharing, celebration, joint action, and common life. Fourth, there is a way of worship to experience, to dwell within and from which to perceive the world.[4]

This kind of formation cannot be provided by the National Professional Qualification for Headship, nor should it be expected.[5] That framework, quite legitimately, has other purposes. It cannot deal adequately with the notion of spiritual leadership, beyond some rudimentary attention to the need for vision, for personal values and for self-knowledge. It cannot sponsor a sense of vocation, for it has no mandate to connect the educative task to the personal call of God to each person to match their gifts with the world's need. And, although it can stress the value of personal integrity, it lacks the rationale for grounding the coherent, integrated approach to the curriculum and learning required by a Christian worldview.[6]

Although mainstream leadership provision in many centers can be intelligent, principled, reflective, professional, practical, relevant, realistic, and empowering—all of which is to be applauded, encouraged, and supported—it still lacks dimensions I consider vital for effective leadership of Christian schools. These include attention to understanding informed by Scripture, doctrinal and moral theology, and spirituality, and insights illuminated by engagement with Christian witness, participation in the sacraments, liturgy, and living tradition. Undergirding the existence of separate Catholic schools, for instance, there is a particular, substantive, thickly developed and tightly integrated network of understandings which contribute to a shared view of life. These understandings include a theology of creation, nature, and grace, with an associated sacramental perspective, together with a Christology and an associated anthropology and ecclesiology.[7]

---

4. Sullivan, "From Formation to the Frontiers."

5. Introduced by the UK government at the end of the twentieth century (and a compulsory qualification for all new head teachers as from 2004) in order to equip candidates for head teacher posts with a standard set of skills, competencies, and areas of knowledge, published in 1998 by the Teacher Training Agency. See Sullivan, "Skills Based Model," for a critique of the skills-based approach to school leadership.

6. Congregation for Clergy, *General Directory for Catechesis*, 74; Sullivan, *Catholic Education*, 86–92.

7. Sullivan, *Catholic Education*, 105.

Mainstream provision of school leadership training programs seem to me to attend quite well to the extra-personal and the interpersonal dimensions of the work of leaders, but too little to the intrapersonal, that is, to the inner dynamics that influence their action, connecting this to meaning and motivation, to self-perception and self-acceptance, to overarching purposes and a bigger "story." For leadership in faith-based schools, there is a need for more emphasis on personal formation, on orienting the curriculum for service, on modeling and fostering countercultural and prophetic witness, on community-building, and on coping with vulnerability, shortcomings, failure, forgiveness, and healing—and on the role of prayer and worship in all of this.[8]

## AN EXAMPLE OF LEADERSHIP PROVISION FOR CHURCH SCHOOLS

There is a growing literature on Catholic education and on the leadership of such schools.[9] This literature is a sign of much rethinking about Catholic education that is going on across the world. In the UK, as elsewhere, professionally, we have seen the emergence in the last generation of an all-pervading managerialism as a phenomenon affecting many aspects of contemporary life. More recently in this country, a ladder of competencies for school teachers and leaders has been drawn up, providing a framework that can be used in staff selection, induction, deployment, development, monitoring, appraisal and promotion. Although both of these phenomena have positive features, they also present aspects that are problematical.[10] Ecclesially, there is the continuing task of implementing the new emphases within Catholicism that emerged from the Second Vatican Council (1962–65). This process, if past patterns of conciliar implementation are any guide, is still unfinished and is likely to take several more decades. The

---

8. For a recent, penetrating, and thorough analysis of the bearing of Catholic social thought on the practice of management, see Alford and Naughton, *Managing as If Faith Mattered*; and for an examination of the bearing of Christian faith more generally on school leadership, see Kay and Francis, *Distance Learning*.

9. Arthur, *Ebbing Tide*; McLaughlin et al., *Contemporary Catholic School*; Conroy, *Catholic Education Inside Out*; Hunt, *Catholic School Leadership*; Sullivan, *Catholic Schools in Contention*; Sultmann and McLaughlin, *Spirit of Leadership*; Sullivan, *Catholic Education*; Grace, *Catholic Schools*; Hayes and Gearon, *Contemporary Catholic Education*. This literature has continued to proliferate since this was first written.

10. For critiques either of managerialism or of the skills-based model of school leadership, see Pattison, *Faith of the Managers*; Sullivan, "Wrestling with Managerialism"; Loughlin, *Ethics, Management and Mythology*; Sullivan, "Skills Based Model."

very interpretation of the council has been and continues to be charged with controversy within the church. New imperatives in ecumenism and in interfaith dialogue and co-operation present challenges to Catholic educators and leaders, as do changes in the composition of church schools and in patterns of behavior by church members. Significant modifications in styles of—and responses to—authority within the church and society inevitably have an impact upon the types of leadership desirable and possible within church schools. As theologian George Schner puts it: "We are in a moment of reconstruction, passing from one coherent manifestation of identity and authority within the tradition to another."[11]

In response to this changing professional and ecclesial context in the UK, a special program for Catholic school leadership was launched at St. Mary's College, Twickenham, in 1997. It sought to facilitate for students, all of whom were experienced teachers, an integration of academic, professional and spiritual competence, intelligence and wisdom, paying attention to the inner self, to the group dynamics of daily school functioning and to agencies and factors beyond the school that influence its educational, religious and community responsibilities. The currently prevailing sense of "vocational," that is, being relevant to, and equipping people for, the world of work, with careful attention to professional context and ground-rules, was brought into a serious engagement with an older sense of vocation, of living out one's life in response to God's particular call to us to match our gifts to the world's needs, giving witness to the gospel, offering a ministry of service and co-operating with God's grace in communion with the church.

Many features of this MA program addressed issues similar to those dealt with in other, mainstream school leadership courses, for example, strategic planning, curriculum leadership, staff development and the management of quality in learning and work. However, it also sought to immerse students in the church's developing understanding of the nature, purposes, scope, and challenges of Catholic education, by facilitating an in-depth engagement with that faith community's authoritative documents, at international and national levels, and relating these to the realities of current contexts for work, learning, and living. Students investigated the church's understanding of spirituality, of spiritual development, and of spiritual leadership and explored ways to appreciate these critically and to appropriate them creatively. Theological perspectives were drawn upon in order to cast light on the educational endeavor, on moral dilemmas, on the school's

---

11. Schner, *Education for Ministry*, 78.

relationship with the church, on styles of leadership, and on relationships in classrooms and community.[12]

Not only were there differences in some of the topics studied, in many of the resources referred to and in some of the constituencies taken into account, there were also differences in how the course was conducted. Formation, according to the description given in section 2 (above), rather than training, was seen as central. Formation is rooted in the worshipping community, and it seeks interconnectedness between our thinking, feeling, acting, belonging and worship. Its goal is the development of discipleship, which requires discernment and the capacity for initiative, responsibility, creativity and improvisation rather than mere conformity, repetition, and obedience. Students were expected to relate their academic reading and writing to their worship, church membership, personal spiritual growth, pedagogy, and professional practice. Perhaps controversially, prayer was a regular feature of classroom experience, framing our work together, placing it in the wider context of God's purposes, relativizing authority structures, reducing distance between students and lecturers, keeping in perspective the importance of particular topics, recognizing the place of work in our lives and the connections between this and all the other dimensions that comprise who we are and that affect us. While constantly fostering critical questioning of all our assumptions and practices, as is appropriate for such a level of study, we spoke explicitly from faith and to faith. In examining the unfinished "script" of the church's educational, spiritual and theological reflections, and using this to cast light on their teaching and school leadership, students not only came to see their work in new ways, but also to see differently elements within the tradition itself and to see new connections between the parts of its "ecology" and the "economy" of salvation. I believe that in making connections and in raising questions, their insights make an important contribution to the cutting edge of (intra-ecclesial) applied theology, as well as to the wider understanding of education.[13]

---

12. For a rationale and analysis of this program, see Sullivan et al., "Story of an Educational Innovation."

13. While there are no published evaluations of this MA program, it went through a successful external inspection in 2001 and enjoyed throughout the period described almost a nil dropout rate; and a very high proportion of its students were extremely successful in gaining promoted posts in their own or other church schools as heads or deputy head teachers, or in dioceses as senior officers in the Catholic school system. More important, many individuals claimed that their personal understanding had been transformed, their sense of vocation renewed and deepened, and their schools revitalized.

## POTENTIAL CONFLICT

The existence of faith schools in a highly secular and pluralist society is controversial.[14] Thus, efforts to justify the provision of separate leadership training opportunities for such schools might be expected to be controversial, not only beyond the faith communities, but also within them. I comment briefly here on the differing perspectives of teachers' unions, government, and faith communities.

First, teachers' unions and associations, which have a major stake in continuing professional development and advancement opportunities for their members, may be concerned about religious requirements that they consider intrude unwarrantably into private lives, or which undermine equal opportunities for some colleagues working in church schools. They will wish to protect professional activities, training and education from interference from the church. There may be occasions when prevailing professional norms appear to clash with the mission and ethos of church schools, or with the demands of discipleship, which might appear to ask too much of staff.

Second, governments, conscious of the need to be demonstrably upholding equity, and anxious not to be seen favoring any particular section of the community, may be wary of conceding too much to any particular faith group, with regard to funding, training or any modifications in regulations that frame the organization of education or that are put in place to ensure quality of provision. No Western government in secular, plural, and highly secularized societies wants to appear to be operating as an arm of the church or to allow any creeping sacralization. Furthermore, the government in the UK faces criticism from some quarters that its positive policy towards faith schools undermines the common good by showing partiality towards one section of the population. However, in the attempt to stress the contribution that their schools should be making to the development of citizenship and to the promotion of the common good, I believe that Anglicans and Catholics have a creditable record. If generally Anglicans have stressed the service role of their schools, in contrast to their role in nurturing the faith of believers, more than and for longer than has the Catholic

---

14. For examples of philosophical, theological, political, and educational literature that casts light, directly or indirectly, on many of the issues arising out of church-state relations in education, see Benne, *Quality with Soul*; Callan, *Creating Citizens*; Dwyer, *Religious Schools v. Children's Rights*; Fraser, *Between Church and State*; Gascoigne, *Public Forum & Christian Ethics*; Douglass and Hollenbach, *Catholicism and Liberalism*; Levinson, *Demands of Liberal Education*; Marty and Moore, *Education, Religion*; Nagel, *Equality and Impartiality*; Stiltner, *Religion and Common Good*; Thiessen, *In Defence of Religious Schools*.

community, the gap between their two types of church schools is rapidly diminishing. It seems to me that there is a real concern in many quarters to recapture the distinctive dimension of Anglican education, without loss of its traditionally inclusive style. And, in parallel fashion, there are real efforts to ensure that in Catholic schools the gospel imperative towards inclusiveness is properly engaged with, without loss of distinctiveness.

Third, faith communities, fearing what for them is the threat of increasing secularization, and holding to the view that neutrality or impartiality in government educational policy is often neither equal nor benign in its effects, will wish to stress the importance of differentiation of treatment, if their particular needs are to be met. Defending their "corner" in education, in this case, referring to separate schools and to adequate and appropriate provision for leadership training for them, is linked, in their minds, with providing the conditions for the healthy maintenance of their community's present life and future flourishing. A legitimate concern here is that if teaching is conceived of as a vocation, if school leadership is envisaged as a form of ministry and if church schools are considered to be a central part of the church's mission and both drawing from and contributing to its living tradition, then church schools, to be authentic in their identity and purpose, require both a high degree of personal investment from each teacher and a substantially corporate approach from staff. There will be a strong brand and a strong culture. This poses difficulties for those who do not feel comfortable with this strong brand. Yet, "if faith-based schools and agencies become conformed to government expectations and ways of doing things, they lose much that is valuable about their distinctive approach."[15]

One kind of tension or conflict about faith schools, more specifically, church schools, and even more narrowly, Catholic schools, that may become more marked in the future than it has been in the past, is disagreement *within* the faith community as to the purposes and priorities of "their" schools and to the expectations of leaders of those schools. Referring to my own Catholic community, the move from religious or clerical leadership of church schools, now almost complete in many parts of the world, the professionalization of governing bodies, (whose work requires active citizenship and responsibility rather than "rubber-stamping" what the head decides and simply being a supporters' club), the emergence of more confident forms of lay spirituality, the growing numbers of people who are theologically literate, a more independent religious press, more open communication between and less subservient relations between people and their clergy—all these features may well lead to more vigorous debate about

---

15. Glenn, *Ambiguous Embrace*, 40.

the characteristics of Catholic schools, and therefore about their leadership, than was seen in earlier generations when it was crucial for a minority and slightly alien group to present a united front to government and society to fight for "a place at the table" where educational policy was decided and resources were allocated.

The implication of my approach to the question as to whether school leadership preparation programs for church school staff should be carried out wholly together with staff from mainstream schools, entirely separately, or in some kind of mixed economy is that the last of these three is required.

## DANGERS OF OVER- AND UNDEREMPHASIZING DISTINCTIVENESS

I have argued that, once separate faith-based schools are allowed to be part of a system of educational provision, it is necessary also to allow for partly separate provision of leadership preparation programs. Without this, justice cannot be done to the special nature of such schools and they will be undermined. As a result, the educational system as a whole will be the poorer. There are dangers, however, for teachers, pupils, and parents, as well as for governments, citizens and members of the church, if the distinctiveness of church schools is emphasized too sharply.[16]

First, key aspects of the Christian worldview are deeply controversial. Disputes arise about how to interpret tradition, how to express doctrine, how to order worship, how apply moral teaching, how to build the ecclesial community, how to exercise authority within it, how to communicate with outsiders, and how to assess relative priorities within all these areas. The task of establishing schools based on a distinctive worldview is not straightforward if that distinctiveness is open to question and if its parameters are unclear. There is not, at the present time, nor is there likely to be in the foreseeable future, a consensus among Christians about education. Clarifying distinctiveness is not a process that should be kept "in-house," that is, merely among church members; it is one that will benefit from dialogue with other Christians, with members of other faiths, and with our secular colleagues.

Second, at any one time, at least some aspects of the church's teaching and practice are in a state of flux; there is disruption and discontinuity as well as stability and continuity. A tradition and its canons tend to lay down what should be preserved. They also provide resources with the capacity to

---

16. I borrow heavily in the following four paragraphs from Sullivan, *Catholic Education*, xiii–xiv.

authorize creative responses to new demands. The church exists in history; its boundaries shift in response to changing circumstances, emerging opportunities and new threats. Outside influences affect the internal balance at any particular moment. Any social organization maintains its cultural identity by adjusting to the changing practices of others as well as by the unfolding of its own internal logic. The church shares in that process. The task of establishing separate schools based on a distinctive worldview cannot be settled or secured except temporarily and provisionally, since that distinctiveness derives partly from responses to circumstances, factors, and developments that are outside the church's control and that are themselves undergoing constant change. Part of this flexibility depends on proper engagement with and a real appreciation of these changing circumstances, factors, and developments; without this, separate training for church school leadership will become irrelevant and out of touch with important realities.

Third, from a faith perspective, to commit oneself too readily to any particular form of distinctiveness is to run the risk of idolatry. In such cases, human achievement is misread as the work of the divine, the signpost is treated as if it were the destination, and provisional signs of promise are falsely taken as indicators of permanence and possession. True discipleship requires us to be open to a God who still speaks, one who is leading us, through the Holy Spirit, into a greater fullness of truth, and a God who transcends the church. This process of being led further into truth is unfinished. By turning inwards too soon, defending what we already have, we also run the risk of slipping into complacency, as if we believe we have all that is necessary and have nothing further to learn. Such a stance would lead to isolation, thereby contributing both to our own impoverishment and to a failure to communicate the gospel as effectively as possible.

Fourth, the desire to provide separate schools that have a mandate to offer religious formation in a holistic manner can lead to the temptation to overemphasize distinctiveness in various ways that are damaging. One can exaggerate distinctiveness both by ignoring how much has been borrowed from others who are outside one's community or tradition and also by downplaying how much is still shared with them. This is to distort reality. One can undermine the constructive potential of distinctiveness by overprotecting and isolating it. This leads to a failure to engage in dialogue and so to an abdication of responsibility for the educational welfare of others. One can promote distinctiveness so strongly in the pluralist marketplace of educational services that such promotion slips into appearing not so much a positive advocacy of a set of ideals, but more a negative critique of the stances of others. This can be divisive. One can construct the distinctiveness in such a way that schools based on it become elitist. High hurdles are set on entry, thereby ruling out many students and teachers who could otherwise have benefited from membership. Expectations are so demanding that students and staff who fall short of these requirements experience defeat and despair. This type of emphasis could make faith-based schools vulnerable to the accusation that they are exclusive.

In contrast, if distinctiveness is constrained, for example, by insisting that prospective leaders attend a program intended for all schools and then undergo evaluation by criteria that apply to all schools, there are likely to be several damaging side effects. First, for those wishing to work as heads in church schools, they could well up end having to jump over two sets of hurdles, instead of one. If they wish to be accredited as worthy of headship, they will need to attend National Professional Qualification for Headship programs. If they want to exercise that role in church schools, they will also need to take part in additional in-service courses arranged by dioceses, church colleges, and other bodies, courses that address the specific requirements, contexts, and constituencies of the faith community. This is expensive, burdensome, and time consuming.

Second, "double immersion"—having to go through two separate and different kinds of leadership preparation, one secular and one spiritual—might give the impression that what is needed for church schools is an "icing" on a "cake" that is already baked. In this way, the additional elements are "bolted on" after the main job of preparation is done. This could lead to a situation where the secular and the spiritual are kept in isolation from one another, to the detriment of both. Either there is an excessive accommodation to the secular agenda or an excessive spiritualization of the way church school leadership is envisaged. For the individuals preparing for headship these need to be properly integrated, rather than kept in separate compartments. State provision of leadership preparation is likely to include school development planning and strategic direction, performance management, curriculum leadership, communication skills, and marketing of the school. These necessary features need to be brought into dialogue with theological literacy, personal spirituality, communion with the church, and a sacramental perspective. This would assist the process of integrating the apparently secular with the apparently spiritual. An incarnational faith needs a proper appreciation of the material and the political, of technology, and of the "tools" of management, if it is to be fruitful, while effective educational leadership needs to be informed by a coherent, well-founded, and inspirational vision, a core of values, and a set of practices that connect a worldview to building a character and a community.

Third, just as the church's educational vision and priorities benefit from facing the challenge of real engagement with professional norms and the government's policy agenda, so too the alternative perspective offered by ecclesial views on human nature and needs, on education and development, on authority and leadership, on values and community, prevents too unquestioning an acceptance by teachers and school leaders of current agendas, bandwagons, assumptions, and orthodoxies. School leaders' capacity to serve the common good over the long term—both in church schools and in other schools—will be enhanced if they are critically discerning about the purposes being pursued. In the ongoing dialogue between church and state (and between other faiths and the state) about educational provision and on provision of leadership preparation opportunities in particular, there is a gain for society in drawing upon, engaging with, though not in being dictated to by, the resources of the living traditions of the faith communities. Dwelling in these communities there is much practical wisdom, for education, for leadership, and for human flourishing.

# 8

# The Dynamics of Ownership

RELIGIOUSLY AFFILIATED SCHOOLS AND colleges are sites where educational and religious priorities intersect. They are also sites which function simultaneously as workplaces and as political communities. There can be mismatches or even clashes between different imperatives. Those charged with espousing the mission of church schools and colleges must demonstrate understanding of and commitment to its particular tradition; yet major aspects of the tradition are contested, both among adherents and by those external to it. Leaders have to be insiders to this tradition, critically familiar with it, capable of taking it forward and inspiring others in its service. At the same time they must engage in the discipline of talking to different types of people who are outsiders to (at least parts of) the mission, for the sake of ecumenism, for interfaith dialogue and harmony, for the sake of inclusiveness, and for pastoral effectiveness.

This chapter is a contribution to the exploration of religion in the workplace. My focus is the intersection of different types of identity, affiliation, and commitment among staff in religiously affiliated schools and colleges. The promotion of the mission is affected by the diverse perceptions and affiliations of groups within the institution and the different kinds of interaction between them. A spectrum of responses to the mission is examined. In the face of the range of responses, leaders must combine unflagging zeal for the mission with a discerning reading of the realities of their situation and they must develop a political wisdom that allows them to be effective in the realm of possible. They must exercise leverage in order to carry out the mandate entrusted to them but at the same time they need to show restraint in order to maintain a healthy, effective, and harmonious working atmosphere. Their task is to promote learning, to protect and advance the religious mission, to exercise professional responsibility, integrity and initiative, and to respond wisely to the politics of the mini-cultures that operate either openly or in the shadow side of the institution. A strong ethos can be a foundation for a truly collegial ethos, but it can also slip into measures that are experienced as oppressive by those who feel distanced from the mission. Where there is a strong ethos, confidence can lead, in some cases, to complacency, while in others it issues in creative appropriation. Where the religious ethos in a church school or college is relatively weak, too ready an accommodation to secular perspectives, to doubters, dissenters, or adherents of alternative worldviews can erode the ethos even further and undermine the mission. A mixture of bold advocacy and cautious sensitivity is required if promotion of the mission is not be come across as naïve, crude, or insensitive to the alignments and affiliations of staff. When promoting the mission in the workplace, a balance has to be maintained: pervasiveness and permeation are desirable and to be striven for; at the same time, this process must not become intrusive or oppressive.

First, I comment on the term "ownership" used in the context of one's work, acknowledging its potential abuse but arguing for its continuing value as something worth aspiring to and developing with oneself and others. As deployed here, "ownership" pays attention to important features of the subjective dimension of work. Second, I bring out the range of responses to the mission that can be displayed by staff, distinguish between the demographics and the dynamics of ownership, and relate staff responses to the shadow side of institutional life. Third, I propose a threefold analysis of ownership, proprietary, professional, and participative, as relevant to and necessary for faith-based schools and colleges. A particular feature of my approach is to reflect on the dynamics of ownership of the mission of faith-based education in schools and colleges by drawing upon literature that comments on the world of work more generally, since I believe that this literature casts light on some of the interactions that take place with regard to mission implementation, those interactions that lead to commitment and those that lead to resistance.

## OWNERSHIP: USE AND ABUSE

In her coruscating critique of many features of the modern workplace, *Willing Slaves*, Madeleine Bunting says that "two of the most ubiquitous and fraudulent words are 'empowerment' and 'ownership'; companies claim they want their employees to be 'empowered' and to 'own' their jobs."[1] In general her thesis is that, far from feeling more in control of what they are

---

1. Bunting, *Willing Slaves*, 116.

doing, and experiencing ownership or empowerment, many workers feel more tightly controlled, more constantly directed, and more intrusively overseen (even if the iron fist is wrapped in a deceptively velvet glove). Bunting is particularly critical of what she calls "missionary management." She argues that we live in a context where work has increasingly become the main provider of key categories of our experience, "time structure, social contact, collective effort or purpose, social identity or status and regular activity. . . . This gives employers unprecedented purchase over our lives: how they are organized, how we perceive ourselves, and how we shape our relationships outside it."[2] Furthermore, technology has exacerbated this situation, significantly reducing the gap between work and private life, for example, through mobile phones and email.[3] She complains of the way "corporations attempt to mold and manipulate our inner lives through new styles of invasive management," styles that "reach after parts of the employee's personality which have hitherto been considered private in order to unlock the required commitment, high performance and overwork."[4] Here I merely note the suspicion and cynicism with which attempts to promote empowerment and ownership are often met. These terms are open to abuse, as is shown in a recent analysis of religion and the workplace by Douglas Hicks, who suggests that "as the language of empowerment has been employed to give a false sense of agency or control to workers, so, too spirituality talk has the potential to take unfair advantage of workers."[5] If this is true of work in general, surely the temptation to employ "missionary management" language and techniques, tendentiously promoting ownership and empowerment, might be expected to be a phenomenon even more marked in church school and colleges.

In this chapter I explore the special challenges that religiously affiliated workplaces face as they seek to link their religious mission to modern approaches to leadership and management, approaches that aim to integrate subjective dimensions of work with its more objective features. Participation, transparency, ownership, and equity are central to the subjective dimension of work.[6] The subjective dimension of work is concerned with the intrapersonal; that is with how work harnesses, ignores, or conflicts with the sense of meaning and purpose and the springs of motivation of employees. It recognizes that workers need to feel accepted and respected,

---

2. Bunting, *Willing Slaves*, xvi.
3. Bunting, *Willing Slaves*, xx.
4. Bunting, *Willing Slaves*, xxv, 92.
5. Hicks, *Religion and the Workplace*, 41.
6. Alford and Naughton, *Managing as If Faith Mattered*, 142.

that their views are taken into account, that they make a positive difference, and that they are treated fairly. When considering the subjective dimension of work a person asks, "What is work doing *to* me as well as *for* me, and *for others*?"[7] Leaders must ensure that the central purposes of organizations are pursued, that the overall "system" and structure set in place to implement the mission is maintained intact, and that efficiency, economy and effectiveness are kept in view; without attention to these objective requirements the organization would become chaotic, collapse and go bankrupt or be taken over. Without attention to the subjective dimension of work, however, they would jeopardize the moral and spiritual health of people who work for them, and thus eventually also undermine the mission.

Thus, although we should beware abuse of such words as "empowerment" or "ownership," this should not obscure their real role and value in the realm of work. A strong sense of ownership is likely to influence institutional effectiveness, staff satisfaction in their jobs, personal and professional growth, and staff retention. The lack of it is likely to lead to converse results. Ownership of the mission of an organization is needed to combat pressures and temptations to address competing priorities. This is all the more true in religiously affiliated institutions. The task of discernment of the dynamics of ownership of the mission is made more complex when we take into account, first, that "some employees understand that their work is an integral part of their religious life" and, second, that "Christian business leaders [can] uncritically conflate their own individual religious values with organizational religious values."[8] The first feature is a positive asset for a religiously affiliated educational community, provided that there is congruence between the interpretation by leaders of the religious life and that of the institution in which they work; without this congruence of interpretation the centrality of religion in an employee's motivational make-up might even be distracting for the individual concerned and disruptive for the institution. The second feature—the identification and conflation by leaders of their own religious values with that of the organization—can sometimes also be an asset, in terms of contributing to integrity in action, synergy of effort, persistence in the face of difficulty, clarity of conviction, and resonance in communication. It runs the risk, however, of doing much damage to other people's consciences, of inviting hypocrisy by employees who fear the possible outcomes of disagreement with the values of school or college

---

7. Alford and Naughton, *Managing as If Faith Mattered*, 128; emphasis in original, except emphasis on "others" added.

8. Hicks, *Religion and the Workplace*, 107, 126.

leadership, of forcing compliance instead of the much harder work of inspiring and eliciting commitment.

## RESPONSES TO THE MISSION

In societies that are not homogeneous, which is the situation that prevails in contemporary democratic, secular, and pluralist culture, there will be many different responses to the mission. Some people embrace it; others undermine it; some ignore it; some wait and see; others test it; some ridicule it. In some church schools and colleges, there is a clear majority of people who subscribe strongly to the mission; in others, such people constitute a beleaguered minority. Even when people are agreed on a set of goals, values, or priorities, this does not necessarily mean that they either interpret these or act on them in the same way. Depending on their own context and histories, their strengths and weaknesses, their virtues and vices, their role in the organization, there will legitimately be a variety of ways of contributing to an institution's mission, sharing its charism, and developing its ethos.

Who speaks for the organization? Who is marginalized? How does the mission of religiously affiliated schools and colleges appear when considered from different positions within the organizational structure? Roles, remits, and rights can sit awkwardly side by side. Simon uses the phrase "the demographics of ownership" to analyze the numbers and positioning of staff in relation to the mission. She distinguishes between those who are fully and effectively contributing to the mission; those who are committed but not yet equipped to contribute effectively; those who are comfortable with the mission but see it as someone else's job; and those who are alienated from or indifferent to the mission.[9] The effect of these various degrees of proximity to and distance from the mission is influenced by the positioning of staff as well as by their professional effectiveness and political persuasiveness. Thus if those close to the center of influence and decision-making are distant from the mission, this can have an effect disproportional to their numbers. If those at the margins are the ones with enthusiasm for the mission, their voices may not be heard.

Although I have found useful Simon's phrase, "the demographics of ownership," I have preferred to adopt a modification of this, "the dynamics of ownership," in order to bring out more clearly that the positions of people in relation to the mission are not static or fixed. Rather they are constantly in flux, shifting and interacting in complex ways. While the demographic detail is useful and necessary in clarifying where we are at any particular

9. Simon et al., *Mentoring for Mission*, 44.

moment, with regard to getting a view about relative commitment and resistance, staff cannot easily (or accurately) be pigeonholed as committed to or alienated from the mission. Those who begin by being committed can lose this commitment through a mixture of personal and institutional experiences. Those who begin as complete outsiders to the mission can be brought within the fold, to a greater or lesser extent, depending on how the mission is interpreted and how they are treated as individuals. Changes in leadership, in organizational culture, in team membership, in role, in the provision of staff development opportunities in relation to the mission, apart from personal changes of belief or affiliation outside the workplace, can all make a significant difference to how people place themselves in relation to mission.

Gerard Egan reminds managers of the need to become fully aware of the "shadow side" of their organization: "the unspoken, unacknowledged, behind-the-scenes stuff that stands in the way of getting things done efficiently, or even getting things done at all."[10] "The shadow side consists of all the important activities and arrangements that do not get identified, discussed, and managed in decision-making forums that can make a difference."[11] Among the categories of shadow-side activity, Egan includes organizational culture and social systems, individual styles and behavior, internal politics, and the hidden curriculum that is conveyed.[12] In the shadow side there is the hiding of defects, unwritten rules of conduct, deliberate ignoring of policy, alternative renderings of priorities, and the putting up of facades. In the shadows one might find indifference, naivety, and cynicism as well as structures of influence that parallel rather than overlap with official structures. Egan identifies the damage caused by leaving the shadow side in place as including psychological, social, and financial aspects. It can disrupt relationships, distort priorities, undermine productivity or effectiveness, waste time, blur communication, lead to confusion, and dissipate concentration of focus and energy. The shadow side is the place where good practice is ignored or insufficiently built upon and where poor practice is left uncorrected. It can also be a place where the past exerts too strong a hold or where change meets its strongest opponents.

In considering the dynamics of ownership of mission in church schools and colleges, I find useful Egan's analysis of the different internal stakeholders of an organization—so long as it is recognized that in reality people play several roles at once, can shift their position and allegiance and

---

10. Egan, *Working the Shadow Side*, xi.
11. Egan, *Working the Shadow Side*, 4.
12. Egan, *Working the Shadow Side*, 8.

adopt particular stances in relation to specific issues and circumstances; we should not assume that they permanently play the same role, either in the public domain or in the shadow side. As Egan describes:

* *partners* are those who believe in and actively support the institutional agenda and have a good relationship with its sponsor;
* *allies* are those who believe in the agenda and, at least with the proper encouragement, will support it;
* *fellow travellers* are players who like the sponsor and therefore support the agenda, at least passively;
* *fencesitters* are players whose position on the agenda and/or feelings toward the sponsor are not clear;
* *loose cannons* are difficult people who cause a great deal of damage even though they might not be specifically against the agenda or its sponsor;
* *opponents* are players who oppose the agenda but not the sponsor;
* *adversaries* are people who don't like the sponsor and therefore reject the agenda;
* *bedfellows* are players who like the agenda but may not know the sponsor well enough or distrust him or her;
* *the voiceless* are stakeholders who have little power.[13]

Egan offers valuable advice about these categories of people. Here are some examples:

> The biggest mistake with respect to allies is to take them for granted. . . . Some fencesitters sit on the sidelines until they see which party is to be the likely winner. . . . Opponents may feel that some competing agenda has more merit or have some personal hidden agenda that will be thwarted by the sponsor's agenda. . . . The voiceless may be used by your adversary. Pay attention to their concerns.[14]

In the face of such diverse responses and stances, leaders need to be discerning about who stands on what side, on which issues and in what manner in order to act wisely themselves, deploying their knowledge of

---

13. Egan, *Working the Shadow Side*, 220–22.
14. Egan, *Working the Shadow Side*, 220–22.

the cultural realities of the workplace and communicating with tact, clarity, sensitivity, and cogency.

## THREE TYPES OF OWNERSHIP

At this point I wish to distinguish three different types of ownership: proprietary, professional, and participative. The first, proprietary ownership, relates to authority and possession; the second, professional ownership, influences the degree to which there is scope for autonomy and initiative and respect for difference within the guild responsible for implementing the mission; the third, participative ownership, is concerned with the nature and quality of the community in which the mission is carried out. I do not claim that these three, taken together, provide an exhaustive account of all the desirable possible types of ownership; however, I believe that they do provide useful examples of the kinds of ownership to be striven for. I shall also argue that all three types of ownership are required.

### Proprietary Ownership

Proprietary ownership is about who owns the site and the buildings. This usually relates to a body that endures over a lengthy period of time. It is also about who appoints the principal or institutional leader and who oversees the continuing effective functioning of the raison d'être of the organization. Thus it is about who is charged with a mandate to promote the special nature of the school or college as an educational community to be conducted according to the worldview of a particular religious faith. Crudely put, it is about who is in charge, who legitimately directs, whose voice is authorized to hold sway, regardless of what may happen in the shadow side. Proprietary ownership relates to who the institution belongs to, who can speak for it in the public domain, who has to be consulted before major changes affecting it may be implemented. Usually such owners have close links with regional and national and religious bodies to which they belong as members of the same "family of faith," bodies that jointly represent the interests of faith schools and colleges in dealings with legislators, the executive and policymakers. Proprietary ownership need not (but may) entail close involvement in the day-to-day running of the institution. This is usually left to leadership and management, as opposed to the governance function which restricts itself to general oversight, mission protection (and associated boundary management), the appointment (and calling to account of) senior leadership.

Proprietary ownership is a necessary element for an institution. A mission does not rest on thin air; it must be located, embedded, and protected if it is to have a chance of being promoted. However rickety and deficient institutions are, nevertheless they function as vehicles for the spirit, for religious mission and ethos, as bodies for incarnating this, as offering structures for advocacy, advancement, assimilation, and appropriation. While it is true that institutions can only too easily inhibit mission, that structures can stifle the spirit, that organizations can obscure the good news, discourage authentic discipleship, undermine confidence, and erode enthusiasm, these are malfunctions to be put right, not necessary features. They are permanent dangers but they need not be permanent realities. Proprietary ownership facilitates in an institution several key features which collectively serve to protect its raison d'être: tenacity of purpose, longevity, stability, and identity in the face of difficulty, change, loss of confidence or of commitment. Just as the institutional element, along with its connotations of history, tradition, and authority, is part of the religious life, as was seen so clearly one hundred years ago by Hügel,[15] so too the proprietary aspect of ownership is a key component in the long-term endeavor of running faith-based education.

## Professional Ownership

Proprietary ownership may be essential for faith-based educational institutions, but it is never sufficient. Without the second kind of ownership referred to here, professional ownership, a faith-based school or college would remain an empty shell. It needs the daily implementation of the mission from the guild of professionals—expressed in pedagogy, assessment, and curriculum, and, in higher education, in research and scholarship. Professional ownership should build on and flow from proprietary ownership, though given that many faith-based schools and colleges have a very mixed composition of staff, it is likely that the professional expression of the mission will be diversified and complicated not only by the differences that stem from curriculum specialisms but also because many teachers, lecturers, and professors will not belong to the host faith tradition. Even those who do affiliate with this tradition may have experienced a thoroughly secular induction into the practice of teaching and of scholarship, to such a degree that they find it difficult to articulate or to see connections between the religious and the academic mission.[16]

15. Hügel, *Mystical Element of Religion*.
16. Sullivan: "Vocation and Profession"; "Responsibility, Vocation and Critique."

PART TWO | LEADERSHIP

Teachers are not merely technicians, who put into practice prespecified procedures laid down in textbooks or manuals. They are centers of initiative and decision-making in their own right. Of course, scope for initiative does not mean total control; professionals are constrained by the purposes of their institution and the goods of the practice they serve as well as by the ethics of their profession and the specific remit of their particular responsibilities within a structure of jobs. Professional ownership is needed if staff are to have the freedom to exercise judgment and creativity in meeting norms, in interpreting priorities, and in matching applying practices to meet the needs of particular people. There is an intimate connection for professionals between a sense of self-directedness and an acceptance of responsibility. More than obedience and compliance is required for the complex and sensitive tasks they have to carry out. As the Croatian theologian Miroslav Volf puts it, "Workers should be able to set goals in their work role and pursue them, or at least be able to identify with the goals that management sets for them. Any action a human being is pressurized to do but which she has not made her own goal contradicts her nature as a personal being."[17] In the context of education the carrying out of tasks over which they have no control or discretion is likely to inhibit quality teaching and authentic learning, by students as well as by staff. Leaders and managers need to leave sufficient space "on the ground" for professionals to use their judgment in how to they deploy their talents and draw upon their experience. This has a double benefit. As Alford and Naughton, writing about the bearing of faith on management, put it, "Firms organized subsidiarily stand to benefit more fully from the expertise of those in top management, who are freed to concentrate on long-term or large issues. They stand to benefit from the judgment and initiative of subordinate individuals and groups."[18] Thus it is incumbent on educational institutions to facilitate as much professional ownership as is compatible with the principal goals of the faith tradition.

One way to describe such professional ownership is, to use a phrase from psychologist Robert Kegan, hiring the "psychologically self-employed."[19] I take this phrase to mean that despite the fact that someone else devised our job, set the parameters for our role, and even calls us to account for how well we meet their priorities, this does not necessarily leave no space for creativity or for us to put our own stamp on the work. As Kegan (quoting Roland Barthes) puts it, "The discrepancy that matters

---

17. Volf, *Work in the Spirit*, 175.
18. Alford and Naughton, *Managing as If Faith Mattered*, 78.
19. Kegan, *In Over Our Heads*, 170.

is not between 'what I am doing' and 'what they want me to do,' but rather between 'what I am doing' and 'what I want to be able to do.'"[20] When this discrepancy is transcended, then professional ownership is possible.

Kegan offers a very useful analysis of key aspects of being a worker, all of which I believe apply to professionals. He says we are expected as workers:

1. *To invent or own our work* (rather than see it as owned and created by the employer)

2. *To be self-initiating, self-correcting, self-evaluating* (rather than dependent on others to frame the problems, initiate adjustments, or determine whether things are going acceptably well)

3. *To be guided by our own visions* (rather than be without a vision or be captive of the authority's agenda)

4. *To take responsibility for what happens to us at work externally and internally* (rather than see our present internal circumstances and future external possibilities as caused by someone else)

5. *To be accomplished masters of our particular work roles, jobs, or careers* (rather than have an apprenticing or imitating relationship to what we do)

6. *To conceive of the organization from the "outside in," as a whole; to see our relation to the whole; to see the relation of the parts to the whole* (rather than see the rest of the organization and its parts only from the perspective of our own part, from the "inside out")[21]

In my view, none of Kegan's first five points here either implies or requires an unduly individualistic understanding of or approach to professional ownership; his final point directly contradicts such a narrow interpretation. They do, however, set a challenge for leaders of institutions that have an explicit and demanding mission: How will they manage the dynamic interplay between their own executive authority and the expertise authority of professionals? I will say a little more about the community dimension at the end of my treatment of participative ownership (below), but here I wish to focus on the voluntary aspect of a professional's motivation.

While Kegan's notion of being psychologically self-employed requires a high degree of voluntariness and thus implies the absence of coercion, this

---

20. Kegan, *In Over Our Heads*, 170.
21. Kegan, *In Over Our Heads*, 15–53.

does not rule out the exercise of strong influences which we might choose to accept. Being a professional involves, among other things, establishing the right distance between oneself, the service one provides, and the recipient. The self can intrude too much, distorting the activity, and imposing on the recipient, leaving them, in this case, the student, with insufficient space for *their* initiative. This is establishing too little distance, or underdistancing. However, the self can remove itself too much, rendering the service mechanical rather than personal. This is overdistancing. Philosopher Mike Martin puts it thus:

> Proper professional distance is a reasonable response in pursuing professional values by avoiding inappropriate personal involvements while maintaining personal engagement and responsibility. In contrast, underdistancing is the undesirable interference of personal values with professional standards. And overdistancing is the undesirable loss of personal involvement, whether in the form of denying one's responsibility for one's actions or in the form of failing to care about clients and community.[22]

In the case of underdistancing one's own feelings intrude too much on the other person and on the activity; in the case of overdistancing, they are insufficiently engaged. When there is underdistancing, what the professional wants dominates the activity; when overdistancing occurs the professional fails to own their actions or the results of these.

Another—perhaps more contentious—point about voluntariness, is that in many countries, certainly including the UK, teachers and lecturers freely choose, subject to no external pressures, to work in church school and colleges. Such faith-based institutions constitute a relatively small minority, surrounded by a much bigger majority of institutions that are secular in ethos, so that employment prospects are not at risk if one rejects the tenets they hold dear and the mission they seek to promote. Although there must still be respect for professional ownership, as I have described it, leaders of educational institutions based on a religious foundation do have a right to expect a level of congruence between the work of their professionals and the religious ethos for which they have a mandate to promote. If they object on principle to the salience of religion within such educational institutions, professionals should take their talents elsewhere rather than resentfully resist or seek to undermine the raison d'être of the body that employs them. Mike Martin says that religious groups have the right to "modify secular professional standards—within limits of basic decency and informed

---

22. M. Martin, *Meaningful Work*, 86.

consent—to serve religious ends."[23] I would prefer to say that religiously affiliated schools and colleges have the right to promote their mission by setting professional goals and standards in a wider context and to direct them towards goals that are more all embracing than, though not in contradiction to, those usually pursued by professionals.

Up to now I have not adequately attended to the specialized knowledge, training and expertise possessed by professionals. This expertise—together with the high regard for the central goods promoted by professionals (for example, health, justice, education) and the ethical codes (implicit or explicit) that govern provision of the service—is the basis of the professional's authority. In schools and colleges this expertise will be subject knowledge in some curriculum area (or areas) as well as other kinds of knowledge, such as that about child development, about pedagogy, and about research methodology (in universities). Just as the intellectual element, along with its connotations of critical questioning and independent thinking, was considered by Hügel to be an essential part of religious life,[24] so too the professional aspect of ownership is a key component in faith-based schools and colleges. Indeed intellectual confidence and independent thinking are key ingredients in effective professionalism for teachers and lecturers. Perhaps controversially, I would claim that part of what it means to be a professional teacher or lecturer in a church school or college is to make links between the mission and one's work, to show the bearing of one upon the other. I do not expect this to be a one-way affair. Critical questioning, based on one's academic and professional expertise, can be applied to the religious tradition and its functioning as well as to academic and professional issues. It would be wise for leaders to be open and responsive to such criticism and questioning. There are no unaskable questions and there are no unquestionable answers in a learning and an educative community; this includes faith-based educational communities.

## Participative Ownership

The third kind of ownership I wish to refer to, I call participative. Participative ownership refers to features that jointly contribute to the development of a high quality community in a democracy where it is assumed that there is basic equality of worth to be attributed to each person. In contrast to proprietary ownership, which limits its focus to those with the authority of possession, and in contrast to professional ownership, which limits its focus

---

23. M. Martin, *Meaningful Work*, 160.
24. Hügel, *Mystical Element of Religion*.

to the (much larger number of) those with lengthy training, specialized expertise, and whose work is governed (explicitly or implicitly) by an ethical code that preserves the special nature of the goods of the service, (for example, critical thinking and autonomy), participative ownership widens the circle of concern to everybody within the school or college. Thus, many of the values, qualities, and practices that facilitate professional ownership also apply in the case of participative ownership. However, whereas, in that case, this stemmed from an acknowledgment of the authority of expertise, and the ensuing need, if they are to carry out their role properly, for certain kinds of discretion, initiative, and autonomy, in the case of participative ownership, the promotion of key values, qualities, and practices flows simply from a concern to create a flourishing community, one that treats all its members as worthy of respect, dignity, with rights to be consulted about what affects them, to be heard, to be supported and challenged to develop. A concern to promote participative ownership leads to checking that all members of a community have been invited to contribute, that their voice is heard, their contributions are affirmed, their efforts are encouraged and rewarded, their interests are taken seriously, that they share in the community's celebrations of identity, progress, and achievement.

Professional ownership could be in danger of becoming elitist, protecting the guild against outsiders, exaggerating the needs of specialists, at the expense of other members of the school or college community, for example, students and support staff. Participative ownership seeks to transcend such divisions, embracing all members of the community, aiming for as high a degree of inclusiveness as possible. There will be limits on participative ownership, limits imposed by each of the other types of ownership. Proprietary owners will set parameters and boundaries about what is prescribed and what is proscribed. This relates very closely to the essential nature of the institution and its raison d'être, for example, as a church foundation. If professionals are to do their job properly, they too will set down considerable limits about what must and must not be done, in areas that relate closely to their role in promoting learning, maintaining educational standards, and developing new knowledge. Even after appropriate requirements have been laid down as a result of proprietary and professional ownership, there should still be a great deal of room left for the exercise of participative ownership. Proprietary owners can be tempted to seek to impose more than is required for the exercise of their responsibility. The same is true of professionals. Participative ownership acts a kind of counterbalance to temptations to extend the authority of these groups beyond the proper limits.

All three types of ownership are required for the effective flourishing of church schools and colleges and of other faith-based educational institutions. Proprietary ownership protects their special nature: without the exercise of this kind of ownership the institution might soon lose its way, betray its past, and fail to carry out its mandate. Without the exercise of professional ownership, however, proprietary ownership would stay at the level of theory and formality, lacking any substance or reality. Professional ownership ensures that the church school or college is an educative organization, one that promotes critical thinking and one that takes learning seriously. Participative ownership makes it possible to show more clearly the practical implications of connecting the first two types of ownership, the religious mandate and the focus on learning. Participative ownership rehearses for all what it means to live in the light of the first two forms of ownership, integrating them and deploying them in a way of life that can be extended beyond the walls of the school or college.

Much of our learning occurs in the context of a community. A failure to attend to participative ownership leads to a neglect of important aspects of the way we learn, both religiously and academically. Thus participative ownership is needed, not only because it is a necessary prerequisite for promoting democracy, important though this is, but also because the construction of community is a prerequisite for growth in faith and for growth in academic development. Theologian Frederick Aquino has recently written about communities of informed judgment, stressing the important role played by the community in the way we come to know. "Proficiency in reasoning stems from induction into a community with vibrant practices, nurtured by exemplars of skillful judgment.... A vibrant tradition is indispensable for acquiring and passing on requisite qualities of informed judgment.... A community learns to share the cognitive load."[25] I take Aquino to be reminding us that learning, at all levels, requires mutual confidence and collaboration, stems from a high degree of interdependence, and makes progress by resting on many shared assumptions and common frames of reference. If proprietary owners in church schools and colleges issue the call for commitment, professionals show its grammar and the educational community provides conditions for its emergence, development, and application.

\* \* \*

I have already indicated an echo of Hügel's threefold analysis of religious life in the first two forms of ownership referred to in this chapter, suggesting

---

25. Aquino, *Communities of Informed Judgment*, 3, 121, 128.

that proprietary ownership links with the institutional dimension of religion and that professional ownership (in schools and colleges) is a (partial) expression of the intellectual dimension. I also see some (again, admittedly only partial) parallels between Hügel's third dimension, which referred to the spiritual and the personal—interpreted by Hügel in a very comprehensive way—and what I have described as participative ownership. I have taken the liberty of assuming that, if he were alive today, Hügel would adopt a more communal understanding of his third dimension of religious life, the experiential, existential, personal, and spiritual. He argued strongly that the church should maintain a creative tension between (and integrate as much as possible) the institutional, intellectual, and spiritual dimensions of religious life. He acknowledged that each of them is open to abuse, if taken on its own, uncorrected by the other two. I argue, in a parallel way, that each of the three forms of ownership described here, proprietary, professional, and participative, are necessary for church schools and colleges, acknowledging that each is open to abuse if not balanced by the other two. Leaders charged with addressing the challenges of promoting the mission in the face of a variety of responses need to take into account the dynamics of ownership. They must have personal conviction and courage; this gives them something to communicate and the capacity to do so in the face of difficulties and opposition. They need discernment as they read realistically their situation and context; this prevents them from acting inappropriately. They also need highly developed political skills of tact, sensitivity, and persuasiveness if they are to deal adequately with different interpretations of the mission and with different perceptions of how it is being implemented. An appreciation of the dynamics of the three types of ownership analyzed in this chapter should equip them to offer positive but not domineering leadership, to be invitational but not intrusive in their style and to serve as reliable yet sensitive advocates of the mission.

# 9

# Leading Values and Casting Shadows in Church Schools

IN THIS CHAPTER, THE image of "shadows" will be explored in terms of its possible relevance for understanding some features of the educational landscape in church schools. In particular, I suggest that an exploration of the shadows cast by certain emphases within school leadership will prompt us to attend more carefully to the moral dimensions of such leadership and its associated modes of communication and persuasion. The notion of shadows will be used to represent side effects or consequences, usually unintended, of current practice. I suggest that a retrieval of certain Aristotelian insights on rhetoric will assist heads in their moral leadership role.

## SCHOOL LEADERSHIP AND VALUES

There has always been a close association between head teachers and the advocacy and expected exemplification of the key values upheld by the school.[1] Heads represent and symbolize the school as public persons. They have a mandate from the governors (themselves representative of the wider community) to exercise both leadership and initiative in pursuing certain values and goals. Heads are authorized, given the authority, through their position, to be leaders and not simply managers.

Values are at the very heart of work of heads. They have to articulate the central values of the school, inspire others to pursue these values, promote and explain them with all partners and constituencies, and defend them from undermining influences from within and without. Then heads

---

1. Treston, *Creative Christian Leadership*; Higginson, *Transforming Leadership*.

must secure their permeation throughout the life and work of the school, and, above all, reconcile them one with another (for values can conflict); there is also the need to reconcile those who interpret these values differently. Many aspects of school call for the expression, exemplification, and facilitation of values. Decisions about pupil admissions, grouping, assessment and exclusions, about curriculum content and policies, and about approaches to behavior management, sex education, equal opportunities, special educational needs and multicultural education—all have a values dimension. So too do decisions about staff development, promotion, and appraisal, about institutional self-evaluation, and about the budget and time allocation. Whatever a head attends to conveys a value statement, as does every omission.

The centrality of the head in promoting values raises a difficulty as to the respective rights of other members of the school community. Schools can appear in a very different light to the people who have a vested interest in what goes on in them. Among these "stakeholders" we can include pupils, parents, governors, trustees, teaching and support staff, not to mention local education authorities, dioceses, parishes, central government, and the various communities within which the school is located. In each case, what is important about a school, what it is aiming for, the gap between claim and achievement, its strengths and weaknesses, its burdens and benefits will appear in a different light. The insights of some "stakeholders" will be scarcely recognizable to others. Even among the teaching staff there are often marked differences of perceptions between those in senior management (who have to spend a considerable amount of time responding to people outside the school) and more junior teachers (whose energies are mostly taken up with meeting the needs of their pupils.)

All institutions and communities are likely in practice to fall short of their own projected ideals; if this were not so, there would be no need for further striving. Ideals can serve as guiding lights to show us the direction in which we hope to travel. They provide a framework for the essential projects of our particular community. They set goals, however distant; they inspire effort, for the destination is believed to be worth the rigors of the journey; they set parameters for action, for some styles of operating are in keeping with the ideals and others would be ruled out as incompatible with them. Gaps that open up between ideals and current reality can be experienced by people working within schools as paths that are illuminated by the ideals or alternatively these paths can be experienced as cast in shadow by our failure—and that of others around us—to live up to them. In the case of the former, we acknowledge that there is more still to be done; but we know where we are going, and our eyes are directed towards the goal and the steps which we believe will take us there. In the case of the latter, we are only too aware of the gap and the distance to be traveled seems overwhelming.

Our sensitivity to any gap between ideal and reality is heightened when we identify the increased attention given to "rhetoric" and to scrutiny. By "rhetoric" I am referring to the various ways in which schools "market" their wares: glossy prospectuses, open days and evenings, the appointment of press officers, documentation, and attention to "house style" in the presentation of all communications with parents and the wider community. Many schools have even produced video- or slide-tape presentations for display in potential "feeder" institutions. By scrutiny I am referring to the range of ways that teachers find their work being monitored and evaluated: through individual staff appraisal, school inspection, institutional self-evaluation, examination results, publication of other data about schools in comparative league tables, reporting progress to governors and to parents on published action plans. Both "rhetoric" and scrutiny are experienced as pressures by teachers, even when they accept the reasons for them. The combination of "rhetoric" and scrutiny can also, in a context of strong leadership, be experienced by some teachers as management by manipulation, especially if they feel that they had little real say in contributing to the "vision," mission, or espoused values of the school and if the criteria to be used in evaluation are not ones they fully share or recognize as the most important.

However strong an emphasis is given to leadership, a school cannot operate effectively without a high degree of consensus. Any failure of effort by a head to maintain such a consensus would invite accusations of autocracy or high-handedness and elicit compliance at best, or even outright resistance, on the part of staff. Certainly the notion that an ethos could be imposed would be strange, if not a complete contradiction of terms. It would be difficult for teachers to model independence of thought, self-evaluation, critical engagement, sensitive responsiveness to particular situations and the qualities of creative teamwork, if they were patently subject to rules laid down from on high without their involvement, exposed to scrutiny by yardsticks they had no part in negotiating, expected to be unquestioningly loyal to all aspects of current practice and inexorably consistent in implementing school policies, displaying uniformity but without the give-and-take, compromise, sharing, and interaction of true collaborative effort.

## SHADOW SIDES

Schools, like other organizations, reveal a "shadow" side as an important element of their ethos, a side which we should recognize and engage with.

Egan devotes a whole book to *Working the Shadow Side* of organizations. He expects managers to be sensitive to the shadow side, which consists of "all the important activities and arrangements that do not get identified, discussed and managed in decision-making forums that can make a difference."[2] The shadow side will be found in covert assumptions, actions, expectations, habits, all of which impact upon the way things are both perceived and done, but which are never properly spelled out or publicly justified. The expenditure of staff time and energy will be affected by this shadow side, which has the capacity to obscure or even to hinder the implementation of the mission of the organization.

There are many aspects to understanding the shadow side of organizations. It will include recognizing those insights, talents, and qualities of staff that are, as yet, not drawn upon. It will involve penetrating behind attempts to hide defects and shortcomings in the quality of work being carried out and to gloss over the less pleasant aspects of our dealings with one another. It should enable leaders to identify some of the unwritten rules or assumptions of the organization and some of the human factors which affect practice: "revenge, lust, greed, hatred, ambition, pride, dishonesty, and stupidity."[3] To these we might add insecurity, laziness, fear of rejection, desire for social acceptance, and wanting to feel that our work makes a significant and valued contribution. Egan believes there are expensive consequences for organizations that fail to address their shadow side: these will be psychological, social, and financial.[4] Prudent, steadfast and constructive confrontation should be carried out by managers if the shadow side is to be properly addressed.

I have chosen Egan's work as representative of a whole genre of management literature, for it offers a wealth of insights and strategies to leaders. However, those on whom his advice is practiced might feel that by becoming more skilled, their managers find it even easier to manipulate them. For example, the emphasis on the need for a strong culture within organizations, and for staff alignment and attunement with this culture, if they are to achieve their goals, together with the naming of obstructive elements and the analysis of helping and hindering factors, all cumulatively suggest that staff are not viewed as collaborators in a joint enterprise, participants in a living tradition, or partners in a debate, but as human resources to be deployed efficiently. Egan analyzes these resources as partners, allies, fellow travellers, fencesitters, loose cannons, opponents, adversaries, bedfellows

---

2. Egan, *Working the Shadow Side*, 4.
3. Egan, *Working the Shadow Side*, 27.
4. Egan, *Working the Shadow Side*, 44.

and the voiceless.[5] Their respective roles and the appropriate responses called forth from managers appear in Egan's analysis to owe little to moral insight and evaluation and everything to their potential as servants of an externally set mission.

Egan's study of the shadow side of organizations (admittedly not written with schools in mind) is useful in reminding us of the subversion, special interest groups, and idiosyncratic behavior which need to be acknowledged if a strong culture is to be built. However, it also exemplifies some concerns relating to school leadership already raised in this chapter. For what some might experience as clear direction and guidance, others might experience as interference or unwarranted constraint, so that emasculation rather than empowerment is the outcome.

This situation is more complex in the case of faith-based schools that have a close relationship with a church. There are various metaphors or ways of understanding church available in theological literature, for example, as institution, herald, mystical communion, sacrament, and servant.[6] Each of these models has particular insights; but each of them is also open to distortion and imbalance if treated in isolation from the others. For example, those who adopt the institutional model can fall into the danger of identifying the church only with its formal structure; they can be doctrinaire, rigid, conformist, and, by mistaking the official church for God, even idolatrous. The herald model may oversimplify the process of salvation, conveying an impression that the *only* task of the church is the proclamation of the gospel. The mystical communion model may raise expectations about its life which are impossible to satisfy and may, through lack of emphasis on formal structure, lead to confusion when there are disputes to be settled. The sacramental model can be heavily theological and hard to communicate, undervalue structure, and attend insufficiently to its mandate for mission. The servant model can run the dangers of reducing the gospel to good works, uncritically accepting secular values and neglecting the spiritual dimension of church life.

If church schools, like other organizations, have their "shadow" side as an important element of their ethos, this is likely to be influenced by the respective "shadow" sides of the models of church upon which they draw. Within the Catholic context, some cultural analyses have identified a "shadow" side to various expressions of that faith. For example, Rohr and Martos make a number of criticisms.[7] They accuse many Catholics of neglecting

5. Egan, *Working the Shadow Side*, 220–22.
6. Dulles, *Models of the Church*.
7. Rohr and Martos, *Why Be Catholic?*

much of their own tradition, of failing to display a concern for the common good, of focusing more on external observance than on inner conviction and conversion, of uncritically accepting the norms and expectations of society. Too often, they say, the Catholic Church is strangled by institutionalism, hierarchy, and control; it is over clerical, is male dominated, leaves little room for creative responses and ministry by laypeople, is inadequately scriptural, and its reliance on sacraments can slip into a mechanical ritualism. To the extent that church schools share in the defects of the wider church from which they stem, their ethos will be overshadowed by some of these shortcomings.[8]

## DEBATE, CLARITY, AND UNCERTAINTY

Too much emphasis on promoting the mission can fail to allow for contradiction and resistance when communities are debating purposes as well as procedures. Eliciting optimal performance and commitment from staff requires a critical engagement which will enable them to grapple creatively and constructively with the challenges and opportunities coming from beyond the school. Such engagement will help them to identify the internal tasks that flow from a mission they have helped to articulate. It will prompt them to identify and respond to potential clashes between the various values being promoted through the overt curriculum and those which seem privileged through the "hidden" curriculum of the school, for these two sources of values can either cohere or fragment, they can reinforce or contradict each other.

A morally sensitive style of management will seek to facilitate situations where teachers do not feel manipulated, crushed between "rhetoric" and scrutiny, pressurized by an externally imposed mission and hostile evaluation procedures, or co-opted into the service of a public image which bears little relation to the reality they experience daily. It will encourage them to reflect on the ends being pursued in schools and to reflect on their progress towards these ends, to play a full part in both recognizing and reconciling conflicts of values. There must be room for contention, contradiction, questioning, critique, and debate about purposes as well as procedures.

Yet it has to be admitted that, however involved teachers may be in the process, demands for greater clarity about goals may cast shadows or leave in their wake unintended side effects. There are two aspects to be considered here. The first is pointed out by McLaughlin. "Too much emphasis on clarity can in some circumstances be unhelpful." It might lead to "bringing

8. Brennan, *Christian Management of Catholic Schools*, 80.

into focus the full extent of disagreement between teachers," which could result in "the inhibition of practical consensus and effective action. Ambiguity has a constructive and lubricative role here."[9] Frequently staff are able to work together with a reasonable degree of camaraderie, consistency, and coherence towards the implementation of goals about which they have reached a minimal level of agreement, even though further probing would reveal considerable levels of variation in interpretation and prioritizing among such goals or even substantial personal disagreement about their interpretation or application.

The second reason why attempts to reach a greater clarity about goals can create tension or uneasiness among teachers is that uncertainty is integral to the nature of teaching. Classroom exchanges are dramatic and unpredictable, requiring personal creativity, not mechanical application, on the part of the teacher. Judgment as well as technique is needed. This point is brought out particularly well by Buchman and Floden.[10] Assessments of student learning are uncertain, for there can be many possible reasons for giving either the right or the wrong answer to a question. The effects of our teaching are uncertain, for general trends or "outcomes" from our work may not apply to particular children. There are uncertainties among teachers about content which are based not only upon inadequate grasp or misunderstanding but also on radical disagreement in interpretations, for example, about historical or scientific theories or aesthetic judgments, not to mention the conflicts over moral values already alluded to. There are also uncertainties as to the nature and extent of the teacher's authority.

In church schools there is the added problem of fostering a balance between faithfulness to tradition and openness to the experience and insights of present members of the school community. Fidelity and creativity do not have to be seen as opposed to one another; they can be held together. There are resources within the church and its theology which cast light on this task of embracing both fidelity and creativity, including, for example, notions of living tradition, the development of doctrine, a prophetic reading of the signs of the times and inculturation. In the attempt to put the gospel into practice, fresh interpretation, not mere repetition, can be a form of bearing witness and making a contribution. On the other hand, in the context of encouraging pupils and staff to engage with the missionary imperative of the gospel, we may find that the effort of appropriating a text which at first appears to be alien or external to us, if followed by appreciation of its meaning, can lead us to a deeper self-discovery and a sense that life is both

---

9. McLaughlin, "Values, Coherence and School," 459.
10. Buchman and Floden, *Detachment and Concern*, 21–26.

enhanced and liberated, rather than diminished and constrained. Furthermore, our thinking about leadership and mission in church schools could benefit from theological studies of the reception of doctrine by the faithful and the nature of consent required within the church.[11]

## RHETORIC RETRIEVED

If heads are to avoid slipping into manipulation, they might usefully retrieve some insights on rhetoric from Aristotle. The term "rhetoric" is often used in a pejorative sense. We tend to associate the word with an empty claim, something which cannot be substantiated, or with idealistic aspirations which are removed from reality, or with high-blown language which seeks to persuade by appealing to deep-seated hopes and desires which escape the grip of reason. Aristotle, however, used the word very differently. He had a rich and fertile understanding of the term. His analysis of rhetoric, which brings together a concern for the art or practice of persuasive skills, moral wisdom and logical reasoning, is a fruitful source for a better understanding of what is at stake in combining a concern for character, communication, and quality in school leadership. I shall treat his remarks on rhetoric both sketchily and unduly schematically because of brevity of space and in order to relate them to the issues discussed in this chapter.

Aristotle refers to three types of rhetoric: deliberative, forensic, and epideictic. The first is concerned with what is advisable; the second with what is just; the third with what is admirable. It is the deliberative rhetoric which is most called upon within the tasks of school leadership, although there is also a need to exercise each of the other types. Aristotle also discusses three interconnected foundations for persuasion: character, emotion, and reason. All three are needed by school leaders; none can be dispensed with, for they are inseparable within the act of persuasion.

According to Aristotle, audiences wish to see three qualities in an orator: good sense, virtue, and goodwill. Each quality reinforces the other during the process of persuasion. (For the rest of this chapter let us take the orator to represent the head teacher.) The first quality, in the school context, elicits the judgment that the head has not been deceived by events or reports of events; s/he has "read" the situation perceptively; s/he has cogent reasons for what s/he is advocating, even if all the evidence is not immediately to hand. The second quality encourages listeners to trust the head, because his/her motives are judged to be, not self-regarding, but directed towards the good of the school as a whole and in harmony with sound ethical principles,

11. Bliss, *Understanding Reception*; Finucane, *Sensus Fidelium*.

not all of which are necessarily spelled out at the time, but which can be assumed to be operative within his/her character. The third quality, goodwill, may be taken here to mean that, even for the sake of the good, the head will not seek to dominate, threaten, undermine or manipulate the staff in any way, but rather adopts an attitude of positive regard for them and aims at their well-being, as well as that of the school, as s/he perceives this.

Several of the themes of this chapter can be illuminated by reference to Aristotle. First, I have indicated the concern that efforts by leaders to be persuasive can be experienced as manipulation. Aristotle reminds us that the mode of persuasion must be related to the political or community context. In a democracy we should beware of flattery, appeasement, demagoguery and even reliance on mere logic. The first two of these modes of persuasion are unworthy of communication in a democracy; in addition, they are variants of manipulation and inappropriate in a school. The third of these modes of persuasion constitutes an abuse of popular emotions rather than an ethical harnessing of them towards a clearly identified good. In the case of the fourth, neither the validity of an argument nor mere cleverness in a speaker renders an argument automatically persuasive; for "logic is not audience-specific [but] persuasion is."[12]

Second, I have recognized that, despite the great diversity of views and inevitable conflict about values, for a school to be an effective educational community, there needs to a means of reaching high levels of agreement about key priorities and the values which underpin them. This agreement cannot be compelled; it must be elicited or won through the free exercise of judgment. Disagreement cannot be ridden over in a rough-shod manner; it needs airing, fair treatment, and sensitive responses. Aristotle constantly alerts us to the importance of argument as the center of the art of persuasion. There must be no premature closure of the arguments, simply to convey the impression of consensus. On the other hand, it also has to be recognized that frequently decisions have to be arrived at and action taken without the benefit of prolonged inquiry, examination, reflection, or debate.

Third, I have acknowledged some of the various ways in which teaching operates in the realm of the uncertain. In the context of arguing for priorities and policies no greater certainty should be claimed than is warranted by the nature of the issue which is at stake. Schools are not research institutes, piling up evidence; they have to be satisfied with the reaching of agreement and, if fortunate, conviction, but they will rarely be in a position to claim proof for the theories or viewpoints which are the basis of decisions.

12. Garver, *Aristotle's Rhetoric*, 150.

Fourth, the notion of alignment of staff with the mission has emerged as both an essential element among the tasks of school leaders, yet also problematical in that perceptions of value, of the constituent elements of well-being, as well as the likely effects of various policies, may differ from the leader's judgment on these matters. Ownership of the mission is a legitimate goal, but not all will be ready for it; some will have to be helped to grow towards such readiness. Not all staff will be equally perceptive about or oriented towards the good. Some will be shortsighted about what is needed, blinded by self-interest or insecurity, ill-informed or prejudiced, immature, or simply unable to weigh all the relevant factors. This is not to suggest that school leaders are themselves immune from these defects or distortions of perception.

Fifth, if trust and credibility—which does not imply gullibility on the part of audiences—are at the heart of persuasiveness, then school leaders must accept that "being a good speaker seems in many ways to depend on being a certain kind of person, rather than possessing a body of knowledge."[13] If too much distance has been kept from staff, or if staff do not feel that they know their head sufficiently, then one of the springs of persuasiveness cannot function. For if showing oneself as trustworthy is an integral part of persuasiveness, then it is imperative that heads share part of themselves, their emotions and evaluations. Such openness or vulnerability facilitates the ability of staff to "read" their head and must be demonstrated prior to their granting of trust.

Sixth, Aristotle reminds orators (in this case, heads) that they must be realistic in their assessment of how things appear to various parties with whom they have to work. They deal with arguments "as they are *received*, rather than as they are *conceived*."[14] This does not necessarily imply that each person's "vote" counts equally in the weighing, but it does suggest that wide and regular consultation of all "stakeholders" will help in keeping a finger on the various "pulses" and perceptions.

This is closely related, seventh, to Aristotle's emphasis on proper attention being given to the emotions in any attempt to be persuasive. He does not see our emotions as disconnected from our beliefs or our evaluations. Emotions are not separate from our assessment of an actual or desirable situation; emotions have a cognitive dimension. Nor is recourse to the emotions for Aristotle in contradiction to a concern for ethics. Indeed, rhetorical argument, for him, is essentially ethical, for without the ethical dimension and a concern for character, "argument will be pure calculation,

---

13. Garver, *Aristotle's Rhetoric*, 20.
14. Roland Barthes, quoted in Garver, *Aristotle's Rhetoric*, 280; emphasis in original.

and an act of argument nothing but technique."[15] Furthermore, "the emotions are continually at work in good decisions,"[16] being either "generated, destroyed, deflected, intensified or minimized."[17]

Finally, we may claim that if we follow Aristotle's treatment of rhetoric, we will hold together, rather than keep apart, deciding what to do and getting others to do it. School management will be simultaneously a political and a moral activity. Perhaps this is a partial application of the biblical advice that we should be as wise as serpents and as gentle (or as innocent) as doves (Matt 10:16).

## THE NEED FOR MORAL PERSUASIVENESS

The competency approach tends to focus much more on management than on leadership. The importance of developing a coherent philosophy of education and a set of values is neglected. Preparation for school leadership should include an emphasis on character, integrity, imagination, vision, philosophy, wisdom, judgment, and resilience. It should foster sensitivity to the differing cultures, contexts, ethos, and value frameworks that prevail in schools. Heads need the qualities and skills associated with a retrieval of an Aristotelian view of rhetoric if they are to inspire colleagues, pupils and their parents to act according to worthwhile purposes and values. Furthermore, an assimilation of this view of rhetoric will help them to acknowledge that people not only serve purposes, but they also have purposes of their own.

If their advocacy with regard to upholding the school's mission is to be persuasive, school leaders will need to display vision and imagination, self-confidence and conviction, intelligence and clarity in the task of communication, courage in the face of opposition and difficulty, patience with those who fall short, and persistence over time in the never-ending effort to maintain a consensus. Like teachers who require the political skill of securing from their pupils the vote of attention and effort in the classroom, so heads have to demonstrate the political skills needed to mobilize staff to work together in putting into practice the values espoused by the school. Rhetoric is central to this task.

The art of moral persuasiveness will be needed to ensure that the response of the school to governmental demands for "zero tolerance" of bad pupil behavior and poor staff performance is one that harmonizes with

15. Garver, *Aristotle's Rhetoric*, 184.
16. Garver, *Aristotle's Rhetoric*, 108.
17. Garver, *Aristotle's Rhetoric*, 119.

Christian principles. It will also be required in the engagement with pressures to increase monitoring, to ensure not only that such monitoring does not become increased surveillance for increased compliance but also that relationship is always treated as more important than measurement. The celebration of achievement and success is another area where rhetorical skill should be exercised with care. The use of inappropriate yardsticks and criteria can distort the mission of the school to include the efforts, talents and perspectives of the socially disadvantaged, the marginalized, the unchurched, and all those with special needs. Even in the very process of displaying strong leadership, effective advocacy, and moral persuasiveness, the head should always be aware that, despite any hierarchical status which she or he enjoys and notwithstanding any authoritative mandate from which she or he benefits, priority must be given to common discipleship. If this is not remembered, the head's role in the value leadership will merely *add* to the shadows, rather than assist people to move out from them.

# 10

## Living Logos
### *Christian Leadership*

IN THIS CHAPTER I first make some general comments on aspects of the challenges facing Christian leaders. Then I shall draw your attention to key ideas that are articulated in a recent, short but fertile, book on leadership, by Thomas Sergiovanni. Finally, in the more exploratory part of the chapter, I will take liberties with the phrase "living logos" as one, potentially interesting, entry point into appreciating some important, complex, bewildering and rather awesome dimensions of Christian school leadership. I hope that by unpacking the ramifications of that phrase, "living logos," I can approach what will turn out to be a well-recognized and very familiar challenge, but from a fresh angle.

## ASPECTS OF LEADERSHIP

In reflecting on leadership in general, three dimensions spring immediately to mind. First, there is ethics, which raises the question: What should we do? Without an ethical component in their make-up, leaders are criminal. Second, there is politics, which prompts us to address the question: How can we mobilize others in order to carry out the answers we give to the ethical question? We have to get the vote of attention, develop coalitions, minimize opposition to what we see as the good, harness energies, and elicit commitment. Without a political component in their armory, leaders are ineffective, no matter how fine or noble their ideals. Third, there is spirituality. Of course, there are many competing definitions of spirituality, but for today let me suggest that spirituality, among many other things, helps us to answer the question: How can we maintain integrity in the struggle for and the gaps between the ethical and the political? Without the spiritual dimension, who are we? We are nobody.

These three dimensions, I venture to suggest, apply to all leaders, in any context. When we try to be more specific and come to reflect on Christian leadership, I think we can identify a whole range of "ingredients" or contributing features. Here I pick out nine characteristics of Christian leadership, all of which could be displayed if we functioned as living logos. The order in which they unfold here, apart from the first point, is not especially crucial.

We can begin, surely, by claiming that Christian leadership is rooted in discipleship. It is based on the life and teaching of Jesus the Christ. It is informed by such teaching; it is formed by relationship with Christ; it is transformed by ongoing conversion in the various dimensions of our lives.

Second, this leadership is for service, not for lordship. It hopes to serve, rather than to be served; to be rewarding for others, rather than to "rake it in" for oneself. It addresses the needs and builds up the dignity of others; the self-fulfillment of leaders, though it may be an outcome, is accidental and not in the forefront of their minds; self-aggrandizement through the trappings of office is a temptation to be avoided. According to Bonaventure, writing in the thirteenth century, there are six essential virtues of the servant-leader. These are zeal for righteousness, fraternal love, patience, an exemplary life, wisdom, and devotion to God.[1] Together these virtues comprise a good description of what I mean by a living logo. This feature of Christian leadership is closely connected to the third aspect to be picked out here. The attitude to be adopted towards the objects and areas of our responsibility is that of stewardship rather than of ownership. In the case of a school, the curriculum, the department, the staff, the resources, and the budget—none of these are ours; we hold them in trust on behalf of others and in due course, we must be ready to give an account of our use, our stewardship.

My fourth and fifth characteristics of Christian leadership are also closely related. The style of ministry we exercise should be collaborative; that is it should promote the participation and empowerment of as many as possible. Many voices should be heard, many views should be canvassed, tasks are to be shared, teamwork to be fostered and mutuality and reciprocity encouraged. This is unlikely to happen unless our style is invitational. It must be noncoercive. The spirit cannot flourish in an atmosphere of force;

---

1. An emphasis on these virtues pervades Bonaventure's life and works. See Sullivan, *Lights for the Path,* 85–111.

its healthy growth draws on the oxygen of freedom. Imposing our will, by sticks or carrots, can at best arrive only at compliance, not commitment.

The final four characteristics follow in different ways from one or more of these first five. There will be acceptance of vulnerability and forgiveness of failure as a means of learning. A punitive ethos merely makes people defensive, avoid risks and cover up mistakes. Despite the gentle treatment of shortcomings, and alongside affirming and encouraging people, there will nevertheless be a constant striving for perfection in as many aspects of school life as possible, because such striving is part of what it means to be oriented to the kingdom. The struggle for excellence is integrally related to aspiring to sanctity, to be worthy of sharing God's life more fully. This improvement plan, learning journey or pilgrimage requires of us that we are truly open to the Spirit. The possession of truth is not securely in our grasp. God's Spirit invites, prompts, hints, and whispers to us from all kinds of directions and via all kinds of sources. The Spirit communicates, both from among our recognized membership and from well beyond its boundaries, from those of whom we approve and those whose approval we seek, as well as from those of whom we disapprove or perhaps even fail to recognize at all. The learning organization can "read" the signs of the times and interpret the promptings of the Spirit because of its quality of alertness and its willingness to be humble, open, and receptive. Finally, Christian leaders, like effective leaders in many walks of life, constantly connect the mundane activities, their own and that of others, to a bigger "story," one that is ennobling, motivational, purposeful, and meaning giving. This particular characteristic will be returned to when I focus on the notion of living logos later on.

## IDEAS-BASED LEADERSHIP

I want to refer to a book by a well-known writer on leadership, Tom Sergiovanni. I will quote him extensively so as to bring out a particular line of argument proposed in his latest work. He talks of leadership being based "less and less on personalities, less and less on positions, less and less on mandates and more and more on ideas. Leadership that counts is far more cognitive in orientation than it is personality based or rules based."[2] "What leaders stand for, and their ability to communicate ideas and meanings in a manner that inspires, is compelling, and makes the work lives of others more significant."[3] Sergiovanni suggests that we should not ask staff to fol-

2. Sergiovanni, *Leadership*, x.
3. Sergiovanni, *Leadership*, 8.

low us because of our position and the system of roles, expectations, and rules that we represent; nor because we will make it worthwhile for them if they do follow us.[4] "Teachers ought to follow their heads not because they are clever manipulators who know which motivational buttons to press, or are pleasant persons who are fun to be with, but because heads stand for something."[5] This is where my notion of "living logos" will apply.

In support of his argument about ideas-centered leadership, Sergiovanni quotes Howard Gardner, who has made important contributions on leadership as well as his even more celebrated work on multiple intelligences. "What are the ideas (or stories) of the leader? How have they developed? How are they communicated, understood, and misunderstood? How do they interact with other stories, especially competing [ones]. . . ? How do key ideas (or stories) affect the thoughts, feelings, and behaviors of other individuals?"[6]

I remember once, when working with a fairly new head, helping him to reflect on his achievements, where he had make his mark, and what impression he had given others as to what his "bottom lines" were. We asked his deputy to come in and simply identify three priorities of the new head that had come across in the first six to nine months. The head was dismayed that, despite his best intentions, the deputy named three quite different priorities from those espoused by the head and failed to mention any of the three he had previously identified for himself. What cultural script might an acute listener hear from your school and from you personally, after being in your company for a few months?

Sergiovanni speaks about the management of meaning as a basic competency of a leader. He claims that good leaders connect seemingly mundane routines to the larger purposes and meanings that define "who people are, why they are in the school, why the school needs them, and why their participation with the school is worthwhile."[7] This brings us directly to my exploration of the notion of "living logos."

## LIVING LOGOS

I am playing with two different pronunciations and meanings here. In the secular world, we are familiar with company logos and advertising slogans: Nike's "Just Do It," Coca Cola's "The Real Thing." Many of these are visual

---

4. Sergiovanni, *Leadership*, 28.
5. Sergiovanni, *Leadership*, 29.
6. Howard Gardner, quoted in Sergiovanni, *Leadership*, 35.
7. Sergiovanni, *Leadership*, 52.

creations, easily recognizable images that identify the product or the company or business. Many organizations develop a house style, to be used in all internal and external communication, for example, in memos, policies, and advertisements. A logo is a compressed meaning-bearer, a symbol, a form of economic and rapid communication. It functions in some respects rather like an icon or even a sacrament. Sacraments are concentrated versions of the kind of work God does at all times and in all places. They are privileged moments of encounter, but not exceptions to the norm. They are the great examples of what God is doing all the time. They are visible, small-scale representations of what is happening on the macro level invisibly. I want to suggest that school leaders in general, and Christian school leaders in particular, function partly at least like logos, in this first sense of the word, a compressed symbol, an embodied form of communication about what the school stands for.

I also want to draw upon the notion of logos as used in the Bible, especially in the prologue to John's Gospel. The word *logos* here has many, fairly closely connected meanings: word, argument, discourse, speech, story, book, reason. To claim that leaders are living logos in this sense is to suggest that they embody, proclaim, and facilitate the key meanings of the school and the significance of its work. As living logos they address the questions: Who are we? Why are we? What might we be? What do we stand for? They symbolize and give explicit expression to the school's vision and goals, its raison d'être, and its mode of operation.

They do this in a way similar to the way a monk's habit and bearing or posture is meant to be an outer sign of an inner frame of mind. Once training in posture was an accepted part of education. Close connections existed between the position taken on an issue and the position in which the body is held. The gestures, motions and postures of the body register an inner state. According to this view, the body was to be "read," and there was a blurring of the borders between the physical presence of the teacher and the contents of a lesson. "In the disciplined person the body is the perfect mirror of the soul. That means that learning to walk and gesture elegantly, to speak persuasively, to hold the head and the body in dignified, grave, modest gestures, and to compose facial expressions appropriate to any given emotion, are the first steps in the cultivation of virtue."[8]

I am not suggesting that, as part of their preparation for headship, teachers should take lessons in deportment, merely hinting that the visible and audible presence and demeanor of the leader mediate the inner meaning and significance of the school and its priorities. The musical

---

8. Jaeger, *Envy of Angels*, 12.

metaphor—in which the body was "tuned" to ensure the inner world reflected the harmonics of the outer world—was well known in the eleventh and twelfth centuries. A closely linked metaphor was that of teacher as seal and student as wax receiving his imprint. Students learned by "reading" their teachers—their character, habits, and attitudes as well as their words and deeds. Leaders as living logos are in some ways like seals, offering an imprint of meaning and significance. What kinds of "reading" are done by your pupils, your staff, your peers, your governors, and visitors to your school with regard to your demeanor, priorities, philosophy, and style? When these groups or constituencies "read your meter," what do they come up with?

As living logos, leaders have the capacity to deepen the sense of meaning that people find in their work, to appreciate what kind of difference they are making and aware of how their particular roles aid and abet the accomplishment of the school's mission. Living logos, as I use this term, so affirm people's contributions that they know what would be lost if the place was closed and that this loss would really matter. Living logos bring out the symbolic significance of what we all do and say.

Different kinds of "reading" (and "joined-up" thinking) are needed for this role. Heads have to read the reality, circumstances, situations, and contexts in which they work. They have to read souls and the people around them. They must read themselves and the effects they have on others and how they respond to these others. Many factors influence the quality of the different kinds of reading that we carry out. These factors include, first, our experience, memories, and assumptions; what we bring from the past orients us for the future. Second, our knowledge, maturity, and intellectual capacity make a big difference in what we can do with what we receive or read. Third, our hopes and fears and the state of our feelings; these will inhibit or enhance our receptivity. Fourth, our purposes and priorities, both long and short term, will color and shape our responses. Fifth, what else we are doing and learning at that time in our life will have a bearing on what we can get out of our study or reading. Sixth, who we are with, the company we keep, can significantly modify what we take in. Seventh, our attitude towards and our relationship with the "text" or speaker can make all the difference for us in either leading us to accept or reject the content of communication. Eighth, the clarity and quality of the "text" itself obviously has a bearing. Ninth, chance and unforeseen circumstances and connections can prompt us to make certain kinds of links not intended by an author or that would not have been possible to us at other times. We should not forget, as a tenth factor influencing our reading, our character and its moral and spiritual dimensions. All these factors make a difference in important ways to what we get out of what we read. There are clear connections here between our being living logos and the kind of sense we can make of what we interpret.

In the light of such "reading," school leaders need the ancient art of rhetoric, which is all about moral communication, not about sound bites, nor about pulling the wool over people's eyes. Rhetoric is about establishing a match between a message, its sender and its intended audience.

Unfortunately, rhetoric is often associated with something negative and untrustworthy. Huxley, when told he was using rhetoric, replied that he would never "plaster the fair face of truth with that pestilential cosmetic, rhetoric," which, as Chesterton points out, is as fine a piece of rhetoric as any.[9] Too often rhetoric is considered to be insubstantial fluff, fluff employed to advance covert designs upon an audience. To accuse someone of using "mere rhetoric" is to suggest that they are dressing up the poverty of what they have to say in "false verbal vestments." In an age of spin doctors, we suspect forms of political ventriloquism: Whose words, whose voice is behind the speech? "Read my lips" is a phrase fraught with danger: Does it promise clarity, honesty, reliability, and courageous commitment? Or does it indicate empty promises, recklessness, pretense, and superficiality? The American politician Bob Dole many years ago was exposed and ridiculed for his false rhetoric—the *Guardian* said of him that this required "a surgical operation to give a mute an artificial larynx" and "verbally, Dole was being asked to make, in one evening, the leap from the speaking clock to the Desiderata."[10] In this case, it might be suggested, this politician could not function effectively as a living logo.

But heads do have to function as effective moral communicators, for values are at the very heart of their work. This work includes articulating the central values of the school, inspiring others to pursue these values, promoting and explaining them with all partners and constituencies, defending them from undermining influences from within and without, securing their permeation throughout the life and work of the school, and, above all, reconciling them one with another (for values can conflict) and reconciling those who interpret them differently. Many aspects of school work call for the expression, exemplification, and facilitation of values, for example, the prospectus, decisions about pupil admissions, grouping, assessment and exclusions, curriculum content and policies, approaches to behavior management, sex education, equality, special needs, and about staff—selection, development, promotion, appraisal, as well as institutional self-evaluation, budgets, and time allocation.

---

9. Chesterton, *Victorian Age in Literature*, 13.
10. *Guardian*, Sept. 18, 1996; further bibliographic information unavailable.

In their role as moral communicators and as living logos, I believe that school leaders can usefully learn from Aristotle's treatment of rhetoric. According to Aristotle, audiences wish to see three qualities in an orator (one of the head's roles): good sense, virtue, and goodwill. Each quality reinforces the others during the process of persuasion. The display of good sense elicits the judgment that the head has not been deceived by events or reports of events; s/he has "read" the situation perceptively; s/he has cogent reasons for what s/he is advocating. The presence of virtue encourages listeners to trust the head, because his/her motives are judged to be, not self-regarding, but directed towards the good of the school as a whole and in harmony with sound ethical principles. Goodwill may be taken here to mean that, even for the sake of the good, the head will not seek to dominate, threaten, undermine, or manipulate staff in any way, but rather adopts an attitude of positive regard for them and aims at their well-being, as well as that of the school, as s/he perceives this.

Let me return to another aspect of the importance of reading. Christian leaders should learn how to do all this "reading" in a particular way and in a particular spirit—with the church. This involves connecting our stories to the treasury of past stories of Jesus and to the ongoing, living tradition of the church. For this to happen we have to make within ourselves a home for Scripture, to be at home with God's word and to see ourselves as one among many home bases that God uses to evangelize others. Then we will be able to use Scripture "for teaching, for refuting error, for guiding people's lives and teaching them to be holy" (2 Tim 3:16).

My emphasis on leaders as living logos is simply meant to underline that the world building via the word that is part of being an effective leader requires relationships of reciprocity, bolstered by hospitality, gift giving, forgiveness, love, listening, and sharing. You have to be there for that to materialize.

Being a living logo means we have to see the bigger picture but not forget the particular person in front of us. Our vision must be large, but our capacity to read and respond to the small print of our human encounters must be kept in good shape. Having a helicopter mind that enables us to rise above the forest and "read" the landscape should not prevent us from appreciating and engaging with the concreteness of each "tree" when we walk through that forest. That would be to lose the incarnational principle and foundation of logos. "The virtues of serving, caring, respecting, empowering, and helping without asking for anything in return are far more powerful "motivational devices" than is the artful manipulation of motivational science that seeks to trade fulfilment for compliance."[11]

Being a living logo involves connecting our voice with our touch, or, as some describe it, walking the talk, incarnating the espoused ethos, living out the mission. As a living logo the leader's self (and not anything external to her or him) is her or his primary management "tool." Robert Starratt puts it thus: "Our sensitivity to issues, our ability to carry around the whole school in our head, our ability to remember, our ability to read the unspoken messages, and our ability to see the connection of the present decision to the long-range plan—all these enable us to become this 'primary tool.'"[12]

In the end any kind of leadership at a distance has severe limitations. Writing memos, documents, policies, even creating videos and broadcasting messages, cannot replace our presence as living logos. We have to be there and we have to face people if we are to move them in any worthwhile way. Being there involves authentic presence, with our real, rather than with our ideal selves. Being there depends on our being both centered and grounded. To be personally centered entails a balance between doing and being, between being proactive and reactive, between having theoretical perspectives on and adopting practical approaches to our work. This ensures that we have a recognizable and harmonious "story" to convey, one that is ours, one with which we resonate, one we "give off" by being living logos. To be grounded means that we are rooted in reality, and that we connect to the bigger picture, rely upon deeper values, and are sustained by a wider web of concern and relationships. This ensures that the story we have to convey, the logo we represent or embody, is neither merely personal nor parochial but of greater significance and therefore of wider appeal to others.

To live up to the expectation that in our leadership we should operate as living logos is very daunting, for we know in our hearts that we are all vulnerable, fallible, incomplete, and wounded. But we are not alone. Grace is all around us and, if only we could see them, there are guardian angels, in all kinds of shapes, sizes (and disguises), who hover all the time by our side, ready to help us carry the load. It is in God's sea that we swim; and God will not let us drown.

---

11. Sergiovanni, *Leadership*, 69.

12. Robert Starratt, *Transforming Educational Administration*, quoted in Loader, *Inner Principal*, 96.

# 11

# Succession Planning for School and Church

## THE CHALLENGE

On the world's political scene, it seems clear that many regimes and leaders take little thought for the long-term health of their nations; short-termism bedevils too many political decisions that affect health, the economy, climate, education, and social welfare. The next election, the next source of funding, the next ally, the next favorable headline or media presentation—these are to be secured, even though the long-term needs of the people might be neglected in the process. As we have seen recently in Tunisia and Egypt, and also elsewhere, for example, in Zimbabwe, leaders remain in power until the very last minute, refusing to leave office when they have clearly lost any popular mandate to rule. Rarely is enough thought given to succession planning, to who will take up next the reins of responsibility, nor to how current initiatives will be sustained in the long run, rather than simply be allowed to run out of steam and then to be replaced completely under new leadership.

So too, in the church, we see in many places a crisis of provision of leadership for the future, both in parishes and in the church's schools. Many priests are in the twilight years of their role. Despite occasional positive blips, on the whole the supply of incoming priests to serve the people of God is seriously inadequate and unable to step into the shoes of their predecessors. Although various strategies are being tried, with regard to twinning or grouping some parishes and closing others, on the whole, and in comparison with the seriousness with which businesses consider succession planning, the continued flow of staff recruitment, and strategies for developing the skills and talent already at their disposal, the church falls far behind in such matters.

It might be thought that a major task of a parish priest is to help identify the gifts of the people entrusted to his pastoral care, to foster such gifts, to encourage their generous deployment, and to help in the process of a coherent ordering and integration of these gifts in service of the common good. Holding onto all the significant tasks in a parish and having to make all the significant decisions with regard to its functioning is a disastrous approach, one that is likely to leave the clergy burned out; at the same time it is an approach that is bound to fail to animate God's people to respond appropriately to the call of the gospel and to the needs of their community. In the light of demographic patterns, social and cultural changes, the declining numbers (and increasing age) of clergy, the church should face up to the challenges of equipping God's people for new forms of ecclesial life and organization. While we live *sub specie aeternitatis*, conscious of God's abiding presence with God's people, and do not have to jump onto every bandwagon out of panic that we may be left behind or that the gospel will be rendered out of date and irrelevant, nevertheless, it is incumbent on us to read the signs of the time shrewdly and to be prepared to reconsider approaches that might have served us well in the past but which should not be clung onto as idols or obstacles that prevent new ways to respond to God's call. Engaging the members and potential leaders of the church entails, among other things, giving thought to succession planning. Succession planning is about all the steps that could be taken to ensure, not only that current leadership and ministry roles are being renewed, but also that new types of leadership and ministry are envisaged and prepared for. It means that invitations are being issued to people to accept responsibility, that support is provided and that resources are properly and equitably available. It also means putting in place many different modes of equipping people, drawing on a wide range of ways to train people, to enhance skills, and to evaluate effectiveness. As a learning church, we still have much to learn about learning, about human development, about the effective deployment of human resources, and about evaluation of how effective we are in living out our mission.

In Catholic schools in my own country we read constantly that there is a continuing crisis with regard to the numbers of suitably qualified and experienced people coming forward for senior posts, especially at principal level. Although there often have to be re-advertisements for head teacher posts in schools, this happens much more frequently in the case of Catholic schools, thereby incurring considerable expense both for adverts and for the selection process. Despite initiatives in various parts of the country, the issue of succession planning remains very high on the agenda.

For more than twenty-five years, I have believed that it is part of the duty of an educational leader to gradually hand over, in carefully managed stages, more and more elements of his or her portfolio of tasks and roles to others. Obviously, to do so too quickly would be to abdicate one's own responsibility and would be damaging to the organization for which one is responsible. However, if one fails to facilitate such handing on, there seem to be at least three possible deleterious side effects. First, given that part of the role of a leader is to look ahead, to scan the environment, to recognize both challenges and threats on the horizon and to prepare the organization to get ready to face these, to the degree that he or she is bogged down in the day-to-day running of an organization, there is less time available for this necessarily future-oriented dimension of leadership. As a result, both icebergs (which threaten to capsize the vessel) and helpful tides (which might transport it to safer places) might be missed. In this way, leaders fall short of one of their principal duties through insufficient reduction of other duties. Second, if anything happened to them (through illness or accident or other misfortune), and as a result they could no longer function as leaders, the institution would be more vulnerable than it should be (in such an interim period between leaders) to the vagaries of change, external pressures, and internal uncertainty or even turmoil. Third, by failing to engage in serious succession planning, the understanding, gifts, level of confidence, and readiness of members of the community to take on new roles will be inadequately developed.

I have endeavored, in my own career, to ensure that when I move on to a new post, there has been a gradual handing on of the baton, a detailed sharing of how and why things have been done in my own particular way, opportunities for colleagues to rehearse, wherever possible, the roles I have carried out—and all this among a range of colleagues, in order to distribute or spread capacity to maintain continuity. Of course, this has to be done in such a way as not to constrain the future, or in order merely to extend one's legacy. As one prepares to leave, it is important to display a humble awareness that one's leaving may provide an opportunity for the members of an organization to consider if they wish to review the necessity for the post that is being vacated; perhaps it should be discontinued; perhaps it should be modified; perhaps the duties linked to it need to be redistributed. Succession planning is also greatly helped by post holders having the wisdom to judge the best time to step down, when to let go of the reins of office. Although each of us is irreplaceable, none of us is indispensable. Recognizing when one has done what one can and when it is time to allow others the chance to move things forward in their own way—this is a blessing both for the individual and for his or her community.

Another way of making these comments on succession planning is to say that leadership is less about what leaders do themselves and more about what they enable others to do. While leaders must show the way by personal example, holding onto the trappings of office and making all the decisions should not be marked features of their period of office. Instead of asking "What did I achieve?," they should ask, "How did I help others to grow?" Unless Catholic schools can be places where personal and professional growth is encouraged and fostered, they cannot function effectively as contexts where the gospel is realized, made real. This is also true of the parish.

Succession planning is, of course, not the only element missing that contributes to a situation where Catholic schools and parishes face an uncertain future in terms of leadership and sharing of ministries. There are many factors that cumulatively contribute to a shortage of applicants for senior posts in Catholic schools and a shortage of people coming forward to train for the priesthood and other ministries. With regard to schools, there are many other factors at work, apart from succession planning.

Let me offer some examples of these other factors, before I focus especially on succession planning. I have identified four of these factors in my own context, the UK, and I leave it open to readers to decide whether any of these might be relevant in their own context. First, Catholic school provision of religious education for older teenagers seems patchy: often it fails to excite students about the worth of studying religion, and it does not show the bearing of such study on other curriculum areas; nor does it promote a sense of vocation with sufficient conviction. Second, Catholic higher education has been weak in adding value to normal higher education provision, especially in initial teacher education, where meeting the state's requirements has dominated time and energy, leaving little scope for explicit and in-depth Christian education to be addressed. Weaknesses in Catholic higher education are not helped by the rather remote relationship between bishops and church-affiliated higher education institutions, nor by the apparent lack of interest or engagement in scholarship by bishops. Here what seems required of potential bishops is a safe pair of hands that will not rock the boat or question traditional ways of being church. The low priority given to theological literacy in Catholic higher education contributes in turn to a failure to promote distinctiveness or to adopt confident approaches to staff selection for mission. Third, advanced level provision of continuing professional development in Catholic educational leadership—with honorable exceptions—remains weak in the UK. Sometimes what is on offer is not respectable academically, not distinctively Catholic, and it fails to integrate properly the professional/practical, the educational/academic, and the spiritual/theological dimensions. Fourth, despite much excellent work in all sectors of the Catholic "system"—in parishes, primary and secondary schools, colleges and universities, seminaries, diocesan offices, youth ministry—the various parts of this system are not strongly connected. We lack ways across the system to enthuse, promote, reinforce, support, encourage; we need to get better at celebrating effort, contributions, success, progress, and influence; and we need to find ways to learn from good practice wherever it occurs in the Catholic network.

Unfortunately, in some parishes, the galvanizing of God's people to offer their experience, expertise, insights, energy, and gifts is stifled or hindered by poor communication between clergy and laity and a failure to challenge laypeople to identify and develop their gifts and to harness them for the church. The reality is that many parishioners are better educated then their clergy and exert high levels of responsibility in their daily lives, yet seem to have little influence on the public face or daily life of the church.

## WHAT MIGHT BE DONE?

In part 2 of this chapter I outline what seem to me to be some of the principal steps or elements of succession planning for Catholic schools and parishes. While some of these will apply more closely to schools and others will be more appropriate for parishes, I hope there will be sufficient overlap that the elements identified might have some relevance for both sectors.

First of all, in succession planning there must be clarity about what the role is that is being prepared for. While this might seem to be obvious, such clarity cannot be taken for granted. Making explicit the purposes and functions of leaders or other roles or ministries is a task that some might assume has already been done and that does not need to be revisited. However, unless there is agreement about what is expected of role A, B, or C, the community cannot effectively take steps to prepare people to take on this role. There might be new needs to be addressed which require new types of responsibility. Roles that were important in the past might now have become either redundant or of lower priority. Thus succession planning might lead, not simply to planning for replacement, but perhaps also to the development of new roles.

Second, there needs to be clarity about the kinds of knowledge, skills, virtues, and qualities that are required for the role or task to be carried out well. These might be similar in kind to those currently being exercised, but not necessarily so, since the context might have changed since current officeholders were appointed and new challenges and opportunities might have arisen. In the world outside of church there will often be careful assessment of the nature of the job and the kinds of capacities needed to fill it adequately, with clear discrimination between qualities, skills or knowledge that are essential and those that are desirable. It is important here to separate out "capacity for" from "has experience of." The former has its focus on the future, on potential, while the latter is fixed on the past and actual achievement, but not on what could be achieved.

Third, there need to models or exemplars of good practice, in order to demonstrate the kind of activity and the quality of activity that is desired. Such models or exemplars might be provided by current officeholders. On the other hand, one might need to go elsewhere to observe the kind of activity that is desirable, or at least to compare current practice "back home" with alternative ways of doing things. This is where better connections across the Catholic "system" can help—by making people aware of where initiatives are being attempted, where pockets of good practice can be identified, where role models can be observed and talked to, so that their experience is drawn upon and their insights properly weighed. Not all good ideas or practices are transferable to other contexts; some ideas or practices that failed in one context should still be considered for elsewhere; and so it is important to seek to identify what in the local context has helped or hindered progress when an initiative has been attempted.

Fourth, a supportive and encouraging professional ethos is vital. Fostering learning, sharing successes and defeats, acknowledging high and low points and questioning about principles and practice—all these play a part in developing the right ethos. Sharing vulnerability is a major high road to personal and professional growth. There is no real learning without risk of falling short. It must feel safe to take such risks; there must be opportunities to share worries; remaining only in our safety zone will prevent growth.

Fifth, each of us benefits from opportunities to practice bite-sized parts of a bigger role than those that we are enacting at the moment. Such rehearsals should be attempted with a safety net (that is, under supervision and with the possibility of being rescued if things go badly wrong). Feedback on our attempts to try out responsibilities beyond our current remit should be provided by more experienced mentors. Prompts for reflection and self-evaluation should be readily available. In a school, teachers might be encouraged to lead an assembly, chair a meeting, be involved in timetabling, observe a selection interview, or try out using a lesson observation pro forma alongside a more experienced educator as they observe someone else's classroom practice. A parishioner might be offered a chance to offer a post-communion reflection, lead a midweek prayer service, chair or act as scribe for a meeting, organize a trip or a social activity, or contribute to a welcoming ministry. These opportunities to try out a role should be repeated, rather than experienced as merely a one-off occasion.

Sixth, succession planning depends on there being in place serious attempts at eliciting feedback from those working "under" current office-holders, for example, pupils/students, teachers, other staff, parishioners. The purpose of such feedback would be, not to be judgmental, but to ascertain what, with regard to current practice, is going well and what is going less well; it can also help in identifying if there are any gaps in provision. Such evaluation should include parties external to the work situation, for example, parents, inspectors (ecclesial and secular), clergy, trustees, or others. This feedback should inform step 1 (above); it will also prove useful for other steps being outlined here.

Seventh, information from the feedback sought in step 6 should be available to junior staff (in school) or to parishioners in general, so that they can see how their own perceptions and evaluations of how tasks are being carried out are matched, reinforced, extended, contradicted, or qualified by those of other parties. When we encounter differing assessments of how roles are being exercised, this can provide quite a jolt and sometimes it constitutes a valuable learning experience. It can open our eyes and deepen our sensitivity to come across perceptions that contrast with what we thought was the case.

Eighth, it would greatly help succession planning if collaborative initiatives could be developed across a diocese, religious order, or local area to foster exchanges of staff, limited secondments, wider sharing and learning (I deliberately avoid the term "training") opportunities. Such exchanges should include opportunities for staff to compare how different institutions establish different priorities and develop different strategies for addressing their mission. They should also foster a spirit of camaraderie among cohorts of potential leaders. What is not wanted here is any encouragement of insistent or competitive individualism.

Ninth, opportunities for mentoring and coaching for individual guidance should be available. These opportunities should be offered carefully because some people might want to experiment with a role or wish to seek advice about what is entailed in taking on a particular task, but at the same time they might want to retain the right not to proceed if it turns out to be too difficult or not what they hoped for. Thus the chance to experiment and the seeking of advice need to take place out of the limelight and with a degree of confidentiality. But it can be made known that members of staff and parishioners with some experience of various roles and tasks can be approached and are willing to serve as mentors or coaches "behind the scenes" and without those seeking them out having to confirm their commitment to taking up such roles afterwards. Mentors and coaches should avoid being too prescriptive or intrusive in how they support those who come for advice or guidance. Their role is to listen, to share experience, to offer but not to impose. "This is what works for me . . . I have found it helpful to . . . You might want to think about . . . Suppose you did it this way round . . . Why do you think it worked out like that? How might you tackle that differently next time?" Their task in mentoring is not to produce clones of themselves but to create the kind of learning space in which mentees can grow into a role in their own way, in safety, with the support of someone with some relevant experience (but who is not necessarily an expert).

Tenth, there needs to be in place in schools and parishes, but also at diocesan level, strategies for identifying potential leaders and encouraging them to access both normal and accelerated learning opportunities. Of course, this cannot happen without there being clarity as to what the role is and also about what are the key qualities, skills, and types of knowledge needed to carry it out. Schools, parishes and dioceses need to ask themselves: How will we recognize who might be able to take on particular tasks or who could grow into being a leader in some aspect of our mission? What kinds of signs might tell us who to approach? How do we identify potential? How do we smooth the path for people to respond to our invitation to undertake some formation or learning? What is the role of our community in helping people hear and embrace the call to discipleship in particular ways? If we are to avoid favoritism and if we are to be inclusive, how do we ensure that as many talents as possible are identified, affirmed, and, where possible, strengthened and coordinated in service of the community? Who will be responsible for such discernment and how will they go about it? Are procedures transparent and accountable to the community, so that they can be modified, extended, or enhanced, as appropriate? Once people have been identified as possible future holders of roles or as potential leaders, what learning opportunities will be made available, by whom, when, and where?

Eleventh, in order to give credibility and transferability to any learning opportunities, it would greatly help if there was in place a multilevel (and at least partly accredited) framework of advanced academic and professional learning opportunities, catering from induction through to retirement. Such a framework goes beyond the remit or capacity of a particular school or parish. It would need to be arrived at by consultation and collaboration with the wider church (at diocesan or regional level) and probably also with a university, with all working together to ensure that learners experience an integration of intellectual, practical/professional, and personal/spiritual dimensions. A framework of accredited learning opportunities, stretching from the most basic skills to very high levels of ministerial formation, would avoid parishes and schools having to invent the wheel over and over again; it would facilitate their drawing upon wider fields of candidates, and it would encourage transferability of learning beyond the local area or context where it was originally gleaned. It would also encourage a climate of learning as integral to the flourishing of the church and its institutions and agencies.

Twelfth, to support all the above, succession planning also benefits from a rigorous yet supportive framework of appraisal, one that facilitates in-depth self-knowledge and self-evaluation in relation to tasks and roles. In the parish context, where many roles and tasks are carried out by unpaid volunteers, the degree of rigor is likely to be considerably less than it should be in the case of paid professionals in the school sector. However, in both cases, appraisal can greatly boost our capacity to grow, to check out how our contribution is being received by others, to identify how we might make improvements in what we do, and to discern what kinds of help we need in doing so. Built into the appraisal process can be a concern for mutuality and reciprocity, underlining the service orientation of roles. Three particularly powerful questions posed by an appraisee to individuals or groups he or she seeks to serve can help here: First, what am I doing that you find helpful? Without knowing the answer to this, one might drop a practice through lack of awareness of how it is being welcomed. Second, what am I doing that you do not find helpful? Again, feedback from this question might indicate which practices should be dropped. Third, what am I not doing that you would find helpful? It is likely that this question would lead to some suggestion that could be taken on board; but even if the appraisee finds that she or he cannot follow up a particular proposal or request, at least they have the chance to explain why not.

\* \* \*

While we can be confident that God's Holy Spirit abides with the church and her schools, and although we can be sure that the gates of hell will not prevail against them, nevertheless, we would be seriously at fault if we failed to do what it is in our power to do to sustain and promote the mission. Equipping people to carry out their roles appropriately, with confidence and joy, but also effectively and wisely, is integral to building a community based on the gospel. Succession planning—and the steps associated with it that I have outlined above—is a major responsibility of the ecclesial community. Although some of these steps would be difficult for one school or one parish to manage on their own, many other steps are within reach even for individual schools and parishes, do not require high levels of financial, technical, or expert resources, and offer the promise of a more involved, more open, more confident, and better informed pilgrim community.

*PART THREE*

# Education as a Spiritual Endeavor

## INTRODUCTION

For some the classroom is a place of strife, both for the teacher and for the student. For the teacher—facing some students who don't want to be there, who are not ready to be there, whose parents don't buy into the values and vision of the school, whose home life does not provide an ethos or ambience that supports what the school is trying to offer their children; and where resources are tight, in some places where the buildings are not fit for purpose, or where it is hard to recruit or to retain teachers—teaching can be a wearying business, disappointing in the response it receives, always demanding more of you than you feel can be given. There is always the danger of stress, burnout, loss of energy and enthusiasm; at such times, the struggle seems too much to bear. This applies as much to principals as to faculty. And for some students too, school can be a difficult place, for all kinds of reasons. In such circumstances it may seem very strange to say that classrooms can be holy places, places of blessing—for both teacher and student. But I believe that is indeed what they can be, even though it is not always so.

Our teaching does not produce objects which can be counted, weighed or measured; instead our teaching transforms subjects, who elude measurement and who transcend even our best attempts at assessment. We are in the business of reading our students, our curriculum subjects, and ourselves in the light of our understanding of and our response to God; and then enabling our students to read themselves in this light too. We need to see our students as possessing a story that we should be ready to hear and learn from. Students, like all children, have an amazing radar for reading us and telling whether we are authentically walking the talk, living what we say. They detect when we are being real or simply going through the motions, without really believing what we tell them.

As teachers, we are in the inspiration business. We are meant to detect and affirm and then to reinforce the emerging gifts of our children, to fire them up, to breathe the oxygen of encouragement into them, to fan the fragile flames of their enthusiasm, to help them pay attention to their world and to care for it wisely and lovingly. This means we have to care for them wisely and lovingly. If we are to sustain this work, it also means we have to care for ourselves wisely and lovingly. In the process we are rightly expected to care for standards of learning, but this does not mean that we are in the standardization business; we are not producing batches but responding to precious, unique individuals—and doing so as precious, unique individuals ourselves, each of us with unique needs and special gifts.

We can make the classroom a holy place by the way we try to meet students' needs, by the quality of the relationships we establish with them, by our hard work, by our regular and punctual attendance, by our thorough and conscientious preparation and planning, by our marking of work and assessment of progress, and above all, by our readiness to listen. Our own good example, our enthusiasm, our combination of challenge and support, together with the way we model collaboration with our colleagues—all these help towards making classrooms holy places.

There are several ways that we can connect teaching with the fostering of a Christian school ethos. First, teachers who provide hospitable spaces for learning are offering a great gift to their pupils, something precious; that something is themselves. Each teacher is an expression of one of God's gifts intended for the benefit of students. Insofar as each teacher is different, then her or his particular gift cannot be offered by anyone else. The more of themselves that teachers, share, the richer students will be.

Second, by imparting their curriculum expertise, a teacher opens up the world as seen from a particular perspective. By breathing life into this subject area a teacher makes it a possible vantage point from which to see the world. We can find something special, valid, useful and enriching through every one of the areas of study. Even what seems a purely secular activity, like teaching a person to read, can be a soul-shaping process.

Third, it is possible, through the different subjects and topics we teach, to open up perspectives on God's world, people, purposes, call, and grace. The teacher's task here is to help students find connections between those aspects of their experience and learning which can be described in secular terms and the language and worldview which flow from faith. God is as close to us in the laboratory, sports field, playground, classroom, library, workshop and cloakroom as in private prayer, public worship, the words of Scripture and sacramental practice, although, on our side, we may be less aware of that presence. Whatever we study, we are in the domains of the one who "is before all things, and in whom all things hold together" (as it says in Col 1).

And fourth, we help make the classroom a holy place when we are conscious that we are working with students who are whole persons, even though we are dealing, at a particular time and place, with a narrowly prescribed skill, or a particular notion, or a small drop in the ocean of knowledge. The lives of students are multidimensional, with unforeseeable reverberations potentially sparked off in any compartment of their being by an apparently mundane aspect of learning. Even an arid exchange in a classroom can stimulate something vital within the student, without the teacher ever being aware of this; at the same time, even the most religious subject matter can leave a student unmoved and be experienced as a spiritual desert.

Teachers can serve as mediators of God's grace. They do so by their passion for what they teach; by their compassion for who they teach; by their professionalism in how they teach; by their openness to and for dialogue with students, parents, and colleagues; by their wisdom; by their commitment and dedication; and by their ability to let go. By sharing their humanity and how they evangelize through their witness and behavior. They hand on the holy by the way they handle the ordinary things of life and the ordinary gestures of human exchange. I believe that teachers can make a huge difference—through what they know and their love for this; through their character and personality; through their skill in communicating and enabling learning; through their patience and perseverance; through the professional quality of their relationship with students; by the special way they exercise their art and craft.

Each of the three essays in part 3 in some way contributes to the claim that education is an essentially spiritual endeavor. What are the classroom verbs for being spiritual? Be present. Pay attention. Listen. Wait. Welcome. Invite. Be hospitable. Share. Bless. Give. Forgive. Reconcile. Heal. Celebrate. Encourage. Be vulnerable. Pray. Insofar as teachers are doing some of these, then they are helping to make their classrooms holy places.

Chapter 12 presents an alternative to the prevailing emphasis on what constitutes knowledge—knowledge as the fruit of scientific method, something that is objective and detached from the self. I argue for a critical retrieval of premodern approaches to knowledge that were promoted within the Eastern and Western Christian tradition, approaches that are spiritual in nature. I propose that spiritual modes of knowing should be considered alongside other forms of knowing, in service of a richer, more holistic approach to higher education, one that does justice to the multidimensional aspects of human nature, development, formation, and flourishing. Students should be offered opportunities to become familiar with complementary modes of knowing that are likely to extend the repertoire of the ways they read and respond to the world, other people and their experience of life. Such premodern Christian approaches privileged self-giving and self-control, rather than mastery over or control of what was investigated. Their epistemology viewed intellectual, moral, and spiritual virtues as intimately interconnected. They considered knowledge to be something revealed and given rather than constructed or exposed by our methodology. The chapter considers the educational potential for students today of learning from the premodern emphasis on knowledge as dependent on both ascetic training and affective formation, as entailing capacitation (being attuned to or fitted for external reality), and as promoting self-knowledge and transformation. I contrast premodern and contemporary approaches to knowledge through the metaphors of pilgrim and project manager.

The focus of chapter 13 is on the personhood, self-awareness, and interior life of teachers, how they are present to their students, rather than their academic subject knowledge or their professional competence. After briefly acknowledging some of the high expectations and challenges faced by teachers in Catholic schools and the various polarities they need to hold in creative tension, I outline the complex set of factors that influence how the personhood of teachers is brought into play with students before introducing and explaining the notion of perichoretic pedagogy: the interaction between teacher and student that can become a mutual indwelling. I suggest that gentleness—not usually treated in the literature about teaching—can foster real presence in the classroom.

Chapter 14 turns to a neglected aspect of Christian anthropology. Any approach to education cannot help being influenced by the understanding of human beings held (whether explicitly or implicitly) by the teacher. The Christian teacher needs to work from a Christian anthropology or understanding of human personhood. In the literature on Christian anthropology, because of the centrality of the notion of human beings made in the image of God, much attention has been given to various human capacities and activities, but less attention has been given to human receptivity. The focus of this chapter is on vulnerability as an important feature of human nature as receptive to and affectable by a range of external influences. I argue that vulnerability has positive as well as negative connotations and implications and that among such positive implications is that vulnerability renders us open to the divine as well as to unwelcome life experiences.

Beyond treating vulnerability as an inescapable condition of human life, the chapter explores the choice between responding in such a way as to close ourselves off (insofar as this is possible) from external influences or to open ourselves up to them. I claim that vulnerability is a prerequisite for learning, for loving relationships and for opening ourselves to the divine.

# 12

# Pilgrims or Project Managers
## *Premodern Challenges for Contemporary Students*

### INTRODUCTION

Education privileges particular ways of knowing and, at the same time, it marginalizes or ignores other ways of knowing. I think it is important for university students in any discipline to be introduced to the history and philosophy of that discipline. They should be helped, within the context of their chosen discipline, to become aware of:

- The questions considered worth pursuing
- Representative answers given to those questions
- The methods of investigation recommended, the kinds of evidence counted as relevant and the modes of argument considered valid
- The acknowledged limits of those methods of inquiry and types of evidence
- The central concepts, leading paradigms, and canonical texts that are deployed for organizing and ordering knowledge
- The modes of evaluating and testing knowledge claims
- Leading exemplars of the discipline who have shaped its development
- Areas currently under dispute or where is scope for alternative interpretations
- Acceptable style of presentation

- Connections with and differences from "neighboring" disciplines

In a context of constantly expanding, yet also fragmenting, knowledge and ever greater specialization in academic disciplines, and with new subdisciplines emerging all the time, it becomes more and more difficult to help learners to discern how to develop a stance toward the circle of knowledge as a whole. If scholars become dependent on external funding sources, from government or other agencies that are uninterested in supporting the humanities and overconfident in the undoubted benefits of science and technology, funders who expect a tight connection between higher education, employability, and the needs of the labor market, this leads to the neglect of existential and spiritual concerns and a failure to take seriously questions about meaning, purpose, and overarching, life-guiding values.

One advantage of revisiting the premodern worldview—faced with the fragmentation of academic disciplines, constantly being differentiated into ever more tightly prescribed and specialized subdisciplines, the loss of confidence in any metanarratives that explain our place in the world, the frequent assumption that there can be a disconnection between academic work and any particular moral tradition, and the erosion of trust in any possibility of our attaining truth—is to learn from its strong sense of the coherence, integrity, and harmony of creation, its conviction that there is an objective order to be found in the world and its assumption that there is a necessary connection between, on the one hand, our moral character and spiritual state and, on the other hand, the effectiveness and comprehensiveness of our cognitive reach.

My focus here is on approaches to knowledge and, in particular, assumptions about the qualities needed by learners to engage in such approaches to knowledge. My hope is that, by recommending that students in higher education are given the opportunity to reflect on unfamiliar assumptions, notions and practices from the past with regard to knowledge, they are unsettled enough to allow themselves to take seriously these alternatives to current presuppositions in the academy about accessing knowledge.

The chapter is divided into five parts. First, I explain what is entailed by an attempt to engage in a critical retrieval of past ways of thinking and practice. Second, I contrast premodern Christian and contemporary secular approaches to knowledge. In part 3, the focus is on the importance attached to the promotion of self-knowledge and the notion of habitus among premodern Christian educators. Here, as an illustration of significant differences between contemporary and previous understandings of the student's role, I introduce the images of the student as pilgrim and as project manager. In part 4, I explain the nature, purpose, and scope of ascetic training, perhaps the most distinguishing feature of premodern educational approaches to knowledge. Finally, I conclude by revisiting the metaphors of pilgrim and project manager, arguing that what is implied by both these metaphors has a legitimate role to play in universities today—and therefore that the legacy of the Christian tradition continues to supply resources that can potentially enrich the learning of contemporary students.

## CRITICAL RETRIEVAL

Retrieving thinking from a previous era can give us distance from the present and enable us to see it with a mind strongly informed by and familiar with quite different ways of living and thinking. Historical perspective can help us to become sensitive to those modern assumptions about learning and knowledge which, by going unexamined, have become so automatic as to be unduly limiting—aspects of our thinking that are unduly influenced by our cultural blind spots. As Michael Casey notes, "There are elements of universal human experience that are overlooked in our culture that can be rediscovered by paying attention to the insights from another time and situation."[1] Some familiarity with approaches to knowledge that were customary in the past can stimulate us today to loosen the grip of what is often taken for granted in higher education and to open up the possibility of imagining a different future. Awareness of alternative approaches to knowledge can serve as a counterweight to presentism and belief in the inexorable march of progress.

A capacity for mental time travel is an important item in the toolkit for any academic discipline. It is only too easy for us to accept the dominant assumptions of our era as if they are so obvious that they do not need to be questioned. Teachers and students need, at least provisionally, to escape from such assumptions, which can function as dogmas. They need a safe space in which to question current assumptions and imagine alternative ways of thinking. One way of achieving this is via a critical retrieval of earlier forms of wisdom.

Such attempts at retrieval, if they are to serve as liberating in the present, should avoid two unhelpful alternative stances. First, they are not about trying to reinstate the past as it once was, in the hope that this would be a remedy for our current ills. This would be practically impossible; the conditions that made past assumptions feasible pertain no longer. Restoration is not in order. Second, they need to take past ways of thinking and practice seriously enough to allow them to challenge any presentist tendency to

---

1. Casey, *Sacred Reading*, viii.

treat our contemporary human experience as having universal validity or ultimate authority. Thus, we should avoid idolizing either the past or the present. What is required is a dialogue with the past, learning from past wisdom, becoming conscious of its insights, yet also of its blind spots, and allowing this to inform our current discernment of our own situations. That dialogue with the past should be neither servile nor cynical. It should embrace charitable appreciation with critical discernment.

In retrieving some aspect of past thinking and practice, there is more than mere imitation or repetition. Instead, in the process of rediscovering something from the past, one assimilates it but also transforms it by bringing into contact with the present situation. The source—in this case, premodern Christian perspectives and practices with regard to approaching knowledge—needs to serve as a dynamic wellspring or fountain, infusing something new by creative adaptation into current ways of thinking and acting with regard to knowledge acquisition. In this way, careful retrieval of the past can lead to what Johann Baptist Metz referred to as "productive noncontemporaneity."[2]

Thus, I see critical retrieval as drawing out the conceptual resources and constitutive practices inherent within a tradition (whether that tradition be religious, spiritual, intellectual, political, social, or cultural), but doing so in a way that probes carefully for their ongoing relevance and potential applicability. It is a looking to the past in order to help us to look beyond our present horizons and to enrich ongoing debates. Such retrieval in no way precludes engaging with contemporary sources of wisdom, many of which will advance beyond past insights. Our efforts at retrieval run the risk of being superficial, with too easy a lifting from a past that is not fully plumbed to a present that too automatically dominates and distorts a proper reading of that past. As Henri de Lubac observed, "It sometimes takes a lot of arid archaeology to make the fountains of living water well forth anew."[3]

## ASSUMPTIONS ABOUT AND APPROACHES TO KNOWING

The purpose of educational efforts is to nurture, discipline, and resource the outlook and the development of students, equipping them to read and respond to the world. Readiness to learn is connected to maturity, motivation, and formation or training. Relationships, community-building, personal virtues, spirituality, and habits—all play a part in the process of accessing

2. Sarisky, *Theologies of Retrieval*, 193.
3. Lubac, *Paradoxes of Faith*, 58.

knowledge. Yet these are often neglected. Contemporary cultural scripts emphasize a therapeutic, technological, and consumerist outlook. It is often assumed that everything can be treated, fixed, and possessed. The difference between informational reading—where we extract from a text something with potential pragmatic benefits—and formational reading where we open ourselves to be shaped by the text—is insufficiently appreciated. The mutual interaction in learning of physical, cognitive, emotional, and social aspects of human development is lost sight of in the higher education context, to a degree that would not happen in primary education or in educational provision for those with special needs. Too often, university education ignores the fact that the powers of the mind are connected to the qualities of the person. In contrast to much current thinking, for premodern Christians, education proceeded on the assumption that there is an inherent order in what is studied to which we need to accommodate ourselves; we need to be made ready to fit that order—one that is external to us—so that order can be mirrored in us.

An obstacle here is radical individualism, when autonomy is so emphasized as almost to render us monads, disconnected from one another; as if we are independent and self-made people. Furthermore, too often students think of themselves as detached from what they are coming to know; learning is considered to be separate from other aspects of their life (physical, moral, their habits, the company they keep, what else they give their attention to). Knowledge is something external, accessed at a distance—seen but not internalized; it is available at a glance and achieved at no real cost; it is not self-involving and requires no deep personal change. An encounter with the apparent weirdness of past assumptions can serve to offer a counterweight to current modes of thinking about knowledge and complement contemporary education by proposing alternative ways of thinking about what is worth learning and how one might equip oneself to learn.

For premodern Christians, intellectual engagement occurred in the context of belonging to a community and sharing in ritual activity. Community life and ritual activity reinforced classroom learning in shaping not only minds but also bodies and character. This was education as initiation, where students were becoming inducted into being insiders to a living tradition. Gesture, posture, and clothing mattered. Theodore of Mopsuestia (ca. 350–428) is an example of how all this was central to the teaching of a typical Christian thinker.[4] Such patristic figures as Gregory the Great ("Pastoral Rule"), John Chrysostom ("On Vainglory and the Right Way for Parents to Bring Up Their Children"), Basil of Caesarea ("Address to Young

---

4. Schwartz, *Paideia and Cult*.

Men, on How They Might Derive Benefit from Greek Literature"), Benedict of Nursia ("Rule"), and Cyril of Jerusalem ("Procatechesis") faced, as we do today, "pluralism, syncretism, and materialism, grappling with fallout from plagues, economic upheavals, and the mass migration of peoples."[5] Kyle Hughes points out that they, too, had to address such questions as: "Who are we as teachers? Who are our students? What are we teaching? How are we teaching? How do we plan for growth?"[6] Byzantine Christians, despite their noted emphasis on and prioritization of spiritual knowledge and wisdom, never denied the necessity for and value of secular knowledge and their mainstream teaching was never anti-intellectual. While they approved of secular learning, they always set this in a context in which such learning was located, guided and enhanced by prayer, piety, humility, fasting, and obedience—and, more generally as open to illumination from divine revelation.

Students today do not envisage that their tasks include being engaged in a spiritual struggle for self-improvement. They are ready to accept correction in matters of technique but not in matters of character; they would consider any attempt made by their teachers to comment on their personal habits and lifestyle as being irrelevant to their coming to know; it would be taken as an affront to their dignity and an unwarranted intrusion on their privacy. Being advised to maintain scrutiny of their way of life, because this may be impeding their path to knowledge, would sound too much like opening themselves to judgmentalism, a cardinal sin in an age of moral relativism. Their inner world of thoughts, desires, emotions, and imagination is generally considered to be out of bounds and beyond the remit of teachers today, but that inner world would have been treated as highly pertinent to those wanting to walk the path towards knowledge by most premodern Christian thinkers, whether from the Eastern or the Western tradition. The very notion that acceptance of spiritual direction might constitute an integral element of intellectual growth or that holiness may be associated with sound interpretation would sound ludicrous to most students—as it would to their teachers.

The alien nature of ascetic education of the kind promoted by Dorotheus of Gaza (ca. 506–560/580)—to be commented on in part 4 (below)—emerges starkly when it is confronted by the shallow view held by many contemporary students, that our choices are unfettered by consequences; that they can be made and unmade equally freely, in each case, as if starting from scratch. In reality, past choices change who we are in ways we are often

---

5. Hughes, *Teaching for Spiritual Formation*, 9.
6. Hughes, *Teaching for Spiritual Formation*, 13.

quite unaware of; they constrain future choices because they leave a residue, have an imprint, become embedded in us; they influence our attention, our perceptions, our will; they modify our desires, priorities, and purposes. Individual acts quickly slip into habits, which then shape and reinforce settled dispositions. Reversing past choices and changing direction, while not impossible, often turns out to be much less easy than anticipated.

The medieval historian Stephen Jaeger shows how the discipline of the body was considered across the medieval centuries to be a "composing" of the inner person.[7] Just as a musical instrument can be "tuned" to reflect and act as a medium for the laws of harmonics and musical proportion, so too the body can be "tuned" to reflect and mediate appropriate and fitting human behavior. Here, "dress, gesture, speech, tone of voice, table manners, posture and gait are the point of departure for the cultivation of virtue."[8] In the twelfth century, Hugh of St. Victor's treatment of the discipline of the body, the role of example and imitation, and the influence of living in community on student learning—all combine to promote rationality, realism and virtue in service of wisdom.[9] For a brief overview of medieval understandings of teachers and scholars, of scientia and sapientia, the inextricable links between intellectual, moral, and spiritual virtues, and similarities and differences between the ethos of medieval and modern universities, see my book *The Christian Academic in Higher Education*.[10] For most medieval thinkers, knowing was always linked to a way of life that seeks to be in tune with reality. Their view was that, unless we are doing the truth, living in harmony with it, in accordance with it, then we are out of touch with truth; in other words, only by living rightly can we come to the truth. They held in common the notion that the world is ordered rather than random and that we have to accommodate ourselves, as individuals and as communities, to that order, an order that is not constructed by us and that exists prior to our plans and priorities.

They also shared an emphasis on the necessity for dependence on spiritual authorities and epistemic guides, not just as sources of information, but with regard to how we need to be transformed so as to be capable of receiving knowledge. Behind the stress on the need for such guides was a sober assessment of our capacity for accessing truth: there are seriously negative cognitive consequences if our minds are disordered, our attention is distracted, our appetites are untamed and unruly, our energies are

---

7. Jaeger, *Envy of Angels*, 13.
8. Jaeger, *Envy of Angels*, 106.
9. Sullivan, "Hugh of St. Victor"; see ch. 3 of this book.
10. Sullivan, *Christian Academic in Higher Education*, 55–74.

dispersed, our emotions are in a state of turbulence, our desires and priorities are conflicted. Where these are features of our life and where our behavior is unethical, we are likely to suffer from self-deception, distorted perceptions, and become prone to unwarranted judgments.

Minds clouded by sin and modes of behavior distorted by habits and wills out of line with God's purpose for us, could, according to premodern Christian thinking, be reformed, corrected, and realigned with what God intends for us, leading us to truth, flourishing, and, in cooperation with God's illuminating grace, to salvation. Healthy growth and reliable access to learning was linked by most premodern Christians to living by the virtues and to openness to the light offered by God, a light which could enhance our powers to see, know and accept truth. A crucial insight they shared was the role played by the emotions and the will and especially love, in our capacity to recognize truth and to live rationally. Modern educators would do well to learn from their Christian predecessors the role played by the virtues in reordering humanity, the inseparability of love and knowledge, and the ways that openness to God's illuminating (and healing) presence can reinforce and enhance our natural (also God-given) powers.

Current emphases on critical thinking, problem-solving, analysis, the deployment of information technology and other communication skills, a sense of social responsibility, a capacity to contribute to local and global citizenship and to deal with complexity, diversity, and change—all these are important and valuable features of higher education today. However, one might question whether enough is being done to enable students to arrive at self-knowledge. Furthermore, does higher education today sufficiently emphasize the ability to internalize and appropriate what is read, and to allow oneself to be "read" by what one reads. I am drawing attention here to the need, within education, to help students to work on their inner self and their personal growth. In the face of a plethora of external sources of information, students also need their attention to be drawn to their inner resources—with which they will have to face life's challenging situations and cope with external forces and pressures. These inner resources include emotional intelligence—understanding and wisely regulating their emotional repertoire—and careful reflection on the habitus they are developing. The habitus we develop mediates between the subjective world we inhabit and the objective world around us; it functions between the student and what they seek to know or to be able to do; it enables or hinders access to knowledge. Cultivating the right habitus used to be considered a task that is intrinsic to and essential for educational development. As Mary Keator points out, "Educators need to recognize the importance of ordering the classroom space but they also need to recognize the importance of helping students to re-order their inner space."¹¹ Echoing this view, Inbar Graiver notes:

> In the modern West, our ability to influence external reality has far surpassed the power we have over ourselves. While we have developed a tremendous power of bringing the environment under our control, we quickly lose our self-control, helplessly swayed by emotions of lust, greed, pride, or envy. Monastic asceticism enabled Christian believers to free themselves from this compulsion and become masters of their own mind and experiences, thereby aligning themselves with God.[12]

One way of articulating a major difference between premodern Christian and contemporary secular approaches to knowledge acquisition would be to say that, for the former, the student is treated as a pilgrim, whereas for the latter, the student is envisaged as a project manager. The pilgrim leaves behind much of the baggage of life, and risks much discomfort, feeling drawn towards a goal that exerts a pull on them, one that will demand personal and lasting change. The project manager efficiently constructs a path, driving towards a goal they have often set for themselves; the journey entails filling up at various knowledge stations, but does not require deep-seated personal change and after which they are free to make quite a different journey—as if the prior journey had not taken place. The student as pilgrim finds herself acted upon, becoming porous, attuned to, and opened up before something (or Someone) external to themselves. The pilgrim is remade in some way by the experience. The project manager remains in charge and in control of what happens. Such a person remakes (some aspect of) the world in his or her use of its resources.

To finish this section, three further observations by recent commentators on defects in modern approaches to knowledge might be made. First, Paul Griffiths laments the questioning of authority and the concern with preliminary issues of method and justification (intellectual attitudes and concerns typical of modernity) partly because these tend to lead to "the endless deferral of commitment" and partly because they rest on the twin assumption that "the individual is the locus of value" and that the educator's task is to "maximize the individual's knowledge of alternatives and capacity to choose among them."[13] Second, Hanna Lucas alerts us to the way that "our epistemology does not envision a *capacity to receive* truth, but

---

11. Keator, *Lectio Divina*, 190.
12. Graiver, *Asceticism of the Mind*, 188.
13. Griffiths, *Religious Reading*, 68.

rather the capacity to *construct* truth."[14] And finally, Vartan Gregorian notes that present practices in higher education make it "difficult for students to integrate knowledge . . . there is no differentiation between consumption and digestion, between information and learning."[15] In the following two sections I will suggest that key features of premodern approaches to knowledge—for example, the emphasis put on self-examination, on ascetic training and affective formation—can assist students in learning how to become less self-centered, to commit themselves more fully, to nurture their capacity to receive, and to internalize what they are learning, all of which increase their ability to integrate the diverse aspects of their education.

## SELF-KNOWLEDGE AND THE HABITUS OF THE LEARNER

Without a mature self-knowledge—a discerning awareness of our internal dispositions, our habits of thinking and acting, and the way we orient ourselves in relation to situations and experiences, we are more likely to find ourselves adrift in the midst of the conflicting pressures upon us, often confused and liable to make decisions that are incoherent and thus self-defeating. Our subjectivity is not something quite separate from our scholarship; indeed subjectivity saturates and shapes all attempts at learning. To be adequately self-reflexive we need to work hard to detect and discern how our attention, perceptions, thinking, priorities, judgments, and evaluations are linked to our location, context, autobiography, commitments, aversions, hopes and fears. As husband and wife Douglas and Rhonda Jacobsen point out: "Our ideas and values are connected to each other in complicated webs of relation and reference that have as much to do with our autobiographies as with pure logic."[16] The kind of person we have become cannot help but simultaneously enable and hinder our access to knowledge.

A useful term here, to help us appreciate the significance for our ability to access knowledge, is the notion of habitus. *Habitus* is an acquired pattern of thoughts, judgments, outlook, values, behavior, and taste as an outcome of internalizing standards and expectations from exemplars and significant others, from culture and social structures. Our habitus occurs below the level of consciousness, in the interplay between our environment, the social structures and activities in which we engage, the choices we make, the decisions we take, and our regular mode of being, of interpreting and

---

14. Lucas, *Sensing the Sacred*, 203; emphasis in original.
15. Gregorian, "Higher Education," 149.
16. Jacobsen and Jacobsen, *Scholarship & Christian Faith*, 56.

engaging the world. Premodern Christian educators, both in the patristic period and during the medieval centuries, put great emphasis on the importance of fostering in students an appropriate habitus. Stephen Jaeger connects habitus to the following cluster of words: attitude, inner posture, frame of mind, stance, and position.[17] It has obvious links with the clothing or habit worn by a monk or nun and the notion was extended to refer to posture understood as "both the position taken on an issue and the position in which the body is held."[18] Premodern Christian teachers took it for granted that motion and gesture, the way one carried oneself, one's emotions and impulses were interactive and mutually influential on how well we learn. For them it was natural to believe that the motion of the body is perhaps the most visible means of registering the inner state. Therefore education in manners was necessary because it was intended to train students to govern their impulses. In our age, when there seems to be a disconnection of morals and manners (personal habitus) from learning and an assumption that the operation of our intellect occurs quite separately from our passions, premodern assumptions about habitus can seem strikingly alien, yet also salutary.

Medieval historian Ayelet Even-Ezra distinguishes habitus from, on the one hand, an as yet undeveloped and merely potential ability and, on the other hand, sporadic, individual action; one's habitus is an already acquired ability that is also an abiding characteristic. She explains habitus with the following example: "In the field of learning, *habitus* is neither one's potential ability to learn French one day nor the actual speaking of one sentence or another at this or another moment. Rather, it is one's complete, internalized skill at speaking French."[19]

It is to be noted that our habitus is related to, indeed exerts a strong influence on, our worldview, but it works at a deeper level within us than our worldview. A worldview influences what we take in, what we notice, what we accept and how we perceive messages being sent to us by various individuals and groups. Our worldview filters reality for us; it helps us in deciding where and how we fit incoming lessons or messages into what we already hold, know, and are committed to; and what we do afterwards with what we have assimilated and learned. Worldview is about configuration, interconnectedness and mutual reinforcement in those leading perspectives we have that function as the keys to our main perceptions of reality and our judgments, but our ideas and viewpoints neither emerge on strictly logical

---

17. Jaeger, *Envy of Angels*, 9.
18. Jaeger, *Envy of Angels*, 10.
19. Even-Ezra, *Ecstasy in the Classroom*, 21.

lines nor do they get deployed on purely logical grounds. Rather they are embedded in a pattern of behaving and belonging that "carries" whatever reasoning goes into them beyond any strict remit that flows from reason alone. That is, people are formed (and sustained) in a worldview largely through the company they keep, the practices they engage in, and the lives they lead—this is their habitus. Their worldview gives them some kind of picture of the whole and a sense of meaning within the flux and ambiguities of life. It is rough and ready rather than sharply shaped; it is often not reflected upon, nor articulated; it operates clandestinely rather than explicitly in many cases. It can contain irreconcilable elements in such cases. Worldviews function partly as ways of framing the world for us, giving us a handle on it; they filter the world for us, so we can cope with parts of it without being overwhelmed by the sheer buzzing confusion of it all; they also help us to order it in terms of what we give our attention and energy and effort to and they help us to prioritize certain values without having to agonize each one out serially. For the most part our worldview is built on the prior foundation of our habitus. And that is why it is incumbent on educators to alert students to the influence of habitus on their capacity to learn and thus to the importance of growing in self-knowledge.

## ASCETIC TRAINING

Perhaps the most obvious difference between premodern and contemporary approaches to knowledge is the stress put in earlier times on the need for ascetic training and affective formation. We are familiar with the notion that disciplined training is a necessary prerequisite for sporting and musical achievement, but seem reluctant to appreciate the need for such training to be applied to our bodily practices, our emotions and desires, or those things to which we give our attention, treating these as disconnected from our efforts to come to knowledge in diverse fields. In this section I describe key features of ascetic training and end with a brief mention of two elements associated with it: first, affective formation, and second, the connection between cognition and character (in other words, the role of the virtues in our path towards knowledge). I do not have space here to treat two further features that were central to premodern Christian assumptions. The first of these was the vital importance attributed to communal learning—how participation in a like-minded community played a crucial role facilitating learning in depth, learning that could genuinely be assimilated, internalized, and put into practice. An influential secular example of similar thinking can be found in the notion of "communities of practice."[20] The second is what was perceived as the culmination of education, the capacity to engage in contemplation, considered as the highest stage of knowledge, reached only after and through the possibilities afforded by disciplining habits of attention, various kinds of ascetic training, and affective formation, allied to the development of the virtues.[21]

The need for ascetic training comes to the fore if we ask: What in us gets in the way of learning? What aspects of our nature—our desires, our feelings, our habits, our patterns of thinking, our priorities, our ways of attending to and engaging the world, our use of language and how we speak—need to be pruned, purged, reined in, purified, redirected? Traditionally, ascetic training aimed at discernment of how the senses are being used and how time and space are being used; recognizing and dealing with distractions; becoming conscious of what is besieging (obsessing) us. Spiritual teachers encouraged their students to question themselves. What are our energies being given to? Are we aware of our addictions? Do the routines and rhythms of our lives enhance or inhibit our capacity to learn? How are our hopes and dreams, our fears and anxieties, our virtues and vices affecting what and how we learn and what we do with what we learn? What are our inner resistances that we need help to overcome? What is closed or cluttered or crowded in our minds and hearts that might be an obstacle to the openness to learn and to change required of us if we are to develop? Have we areas of defensiveness where we block off questions or probing? In today's language, they might have asked students to become aware of their "no-go" areas, their "black holes" which cannot be entered.

Ascetic exercises were intended to engage with these aspects of life, so that they could be brought into line with the deepest purposes, the long-term goals, and the ideals aspired to by students. Ascetic education sought to bring people to recognize the dangers of self-indulgence in the pleasures of the flesh, whose attraction draws one away from higher goods and then to teach them how to ward off distractions that fill our time, disperse our energies, and obstruct us from the necessary focus on our relationship with God, virtuous living, and a healthy engagement with other people and creatures. In serving to free people from bondage to the world outside ourselves, ascetic education creates a space for the development of our inner resources. It also enables us to recognize, to receive, and to embrace spiritual wisdom, whereas what the world considers wise is incapable of

---

20. Wenger, *Communities of Practice*.

21. For a modern application of contemplative practices to secular university education, see Keator, *Lectio Divina*.

either comprehending or revealing the wisdom that comes only from God. Asceticism, whether carried out by individuals or under the supervision of a spiritual teacher, was a form of voluntary dispossession of what were considered to be lower goods in order to make oneself receptive to higher goods. Hughes quotes a definition given by Greg Peters: "Asceticism, as an essential component of spiritual growth, is the voluntary abstention from food and drink, sleep, wealth, sexual activity, and so on (for a period of time or permanently), for the purpose of maintaining inner attentiveness to God and achieving union with God."[22] Or, as Inbar Graiver describes it, "In a religious context, asceticism involves a voluntary, sustained, and systematic program of self-discipline and self-denial, in which immediate gratification is renounced in order to attain a higher spiritual state."[23]

Far from being based on a contempt for the body, ascetic training was part of a spiritual tradition that believed such training paved the way towards authentic freedom. What they had in mind was freedom *from* aspects of our nature that threatened to impede our development, constrain our horizons, imprison us by unworthy attachments—and freedom *for* a more exalted life, one lived in relationship with God and thereby with inner coherence, and in harmony with creation and other human beings. Adherents of this tradition held the optimistic belief that human inclinations and nature could be changed for the better through a combination of ascetic practice and the operation of divine grace. The self-control sought in asceticism differs from the self-rule held in mind in our current emphasis on autonomy, a self-rule that sees externally imposed discipline as an obstacle to freedom. Premodern Christians, in contrast, saw externally imposed discipline as an aid to the authentic development of inner freedom and enabling access to truth. Ascetic practices might include self-examination, concentration, renunciation, testing one's ability to resist temptations and to cope with bodily and spiritual suffering, and putting oneself in the care of or under the guidance of a mentor.[24]

For Dorotheus of Gaza, one of many exponents of ascetic education, a strong connection exists between the cognitive and noncognitive dimensions of our being. Such education operates simultaneously as therapeutic (or healing), disciplinary (or corrective) and transformative of bodies, emotions, minds, and spirits.[25] Habit formation is central, with regard to pat-

---

22. G. Peters, *Monkhood of All Believers*, 93, quoted in Hughes, *Teaching for Spiritual Formation*, 11n34.

23. Graiver, *Asceticism of the Mind*, 5.

24. Horujy, *Practices of the Self*, 29.

25. Champion, *Dorotheus of Gaza*, 55.

terns of sleep, diet, and careful stewardship of material possessions. Access to truth and the capacity to exercise moral judgment for Dorotheus, as for other ascetic teachers, depend on right habit formation. Jamie Kreiner quotes a later, seventh-century monk from Iran on the dangers of overconsumption of food:

> When the channels of the stomach are filled up and the organs which lead the light from the brain to the heart are blocked, the heart will be overspread with darkness, all the house will be filled with smoke, the limbs will suffer numbness, dejectedness will reign, the mind will be perturbed, the soul will darken, the discernment will become blind, knowledge will be hampered, judgement will be perplexed, (evil) thoughts will be set free, the remembrance of good things will be deleted from the heart, and the passions—the children of darkness—will receive fuel for their fire, will dance with joy, and applaud.[26]

Along with most other premodern Christian thinkers, Dorotheus understood fasting in an extended way, to include not only food, but also the words we use and the things we look at. Thus "the eradication of slander and falsehood, gossip and anger through the 'fasting of the tongue'" as well as guarding or custody of the eyes were both considered to be vital in helping to eradicate passions that prevented true perception and that made us unduly dependent on material things.[27]

It is important here to appreciate that the heart of ascetic practice was not so much curbing carnal desires (though it did require that) but more the capacitation of human nature—the capacity to receive the higher life made possible in relationship with God. Capacitation is a key term in a recent book by Hanna Lucas. The learning that is a fruit of ascetic practice is for her "intimately related to, or even becomes indistinguishable from *capacitation*: the capacity to receive and the capacity to change.... The idea of capacitation involves a sense of openness, acuity, and receptivity; a sense of power and clarity; and a sense of being suited to or made capable of heavenly participation."[28] She contrasts the being made capacious intended by patristic writers—"receptive, open, worthy, sensitive, and susceptible to the transfiguration of our nature that draws us into and fits us for union with

---

26. Kreiner, *Wandering Mind*, 92.
27. Champion, *Dorotheus of Gaza*, 61.
28. Lucas, *Sensing the Sacred*, 6; emphasis in original.

the divine"[29]—with the incapacitation that occurs "through the anesthetic skepticism of modernity."[30]

Affective formation is constituted by two strategies. First one attends to one's desires, emotions, and affections and notes how these are influencing our interpretation of experience, filtering it, distorting it, or enabling us to see it rightly. To the extent that we can recognize who and what is pulling our strings, affecting our motivation, steering our searching, then, to at least a little extent, we are liberated from being trapped in and by our current perspective. Only if we understand the power of our emotions to move us to be blind to some features of life or to misread our environment can we begin to see the point of going beyond mere scrutiny of these emotions, to attempt to regulate them, to redirect them more appropriately. Second, we need training in contemplation, to wait patiently before the object of study, in a way that allows the focus of our contemplation to "get through" to us, to speak to us on its own terms, rather than through the prism of our affective turbulence or our desire to manipulate it or control it for our own purposes. Here there is a connection between being dilated (stretched open, pushed further) and being delighted in a loving relationship with what we study and open ourselves to receive. Only if we learn to wonder at—and to be wounded by—the object of our study—will we allow ourselves to experience its potential power of healing and transformation.

There is no cognition without emotion. Because of their power to hinder or to support our attempts to teach and to learn, perhaps emotions and desires should be considered a category as relevant for educators as race, gender, or class. As Champion, in his study of Dorotheus shows, "Education is education of desire in two senses: it requires desire and affective intensity to direct attention, and it also trains and directs those desires to instill valued moral and affective behavior in ideal students."[31] Affectivity shapes thought and action, perceptions and communal life. Our affections cannot help but exert influence on others and theirs unavoidably impinge on us. Teachers who come across as unable to read the emotional climate in a classroom, who treat this as irrelevant to their educational task, or who neglect to help students examine and regulate their emotions themselves need to learn from their premodern predecessors who were well advanced in matters of emotional intelligence.

Just as there is no cognition without emotion, so too character has noetic effects. "Character can inform or distort cognition; virtue enables

---

29. Lucas, *Sensing the Sacred*, 9.
30. Lucas, *Sensing the Sacred*, 18.
31. Champion, *Dorotheus of Gaza*, 126.

vision; vice obscures it." Baehr connects character traits to our intellectual activity: "*attentive* observation, *thoughtful* or *open-minded* imagination, *patient* reflection, *careful* and *thorough* analysis, *fair-minded* interpretation and assessment."[32] Many intellectual virtues contribute to scholarship: carefulness, fair-mindedness, honesty, humility, intellectual generosity, judgment, open-mindedness, perseverance, prudence, reflectiveness, rigor, patience, empathy, modesty, integrity. Even if the term "virtue epistemology" is one with which many people outside the academic world are not familiar, we commonly employ expressions that are integral to it, when we either accuse someone of being rash in their judgments, of being wishy-washy or timid in making a decision, cowardly in the face of opposition, or gullible when presented with flawed arguments; or we praise someone for being open-minded, courageous in taking a principled stand, cautious in marshaling evidence and argument in support of a decision or viewpoint, robust and resilient in the face of opposition, wise in taking a long-term perspective and balancing and integrating apparently conflicting values and principles. Being intellectually virtuous entails assessing credentials before granting trust, weighing arguments, considering evidence, and interrogating motives (our own and those of others). Closed-mindedness, bias, self-deception, and intellectual pride block the way to knowledge and wisdom; they hinder or obscure the workings of our perception, memory, intuition, reasoning, and judgment. As an antidote to such vices we need humility linked both to patience in the arduous process of learning and to docility (willingness to be taught) and open-mindedness (not thinking I already know all there is to be know about something). Such virtues are among those integral to the kinds of ascetic education I have been referring to above.

## THE PILGRIM AND THE PROJECT MANAGER

In part 2 I contrasted two metaphors or images of the student: as pilgrim and as project manager; the first is concerned with opening oneself up to be changed; the second is about changing some aspect of the world. Both are needed. It is right that students should be equipped to take their place in the world, that their agency is developed so that they can contribute in an effective and constructive way in the world of work, as a citizen and in meeting the practical challenges of daily life. My retrieval of premodern approaches to learning in no way calls in question the need to ensure that students grow in various forms of technical competence, that they are efficient in searching for and deploying data and in bringing this to bear on

---

32. Baehr, *Inquiring Mind*, 1; emphasis in original.

issues and problems in the world. It is not wrong to want them to learn how to be useful and productive. But it also matters a great deal that students are helped to grow in self-knowledge, that they learn how to wrestle with questions about meaning and purpose in their lives, that they are challenged to deepen their capacity for self-examination and self-control, and that they are assisted in giving serious attention to their inner life, the things to which they give their time and energies, so that they become aware of the degree to which the habits they are developing and the company they keep really serve their deepest sense of identity and their long-term purposes. It also matters that they are encouraged to become as adept in their capacity for receptivity and for contemplation as they are in exercising agency in and on the world. Some familiarity with the kind of ascetic training and affective formation that was prevalent in premodern Christian approaches to knowledge could offer students an element in their education which could serve as a counterweight and complement to the assumptions and practices into which they are currently being inducted.

In my view, the church and the university need each other, with each offering perspectives and resources that simultaneously support, challenge and enhance the work of the other. Here I have indicated some of the ways that premodern Christian approaches to knowledge, although they at first sight seem alien to and inappropriate for twenty-first-century universities, might offer a salutary contrast to some of the assumptions that students are imbibing, mostly unconsciously, during their time at university. The possibilities of retrieving such premodern ways of thinking and practice are severely limited, and any attempt to introduce them to students would have to be conducted with care and discretion, bearing in mind the vastly different context and clientele. Nevertheless, Christian tradition, in particular in its premodern emphases, has within it an alternative vision of the educational endeavor. Such a vision, if presented to students, could, at the least, allow them—through an encounter, even if only a brief one, with a starkly contrasting alternative—to become more conscious of the nature of the assumptions that are operative in themselves and in their institutions. And such an encounter, could, at its best, prompt them to consider aspects of their life that deserve serious attention and that otherwise would not even be considered.

# 13

# Towards the Real Presence of Teachers

I THINK OF TEACHING as a life touching another's life and facilitating the emergence of new life, where new possibilities for living are introduced, proposed, modeled, and made accessible and attractive—so that learners feel invited to step into that new life. A teacher might ask herself: What is lighting up my life, giving it energy, direction, purpose, significance and warmth? What is darkening my life, causing stress, fear, tiredness, tension or confusion? And what answers might my students give to the same questions? Perhaps teaching is partly about building bridges between our respective lights and shadows, so that hearts can come into communion with one another. Insofar as there any truth in this view of teaching, then being really present to pupils will be a life-enhancing gift to them.

Teaching is a personal activity in a public arena. There are responsibilities to be carried out and it does matter that high standards of performance are developed and maintained. There is a crucial degree of accountability necessary for teachers engaged in offering a public service and where the development, progress, freedom, and happiness of young people are entrusted to teachers. But teachers are neither mechanics nor functionaries dutifully carrying out someone else's plans; they are centers of initiative and judgment in their own right, requiring a certain degree of autonomy and discretion if they are to have room to develop and exercise vision, imagination, energy, sensitivity, enthusiasm, creativity—all of which are expressions of real presence and each of which enhances real presence.

The focus of this chapter is on the personhood of teachers and how they are present to their pupils, rather than their academic subject knowledge or their professional competence. After summarizing the purpose, as I see it, of Christian education, there are five steps to my argument. First, I stress the importance of teachers as well as the some of the challenges they face in Catholic schools. Second, I outline the complex set of factors that influence how the personhood of teachers is brought into play with students before third, introducing and explaining the notion of perichoretic pedagogy: the interaction between teacher and student that can become a mutual indwelling. Fourth, I suggest that gentleness—not usually treated in the literature about teaching—can foster real presence in the classroom.[1] Finally, I acknowledge a range of limitations that inevitably constrain the degree of presence that it is possible to achieve in the classroom.

The purpose of Christian education is to encourage people to understand, appreciate, internalize, embrace, embody, and communicate the gospel of Jesus Christ by cultivating a Christian lifestyle based on the values of the kingdom of God. Christian education includes activities and experiences that elicit the awakening, nurturing, maturing, expression, sharing, and practice of Christian faith. Catholic schooling is an arena for witnessing to an educational vision inspired and illuminated by Christian faith and tradition in a faithful, realistic, imaginative, inclusive, and effective way.

## THE VITAL IMPORTANCE OF TEACHERS AND THE CHALLENGES THEY FACE

It is difficult to overstate how major a factor is the teacher in Catholic education and in the communication of faith. The teacher's general level of education, self-confidence, enthusiasm for and commitment to the task, familiarity with the tradition, relationship with the church, attitude towards children/young people/adults, as well as his or her ability to ask good questions, willingness to draw on/witness to personal experience, and capacity to elicit trust and to foster cooperation and to promote openness and willingness to contribute in students or adult learners—all these make a huge difference, regardless of curriculum, resources, institution, location, or social setting.

The Sacred Congregation for Catholic Education lists the qualities of the teacher to be looked for: professional commitment, support of truth, justice and freedom, openness to the point of view of others, an attitude of service, personal commitment to students, solidarity with everyone, and a life that is moral in all its aspects.[2] This can be an intimidating list of requirements, and it clearly depends on teachers having a strong sense

---

1. For an argument that complements, along a different trajectory, the case I make for gentleness as an appropriate expression of the teacher's presence to learners and as being space making and life giving, see Burt, "I Have Called You Friends."

2. Congregation for Catholic Education, "Educating Together," §52.

of vocation as well as professionalism. The teacher led by professionalism concentrates on putting into practice the goals expected of the profession's members, using the appropriate methods that she has been trained in and looking for outcomes considered signs of being effective. She lives within an ethos formed during her training and induction and shared with other members of the profession she has chosen. The teacher led by a sense of vocation sees everything she does in the light of responding to a call from God to use her talents for others in this way; this includes her successes, her failures, her guiding values, herself as a child of God, precious in his eyes, regardless of what the world thinks, and the children or students she teaches as made in God's image, worthy of her patience, love, expertise, and self-giving.

Of course, these two ambiences for teaching do not have to contradict one another; they can go together; they can work in harmony. I think the second understanding significantly enriches the first; how we see our role, ourselves, our colleagues, the pupils (and their parents), and what kind of "game" it is we are playing—this can make a huge difference to how we put our professionalism to use, as well as the tone and spirit with which we do so.

The teacher hoping to share Christian faith in a Catholic school faces a range of challenges, for example, holding one's nerve, being true to the best of our living tradition, and remaining open to and invitational towards people with a diversity of views. This requires a combination of emotional rootedness and stability, depth of understanding, and flexibility and creativity in responding to people. Teachers who lack confidence cannot be effective in helping their students. At the same time, being overconfident can be damaging to the development of others. But still, it is important that teachers have self-belief and confidence in the value of what they are doing, and that they are aware that they are modeling how mature adults cope with both conviction and questions.

Teachers are expected to hold in creative tension a range of polarities in their how they relate to their pupils. Such polarities include: control and care; custody and courtship; transmission and transformation; agency and receptivity; being both dialogical and directive; tradition oriented and contemporary; active and contemplative; and being faithful to both text and context. Also to be considered are other polarities teachers must balance, for example, closeness to pupils and distance from them; vulnerability and robustness; bonding and leave-taking (by leave-taking, I mean teachers avoiding creating undue dependency in pupils, and preparing for a self-imposed redundancy: one day pupils will need to do without their teacher). Teachers are expected to be accessible to their pupils, but also, if they are to help them grow, teachers should, in some ways, be disturbing, disorienting, and surprising. They must be both demanding and accepting, challenging and supportive. They need to hold together authority and freedom; structure and flexibility or creativity; constraint and liberation.

All teachers play a role that mediates between the world of adults and that of children and young people. As Leonardo Franchi and Robert Davis point out, "It is in the person of the teacher that we encounter the intersection of inherited culture and contemporary creativity. . . . The educated teacher—the living link between inherited traditions and the hopes and aspirations of current generations—must be conservative/traditional and liberal/progressive: going beyond . . . transient false dichotomies."[3] Franchi and Davis are right in claiming that "the teacher is the human link between tradition, the present, and the future."[4] But that mediating role is complicated by the teacher's position within a network of roles. Alberto Gil and Guido Gili draw on an analysis of speaker roles developed by the sociologist Erving Goffman.[5] There is the *animator*, the person who transmits a message. Then there is the *author*, the person who creates the message. And there is the *principal*, the person, group, or institution in whose name you speak, on whose behalf you speak and who takes responsibility for what is said. While the same person can be all three, the animator, the author, and the principal of communication, the three roles can also be separated and distributed among different subjects. The classroom teacher is certainly the animator, but not necessarily the author of the message and has obligations to the principal. As Gil and Gili note, "When a person becomes part of a group, of an organization or an institution, his communicative acts do not involve *just* his individual responsibility, but even the image and the reputation of the whole group which he belongs to and represents (and conversely, the positive or negative image of the group or the organization is also reflected onto him)."[6] I am not here going into the relationship between the teacher and the church, but it should be obvious that the mediating role of the teacher in a Catholic school—between the church and the generation in school—has an important bearing on both the teacher's experience and how she is perceived by pupils.

To be effective, teachers and educational leaders should go beyond mere competence; they need honesty, humility, humanity, and hope. To sustain these for the long haul, they require conviction (with regard to

---

3. Franchi and Davis, "Catholic Education and Curriculum," 108.
4. Franchi and Davis, "Catholic Education and Curriculum," 114.
5. Gil and Gili, "Transmission or 'Creative Fidelity,'" 329.
6. Gil and Gili, "Transmission or 'Creative Fidelity,'" 330; emphasis in original.

their fundamental principles), courage (in how they put these into practice in face of difficulties, opposition, and disappointments), and compassion (for those on the receiving end of their work). These are deeply personal qualities.

## MEDIATING TEACHERS' PERSONHOOD

Many factors influence how the personhood of teachers is brought into play. Here are nine. First is the mandate they are given—what they are authorized to do, the permission they are given, and associated expectations. Second, there is the level of maturity of the teacher (not necessarily always related to their age). Third, their sense of themselves in relation to the role (their understanding of this and the degree of acceptance and confidence they bring to such self-identification). Fourth, their relationship with students and how well they know them. Fifth, how honest and vulnerable they are willing to be. Sixth, their self-knowledge and self-awareness: their ability to reflect on how they are coming across as a person to students, their alertness to how they are being received, and their ability to reflect on how the job is affecting them as a person. A self-aware and reflexive teacher asks herself: Who am I? What matters most to me in this situation? What is happening in me as I teach? How am I managing myself in this role? How is who I am affecting how I am being received? Seventh, their sense that "this game is worth playing"; that is, their intrinsic motivation; this is quite separate from any sense of success, competence, status, or reward/recognition. Eighth, how well they integrate the intellectual, professional/practical, and spiritual dimensions of the role; most teachers need help throughout their career in managing such integration. Finally, the importance they give to the primacy of being over doing, of interiority over performativity; thereby enabling real presence—to self, students, colleagues, parents, and God.

## PERICHORETIC PEDAGOGY

This brings me to *perichoretic pedagogy*. By this term I mean the way that teacher and student enter into or indwell each other and mutually modify each other in a relationship that parallels the Trinitarian relationship that is dynamic and self-giving, creative and overflowing. *Perichoresis* is a theological term used to describe the mutual indwelling of the persons of the Trinity. Although each person permeates the other two in this relationship, they do not cease to be distinct persons; they do not lose their specific role. Their inner life is made up of both distinction and union, since "persons who have dissolved into one another cannot exist in one another."[7] St. Augustine puts it like this: "So potent is the feeling of sympathy, that when they are moved as we speak and we as they learn, we abide each with the other; and thus they, as it were, speak in us what they hear, while we, in a manner, learn in them what we teach."[8] In other words, teachers and students change each other. Students surprise us by their singularity. They learn something different than what we teach them. They break through our expectations (positive and negative). We experience them as a foreign country. They make demands on us that force us to be more attentive to their otherness, rather than taking them for granted. Although we want them to be like us in some aspect of knowledge or skill, they cannot be a copy; they are—like us—originals. Our courses are intended for the general student, but we face real individuals. The material is new for them; through them, it becomes new for us. Their worlds are (at least slightly) changed in their encounter with us; our world is also changed when we respond to who they are.

Parker Palmer described another kind of indwelling: the way a teacher's knowledge of her subject lives within her.

> The teacher who knows the subject well, must introduce it to students in the way one would introduce a friend. The students must know why the teacher values the subject, how the subject has transformed the teacher's life. By the same token, the teacher must value the students as potential friends, be vulnerable to the ways students may transform the teacher's relationship with the subject as well as be transformed. If I am invited into a valued friendship between two people, I will not enter in unless I feel that I am valued as well.[9]

The teacher has to feel "at home" with the material she teaches if she is to be able to help others to feel invited into it and at home with it. And, as Maria Lichtmann, "Someone needs to be at home for our students to feel welcome."[10] If the teacher feels at home with herself, the material, and her students, her presence to students comes across as authentic and engaged, and this increases the chances that the classroom will feel hospitable to her students.

Perhaps more than most figures from the Catholic educational tradition, John Henry Newman has stressed the importance of the personal

---

7. Volf, *After Our Likeness*, 209. On participation and union with God, see also Borysov, *Triadosis*.

8. Augustine, *On Catechizing the Uninstructed*, 31.

9. Palmer, *To Know as We Are Known*, 103.

10. Lichtmann, *Teacher's Way*, 93.

influence of the teacher, especially in communicating faith.[11] For him, the personal influence of teachers on students displays a living embodiment of an idea in action; it provides an example of how something that is being taught can be significant and operative in a person's life; it enables students to witness firsthand through their teachers how knowledge can transform lives by deepening understanding, providing motivation, reinforcing confidence, facilitating coherence, and guiding action.[12] "Persons influence us, voices melt us, looks subdue us, deeds inflame us," he says in *A Grammar of Assent*, pointing out the power of personal presence and encounter, a power quite lacking in a purely cerebral exercise.[13] The personal presence of the teacher is "the living voice, the breathing form, the expressive countenance" in communication. "Truth, a subtle, invisible, manifold spirit, is poured into the mind of the scholar by his eyes and ears, through his affections, imagination, and reason."[14] Through their personal encounter with teachers, students receive some aspect of that teacher's understanding, attitudes, and commitments; it becomes their own; it comes to dwell in them as a resource for living.

## GENTLENESS

In the midst of language about competence, standards, targets, and outcomes, an important quality which facilitates real presence in the classroom can be neglected. This is gentleness. It is interesting to note that, in proposing areas for further reflection and research, the *Vademecum: Global Compact on Education* refers to "a revolution of tenderness."[15] I hope that the following thoughts on gentleness will contribute to that further reflection. What does gentleness entail? What does it mean to be gentle?

Gentleness is connected to a sense of gratitude. The person or object before me is not mine; it is not my possession; I don't own it; it is given to me; it comes from Another; I did not earn it; it comes as a free gift. A gift I feel grateful for. A gift that I can learn from; a gift which can enrich me.

Gentleness can only lead to an openness to the receptivity of a gift if I am not too full of myself; this can happen only if I do not think I know all I need to know or that I have all I need, or that I already am what I should be. Gentleness then is somehow related to humility, my awareness of my

---

11. Newman, *University Sermons*, 7–8.
12. Sullivan, "University," 546–48.
13. Newman, *Essay in Aid of Grammar*, 89.
14. John Henry Newman, quoted in Crosby, *Personalism of Newman*, 93.
15. Congregation for Catholic Education, *Vademecum*, 35.

limitations and my own need for completion and for correction. Without gentleness in the face of others, I close down the possibility of truly learning from them. I deliberately make myself a lesser person because I fail to open myself properly their own giftedness and goodness. Without humility and the openness that accompanies it, which is a form of freedom, I lock myself in a self-imposed prison.

Gentleness for me is also linked to reverence. What is before me has its own dignity; its worth does not come from me; it is inherent in that person or creature or thing. Rather than grasp it for my own use or pleasure or purposes, first I must see it for what it (or him or her) is; their inherent uniqueness, as something valuable in their own right. To have reverence for someone or something is to approach it carefully, to show respect, to treat as important, to see as a source of value. To have reverence for someone or something is to sense that that person or object has some kind of claim on us. He, she, or it is not something we should be trying to control; they are not a means to our ends; they are an end in themselves.

Gentleness is not the same as weakness, being feeble or passive; it is not the fruit of a false understanding of humility—assuming that I am worthless. These feelings may be forced on us by circumstances and quite involuntary; but they are not virtues in the way that gentleness definitely is a virtue. Gentleness comes from strength. It can be displayed only by a person who has some power to act but who decides to constrain that action, to limit what they do, to hold back some of their energy, force, or vigor they could exert, because not to act with such restraint would be to damage the person or the object. Such self-limitation, is done, not through fear, but through a desire to avoid or at least to minimize the destructive possibilities carried by our words or actions.

Gentleness seems also to be related to appreciation and expectation, in that a gentle attitude towards others is both a sign of and a reinforcing of a sense of their worth, their possibilities, and their capacity for growth and for giving. That leads us to nurture some expectation of them. That makes me wonder: How far do we live up to (or want to live up to) the expectations that others have of us, when their expectations of us are positive? How far do we feel inclined to live down to their negative expectations of us? If people show high regard for us, does that not often encourage us to try to live up to their hopes of us? Do their low expectations demotivate us to give our best efforts? In other words, perhaps gentleness towards others gives them the space, the affirmation, and the will to live more fully into their potential, to be the best person they can be.

The teacher's face and voice give out clues and send out signals about what really matters in her or his life. Students can tell when their teachers are being real or simply going through the motions as they seek to convey messages. As Carrón observes, "If our presence is not a witness to the fullness of life and the change of mentality that faith bring to dealing with all circumstances, its effect will be minimal."[16] Who we are and what matters to us—these come across more strongly than what we know. "Only if I become a presence through the way I live reality do I awaken the interest of others."[17] It is our duty as teachers to grow in our self-knowledge, to be in touch with our deep sources of motivation and meaning, if our teaching is to sound authentic and to come alive for our students, for only then can we be really present to them.

## LIMITATIONS

There are limitations on the degree to which the real presence of teachers in classrooms can be achieved. Sometimes, the mandate given to teachers imposes constraints that call for a narrow interpretation of their role and that give little scope for personalizing their activity. In some cases, a teacher's level of maturity and confidence is insufficient to empower him or her to do more than remain safely within a prescribed role. Then there are other calls on a teacher's energy and commitment than simply those of a particular class; first, there are other classes to be prepared for, taught and whose work needs to be assessed; second, teachers have a home life which makes its own demands. A work-life balance needs to be maintained. Overexertion that leads to burnout will not be a wise deployment of a teacher's energy; nor will it provide a healthy model of personhood to pupils. To replenish the self and the resources which are drawn on in the constant self-giving entailed by teaching, teachers need to attend to their own needs for rest, for affirming personal relationships, and for renewing their sense of vocation. Furthermore, if teachers take seriously their duty to acknowledge, to receive, to respect, to learn from and to respond to the real presence of students in their pedagogical encounters, then doing so will inevitably serve both to provide opportunities for, as well as to cause them to sense constraints on, how much of themselves they can share with and give to their classes.

Teachers should not see themselves as solo performers; rather, they participate in a collaborative ministry. Either explicitly or implicitly, teachers usually work as part of a team, where the contribution of one has implications for the work of others. Just as is the case in the family, where our

16. Carrón, *Disarming Beauty*, 153.
17. Carrón, *Disarming Beauty*, 171.

individual initiatives and responses are affected by the behavior and personality of others (siblings and parents), so too an individual teacher's mode of presence to pupils is enhanced and modified by association with the mode of presence of other teachers. Together they comprise a guild. In the past, guilds played an important role in upholding professional standards in craftsmanship and in scholarship, in fostering fellowship, fraternity, and solidarity, in providing economic support, and in promoting pastoral and spiritual care.[18] Each teacher influences the climate of reception for the others. His or her particular presence and contribution is linked to that of colleagues. That teacher's mode of presence either reinforces the contribution of others or it undermines it. How other members of the guild perceive an individual teacher will be conveyed to pupils even if these teachers never make their views explicit. The acceptance or rejection of my exercise of my role as teacher will be influenced by the pupils' assessment of the general consensus of other teachers about what counts as good teaching.

Sometimes it is incumbent on a teacher deliberately not to accept the consensus of her peers about particular pupils, leading her to treat a pupil with greater compassion, lenience or respect than others (or to withhold these responses if they believe that the judgment of other colleagues about a pupil is misguided). While generally accepting the need for displaying loyalty to and support for one's fellow teachers, this stance cannot be at the cost of personal integrity, the demands of truth and justice, or the duty of care for pupils. Keeping company with other colleagues, in the sense of collaborating and providing mutual support, has its place, but also its limitations.[19]

How I conduct myself as a teacher—the way I am present to my students—will necessarily be influenced and shaped by my perception of their gifts and needs. This perception of mine should take into account my observation of and my listening to the students, as well as being guided by relevant professional literature, the views of parents, and the consensus of fellow teachers who know the students well. My perception of the needs of learners should also be guided by what I believe is true and important for a life well lived, the degree of self-knowledge and wisdom I possess, and by what I am permitted and prevented from doing by those in authority over my work context.

* * *

18. Rosser, *Art of Solidarity*; Courtenay, *Rituals for the Dead*.
19. On teaching as a corporate activity, see Sullivan, "Keeping Company."

The students' trust in the teacher is elicited in the dynamic and unpredictable interpersonal exchange between teachers and learners; it depends on respect for the teacher's competence and character; it relies on consent and cannot be compelled. Trust facilitates a willingness on the part of learners to risk participation and to exercise agency. When trust, consent, and active involvement are encouraged, teachers create the conditions for ownership of learning by students—it becomes *theirs*, a personal possession, not something external or alien, to be discarded as soon as circumstances allow. When this happens, the teacher's real presence to her students has facilitated in them the emergence and more confident expression of their own real presence—to themselves, to each other, to the teacher, and to the subject matter at hand—and, at the same time, it has equipped them to receive the presence of the divine in multiple ways.

# 14
# Vulnerability, Affectability, and Openness to the Divine

AN APPRECIATION OF THE CAPACITY for being moved is relevant for those involved in any form of *psychagogia*—the art of moving souls. This includes teachers, politicians, psychologists, advertisers, lawyers, and those involved in acts of religious communication (for example, preaching, spiritual direction, catechesis, and pastoral care). The tasks of all these are in some way rhetorical in their operation. That is, apart from considering the *logos* or rationality of the message they seek to convey and in addition to being conscious of the *ethos* or trustworthiness and credibility of the message bearer, they have to take into account the *pathos*, the feelings and needs of those they wish to influence. Consideration of our affectability is also helpful for our self-knowledge. In this chapter I explore vulnerability as a key aspect of a Christian understanding of human persons and I argue that vulnerability has positive as well as negative connotations. Although vulnerability is first and always experienced as an involuntary condition, as an unavoidable and uncomfortable feature of human experience, the response we make to such vulnerability can render us open to a better understanding of ourselves and other people, and it can prompt us to become open to the offer of divine grace, love and life. This response—and the ensuing outcome—is not guaranteed, but it remains a promising possibility. My claim is that vulnerability (which entails our affectability by and to others) is a prerequisite for development, learning, healthy and loving relationships, and deification.

There are four parts to the chapter. First, after very briefly setting my treatment of this topic within the wider context of the notion of human persons being made in the image of God, I reflect on the nature of vulnerability and its potential for making us open to the divine. Second, in relating affectability to affectivity, I take into account three recent treatments of the heart as revelatory of important but neglected aspects of human nature (those by Peter John McGregor, Dietrich von Hildebrand, and Beáta Tóth). Third, I explore human responses to the experience of vulnerability, both the temptation to close oneself off (insofar as this is possible) or to open oneself up to something and someone beyond oneself. Part 4 traces the connection between experiences of limitation and opportunities for learning. In conclusion, I summarize the principal points of the argument.

## VULNERABILITY

For St. Augustine, intellect, memory, and will were central to his understanding of how human beings reflected the image of God. Others have located the image in the various ways: in rationality and intelligence, in freedom to choose, in the capacity for understanding and loving God, in symbol use, in creativity, in purposeful action, in self-reflection, in language, and in questioning. The image of God in humanity has also been identified as inhering in the ability to see what is not immediately present to us, in imagination, in dominion over other creatures, in the sense of moral obligation and the operations of conscience. And, of course, the image of God has been found in our spiritual nature, in our orientation to God and our capacity to seek, to reflect on and to respond to God's will. As Nonna Verna Harrison points out, "Theologians and spiritual writers have found the divine image in many different aspects of what we are, what we can and should do, and what we are called to become."[1] Among these, she refers to freedom, spiritual perception, connectedness to God, virtues, royal dignity, and a vital connection to the natural world, reason, creativity, personal uniqueness, community, mystery, and life. She adds, "They are many facets of the splendid jewel that each human person can become." It is notable that vulnerability does not appear in such attempts to locate the features of human nature that make us open to God, perhaps because such attempts focus on our capacity for agency and tend to neglect receptivity.

We find we cannot meet all our needs, secure all our hopes, live fully according to our best aspirations; that the world cannot deliver what it promises; but the realization of this powerlessness—on our part and that of others—seems to make us conscious that there remains something in us that is aware of the possibility of such fulfilment and harmony. Vulnerability can be experienced as either isolating or shared; it can make us feel cut off from others or that we have something in common with them. We

---

1. Harrison, *God's Many-Splendored Image*, 5.

can choose to hide our vulnerability, to resist it, to fear it, to resent it, or to accept its limitation as an essential part of the human condition. We should not confuse fragility with being fallen; these conditions may be connected but they are not identical. Human finitude and fragility are the fine and flimsy wires through which can run the current of God's healing, uplifting, empowering, and fulfilling grace, grace that is invisible in its operation but evident in its effects. The same "wires" transmute our response of gratitude for what we have received into an overflow of that gratitude in the form of generosity towards others.

Stephen Kampowski proposes that our life, given in birth and taken by death, is radically marked by finitude, which can be a source of great fear and anguish. Our finitude, however, does not in itself need to be something negative. It confronts us with the question of our life's meaning and spurs us on to treasure our days. Our contingency, as evidenced in our birth and death, reminds us that we have not made ourselves and that there is nothing necessary about the marvelous fact that we exist. Particularly from a Judeo-Christian perspective, embracing our finitude will mean gratefully accepting life as a completely gratuitous gift and living one's days informed by a sense of this gratitude.[2]

We can consider vulnerability as a mystery to be entered into rather than as a problem to be solved. It can serve to open a door that allows us to enter into the lives of others and into the life of God. As wounded healers who are susceptible to pain, we are not only conscious of our need for help but also enabled to be compassionate to others. Many human and spiritual goods seem to require dilation before delight, being stretched open before being able to receive more; often there has to be a breakdown before a breakthrough is possible. In an age which emphasizes self-protection, self-determination, radical individualism, and autonomy, it seems countercultural to recognize and accept "being given," human interdependence, and ultimate dependency on the divine.

To be invulnerable is to be someone who cannot be affected, someone for whom nothing matters very much; for whom change is unnecessary; for whom mutuality is out of reach. There is no room in oneself to allow others entry and therefore one rules out in advance any prospect of being enriched by others. We are not called to be invincible but to acknowledge our vulnerability, to accept it, to persevere despite it, to learn from it, where appropriate to share it, and, in the light of it, to reach out to others in their vulnerability, and to welcome God's constant and graceful help as we live with and through our own vulnerability as fragile and finite, wounded and

---

2. Kampowski, *Embracing Our Finitude*.

## VULNERABILITY, AFFECTABILITY, AND OPENNESS TO THE DIVINE

wounding people, in need of being forgiven and of being forgiving, in need of correction and completion, of affirmation and encouragement. Our acceptance of vulnerability however, does not excuse us from being willing to be called to go beyond where we are now and to take the risk of opening ourselves to transformation.

Love and vulnerability seem connected: the deeper the love is, the more of the self is implicated and committed. Vulnerability seems a prerequisite for a more expansive existence, a more abundant life. It is no consolation, but salutary, to realize that our wounds, physical, mental, social, spiritual, help to render us more susceptible to our need for God's healing and transforming grace. When things seem to be going well, we are tempted to be much less aware of our unfinished and dependent nature and less focused on opening ourselves to divine life. Only when the props we too often rely on let us down do we become conscious of being held in God's arms, in both our strength and in our weakness. To receive life as gift is to acknowledge that we are fundamentally dependent creatures, dependent both on other people and on God, for our survival, our learning and development, and for our flourishing. Our essential and inescapable dependency renders us also fundamentally equal, in need of others who are in need of us and all in need of God. What we have in common is a capacity to receive God's gifts freely and to share them with others.

Willingness to accept dependency goes against the grain of our current cultural mindset. The Benedictine monk Luke Bell observes:

> The contemporary tendency is to think of our belonging to each other as something negotiated by independent individuals. Yet it is not like that at all. . . . We do not have words; we receive them from other people. We do not have food; we receive it from others. We little by little learn to take part in a conversation that began long before we were there. . . . We can only contribute what we are given. . . . We do not have a history; we receive it from those who are older than us. It is impossible for a separated individual even to survive for long, let alone flourish, in the days following birth.[3]

Such dependency is not an assault on our dignity; it is an integral part of our natural condition as created beings, one that has implications for the moral life, as noted by Alasdair MacIntyre.[4]

Vanessa Herrick and Ivan Mann define vulnerability as "an openness to being wounded (physical or otherwise) which is motivated by love of

---

3. Bell, *Staying Tender*, 32.
4. MacIntyre, *Rational Dependent Animals*.

God and is the outcome of a voluntary relinquishment of the power to protect oneself from being wounded."[5] And they go on to quote Michael Ramsey: "In your service of others you will feel, you will care, you will be hurt, you will have your heart broken. And it is doubtful if any of us can do anything at all until we have been very much hurt and until our hearts have been very much broken."[6]

We can distinguish vulnerability (interpreted broadly) as, on the one hand, a condition that alerts us to our needs and reveals to us the impotence of our appetites to deliver what we desire, and, on the other hand, a willing embrace of vulnerability as an ethical and spiritual stance. Here I focus on the first of these, leaving the second for consideration in parts 3 and 4 of the chapter.

In a recent book review, Kelly Kapic claims that "fundamental need is a basic category for theological anthropology. . . . The characteristics of a creature determine its needs. When these needs are met the creature flourishes, and when they are withheld the creature is harmed. Understanding a creature's constitution, then, helps one better understand how it can flourish, and seeing how it flourishes can help us better appreciate its fundamental needs."[7] For a Christian, one of these fundamental needs is that of having a relationship with God. Kapic claims that "true and full human flourishing requires not just water and food, not just oxygen and human companionship, but also active dependence on God."[8]

And the Jesuit Richard Leonard warns that if we ignore our diverse appetites (physical, emotional, and spiritual), "we can forget where we came from, why we are here and where we are going."[9] We can be misdirected by our desires for status and stimulation, for convenience and comfort, fleeing from appreciating what might be learned from our limitations and insufficiencies, and, in so doing, we fail to realize that, as Mendlewicz notes,

> being vulnerable [is] the condition that makes all our experiences possible. . . . We are not watertight and closed beings. . . . Sickness, death, the anguish of being able to get sick or die, all these are part of our daily lives. But so are solidarity, co-responsibility, or the joy of living in a community. Why, then, when we

---

5. Herrick and Mann, *Jesus Wept*, 5.
6. Herrick and Mann, *Jesus Wept*, 69.
7. Kapic, Review of *God's Provision*, 954.
8. Kapic, Review of *God's Provision*, 956.
9. Leonard, "Season of Joy," 10–11.

talk about vulnerability, do we usually associate it with negative and non-constructive experiences?[10]

Thus, as a condition, vulnerability is double edged: it can make us so conscious of our deficits that it opens a door to depression; or, it can prompt us towards a constructive life of cooperation with others. We might be glad, as Mendlewicz suggests,

> to be free of doubt, inconsistency, sadness, without perhaps noticing that those same experiences are what allow us to experience joy, hope, and love. Imperfection hurts, it is true, but the price of perfection is the impossibility of being affected by otherness.... Without vulnerability, there is no love.[11]

Our being affectable is a sign that we are currently incomplete, and this very sense of imperfection can bring home to us a need for transformation. Mendlewicz warns against two false responses we might make as we become aware of our affectability: "If, in individualism . . . [we] affirm [ourselves] as an autonomous being," thereby aiming to reduce or minimize our affectability, "in collectivism, it is believed that by renouncing decision and freedom in favor of the group" we thereby again seek to minimize our affectability.[12] In the first response we err by a vain attempt at self-defense, while in the second we err by surrendering responsibility for our actions. Both are acts of diminishment. In seeking safety from the negative aspects of vulnerability we close off the possibility of enjoying its potentially positive aspects. But here we should recall Newman's warning, "To be at ease is to be unsafe."[13]

## THE HEART

Our capacity to be moved, to be affected, is closely linked to our affections, those emotional responses we make to encounters and experiences. These can be responses of welcoming, enjoying, and attraction, or they can be responses of hostility, fear, and rejection. Traditionally, to speak about the heart's responses has been a way of referring to the depths of personhood, something central to their being. Although the capacity to love has been included in accounts of what constitutes the image of God in human persons, appreciation of the role of our affections has been somewhat neglected

10. Mendlewicz, *On Vulnerability*, 1.
11. Mendlewicz, *On Vulnerability*, 22.
12. Mendlewicz, *On Vulnerability*, 66–67.
13. Newman, *Parochial and Plain Sermons*, 1:56.

in the literature on Christian anthropology. My brief treatment here of the heart does not associate it with sentimentality, the passions or subjectivism; rather my concern is to link the heart with our capacity to be affected and moved by what life throws at us. I draw on three witnesses to or advocates for the importance of the heart.

The first of these commentators on the heart is the most recent, the Australian theologian Peter John McGregor, in an article that assembles resources for an anthropology of the heart. He begins by referring to common linguistic expressions about the heart:

> One can have soft, hard, warm, or cold heart. To indicate love or affection: I love you with all my heart. To indicate courage: take heart. To describe a person's character: he is a man after my own heart. To indicate knowledge: I knew in my heart. To indicate memory: I know it by heart.[14]

Then he points out that in Scripture the heart is used to indicate a range of human capacities and actions: knowing, believing, willing, conscience, the passions, imagination, and memory. It is, he says, "the place of relationships with other persons, the place which God searches and knows, the place of revelation and the refusal of revelation, and the place of God's indwelling."

After reference to Scripture, McGregor draws on Newman, Guardini, and Ratzinger to make some compelling observations about the role of the heart and human affectivity. I limit myself here to a comment on his deployment of the first two of these thinkers.

From Newman, he links the heart with conversion, an event, or perhaps better, a process, which occurs by touching the heart rather than simply by conquering the reason. McGregor quotes twice from Newman: first to show that conversion is not a merely cerebral process but one that occurs by the exercise of personal influence willingly accepted.[15] "Persons influence us, voices melt us, looks subdue us, deeds inflame us."[16] If we were not affectable, we would not be open to conversion. McGregor's second quotation from Newman refers to the role of the heart in providing the right context for a healthy faith: "A right state of heart . . . is what protects [faith] from bigotry, credulity, and fanaticism."[17]

---

14. McGregor, "Theological Anthropology of the Heart," 228.
15. McGregor, "Theological Anthropology of the Heart," 245.
16. Newman, *Essay in Aid of Grammar*, 89.
17. Newman, *University Sermons*, 234, quoted in McGregor, "Theological Anthropology of the Heart," 245.

## VULNERABILITY, AFFECTABILITY, AND OPENNESS TO THE DIVINE

McGregor's second source for an anthropology of the heart is Romano Guardini. For this theologian of German and Italian descent, the heart is the meeting place between two dimensions of the human person which need to be reconciled and integrated, the sensual and the intellectual, or the body and the mind. "The heart is the place where spiritual mind becomes human soul, and animal corporeity becomes human body"; it is also the place where knowing and loving become united. McGregor agrees with Guardini that "it is only through participation in the life of God that heart truly becomes heart, truly integrated, truly human, truly knowing, truly loving, truly pure, and truly free."[18]

Along with each of these thinkers (including Ratzinger) McGregor is keen to underline a key concern they all share about a disassociation of the intellectual faculty from the sensual-emotional-volitional faculties. When this happens, the use of reason slips into a thin form of rationalism and reference to human affections slips into subjectivism and sentimentality unguided by reason. McGregor describes this disassociation as "a *de-kardiazation* of reason."[19] Bypassing the heart damages both our use of reason and our reliance on our feelings.

My second witness to the importance of the heart is the German philosopher, Dietrich von Hildebrand (1899–1977). In his book *The Heart* he makes six points that have a bearing on this chapter. First, he emphasizes that the heart has equal importance with the will and the intellect, and he notes the danger that attention to the heart can be minimized when too much reliance is put on either the intellect or the will.[20]

Second, he describes an authentic response of the heart as being a value response, one where our focus is not on our feelings in themselves but on the object that we attend to, allowing it to penetrate, to get through, to us.[21] "In the value response, it is the intrinsic importance of the good which alone engenders our response and our interest."[22] As examples of such goods and the affective response they call forth, he proposes the following:

> To be moved by some sublime beauty in nature or in art or by some moral virtue, such as humility or charity, is to allow ourselves to be penetrated by the inner light of these values and to open ourselves to their message from above. It is a surrender which implies reverence, humility, and tenderness. The

---

18. McGregor, "Theological Anthropology of the Heart," 247.
19. McGregor, "Theological Anthropology of the Heart," 250.
20. Hildebrand, *Heart*, 16; 55–57.
21. Hildebrand, *Heart*, 5.
22. Hildebrand, *Heart*, 37.

readiness to let ourselves "be moved" is . . . indissolubly connected with a full and deep perception of certain values.[23]

Third, he distinguishes between psychic states which are caused and affective responses that are motivated.[24] Whereas psychic states happen to us without our willing consent, affective responses stem from our acknowledgment or recognition of something beyond us that we willingly unite ourselves to, as something that matters to us. When we are motivated to respond to some good, our freedom not only remains intact; in the exercise of freedom to reach out to the good, we further actualize or enhance our freedom.

Fourth, he depicts some of categories and features of what he calls tender affectivity:

> Tender affectivity manifests itself in all its categories: filial and parental love, friendship, brotherly and sisterly love, conjugal love and love of neighbor. It displays itself in "being moved," in enthusiasm, in deep authentic sorrow, in gratitude, in tears of grateful joy, or in contrition. It is the type of affectivity which includes the capacity for a noble surrender, affectivity in which the heart is involved.[25]

Fifth, Hildebrand stresses that the value responses and affectivity activated when we are so motivated are neither irrational nor merely subjective. "When someone is moved by a good endowed with a high value to such an extent that he is elevated above the normal rhythm of his life, . . . this does not result from a blurring of one's reason but, on the contrary, from its extraordinary elevation by an intuitive awareness which, far from being irrational, has rather a suprarational and luminous character."[26] Though he acknowledges that there can be affective experiences which have an antirational dynamism, an affective response can be objective if it "conforms to the true nature, theme, and value of the object to which it refers."[27]

Sixth, for Hildebrand, the very quality of a person's life depends on their making affective responses to the goods they discern to be calling out to them. This applies especially with regard to spiritual goods and values. "The world in which a man lives depends upon the breadth and depth and differentiation of his value perception. . . . If a man is to partake as

23. Hildebrand, *Heart*, 10.
24. Hildebrand, *Heart*, 26.
25. Hildebrand, *Heart*, 42–43.
26. Hildebrand, *Heart*, 30–31.
27. Hildebrand, *Heart*, 46.

a personality in the plenitude and glory of the world above him to which value perception opens the gates, it is indispensable that he be 'affected' and that he respond with affective responses."[28]

My third advocate for more attention to the given by scholars to the heart is Hungarian theologian Beáta Tóth. Like McGregor, she is very conscious of the dangers of irrational sentimentalism and of emotionally deficient rationalism; she too laments the disassociation between head and heart. For her, "A Christian vision of human affectivity is vital for our understanding of the human predicament and our relationship to God."[29] Without religious feeling, those things that we claim to believe lose their power to move us—to inspire, influence, or guide us. She points out that "Human affectivity, in being attached to the body and psychosomatic processes, has traditionally been regarded as lying outside the seat of human likeness to God, which has almost unanimously been located in the human intellect."[30] Her important book, which I cannot begin to do justice to here, goes some way to remedying this situation. She brings out the connectedness of reason and the emotions and the essential part played by emotions in intellectual activity. The final point I draw from her leads me directly into part 3 of this chapter:

> The heart is primarily the unified center of the human being, the place of encounter with one's own interiority, the site where one faces one's feelings, conscience, reason, and decisions, and as such, the symbolic site of encounter with God. The heart is the point where one can open up or close off from a relationship with God.[31]

## OPEN OR CLOSED

We find that vulnerability is an unavoidable given of the human condition, one that renders us finite, limited, prone to weaknesses of various kinds, lacking all we need or desire, and ultimately dependent on others. However, there remains the possibility that, instead of resenting, resisting or hiding from this condition, a response which would make us self-enclosed and isolated and that would imprison us, stunting our potential for learning, growth, and expansion of our being, our response can be one that opens

---

28. Hildebrand, *Heart*, 58.
29. Tóth, *Heart Has Its Reasons*, x.
30. Tóth, *Heart Has Its Reasons*, 144.
31. Tóth, *Heart Has Its Reasons*, 153.

us up to gifts from outside ourselves, whether human or divine. Such a response entails an active receptivity and a sense of gratitude.

There is a very close connection between dependence and gratitude; and between both of these and hope and joy. Unless we are conscious of our fundamental dependence on others (and on God), we won't be easily open to the sense of gratitude. If our experience, education and society tells us that we are autonomous individuals who become self-made people, that we can be who we want to be, that we are captains of our own soul or life; if all this tells us that we should not be dependent on others, that something is wrong with us if we have vulnerabilities; then gratitude for what is given to us gets reduced to mere politeness, rather than being truly and authentically gratitude. Our fundamental need is to have a personal relationship with the source and goal of our being, God, as made known to us in Jesus Christ and through the power and presence of his Holy Spirit. Even if all our other basic needs are met, without this need being met we are impoverished and unfulfilled.

I also associate gratitude with gladness, appreciation, receptivity, graciousness, the capacity to recognize what is given as gift, rather than as something earned or deserved. Gratitude acknowledges and affirms the one who is thanked. It confirms that the one who thanks does not take what is offered for granted. Without a sense of dependence and gratitude, hope has little hold on us, and what hope we do have will be more like gritting our teeth in the face of adversity than being lifted up by joyful acknowledgment of the promise inherent in existence.

The Canadian philosopher of the moral and spiritual life, Donald Evans (1927–2018), notes of those who are able to give much to others, that they are able to do so because they are open to receive. He suggests that "they have become open because they have acknowledged and dealt with whatever makes them closed. . . . Their openness is not just a natural endowment, but depends on an ongoing process of uncovering, and letting go of, the ways in which they have been closed to life."[32]

Evans offers three perceptive insights into why people feel tempted to close themselves off from external influence, attributing this partly to an unwillingness to take the risk of forgiveness, both of self and of others.[33] A second factor at work in a refusal of openness he links to fear, fear that any opening up to the influence of others might threaten to make us disappear. In such a case, our attitude might be that "I must remain, at some inaccessible level deep within me, independent and aloof. . . . Insofar as I am closed,

---

32. D. Evans, *Spirituality and Human Nature*, 17.
33. D. Evans, *Spirituality and Human Nature*, 26.

I *am* my armoring.... Thus in my fear of dependence I am very dependent, for my life is dictated from outside."[34] Evans rejects as a false reading of our situation that we face a stark choice between being either "proudly defiant or cringingly submissive."[35] A flourishing life does not hide from, seek to dominate over, or allow itself to be ruled by others. "Insofar as we are closed we are unable or unwilling to enter into genuinely reciprocal relations with the world. Insofar as we are open we move out of this self-isolation to participate in life."[36]

For Evans, a third factor tempting some people to respond to the precariousness of life by closing themselves off is a distorted understanding of our relationship with the divine. Such a person might envisage human agency in relation to divine agency as a zero-sum game: either my action is solely down to me or it is down to God at work in me; the more God is at work, the less I am involved, and vice versa. As if we have to compete for divinity. Or, as Evans puts it, "either I am at the center of the universe and everything else is peripheral or I am not the center of the universe and I am peripheral."[37] But a Christian understanding of human-divine relations holds that the divine nature includes and shares its self-giving in such a way that God's involvement in our life does not suppress, overrule, deny, or cancel out our own initiative, involvement, agency, or responsibility.

While the relation between humanity and God cannot be described as one between equals, we have sufficient evidence of analogous human relationships where people enter into the lives of others in ways that do not threaten their being or their scope for initiative. Parents with their children, teachers with their students, pastors with their parishioners, friends with friends—these can touch, influence, inspire, enhance the gifts, and enlarge the opportunities of those they encounter, rather than suppress or confine them. Anglican theologian Eric Mascall points out that "this openness of creatures to one another and their openness, in association with others, to higher levels of existence and activity is, of course, not the same thing as their openness to their creator, but it is an analogue of it and a tendency towards its realization."[38]

A scholar who meticulously traced the contours of human insufficiency in multiple contexts and who argued that the attempt to be self-sufficient led to self-enclosure and cutting oneself off from the only source of renewal

---

34. D. Evans, *Spirituality and Human Nature*, 31; emphasis in original.
35. D. Evans, *Spirituality and Human Nature*, 32.
36. D. Evans, *Spirituality and Human Nature*, 47.
37. D. Evans, *Spirituality and Human Nature*, 41.
38. Mascall, *Openness of Being*, 147.

was the French Catholic lay philosopher Maurice Blondel (1861–1949). He established a necessary connection between suffering, letting go, and opening to the divine, in the life of faith.[39] What Blondel says about suffering also applies to the acceptance of vulnerability: "Suffering is a rejuvenating bath, an educative process, a revealing sword, the entry of the unknown, inexplicable, infinite, renewing our inner lives."[40] But merely undergoing suffering or vulnerability does not guarantee this outcome; such experience needs voluntary acceptance and active cooperation.

## LIMITATION AND LEARNING

Life presents us with many little deaths: setbacks, disappointments, sorrows, pains, failures—these are evidence of our weakness and vulnerability. We can be hurt. These little deaths can serve as gateways to new life—if we learn from them and grow through them. Awareness and acknowledgment of our ignorance, plus dissatisfaction with such ignorance, is crucial for learning—in earthly affairs—and in matters of faith. You are not open to learning if you are sure you already know all that matters. If you think you know enough already, you are clearly in the dark about your own ignorance. If you think you fully understand a topic, or a person, or a matter of faith, then you are on the way to being lost and closing off further learning.

We know that learning has positive aspects. Through learning we can experience a sense of mastery, of achievement, of excitement, of interest; we can enjoy a feeling of progress. We also know, sometimes only too painfully, that learning can have less positive aspects. In such cases we experience fear, loss, exposure, uncertainty, embarrassment; we can feel intimidated and vulnerable. I believe that, for some of the most important aspects of learning, learning about life and about faith, our weakness is essential to our openness to grace and learning, and I have seen that sharing vulnerability can be a major highroad to growth professionally, personally, and spiritually. People who cannot share their vulnerability cannot learn how to cope properly with it; they cannot grow properly through it. Furthermore, communities that cannot facilitate the sharing of vulnerability and support people in the process of doing so, cannot become communities that promote human flourishing, deep learning, or real spiritual growth.[41]

---

39. Sullivan, "Blondel and the Cost."

40. Blondel, *Action*, 381.

41. See Sullivan, "Vulnerability in Teaching," for an extended discussion on vulnerability in education.

Learning is dependent on facing our weaknesses, shortcomings, incompleteness, ignorance, confusion, guilt, fear—in short—our vulnerability. All this applies to faith learning, as to other kinds of learning. There seems to be an intimate connection between vulnerability and learning, especially faith learning. We cannot communicate the gospel effectively from a position of safety, strength, power, or comfort. Even when the words we use are orthodox and true, what is communicated is not received as the gospel of our Savior who died on the cross. We convey the gospel via our attunement to vulnerability, fully conscious of our own vulnerability and in touch with this, and genuinely open to and accepting of the vulnerability of others.

Many of us know, only too well, that, often, important learning only takes place when we make mistakes—in our words and actions, in our responses to experience, in our efforts. If we didn't make mistakes and get things wrong, we wouldn't have a chance to learn from them. *Felix culpa*— happy fault—we say of Adam's sin. Some mistakes are indeed costly, painful, and we wouldn't wish them on anyone.

Not only is there a connection between our learning and our own vulnerability, but there is also a major potential source of and prompt for learning (including in faith matters) in our encounter with the vulnerability of others—if we allow ourselves to be open to this, in touch with it, letting it reach us and speak to us. Suffering and learning go together. I don't mean simply that we should expect learning to be painful. Teachers do not set out to make their students suffer, though it is their duty to put them on the spot, under some pressure. We only learn from that (or from whom) we can also suffer. If a person or a practice or an idea really matters to us, it has the power to hurt us, to cause us pain. Such pain shows that we are not willing to be closed in, closed off, hiding behind protective walls: we are open to encounter with the person or reality before us. Of course, none of this means that we can't also learn from delight and joy too. But, when it comes down to it, the crack in things is how the light gets in. The imperfections are where humanity is most visible.

Some kinds of vulnerability—the physical, emotional, mental, or spiritual suffering that accompanies vulnerability—can make us angry, bitter, resentful, depressed, overanxious, and determined to protect ourselves as much as possible. If this is our response, we can close down our defenses, hide behind walls, narrow our vision, see things in a black-and-white way— and so reduce our learning; we can hold the world at a distance: we see it or other people as a threat, at least, those who are different than us; we can't relate properly—and if we can't relate properly—from our true selves and open to their true selves—then we can't learn. We freeze in the headlights of the troubles besetting us—and so lose our freedom to see beyond them and see through to a bigger picture. We lose our capacity for flexibility, for openness, for receptivity—for participation, experiment, and risk-taking—in short, we shut off the channels for learning.

What then can suffering and our vulnerability teach us? They can teach us about patience, purification, submission. They can teach us about acceptance, humility, and perseverance. They can teach us about courage. They can teach us to accept the reality of our mutual interdependence (as compared with the radical autonomy claimed by so many in the world). They can teach us how to let go, how to have a more attentive ear, how to have a more active conscience. They can teach us to have a less proud attitude, how to become more open to advice, more ready to accept help (rather than to expect always to stand on our own feet in isolated self-reliance). They can teach us to become more sympathetic to others. They can cut the ground from under our readiness to be judgmental. They can make us more aware of our need, more attuned to the sufferings and needs of others. They can make us more grateful for mercy. Surely, all this is very much about learning how to become people of faith, people who open the door of the self so that God may enter.

Only by falling and failing does our self-knowledge become real. Only by losing or falling short can we appreciate more clearly what we need to do. Only in light of some lack—some distance from what we perceive as good—will we strive towards the light and something more full. Only with vulnerability can our defenses be lowered and our lives be open to enhancement. We can learn how our vulnerability and falling short can open the door of our hearts to God's grace, healing, and transformation. There is a direct link between our difficulties and darkness, our willingness to be open to the divine and both authentic self-knowledge and an enhanced capacity to help others. As Benedictine Sister Joan Chittister observes, "Only the experience of our own darkness gives us the light we need to be of help to others whose journey into the dark spots of life is only just beginning. . . . We all have within us the scars that come from failing to lose once in a while. . . . We need failure to learn that we don't need to win to justify the reason for our existence."[42]

## CONCLUSION

Our vulnerability, weakness, falling short, and sin contribute to, make possible, and provide a prompt for the transformation that God wants to work

---

42. Chittister, *Between Dark and Daylight*, 19, 56, 57.

in us; but we have to allow this to happen. "By virtue of being broken-open to the unprecedented future, we are affect-able by the divine grace immanent in and operative in it."[43] Thus we can claim that vulnerability and the gaps it reveals in us can be both generative and act as a catalyst for change in our response to experience and to others. It can be a resource that serves as "a precondition and expression of trust, mutual respect, responsibility and the possibility of love."[44] An encounter or situation can so interrupt, shock, and challenge us that we find ourselves simultaneously first pierced but then also empowered by the experience to open ourselves to some change of direction and pattern of response to the world and to others. We let go of something in us and let in something that we had either not recognized or accepted before. There is, as a result, something new in us as we risk opening ourselves to an unknown future. Vulnerability makes us aware of a gap in our nature and in our capacities, and this prompts us to be open to the more, something beyond our self-enclosed radical autonomy. When such receptivity includes openness to the offer of divine gift and grace, this does not simply add something that had been missing in us, as if everything else in us was fine and, apart from that missing element, virtually complete; rather it transforms everything within us; it reconfigures, heals, integrates, reorients, elevates, and enhances what was already there.

Of course, we can choose to remain deaf to the call inherent in that interrupting situation or encounter. Our affectability allows us to enter into the lives of others and opens a door for our lives to be touched in turn by them in constant ripples of influence whose contours we can neither map nor control. The affectability that accompanies our vulnerability is a doorway opening a path towards self-knowledge, solidarity with others, sensitivity to divine grace, and transformation. We must choose: either a self-enclosed, defensive, and ultimately isolating and diminishing struggle for safety and mastery in life if we refuse to accept our vulnerability; or a willingness to run the risk of authentic relationality—an openness to and embrace of others that is marked by interdependence, that is subject to uncertainty, and that lets itself be carried forward by the call of love, both human and divine.

---

43. J. Miller, "On the Way," 694.
44. Orphanopoulos, "Reframing Vulnerability," 9.

*PART FOUR*

# Curriculum and Learning

### INTRODUCTION

The curriculum is a context in which there can occur that "fusion of horizons" referred to by Gadamer in his landmark work *Truth and Method*. By this I mean that the teacher's mediation of some aspect of an academic or practical tradition always has in view the student's engagement with that tradition, a mode of engagement that includes a blend of acceptance and reinterpretation, and also, perhaps, of rejection. Thought forms, whether ancient or recent—as mediated by the teacher—come into contact with the perspectives and concerns of students, in such a way as to lead to complex modes of adoption, adaptation, reconfiguration, and reframing. The teacher is entrusted with passing on traditions of learning—cognitive, cultural, social, moral, spiritual, aesthetic, practical, and so forth—with an unstated recognition that, in the process, students will, to some degree, make these their own, but also change them. As Applebee notes,

> These traditions enable and transform the minds of individuals raised within them, and are in turn themselves transformed by those same individuals. . . . [Traditions] provide *culturally constituted tools* for understanding and reforming the world, tools of which we are both heir and progenitor. . . . In mastering such traditions, students learn not only how to operate within them, but also how to change them.[1]

To speak of a the curriculum as a site for the "fusion of horizons" entails a transformative conversation between the culture's past, the teacher's past and present, and the students' present—all of which has implications

---

1. Applebee, *Curriculum as Conversation*, 1, 2, 9; emphasis in original.

for the culture's future. I think that Applebee is right in treating the metaphor of curriculum as conversation as one that is promising and fruitful. This conversation is one that takes place principally between the living, but it does not neglect to include the voices of the past. "Written texts live long after their authors have left the conversation because this process of reconstrual allows texts to be made relevant in new contexts, by new participants. Without reconstrual, the texts would lose their voice and place within the ongoing conversation."[2]

Learning includes all aspects of our nature; it can occur everywhere; and it continues throughout life. Learning can be cognitive—a mental process, to do with our way of thinking and understanding; it can be aesthetic, connected to our sense of beauty or what draws us, what attracts us; it can be kinesthetic or corporeal, to do with our ability to move and to experience the body. Learning can also be to do with the will and the spirit, what we give ourselves to, and therefore about our commitments. It can be something that is either individual or communal, or perhaps both at the same time. It engages the body, the mind, the memory, the will, emotions, imagination and the spirit. Learning has the following elements:

- Attention
- Memory
- Motivation
- Meaning proposed and perceived
- Engagement with and modification of what is proposed
- Meaning and value appropriated and owned

Each of these can be treated without reference to Christian faith, but each of them can also be treated with reference to Christian faith.

The task of educators is to awaken in learners the power to wonder, imagine and question, to think, interpret, understand, evaluate, and appreciate, to receive and give, to live in God's presence—hearing and responding to Word and Spirit. Christian educators should facilitate in disciples the capacity to take on the task of personal integration, and a serious attempt at learning to love rightly; these are lifelong projects that can be begun in formal education. Christian teachers should, whatever the particularities of the context, help their students to develop a sense of the faith and a capacity to receive it, penetrate it, adhere to it, and apply it in their lives. In doing so,

---

2. Applebee, *Curriculum as Conversation*, 40.

they will be mindful of the uniqueness of each student, even in the midst of their common humanity.

The human mind understands, it remembers and it wants. These are basic functions of who we are and what we are like. We are people who look into the depths of things and try to understand them, to make sense of our lives. We are people who cannot help remembering our past experience and how this has left its mark on us (though often this happens in ways in which we are not fully aware). We are people who have needs, who want things, who look ahead to the future. These three functions, our drive to know and understand, our being influenced in the present by memory of the past, and our reaching out to the future to meet our wants—these three can become, for the Christian, the three virtues of faith, hope, and love. Faith is what can happen to our understanding; remembering can turn into hope; and our wanting can be transformed into love. This is not guaranteed, but for us, as Christians, it is a real possibility, if we accept God's help and help from each other. For this we need gratitude and trust, openness to give and to receive. We have to be recreated in faith and hope and love for our understanding, our memory, and our will to become what God really wants them to be. Surely, this is one way we might describe our work in Christian education—helping our students to turn their natural drive to understand, their capacity to remember, and the built-in thrust of their wanting into faith, hope, and love.

And the yardsticks for evaluating our work—the signs of our fruitfulness and effectiveness—what the world calls performance indicators—these yardsticks should not be the requirements of the state, the economy or the media—but those given to us by our faith; these are love, joy, peace, patience, kindness, generosity, faithfulness, gentleness, and self-control.

The purpose of Christian education is to encourage people to understand, appreciate, internalize, embrace, embody, and communicate the gospel of Jesus Christ by cultivating a Christian lifestyle based on the values of the kingdom of God. Christian education includes activities and experiences that elicit the awakening, nurturing, maturing, expression, sharing, and practice of Christian faith.

Educating people in matters of faith is always a delicate endeavor. The way we educate others in faith must be congruent with what we are educating them into: the methods used must match and adequately convey and represent the message. We should be humble. We do not know it all. We are not perfect. Our perspective is limited, incomplete, and distorted sometimes by selfish motives. Other people have the image of God in them. They have something to offer us as well as something to receive from us.

Their dignity should be respected. God is already at work in their lives. In bringing others to the light, the main agent is God's Holy Spirit, not us.

An educator in faith must attend to two sets of questions: those posed by his or her students or audiences; and those posed by the faith community and gospel she or he represents. To ignore the first would be to come across as irrelevant to people's needs. To ignore the second would be to allow this audience to dictate all the terms, topics, and criteria for discussion and offer them nothing new, distinctive or challenging. Thus an educator in faith should ask: Who am I dealing with? What things matter to them? What perplexes them? What attracts them? How are they thinking? What is affecting their thinking? What are their priorities and values? What is being taken for granted? What is being ignored? What is not being mentioned at all? Which voices are surfacing and which are silent?

There is always a need for balance between the explicit and the implicit. To concentrate entirely on the explicit message but without attending to the life that underpins it and makes it credible is counterproductive and self-defeating. To focus only on the way of living but without making explicit the message and story that should be guiding it, challenging it, illuminating and inspiring it, would be to sell people short.

The educator in faith should be sensitive to the hunger for the divine, the inner compass that points beyond the here and now, driving forward for something better, more desirable, that resides somewhere in her or his audience and seek ways to bring this to articulation, to hear it into speech and then to encourage it, support it, reinforce it, and gently bring about an encounter with appropriate treasures from the living religious tradition. These treasures introduce people to new social practices, loyalties, networks, ways of thinking, concepts, and language.

The word "curriculum" means the whole range of educational experiences, formal and informal, provided in an institution. It has been said that there are three types of curriculum: first, the *explicit* curriculum—what is officially taught through the various courses; second, the *implicit* curriculum—what is taught "beneath the surface" by the way things are done, by the kinds of relationships between people, the layout of rooms and buildings, the kinds of behavior that get rewarded or penalized, recognized or ignored; and third, the *null* curriculum—what never receives a mention, what gets left out, or is avoided (this still conveys some kind of message). The curriculum in any particular school or university is influenced by a range of factors; these include the worldviews of the teachers, their understanding of the purpose of education, the nature of knowledge, the learner and learning, the role of teachers and teaching, and the social context in which they are working.

PART FOUR | CURRICULUM AND LEARNING

The essays in part 4 can only touch on some aspects of learning and curriculum. Chapter 15 links integration as a major life task with integration as a priority for university education. First, I explain what I mean by integration as a task for each of us before commenting on what the nineteenth-century Christian educator John Henry Newman has to say about integration in university learning. Then I present five types of challenge that must be taken into account if integration is to be pursued seriously as a priority in university. Finally I indicate some of the ways that faculty might set about addressing these challenges.

Chapter 16 addresses the gap that often opens up between faith learning and other kinds of learning and the neglect, in many churches, of providing lifelong faith formation. It explores what might be entailed by the notion of a "curriculum for life" that equips Christians for their life in a secular society.

The focus of chapter 17 is on the challenge of taking seriously the question of vocation as a key concern for educators in general and for Christian educators in particular. The chapter urges teachers to foster in their students a move from indifference to commitment, suggests ways in which they can help students to discern how best to orient their lives, and draws out some educational implications of adopting vocation as a major theme for consideration in the curriculum.

Chapter 18 brings out some stark contrasts between traditional, religious ways of reading, and the assumptions and approaches that govern the kinds of reading practiced in contemporary education. I retrieve insights about reading drawn from some earlier theological and spiritual traditions, suggesting that these insights have applicability beyond their original settings and beyond the reading of religious texts. I suggest that some familiarity with religious ways of reading would expand the reading repertoire of students beyond the current emphasis which is both consumerist and instrumentalist.

In the final chapter of part 4, chapter 19, I underline the duty of a steward of a living tradition in education to hold together two tasks, which, though integrally connected, are not identical: first, to introduce students to the "text" or the "score" of the tradition, so that they are familiar with it, and, ideally, willing to embrace it as their own; second, to equip students with the skills and confidence needed to "perform" that "text" or "score" in such a way as to bring it to life and to bear upon ever new contexts. There is a dialectic at work between doing justice to the "score" of the living tradition of Christian education and empowering personal rendition of it among learners whose agency is brought into play. In section 1 of the chapter, I explain what I mean by promoting agency in learners. In sections 2 and 3

I draw upon two recent philosophers of education who have commented insightfully on different aspects of the need to develop agency in students. Section 4 outlines the principal risks and benefits one might expect to incur by giving salience to learning agency. Finally, in section 5 I underline the importance, both for their educational and their religious development, of eliciting an original response from those we teach.

# 15

## Newman and Interconnectedness
### *Integration and University Education*

I WRITE AS A COMMITTED (if sometimes uncomfortable and critical) insider to the Catholic tradition, aiming to draw out a particular implication of a Catholic worldview for the priorities addressed in university education. There is a legitimate plurality of views as to what are the key features of this tradition. Even when agreement can be reached as to the constitutive features, there remains a significant degree of disagreement, both as regards their relative priorities and as to how these priorities should be implemented in practice. Views about Catholicism are contentious, not only within the church, but even more so within society more generally.

This applies to many students and staff in Catholic universities, only some of whom attend because they subscribe to the faith that is meant to underpin those educational communities. Present in the mix there will likely be people of many faiths and some people who do not subscribe to any form of religion. While some members of such universities do wish to deepen their understanding of and commitment to faith and therefore are open to faith development initiatives, many will be indifferent to these opportunities and some will resist them vigorously. Nevertheless, it remains the case that one can (and one should) draw out educational implications from the Catholic tradition and take steps to breathe life into them at Catholic universities, so long as these educational opportunities are offered and experienced as invitations, not as impositions. The particular educational priority that is the focus of this chapter is one that is, in many respects, shared by Christians of different denominations and also by many Jews and Muslims.

The curriculum subject religious education (RE) can be distinguished from the various processes that are involved in faith education and development. The focus for RE is on literacy about religion, information, and concepts; RE does not depend on prior commitment; it does not assume membership of any particular faith. Its goal is to promote understanding about religious matters: the stories, Scriptures, beliefs, practices, traditions, and customs associated with a religion, or, more often in recent years, religions in the plural. RE aims to promote informed and intelligent thinking about a religion rather than fidelity to it. It is led by the norms of education rather than by those of the gospel.

When it comes to faith education, the phrase "educating faith" can have two slightly different emphases. The first puts the focus on how a set of activities can make someone's faith more educated in some way: for example, move from being accepted to being understood, from being passive to being more thoughtful, critical, reflective, better informed, more coherent, able to deal with objections. The second puts the focus on allowing one's engagement in the life of faith to educate one: that is, to change one for the better, by crossing the threshold of revelation to see a new world, deepening one's commitment, strengthening one's character, influencing the whole person, not only the mind, but also the affections and the will, including how we treat the body. This is a different activity to RE, but one that can be at least partly assisted and prompted by it, for example, by the critical questioning and deeper understanding of religious matters facilitated by RE. Similarly, engagement in faith development activities can provide experiences that can usefully feed into and be reflected upon in RE. I have argued elsewhere that one should not turn the distinction between education and evangelization into a total separation, indicating several ways that these two activities can mutually reinforce each other.[1]

## THE TASK OF INTEGRATION

We all face the challenge of integration in our lives—becoming one, whole, comprehensive (catholic) person: ordering our drives, needs, and desires; coordinating our gifts, inclinations, and talents; integration through establishing a proper balance of attention both to self and to others; moving towards personal integration. Body, mind, emotions, conscience, spirit, intelligence—all of these need to be gradually built into one "building," a temple of God's Spirit, oriented to God's kingdom, so that we grow ever

---

1. Sullivan, "Education and Evangelization."

more from being an image into a very particular and unique likeness of God.

Educational work for the church calls for both the example of personal integration (in our behavior and in our modeling of discipleship) and the facilitation of conceptual integration, where all elements of knowledge are shown to interact on each other, rather than offer a fragmented curriculum. For catechists, clergy, teachers, and others there needs to be a blend or integration of intellectual development, spiritual development, and professional/pedagogical development. Classroom and educational work needs to be envisaged in terms that can be integrated with kingdom work, professionalism with discipleship. This applies as much in Catholic universities as in Catholic primary and secondary schools. Our personal and spiritual standards and yardsticks should mesh with, be displayed in, and find themselves integrated into our academic and professional standards and yardsticks; the personal/spiritual and the academic/professional should not operate in isolation from each other, nor, of course, should they work in opposition to each other. This will not be easy. On the way to achieving it there will be pain, difficulties, and tension.

Education, throughout history, and in any culture, no matter which worldview prevails in a particular time or place, is about the capacities of human nature and how these are developed, oriented, ordered, and integrated. These capacities include energy, emotions, intelligence, memory, will, conscience, and wonder. While these elements within human beings may be understood differently at different times, and despite the fact that some elements may receive emphasis while others are relatively neglected, nevertheless, all necessarily play a part in our human condition and each of them will both exert influence and be subject to influence during any process of education, whether formal or informal. Even as we might focus, for example, in higher education, on sharpening the mind, on training the intellect, on prompting critical thinking, the faculty seeking to pursue such goals will themselves be people with a "hinterland" of all of the other elements and capacities—other than mind or intellect—aspects of their being which simultaneously work to enhance and to obstruct, to filter and to modify what it is they are teaching. Who we are can get in the way of what we teach, with the effect that the message we seek to convey cannot properly be heard. On the other hand, even when our grasp of what we seek to teach is weaker than it ought to be, and when our professional skill set and repertoire are more limited than they should be, the cumulative effect of all the other elements of our being can sometimes make up for these defects—again because who we are as persons conveys more than the sum of the verbal or intellectual "messages" we try to transmit. In the armory of a wise teacher there must be self-knowledge and an awareness of how the content of her teaching is being mediated by the nature of her character and personality, for better or worse.

John Henry Newman was a strong advocate of the need to be alert to the multiple dimensions of our nature and attentive to the call of integration, in the ways I have indicated above. He contributed importantly to our thinking on such topics as how faith and reason are related, how historical appreciation and understanding of doctrine develops, how laypeople have a crucial part to play in safeguarding the church, how we relate to God, how theology joins other disciplines in the university, learning from them but also contributing to their learning. He championed the sacredness of conscience and its role in helping us become tuned to God. He gave excellent advice about the importance of balancing the needs of the mind, the needs of our spirit, and the needs of belonging to the community. He brought out some key features of an education that is worthwhile, that makes us better people, that equips us for the important things in life. He was a strong believer in the centrality of personal influence, heart speaking to heart; he envisaged teaching as one life touching another life. "Persons influence us, voices melt us, looks subdue us, deeds inflame us," he said in his *Grammar of Assent*, a book that continues to be very important for religious educators in the church.[2] He would agree that the teacher needs self-knowledge. "To gain religious starting points, we must interrogate our hearts, our consciences, the God who dwells there," he said in his letters and diaries. There is for him an intellectual component to faith, one that needs to be cultivated, but it is only *one* component, not the whole. He was deeply aware of the "hinterland" within, the many dimensions of our lives that provide a foundation for our intellectual operations, operations that are never as autonomous or logical as we might like to pretend.

Newman is an exemplary defender of the essential unity of knowledge, believing that every area of investigation points to and depends upon its source and goal—God.[3] His ideal outcome from university education is a true enlargement of the mind . . . the power of viewing many things at once as a whole, of referring them severally to their true place in the universal system, of understanding their respective values, and determining their mutual dependence.[4]

Furthermore, a university professes to assign to each study which it receives, its proper place and its just boundaries; to define the rights, to

---

2. Newman, *Essay in Aid of Grammar*, 89.
3. Newman, *Idea of a University*, 45, 47, 50–51, 99, 137.
4. Newman, *Idea of a University*, 137.

establish the mutual relations, and to effect the intercommunion of one and all. To keep in check the ambitious and encroaching, and to succor and maintain those which from time to time are succumbing under the more popular or the more fortunately circumstanced; to keep the peace between them all, and to convert their mutual differences and contrarieties into the common good.[5]

Clearly, in this vision for a university, the pressures of the market must not rule the construction of the curriculum! For Newman, enlargement of mind and strengthening and deepening of spirit go hand in hand. He has a noble vision of education but also a realistic one. On the need for integration he still has much to teach us. He offers us a vision of an approach to education and to educating faith that is engaged, experiential, and imaginative; it is concrete, rather than abstract; it is very much living and personal knowledge that he promotes. For him, we might say, religious education is in the business of realization, making real. In his life and writings we see intermingled and integrated the interplay of memory, habit, active and critical thinking, prayer, imagination, feeling, belonging, the voice of conscience, our aesthetic sense, the mysterious workings of grace, and the part played by theology and doctrine and the church, plus the power of witness.

I have been arguing that education must support the task of personal integration and that to do so it must take into account the whole person.

> An all-round education seeks to develop every aspect of the individual: social, intellectual, emotional, moral and spiritual. For there is an *ecology of human growth* which means that if any of these is overlooked, all the others suffer.[6]

I have also argued that integration must be striven for both at the personal and the conceptual level. Thus, on the one hand, education should address, work upon, and deploy the multiple dimensions of our personhood; on the other hand, it should assist learners (which means all of us) in relating the different kinds of truth we come to know.

Without the first kind of integration, it is likely that many educational efforts will be unbalanced, unhealthy, or infertile. Without the second kind of integration we gain at best a very limited, fragmented, and distorted picture of truth. For Christians the salvific truth to be found in Scripture and in the life of the church must be related to all the other kinds of truth we find in the world.

---

5. Newman, *Idea of a University*, 457–58.

6. John Paul II, quoted in D'Orsa and D'Orsa, *Explorers, Guides & Meaning-Makers*, 177; emphasis in original.

There are three reasons that drive efforts to connect these different kinds of truth. First, our use of and response to the truths to be found in the world need to be illuminated and guided by God's offer of salvation. Second, the religious truths we learn in Scripture and the church are not to be preserved for a precious, isolated and "holy" part of life; they are to be applied and embodied in our negotiations with all aspects of our earthly existence and the truths associated with these aspects, material, economic, scientific, political, social, cultural, and so forth. Third, the truths we learn from studying aspects of the world can illuminate and help us more effectively penetrate and appreciate the truths of salvation to be found in Scripture and the church.

## CHALLENGES

Any attempt to promote integration as one of the principal tasks of life must face the fact that we are confronted by compartmentalization. Alasdair MacIntyre comments on this feature of our existence:

> Each of the separate spheres of activity through which individuals pass in the course of a day or a week or a month has its own distinctive culture, its own modes of relationship, its own specific norms. . . . As individuals pass from home and family to workplace to school to leisure-time activities and to political or religious associations, they become adroit in leaving behind the roles, norms, and attitudes appropriate to the sphere that they have just left and assuming those of the sphere that they are about to enter.[7]

He laments that, as a result of the pervasive effects of compartmentalization, it has become increasingly difficult for people to find a way to see life whole, with all its parts interconnected; there is no natural position from which to establish an overall perspective and to make evaluative judgments in relation to some architectonic, all-embracing (and external) standard. He wants students to be helped by their university education to integrate all aspects of what they are learning and all aspects of their lives. He takes into account their learning "in the language laboratory and in the chapel, on the basketball court and in the library, in the social relationships of the residence hall and in those of the philosophy seminar."[8] A random collection of experts does not, in his view, make for a university as understood

---

7. MacIntyre, "Catholic Universities," 15.
8. MacIntyre, "Catholic Universities," 18.

in the Catholic tradition. Jean Bethke Elshtain supports his advocacy of integration as a major goal in education: "The student who is formed within an integrative context can, if all has gone well, stand back and assess the standards of human flourishing she has absorbed. Integration offers notions of a plurality of goods as well as ways to evaluate these goods."[9] For Elshtain, what is at stake here is the formation of the character of the student, what kind of person she is becoming. I will return to this in my final section.

Compartmentalization is a well-established pattern within our universities, partly an outcome of a very understandable division of labor between scholars. Aspiring academics learn to see the world through the eyes of their particular discipline and can, in the process, remain ignorant of, perhaps even dismissive of, the methods and insights of other disciplines. Jensen notes the "tendency of disciplines to overextend their valid scope and lose sight of the conceptual limitations built into their formative metaphors."[10] He proposes five reasons for universities to strive to develop interdisciplinary and integrative work. I quote them in full to bring out the force of the case for integration. Without taking the full measure of the case for integration it would be only too easy to cave in before the very real challenges such integration is bound to face. Jensen argues against being satisfied with the current division of labor.

> 1) Even when disciplines are operating on their own turf—on the very problems and phenomena they are created to address—they still cannot offer an exclusive and exhaustive account of what they describe or analyze. 2) Academic disciplines are self-promoting institutions perpetually competing for resources and prestige. Even the research practices and root metaphors of these disciplines are apt to be affected by these dynamics. 3) Academic disciplines serve the broader society, or at least derive their ultimate significance through connections with society. Their structures are apt to reflect the sins and pathologies of the wider society of which they are a part. 4) Academic foundational metaphors are not conceived arbitrarily; probably without exception they reflect some valid and significant feature of reality in their very conception. But our world is complex and multi-dimensional; these metaphors are not inevitable, and they are always subject to re-negotiation and improvement. 5) There really is such a thing as "methodological atheism," and some aspects of academic knowledge reflect a deliberate attempt to marginalize religious authority. Academic scholars should not

---

9. Elshtain, "What Have We Learned?," 136.
10. Jensen, "Faith Integration," 44.

simply take the workings of their own discipline for granted, and assume that faith integration is merely a special task for those interested in interdisciplinary research.[11]

In addition to Jensen's cogent argument for integration in the university, John Paul II also claims that integration should be a key feature of a Catholic university (along with a dialogue between faith and reason, an ethical concern, and a theological perspective).[12] In *Ex Corde Ecclesiae* he calls for scholars to relate all aspects of the truth they investigate to the supreme Truth, who is God.[13] He wants students to develop an organic vision of reality and their teachers to demonstrate that they have integrated faith and life and linked professional competence with Christian wisdom.[14]

There are many challenges to be faced when one considers what is entailed in promoting integration in education. In this chapter I briefly outline and comment on five types of difficulty or challenge. These relate, first, to the amount of subject matter to be covered; second, to relationships between the disciplines; third, to the multiple dimensions of being a person and how subjectivity impinges on scholarship; fourth, to theological differences among Christians; and fifth, to the need for what Newman called "elbow room" or sufficient psychological "space" and time for individual learning to occur in freedom.

One difficulty stems from the sheer amount of subject matter to be taken into account. There seems simply too much to get to know. Mastering a body of knowledge to a level where one may justifiably be confident that one can discern its essential features, key concepts, internal structures, modes of reasoning, and approaches to testing for reality is demanding enough. Without that degree of knowledge one cannot claim to have entered in any adequate way into an academic discipline. If one then attempts to integrate even a single area of knowledge with another area of knowledge, no sound bridges can be built between them without solid foundations on both sides of the bridge. Is there time, in the relatively limited period of formal and accredited study, to do justice to two areas of knowledge, let alone more than two? In addition to the problem of time, this difficulty raises the specter that learning will be superficial, in that, inevitably, in order to make room for addressing more than one subject area, there will have to compromises with regard to curriculum coverage, compromises that put in jeopardy the attainment of appropriate depth of penetration.

11. Jensen, "Faith Integration," 54.
12. John Paul II, *On Catholic Universities*, 15.
13. John Paul II, *On Catholic Universities*, 6.
14. John Paul II, *On Catholic Universities*, 18–19.

A second kind of difficulty is that, if integration is taken to be an educational imperative, depending on their current position (with regard to prestige, funding and the potential rewards available), one discipline might slip into displaying an imperialistic attitude towards other disciplines, lacking humility and failing to display reciprocity in being willing to learn. If the relationship between disciplines turns out to be unilateral, with one subject area providing an agenda, or criteria for judgment, or key concepts, for another, this will reduce the scope for all to contribute as valuably as they might. It will be reductionist in another sense, too, leading interpretation in one discipline or field to be carried out according to the canons, norms, rationality, and priorities of a different one, thereby failing to respect the appropriate degree of autonomy of other disciplines. Ultimately, one cannot claim full autonomy for any discipline; conceptually, each one is interdependent on at least some others and speaking theologically, each, under God, has only a derived or relative autonomy.[15]

Newman was well aware that, where there is no proper balance within the circle of knowledge, academics are likely to claim more than is appropriate for their own particular discipline and acknowledge less than is appropriate for disciplines outside their own. He argued that theology had a rightful place in the circle of knowledge, that when theology is omitted, other disciplines tend to exceed their jurisdiction. Of course, it is also possible that theology itself will act in an imperialistic manner, dictating to other disciplines, or at least unduly constraining them. Even in a situation where no single discipline dominates, the integrative imperative can be open to the danger that it invites undue competition and conflict between disciplines as they come together to produce a jointly constructed curriculum. Humility, restraint, and openness to the other are needed here, as well as well-grounded confident advocacy of the special insights and methods of any particular discipline.[16]

A third kind of difficulty that can arise when academics aim to give high priority to integration in education is that they can be tempted to overemphasize the conceptual and cognitive aspect of knowledge and neglect other dimensions that play a part in our coming to know. Also to be taken into account in the integrative process in education, there is the role of the body, affect, relationships, community, ways of living, the company we keep, aesthetic considerations, and the sheer serendipity of experience. Knowledge has multiple strands, strands it is often almost impossible to unravel.

15. Losinger, *Relative Autonomy*.
16. Sullivan, "Connection Without Control."

As scholars, each of us operates from a complex personal habitus. This *habitus* is an acquired pattern of thoughts, judgment, outlook, values, behavior and taste, a pattern that emerges gradually as an outcome of how we internalize standards and expectations from exemplars and significant others, but also from the culture around us and the social structures that surround us. Thus "our ideas and values are connected to each other in complicated webs of relation and reference that have as much to do with our autobiographies as with pure logic."[17] Our interests, hopes, and fears are intermingled with both our seeking and our finding. Our thoughts are influenced by our bodily and emotional states.[18] Our subjectivity saturates our scholarship.

To be adequately self-reflexive we need to work hard to detect how our attention, perceptions, thinking, priorities, judgments and evaluations are linked to our location and context, our commitments and aversions. Our priorities are modified by our allegiances and affiliations, and the arguments that we find persuasive are linked both to the worldviews we inhabit and the plausibility structures that are significant for us. Our practices carry the seeds of future knowledge within them; they are not simply applications of what we have already come to know. As Iain McGilchrist says, quoting Lakoff and Johnson, "Our conceptual systems draw largely upon the commonalities of our bodies and of the environments we live in."[19] There is an unavoidable interconnectedness between the different dimensions of our being and the complex ways we come to know. No one was more aware of this than the French Catholic lay philosopher Maurice Blondel (1861–1949).[20] In the midst of his huge panorama of the pilgrimage of the human spirit across creation towards God, Blondel points out that "matter is that which can be vitalized, life is that which can be spiritualized and the spirit is that which is capable of aspiring to God and can be deified by grace."[21]

It can be assumed too automatically that what is being integrated is faith and learning, with the intellectual dimension of both being intended. But there are other kinds of integration to be considered too: body and soul, learning and love, learning and hope, faith and justice, mind and heart. In the mix of learning we should aspire not only to equip students to become acute and discerning map readers, capable of interpreting and using the accumulated knowledge made available through the various academic

17. Jacobsen and Jacobsen, *Scholarship & Christian Faith*, 56.
18. Pelias, *Methodology of the Heart*; Springer, *This Is My Body*.
19. McGilchrist, *Master and His Emissary*, 149.
20. Blanchette, *Maurice Blondel*.
21. Blondel, *Être et êtres*, 263. See also Sullivan, "Matter for Heaven."

disciplines. We should also prepare them to become mapmakers, stretching boundaries of knowledge, taking it into new fields and making new connections of their own. Integrative efforts in education can include linking critical appreciation of tradition with creative appropriations of it. Other kinds of integration seek to bring together faith and culture, knowledge and ethics, and coordinating the needs of individuals with the needs of society.

A fourth difficulty is to adopt too quickly some available strongly argued approach to integration, without taking into account possible alternative ways of envisaging the task of integration. It must not be assumed that there is only one, obvious approach to or paradigm for integration. Douglas and Rhonda Jacobsen draw attention to the diversity of Christian models of integration, for example, Calvinist/Reformed, Catholic, Wesleyan, Lutheran, Pentecostal, Anabaptist, commenting that "some of the core theological concerns of non-Reformed Christian traditions simply do not translate into integration-speak."[22] There is much scope here for ecumenical learning. Different Christian traditions relate doctrine and intellectual expression of faith, community, worship, and service in different ways, so that the interaction of Scripture, tradition, reason, faith, and action intermingle in subtle and complexly contrasting patterns. Given that revelation—its nature, scope and relationship to "ordinary" knowledge—is understood differently in the various Christian traditions, it is inevitable that Christian approaches to integration in education will be affected by these differences of emphasis. In analyzing the way that different spiritual traditions have implications for academic life, the Jacobsens provide a succinct summary:

> The contemplative tradition reminds us of the need to make room for divine mystery in our academic interpretations of the world. The holiness tradition points to the fact that the habits we cultivate . . . have the potential to shape our scholarship in subtle ways for good or for ill. The charismatic tradition underscores the fact that reality can surprise us: miracles can happen. It also reminds us that one need not be a scholar in order to be used powerfully by God. The social justice tradition implies that virtually all our scholarship has ethical implications and asks whether our work truly benefits the poor and needy of the world. The evangelical tradition suggests that scholarship connects with faith most powerfully in the practice of apologetics—explaining the world intelligently in a way that promotes belief and submission to God's will for our lives and for the world as a whole. The incarnational tradition encourages us to put academic resources to work in the service of ordinary

22. Jacobsen and Jacobsen, *Scholarship & Christian Faith*, 26.

human beings and to find the holy in the ordinary structures of the world.[23]

The Jacobsens point out that there can be close connections between an emphasis on worldview—marked in some Christian traditions, but not in others—and the place of theory within academic disciplines. The role of worldview features more prominently in many Protestant works on integration in Christian higher education than it does in Catholic ones; Catholic educators can benefit greatly by studying how such thinkers apply Christian faith in service of the task of integration in education.[24] A person's worldview influences what he or she notices, takes in, and accepts. It shapes how they perceive messages being sent to them by various individuals and groups. It orients what they care about. It helps them fit incoming messages or lessons from experience into what they already hold, know and are committed to and, indeed, what they do afterwards with what they are learning now. One's worldview is about configuration, interconnectedness, and mutual reinforcement in those leading perspectives we have that function as the keys to our main perceptions of reality and our judgments.

However, the ideas and viewpoints that comprise our worldview do not emerge on strictly logical grounds nor do they get deployed on purely logical lines. Rather they are embedded in a pattern of behaving and belonging that "carries" whatever reasoning goes into them beyond any strict remit that flows from reason alone. That is, people are formed (and sustained) in a worldview largely through the company they keep, the practices they engage in and the lives they lead. Their worldview gives them some kind of rationale for this and a picture of the whole and a sense of meaning within the flux and ambiguities of life. A worldview is, for most people, rough and ready rather than sharply shaped or clearly defined; it is often not reflected upon, nor articulated; it operates clandestinely rather than explicitly in many cases. It can contain irreconcilable elements, inner contradictions that do not get resolved, but which do not prevent us from living on the basis of the worldview. However, the Jacobsens rightly claim that "the integration paradigm often flounders when applied either to disciplines that are more neutrally descriptive or pragmatic in orientation or to disciplines in which issues of human meaning rarely enter the mix."[25]

23. Jacobsen and Jacobsen, *Scholarship & Christian Faith*, 93.

24. Claerbaut, *Faith and Learning*; Dockery and Thornbury, *Shaping a Christian Worldview*; Dockery, *Renewing Minds*; Downey and Porter, *Christian Worldview and Academic Disciplines*; Harris, *Integration of Faith and Learning*; Litfin, *Conceiving the Christian College*; Sire, *Naming the Elephant*.

25. Jacobsen and Jacobsen, *Scholarship & Christian Faith*, 27.

A fifth challenge relates to both psychological "space" and to time. There must be room for individual growth and freedom. Too tight an integrative "script" can be deadening or suffocating. This applies not only to the room required for experiment and for feeling their way among students, if they are to have a chance to own their knowledge, to assimilate it according to their own priorities and commitments; it also applies to faculty if creativity in their pedagogy is not to be stifled. Furthermore, the results of our educational efforts need time to incubate. Sometimes it will be years after a class or a course that what is learned flowers into life, expression or application. The initial impulse of learning can be separated from later fruition by many intermediary experiences and long periods that appear to be fallow, but where the duration of time allows a deeper level of internalization.

## FOR FURTHER ATTENTION

From the first challenge indicated above, I take it that it is incumbent on faculty to identify the central values, key concepts, and most important claims of their discipline with regard to contributing to the education of the whole person. Without maintaining a sharp focus on what is central, any negotiation within and between subject teams about what should be taught will be seriously hampered. Curriculum design and pedagogical planning cannot help but be "on the move" because of changes in student and faculty composition, the availability of resources, external pressures and opportunities, and so forth; however, faculty should be reluctant to make too many changes too quickly with regard to what is considered "core," even though there cannot be complete agreement about this.

As for the second challenge, universities can set about organizing things in such a way as to facilitate better understanding and mutual appreciation between disciplines. This might be via their systems of hiring faculty, of pump priming interdisciplinary projects, of fostering joint seminars, of encouraging enriched programs of training for research students as well as through curriculum design for undergraduate and taught postgraduate courses. Mechanisms for faculty evaluation and promotion, too, can reward engagement with the institutional mission to promote greater levels of integration in curriculum, pedagogy, assessment, research, and outreach.

With regard to the third area of difficulty, I believe that there is much scope for stressing, much more than is currently the case, the need for self-knowledge as an important dimension of a university education. In the end it will be the student who does the "heavy lifting" in integration—or fails to do so. "In accomplishing the unity of the university curriculum and the disciplines and knowledge within them, one becomes aware that genuine unity resides in the individual intellect of the student. The mere fusion of courses is no guarantee that such unity will take place."[26] It should be possible to invite students to engage in structured reflection on how the questions of their courses relate to the questions of their lives, to model for them how to become aware of the ways that our respective lenses for seeing the world are ineluctably connected to our biology and biography, the company we keep, the pattern of life we are constructing.

Such self-reflection does not have to slip into narcissism or superficial navel-gazing. It can help students to avoid separating their inner and their outer lives, to bring into greater harmony the multiple dimensions of their being. It must be remembered that this task is elusive and unending. But the university can assist students in coming to recognize how their choices have consequences, positively and negatively, and to acknowledge that some choices make later ones much more difficult to make, while some others open the door for us and smooth our path towards building the kind of character that, while flawed (as we all are), nevertheless displays coherence and consistency, that shows what we stand for, that recognizes what undermines our best self and where help can be found in resisting such threats.

I find helpful here the picture of the human person given us by the orthodox theologian Nonna Harrison:

> The human person is able to connect with the different levels of reality in the universe because he or she already participates in them.... Our bodies have received protons and electrons from star dust, atoms from the earth, organic molecules from the biosphere, and genes from the animals. So we share in all the levels of reality in the universe, but on a smaller scale. This means that the human person is a microcosm, or a small world. Because [of this] the human being is able to unite things with each other and with God. Part of being in God's likeness is to serve as a *mediator*.... To mediate is to bring God to the world in blessing and to bring the world to God in receptivity and thanksgiving.[27]

As people who are created from both the earth and from God's breath, our task, Harrison says, is:

> to live harmonious lives, holding together the parts of ourselves that connect us with different parts of creation. As we struggle for harmony within ourselves, we are also contributing to the accomplishment of a much larger task: bringing harmony to the

---

26. Joseph, "Philosophical Foundations of Catholic College," 141.
27. Harrison, *God's Many-Splendored Image*, 127–28; emphasis in original.

whole of creation. We are called to worship God on behalf of the created universe, but we are also called to become peacemakers within the vast and varied creation.[28]

This notion of human beings as mediators between God and creation was central to the thought of Blondel. He too links this task with our identity as a microcosm.[29]

I stress the importance of promoting self-reflection as integral to university education because I believe that we should give very high priority to helping students think seriously about their vocation. I assume here that vocation is about God's call and our response. Our response includes taking into account, first, our *attraction* to a calling; second, our *fitness* for it; third, that the calling addresses a real need in the ecclesial or wider community; and fourth, that this calling is *recognized* or validated by those authorized to do so within this community. "A human being is called when desire and duty become one, when the source of one's deepest longing is at the same time something to which one is obedient."[30]

For believers, their vocation is about who God wants them to be, rather than about any specific line of work. And, of course, the primary and enduring vocation of a Christian is to be a disciple. However, even for non-religious students we can promote serious reflection about vocation in the sense of who they feel called to be, this calling being a blend of calling from within—to be true to themselves—and from without—to serve others. This entails relating a humble acknowledgment of our gifts and talents, together with a sound estimation of our strengths and weaknesses, to a considered evaluation of how we can best deploy who we are among our fellow human beings.[31] The question that should inform the central aim of a university is: What am I going to do with my life?

In order to address the fourth difficulty outlined above, what is needed is a deep commitment to both ecumenical and to interreligious learning. This would be a way to enhance significantly the range of perspectives and ways of interpreting available to scholars and students, as resources for integration. I take it that there is bound to be a connection between ecumenism and education. Both endeavors involve building bridges: ecumenism aims to bridge differences between Christians who come from different parts of the family of faith; education builds bridges between the generations with

---

28. Harrison, *God's Many-Splendored Image*, 131.

29. Blondel, *Action*, 95; Blondel, *Carnets intimes*, 1:307; see also Flamand, *Idée de mediation*.

30. Schwehn, "Lutheran Higher Education," 218.

31. See M. Miller, *Doing More with Life*.

regard to our cultural heritage. The bridge building of education should contribute to ecumenism; the bridge building of ecumenism should contribute to education. The inclusiveness of ecumenism is part of our appreciation of otherness and difference.

All of us—if we are to learn how to live in peace and harmony together—need to get better at appreciating our differences, how to learn from them, how to appreciate them, how to feel less threatened by them, how to grow through encounter with otherness. Indeed, having our worlds expanded is one of the benefits of university experience, and one of the best ways to have our world expanded is to meet with people who think differently from us—in matters of faith as in so many other matters. Our understanding of what is entailed by integration in education would be expanded by coming to an appreciation of how other Christians envisage this task and how they interpret the relationship between faith and the various types of knowledge we develop in studying. Interreligious learning too has much to offer as a resource for greater integration in a university education. Islam, in particular, at this juncture of our history and culture, can be a valuable dialogue partner with regard to the circle of knowledge and how all things hang together in dependence on God as their Creator.

As for the fifth challenge, this requires us, for all our seriousness about integration, not to press too hard, either our colleagues or our students. Invitation, not compulsion, should mark our style of approach to others. Example and encouragement, but not imposition and constraint, are what is needed. A good teacher knows intuitively, not only how to display passion for what he teaches, but compassion for who he teaches, and is aware when persistence can become oppressive of the spirit and an enemy of the lightness of touch that accompanies effective communication (a feature of teaching that Augustine called *hilaritas*).

\* \* \*

I have not argued for any particular approach to integration. One might place one's emphasis on how students can be helped to draw upon several disciplines, while ensuring they are rooted more deeply in one of them. One might concentrate instead on problem-centered learning that depends upon multiple disciplines. One might turn one's attention to meta-cognitional skills, along the lines of the work of either Bernard Lonergan or Robert Sternberg.[32] Or one might focus on large themes in learning as a focus

---

32. Lonergan, *Insight*; Lonergan, *Method in Theology*; Sternberg, *Thinking Styles*.

for integration, as does Martha Nussbaum.[33] An alternative approach to promoting integration in education would be to build on the work of Howard Gardner on multiple intelligences.[34] In contrast, one might construct an integrated curriculum that engaged students in learning the relative scope and limits of experience, authority, intuition, and imagination in relation to various forms of rationality. I have done something much more limited here. I have merely proposed that integration should be a major task in education, as it is in our personal life projects, outlined and analyzed several of the challenges such a task entails, before finally suggesting some of the lines along which these challenges might begin to be addressed within the university setting.

33. Nussbaum, *Not for Profit*.
34. Gardner, *Frames of Mind*.

# 16

# Towards a Curriculum for Life in Christian Formation

LET ME BEGIN WITH two assertions, neither of which I have space to defend adequately here, but both of which influence my motivation in writing this chapter. First, the very close association between what is learned in church and what is learned outside of church—and throughout life—has been lost. Yet the gospel is inscribed in—and conveyed by—lives, lives in which the dividing line between the explicitly religious and the ordinarily secular is porous if not absent. To reduce this gap between faith learning and the other kinds of learning that take place in life, we need to practice telling our faith story, set in the midst of everyday life; and we need to hear the stories of others in their faith journeys. We need to reverse the tendency to separate out church life from everyday life. Such a tendency diminishes our appreciation of God's presence, gives a false and unduly precious and pious understanding of the spiritual, and downgrades the value of our quotidian experiences.

Second, the church's massive contribution to educational provision over the centuries and in so many countries has a significant shadow side: the neglect of ongoing, lifelong faith formation. To use a cliché, but a true one, too many eggs have been put in the basket of schools (and to a lesser extent, in universities) and too few resources allocated to adult faith formation. In order to encourage and equip people to respond to the gospel with their whole self, to embrace their vocation, whatever this may be, and to use their different gifts in ministry or service, there need to be ongoing programs of adult faith formation on the meaning and implications of our baptism and vocation, closely related to the different stages of our life journeys. While the current situation prevails, where, relative to the provision for clergy education, adult Christians receive few opportunities sponsored by the church to grow and deepen in their faith, the kinds of curriculum offered in formal education will often seem out of touch with what students see are the real-life concerns and experiences of adults.

Thus, my concern is that there is a parallel between the gap many students experience, both in school and at university, a gap between the questions emerging from their lives and the questions being focused on in their classrooms—and a similar gap many members of a congregation experience—between the official teaching of the church on the one hand, and the questions and concerns of their everyday lives. I suspect that many pastors, at least those who are close to their parishioners, also worry about this gap, even as they seek to bridge it in how they apply the rules and teaching of the church with flexibility and sensitivity. Finding ways that are both faithful and creative to establish bridges between the world of church and the everyday lives of students has been a constant feature of the work of the religious educator Graham Rossiter.[1] Although his work has been mainly concerned about devising a viable approach to the task of religious education in schools, and developing appropriate resources for this task, there are clearly wider implications for how the church engages her people in lifelong learning about the faith. In the spirit of Graham's pervasive concern to render religious education vibrant and resonant for contemporary culture, in this chapter I address the gap identified above and propose some possible principles and starting points for building bridges between church teaching and the daily lives of congregations.

The danger facing teachers and pastors in their attempts to adapt what they are charged with conveying to their students or parishioners is that they find themselves accused of (or feel unsure as to whether they are guilty of) opening the door to inconsistency, idiosyncrasy, a selective approach to church teaching, and failing to do justice to the tradition they are supposed to be representing. Too much regimentation, too much stress on orthodoxy in teaching and correctness in applying church rules, can come across as alienating, lacking humanity, demanding too much of people and as disconnected from real-life concerns. However, too individualistic an approach by teachers and pastors and a failure to introduce people with sufficient care to the tradition can run the risk of downplaying, or giving a false impression of, its integrity, richness, challenge, and power to transform lives.

There are three parts to the chapter. First, I comment on central features of education and the process of Christian formation, before proposing

---

1. Crawford and Rossiter, *Missionaries to Teenage Culture*; Crawford and Rossiter, *Reasons for Living*; Rossiter, "What Sort of School"; Rossiter, "Religious Education."

two central purposes for such formation. Second, I explore the notion of a "curriculum for life" that would equip people to live as Christians in the secular world. How can we bring significant life experiences and concerns into constructive engagement with the life and teaching of the church? Third, I identify potential resources for developing a "curriculum for life" in Christian formation and raise questions for church communities that resolve to be both more deliberate and more effective in promoting faith formation and Christian learning.

## CHRISTIAN EDUCATION AND FORMATION

Education is about the capacities of human nature: *energy, emotions, intelligence, memory, will, conscience, and wonder*, and it concerns itself with how these capacities are developed, oriented, ordered, and integrated. The way education is carried out is influenced by one's views of oneself, the world or reality, threats, society, the nature, needs, and modes of learning of those to be taught or formed (whether children, young people or those of a more mature age), the knowledge worth passing on, and the needs of one's particular time and place. I believe that education should equip young people with a confident sense of their own identity and perspective, together with a generous receptivity and responsiveness to others. We might say that an education or formation program offers a deliberately structured journey whose goal is to assist learners to grow into their humanity (and thus into their divinity). But journeys are vulnerable to the unexpected. If life is a journey, one in which the unexpected can happen, where the way ahead is not always clear, and along which decisions are constantly called for as to which direction to take, then each of us needs reference points to clarify our location and to orient us for the next step. Religious traditions provide such reference points and a compass to assist in steering a way through life. However, the outcome of formation and education programs is necessarily unpredictable and precarious. Ultimately, what students take into themselves from the learning process, as soul food, for use in the future, is something that cannot be controlled; this is always a free act on their part.

Over generations, people have been instructed in their Christian faith in a wide range of ways: from their mothers by the hearth at home, from sermons in and outside of church, from the liturgy, from hymns, from the work and worship of confraternities and guilds, from stained glass windows, paintings, tapestries, religious plays on festive occasions, through hearing stories from the Bible and the lives of the saints, through pilgrimages, processions and devotions at sacred shrines, and from the experience of pastoral care. At its best, Christian formation displays an interrelation of the moral, physical, mental, and spiritual, a combination of the inner and outer. The linguistic, affective, cognitive, and embodied dimensions of learning are all linked. A comprehensive account of approaches to faith formation—which is beyond the scope of this chapter—would need to take into consideration structures, practices and ethos, each of these being influenced and filtered by the changing contexts and diverse purposes of those involved.

What purposes should guide and govern Christian formation today? Here I focus on just two possible aims, though others could be envisaged. The first is to acquire the mind of Christ; the second is to become a prototype or living embodiment of the gospel. St. Paul clearly states: "Let this mind be in you which was also in Christ Jesus" (Phil 2:5). We acquire this mind of Christ in the context of the church community and its associated practices. What does "having the mind of Christ" mean? What does it mean to think Christianly? It does not mean simply thinking about the Bible, prayer, the church, the sacraments, the saints—necessary although all this might be. For this might be to leave the rest of our thinking—about work, the world of production, politics, taxes, holidays, food, family, sex and relationships, investments, travel—untouched and unconverted. We have to bring into dialogue two kinds of truth—sacred, salvific truth—truth for the sake of our salvation—and all the other kinds of truth that are part of our life. This means that we must bring together and harmonize faith and reason—harmonize them, not compartmentalize them. When electricity was installed into our houses, all rooms were illuminated, not some. In the house of our lives, all our rooms must be illuminated and all dimensions of our being should be seen differently in the light of faith—intellectual, physical, social, moral, economic, political, artistic, as well as spiritual. Having the mind of Christ must engage, not only the intellect, but also heart, imagination, will, memory, and character.

What about becoming a prototype of the gospel as an educational aim for Christian formation? We are called, not only to believe in, but also to become the gospel; not just to hear about and approve of it, but personally and actively to participate in the life and work of God in our world. Not only to be familiar with what God was doing in Jesus Christ, but to live our lives, in all their aspects and dimensions, not only the explicitly religious side, in such a way that they are shaped by and permeated with the gospel. What Christ is for us, we have to be for the world, at least for that part of it that in which we find ourselves placed. Thus, we are not only to benefit from what God offers to us, but also to bear witness to this, by faithfully embodying the good news in our words and actions. As individuals and as church communities we should be like a microcosm of the kingdom, a mini-version, a prototype, a rehearsal; our churches should not be escapes from or hiding places from the world but a sign of what we are all called to become, if we accept God's grace.

We are called to be more than merely beneficiaries of the salvation God has brought about in Christ, though we are that, but also to bear witness to it and to embody it in all we do. Our church communities are meant to be walking explanations of the gospel, like a living commentary on it. Not all are called to be public preachers or traveling missionaries, but all Christians should become the reflectors of as well as recipients of the gospel. Being, doing and telling—or presence, practice and proclamation through example: these are the three dimensions of our Christian mission and the ways people come to learn the gospel. And the more we *become* the gospel, the more opportunities will open up to *speak* the gospel.

For all of us, our task is to learn how to love. This is the way to enter into our humanity and to share God's life. The task of Christian formation is to help us to develop a Christian imagination and sensibility, the capacity to read and respond to the world in the light of the gospel of our Lord Jesus Christ—reading and responding to ourselves, to our neighbors, and to our culture and creation—as we learn *about* Christ, *from* Christ, learn to live *in* Christ together, *with* Christ, *as* Christ in ourselves, and *for* Christ in others.

Christian formation is less about content and concepts and more about verbs and joint activity. It is about worshipping together, encountering the Bible, sharing experiences, welcoming, celebrating, questioning, listening, healing, forgiving, reconciling, remembering, serving others, loving, praying, and, some of the time, learning and teaching more deliberately and explicitly, instead of doing so implicitly, alongside and as part of all the other activities. Such learning helps us to see with the eyes of faith, interpret in the light of truth, and respond with a heart of love.

We would do well today to recapture the notion of the total environment of the Christian community as the principal site for formation. The quality of the community life of a congregation speaks more powerfully than the explicit teaching that occurs within (though of course that has a necessary place). This community life constitutes its implicit curriculum, which is always more powerful in its influence than any explicit curriculum. David Heywood refers to the operation of this implicit curriculum:

> The welcome offered to strangers and occasional worshippers; the demeanor of the worship leader; the content of the liturgy; the scope of the prayers; the relationships in evidence between the worshippers; even the state of the building—all these convey,

often in a far more effective way than any sermon or deliberate teaching event, what the members of a particular local church really believe and value.[2]

Christian formation needs to display the three features of being lifelong, communitarian, and intergenerational. First, we need to beware of restricting formation to the young when it is needed for every age of life. There is no point at which any of us can claim that we are fully formed or fully converted. Second, we should ensure that Christian formation is not merely an induction for individuals, but seek to make much of it a communal process. Third, we need to find creative ways to bring together different generations so that these can enrich and stimulate each other with their various experiences of and perspectives on life.

## LIFELONG LEARNING AND A CURRICULUM FOR LIFE

Any proposal to analyze the needs of the present, with a view to developing a "curriculum for life" runs (at least) two types of risks. First, the nature of one's sociocultural location, upbringing and education, one's minor choices and major decisions, one's gender, race, personality—all these, although they will cumulatively grant one a certain vantage point which enables perception, are also bound to limit what one is able to see, or even to imagine, as important elements in a life worth living. Second, so rapid is the pace of technological and social change, that any attempt to prescribe a curriculum that prepares for and addresses the needs of the present is almost inevitably going to seem, to some degree at least, out of date by the time it has been received.

Learning, ever more deeply, about sacred Scripture, or the teachings, history and tradition of the church will always be essential resources for growth in Christian faith and for daily life as disciples. However, what is also needed, if faith is to be incarnated in all dimensions of life, is guidance as to how these traditional resources assist us in being Christians in the world outside the confines, the protection and community atmosphere, of the church. How do we express and live out our faith in such diverse settings as the home, the office or the factory, the gymnasium or the pub—in all the places of work and leisure? How does faith influence our willingness to volunteer to alleviate some social or pastoral need, for example, to help people experiencing problems with housing, poverty, hunger, debt, drugs

---

2. Heywood, *Divine Revelation and Human Learning*, 85.

and alcohol, loneliness and isolation, mobility, dementia, rehabilitation after prison, or settling into a new country as a refugee? While individual Christians can contribute time, energy and resources in such cases, collective action is often required and this may entail political engagement. How well equipped are Christians for exercising social responsibilities and upholding the common good?

Unfortunately, little help is given to Christians to support their making connections between in-church learning and their daily life situations. David Heywood points out that "lay engagement and influence in the workplace, community and society is vast," but there is "very little curiosity, affirmation, prayer, theological or practical resourcing for these roles at local church level."[3] Referring to the Church of England, Heywood questions whether lay development and discipleship are considered seriously as priorities in most dioceses. He attributes this to the clericalized culture, where ministry is treated as the domain of the clergy, rather than as a natural expression of the vocation all the baptized. His point applies equally strongly to the Catholic Church. Too often, only lip service is paid to adult faith formation that takes account of all the seasons of our life journey and the diverse contexts in which we are called upon to put our beliefs into practice in service of others.

We might ask of Christian formation: How does this fit in with our life story? What light does it cast on our life story? How does it support or challenge our life story? What matters to us at different stages of our lives—what we notice, care about, fear, desire, and value or prioritize—changes in response to the experiences we undergo. As Christian teachers seek to invite others into the faith tradition, the response given to their educational and formational efforts—whether this response be acceptance or rejection, understanding or confusion, distortion or creative modification as it is adopted and expressed—will inevitably be influenced by people's circumstances, contexts, and life experiences.

Can we connect Christian literacy—with its biblical, spiritual, theological, and historical dimensions—more closely and more comprehensively with a literacy for life, in a way that embraces our bodily, emotional, linguistic, scientific, aesthetic, creative, moral, social, economic, cultural, political, environmental concerns? The contexts, currents, courses, and choices of our lives and the corporeal, contextual, and communal aspects of our humanity need to be brought into dialogue with what is touched upon in Christian formation. Thus, coping with vulnerability, death, limitation, suffering, loss, disappointment, guilt, and setbacks all play a part in our

3. Church of England report, quoted in Heywood, *Kingdom Learning*, xi.

journey towards salvation. Similarly, joy, excitement, a sense of achievement, that we make a difference, a positive contribution, finding meaning and purpose—all these are directly relevant to appreciating and responding to our vocation. Christian formation needs to engage the desire for belonging, for identity, for feeling part of something bigger and worthwhile, as well as the inner desire to encounter truth, to see the bigger picture in which we are situated. Within people there is a yearning for love, friendship, warm, healthy, and life-giving relationships, and a capacity to receive and share intimacy.

Education is integral to the church's life and pivotal to promoting mature Christian discipleship. If Christian faith is to lead to an ongoing transformation of lives so that these have a recognizable Christlike character and display a reading and response to reality as God given, then education in the church must provide a multifaceted experience of learning that engages with, listens to, illuminates, and integrates the totality of each person's experience.

I now draw upon two recent books which offer helpful prompts as to how Christian educators and those involved in faith formation might establish links between our life stories and our faith tradition. The first of these books does not explicitly articulate a Christian vision, although it seems thoroughly infused with a Christian spirit. The Hungarian philosopher and polymath Gabor Csepregi published in 2019 a phenomenology of life-defining moments. I will pick out three themes highlighted in this book which seem to me to be fertile starting points for building bridges between the Christian story of salvation and a curriculum for life. These are key experiences, decisions, and models.

The first theme from Csepregi is a focus on key experiences or moments in life. Among these, the author mentions "the birth of a child, a marriage, the commencement of a career, severe illness, retirement, or the death of a loved one."[4] At such times we often modify how we relate to our past, present, and future. Of course, in addition to the key moments in an individual's life, communities also undergo landmark events or experiences in their history which change in significant ways how they see themselves and their world. The author singles out six vital experiences that many individuals undergo: "moments of deciding, of breaking away from actual circumstances, of encountering a model, of immersing in a foreign culture, of listening to a beautiful piece of music, and of experiencing an ethical action."[5] Other experiences he mentions include those of failure, of forgive-

---

4. Csepregi, *In Vivo*, 4.
5. Csepregi, *In Vivo*, 5.

ness and of reconciliation, of achievement or of a "breakthrough" moment when an obstacle no longer seems an impossible stumbling block or when an insight surfaces without our conscious effort. One can envisage fruitful reflections on such moments, with people of all ages, as offering opportunities to connect life stories with Christian learning and formation.

A second theme on which Csepregi focuses is the role of decisions in life. He notes that "Decisions are serious affairs: the 'either-or' of a decision constitutes a fork in the highway of our lives." He distinguishes such decisions from choices, which are much less significant for us, because they do not fundamentally change the nature or direction of life. "We can undo what we have chosen, but we have to live with our decision."[6] Often decisions are made when we face a turning point or crisis (a word which also means an opportunity). For Csepregi, "It is only by courageously making decisions—with the associated risks, uncertainties, responsibilities, and feeling of solitude—that we are able to create a strong and mature personality."[7] Christian formation should include a supporting environment for reflection on, and opportunities to practice, decision-making. Without a robust capacity and willingness to take decisions, we remain vulnerable to the pressures and temptations of prevailing social and cultural norms. This applies to individuals, but also to communities. I have seen, in my own archdiocese, as we prepare for our 2020 synod, how difficult Christian communities can find the process of reaching collective decisions about equipping ourselves to be the kind of church that God is calling us to be. Accepting responsibility for the health of the church and becoming positively involved, exercising properly one's baptismal calling seems to require a revolution in habits of thinking and acting. And if Christian communities find it hard to engage in decision-making within the household of the faith, they will not be optimally equipped to do so as Christians in the world of daily life. Christian formation has a part to play in fostering mature engagement in decision-making.

The third theme to be drawn from Csepregi is the educational role of models. Csepregi defines a model as a person who,

> due to his or her perceived qualities, values, and achievements, exerts a profound and transformative influence on another person.... Models make manifest a discernible value or a selective set of values; they are the incarnation of values in a specific historical epoch and a particular social environment.[8]

---

6. Csepregi, *In Vivo*, 19.
7. Csepregi, *In Vivo*, 31.
8. Csepregi, *In Vivo*, 67, 68.

Such models might radiate vitality, depth, conviction, integrity, and authenticity; or generosity, modesty, or equanimity. They can give us inspiration, confidence, and insight into what we can be if we replicate their qualities. They show us what is possible; by attracting our admiration they motivate us to adopt their way of being, at least, in some aspects of their lifestyle. Although the models we admire and approve of change as we get older, no age is entirely immune from being influenced by the example of those around us (and by those further afield); nor is the process of imitation restricted merely to children and young people. Thus, consideration of the models to which we give attention can provide a salutary bridge between church and world in Christian formation.

The second source, more briefly to be drawn upon here, is by an American Episcopal priest and professor of historical theology, Ephraim Radner. In his book *A Time to Keep*, subtitled *Theology, Mortality, and the Shape of a Human Life*, Radner brings out the implications of the temporal nature of our lives. If, as Radner points out, our "life span is the very means by which human beings relate to God,"[9] then "we cannot pry apart the concrete realities of our life spans from the redemptive claims made about our beings in the gospel."[10] "God's time includes the times that mark our coming to be, our survival, and our passing away: times of birth, growth, eating, learning, sexual engagement, relating, work, birthing, forming, weakening, and dying."[11] Traditionally, Christians have read the Scriptures as if they were speaking about our own times, not a period locked away in the past. They assumed God was as active in their own time as in the times of their ancestors and that he speaks to us, here and now, through these Scriptures. We need to recapture that sense of the immediate presence of God throughout our lives; otherwise our tradition runs the risk of being seen merely as a museum, that is, as offering items for inspection, perhaps interesting, but no longer vitally necessary for life. Being inducted into our Christian tradition should be experienced as a process of being brought into a living presence who speaks directly to the core of our human condition, someone who addresses us personally and who embraces our hopes and fears, our needs and desires at all the stages and seasons of life.

---

9. Radner, *Time to Keep*, 11.
10. Radner, *Time to Keep*, 15.
11. Radner, *Time to Keep*, 8.

## RESOURCES FOR LIFELONG CHRISTIAN FORMATION

To assist us in assembling resources that could support a curriculum for life in lifelong Christian formation, we might take careful note of three writers whose work, at first sight, seems removed from the faith perspective from which we would be operating. The first, by Iain McGilchrist, is a vast and somewhat intimidating, but immensely rich book, based on a rare combination of expertise in both English literature and neuroscience, *The Master and His Emissary*. It seems to me that, although never explicit, underlying McGilchrist's argument there is a deeply Christian sensibility. At the heart of the book is a thorough analysis of the two hemispheres of the brain, the differences between them and how they operate together. One quotation will have to suffice to illustrate this work.

> The world of the left hemisphere, dependent on denotative language and abstraction, yields clarity and power to manipulate things that are known, fixed, static, isolated, decontextualized, explicit, disembodied, general in nature, but ultimately lifeless. The right hemisphere, by contrast, yields a world of individual, changing, evolving, interconnected, implicit, incarnate, living beings within the context of the lived world, but in the nature of things never fully graspable, always imperfectly known—and to this world it exists in a relationship of care.[12]

The first half of this book focuses on the workings of these two hemispheres, while the second part rereads the entire history of Western culture in the light of the scientific points made earlier. A curriculum for life should take into account McGilchrist's insights into how the brain functions, even though at no stage does he refer to the implications for education of his analysis. If grace builds on nature, it is incumbent on Christian educators to understand and appreciate what nature gives to us.

Second, careful consideration of a book by the psychologist Robert Kegan provides pointers to areas that should be addressed in a curriculum for life. Kegan starts from a survey of the principal tasks carried out by adults throughout their life cycle and then he unpacks the range of qualities and skills required to carry out these tasks. These tasks include, among others, parenting, sustaining an intimate relationship over the long haul, engaging in work, participating as citizens in a society where differences have to be encountered and negotiated, managing one's own physical and mental health. "These activities present us with a vast variety of expectations,

---

12. McGilchrist, *Master and His Emissary*, 174.

prescriptions, claims and demands."[13] He points out that a literature has been developed about each of these different spheres of activity, but rarely do these literatures take account of each other, to such an extent that insufficient account is taken of the overall experience of learners (at any stage or season of life) and curriculum coherence is left too often to the student to work out for herself, usually unaided. Thus, "people who write, teach, and shape the discourse about management apparently do not read the literature about intimacy. The people who create the leadership literature do not read the parenting literature."[14] Specialization deepens our understanding of particular aspects of life while failing to attend to its wholeness, unity, and interconnectedness. Again, while faith is not the focus of this book, those engaged in faith formation intended to connect to the real-life concerns of people of all ages would benefit from Kegan's unfolding of the social, psychological, and cultural demands of the different spheres of life. It is striking how frequently Pope Francis emphasizes that pastoral ministry and accompaniment begins with engaging with the reality of peoples' lives.

I find particularly helpful the distinction Kegan makes between "wondering at" and "wondering about." "'Wondering at' is watching and reverencing; 'wondering about' is asking and reckoning."[15] The first is "receptive, contemplation as an end in itself"; it is aesthetic in nature, "the inspiration of the humanities." The second is "acting upon, a means to an end; it is analytic, the inspiration of the sciences."[16] Christian formation should facilitate both types of wonder, facilitating the capacity to reverence as well as to analyze. The former helps us to see rightly; the second helps us to use rightly what we see.

If McGilchrist's and Kegan's work complement and reinforce each other, and jointly provide a sound foundation that underpins the notion of a "curriculum for life," a third writer has contributed valuable insights that offer further building blocks for such a curriculum. Howard Gardner is a foremost exponent of the theory of multiple intelligences.[17] These include linguistic, logical/mathematical, spatial, musical, kinesthetic, self-understanding, and understanding other individuals. His theory challenges educators to realize that, not only do people learn at different speeds, they also learn in different ways. A truly inclusive approach to education and formation will attend to all the different types of intelligence and not restrict

13. Kegan, *In Over Our Heads*, 5.
14. Kegan, *In Over Our Heads*, 6.
15. Kegan, *In Over Our Heads*, 8.
16. Kegan, *In Over Our Heads*, 8.
17. Gardner, *Unschooled Mind*; *Frames of Mind*; *Intelligence Reframed*.

itself to the linguistic and logical. While Gardner's work might not be sufficient on its own as a foundation for Christian learning, it does offer salutary insights that should prompt Christian educators towards a more comprehensive approach to planning learning opportunities for those in their care and it challenges them to extend the repertoire of teaching methods they employ.

In order to harness the insights of each of these three writers into a much more explicitly Catholic vision for the project of developing a "curriculum for life," I would recommend drawing upon Thomas Groome's *Educating for Life*. Here one will find an inspiring outline of a faithful approach to education that is truly holistic and multidimensional, that renders tradition as both vital in itself and as life giving to others, that is inclusive and invitational, and one that combines deep spiritual roots with contemporary cultural relevance. Groome demonstrates how "for life, for all" can be conveyed in curriculum, pedagogy, community and ethos. Key features of Catholicism receive in-depth treatment: "a sacramental consciousness, commitment to relationship and community, appreciation for tradition, cultivating reason for wisdom of life, fostering holistic spirituality, formation in social justice and inculcating a catholic worldview."[18]

Building on these reflections, I propose five questions for church communities that wish to be intentionally formational. First, to what extent does the experience of congregational members *outside* of church color, frame, reinforce, or inhibit their reception of what is offered *inside* church? Second, are the differences (in life experience and perspective) among church members drawn upon as a potential source of learning? Third, to what extent are church members expected to be agents in their own faith learning—rather than recipients of teaching? What scope is given for engagement, responsibility, and initiative in church life, work, and learning? Are church members consulted about decisions in the life of the church? Is their judgment and evaluation invited? Fourth, what kind of balance is there, within a congregation's experience of the church's curriculum, between (i) receiving instruction and teaching (in sermons and beyond) by clergy; (ii) individual guidance and mentoring of parishioners by clergy; (iii) peer ministry and teaching by parishioners; (iv) opportunities for sharing experience and giving testimony; and (v) joint action on projects or in serving others? Fifth, is there encouragement and facilitation of shared reflection on the story of the faith journeys and the struggles, challenges, questions, and insights of church members? I nurture the hope that, if these questions were taken

---

18. Groome, *Educating for Life*, 427.

seriously, and then acted upon, the gap between faith learning and life in the world might be, at least partly, reduced.

Fortunately, God is more patient with us than we are with ourselves. To be too ambitious can be self-defeating. It is salutary to bear in mind Étienne Gilson's warning about school education:

> However heavily we load our programs, and however widely we may diversify them in order to answer the future needs of all our pupils, many of them will feel later on that they have been taught many things they did not need to know, whereas what they did need to know has never been taught to them in school.[19]

Those of us who are committed to Christian formation should remember that the primary agent in moving a person to accept the gospel and all that this entails is not us, but the Holy Spirit, whose work is often invisible to us and who operates according to God's time, not ours. For that we should be grateful.

---

19. Gilson, "Eminence of Teaching," 308-9.

# 17

# Christian Education and the Discernment of Vocation

*From "Whatever" to "Amen"*

CHRISTIAN EDUCATION IS NOT limited to schools. It takes place in homes and churches, in universities and in youth ministry, in service to those in need and while giving and receiving pastoral care, in Bible study and in other kinds of faith study groups and in dialogue with people of other faiths or with those of no religious faith.[1] Its ministers and agents include many more people than professional teachers, or ordained clergy or those belonging to religious orders. In this chapter I focus on a key purpose for Christian education, one that applies, I believe, to all contexts where Christian education occurs: taking seriously the question of vocation. I dare to hope that promoting reflection on vocation is accepted as vital for a wide range of Christians—Catholic, Orthodox, and Protestant (in all their varieties).

A word or act of witness may communicate powerfully quite outside any religious context, while even what appears to be the most explicitly spiritual setting can fail to move some of those who move in its ambience. Thus, while one would be right to expect that Christian educational endeavors would be both deliberate and explicit, there can be nothing guaranteed about the outcomes of such efforts, wherever and whenever these occur. The work of the Holy Spirit in prompting, facilitating and bringing to fruition acts of witness and teaching and in opening hearts to receive these cannot be monitored, nor can it be directed or controlled. As a result, while Christian educators should have enduring and overarching purposes that

---

1. I have treated this range of contexts in Sullivan: *Learning the Language of Faith*; *Communicating Faith*.

guide their work, they must be open to the multiple ways of learning and the mysteries of reception.

Furthermore, Christian education is not limited to the teaching of Holy Scripture or doctrine or moral precepts, embracing, in an intermingled and complex manner, the diverse dimensions of Christian life. Some people deploy the phrase "Christian education" to mean the teaching of the key elements of Christian faith, usually in the context of religious education. Others might have in mind the spirituality of the teacher and how this permeates the outworking of her pedagogy, though perhaps in ways that remain implicit. Others again focus instead either on the celebration of worship or on the provision of pastoral care. An alternative approach, rarely attempted in the UK context, would be to develop a Christian curriculum, one where a Christian perspective on the whole curriculum is articulated and drawn out in each of its constitutive areas. Recently there has been an initiative to unpack the possibilities of developing a Christian pedagogy.[2] However, the focus here is on what I believe should be a central feature of and an abiding outcome of Christian education: taking seriously the question of vocation.

Of course, Christian educators might legitimately wish to privilege other goals, such as the promotion of faith, hope and charity, a love of truth, growth in holiness, a capacity for and a competence in reconciliation, a passion for peace and justice, authentic freedom, a spirit of wonder and gratitude, the emergence of a mature and well-informed conscience. All these should be part of a Christian *paideia*, where learning, virtue, and wisdom feed into character and culture as expressions of discipleship. Taking seriously the question of vocation should be embedded within such a network of supporting goals for Christian education; it is not something that should be seen in isolation from or in competition with these.

My subtitle, "From 'Whatever' to 'Amen,'" is meant to bring out one particular aspect of what is entailed by taking seriously the question of vocation: a move from indifference to commitment. "Whatever," as a phrase that one hears only too often among some young people, seems to me to convey a response to what is being said that combines all the following: Who cares? This is of no significance to me; take that path if you like, but leave me out of it—don't count me in. It suggests distance, cynicism, even sometimes contempt. It seems to imply a refusal to allow oneself to become engaged, a radical individualism, a kind of free-floating sense of independence that allows one to choose, and then to choose differently, if the earlier choice does not satisfy, as if choices do not have consequences, are not part of a

---

2. See Green, "Distinctively Christian Pedagogy."

coherent and unified pattern, and such a stance assumes that all choices can easily be remade, as if from scratch. In this perspective, "whatever" seems to represent the endless postponement of commitment and the very opposite of taking vocation seriously.

In contrast, Amen implies a definite yes to a possible commitment, an acknowledgment of all that is entailed by that commitment, taking its costs and benefits into account; through its conveying of the sentiment "let it be so" it seems to include a recognition that although we are responsible for our actions, we are not in control of our lives, that there is a givenness to which we are responding, an objective order of things not made by us, whose workings we trust. Our Amen transcends particular beliefs and practices; it expresses openness to a way of life; and at least aspirationally, this way of life is unified, coherent—a whole, not a collection of disparate—and possibly mutually contradictory—parts. One might say that the move from "whatever" to "Amen" combines a transition from life offering us a range of items to choose from, each of which has relatively minor importance, to a life centered on something (or for Christians, Someone) of capital importance. I should say that, apart from when it is the first word in a sentence, I spell "whatever" with a small *w*; but I always spell "Amen" with a capital *a*. The transition from "whatever" to "Amen" might be considered a move from the goods life to the good life.[3]

I believe that there is a close connection between, on the one hand, the capacity and willingness to commit oneself in an enduring and wholehearted way, and, on the other, the sense that one is being addressed through the world as a gift (behind which there is a Giver).[4] In promoting reflection on vocation in Christian education I think we should strive to encourage students to *receive and respond to* the supreme author of their lives as they seek to discern the particular shape their lives might take and how they might give themselves in gratitude for the gifts they have received.

In the first part of the chapter, I analyze key features of vocation. In part 2, the focus is on the discernment of vocation. In conclusion, I briefly

---

3. The distinction between the goods life and the good life is made by Gregory, in *Unintended Reformation*, 273. He refers to the goods life as one in which "to be is to buy," a life where people "construct their identity through a never-ending series of acts of self-creation and re-creation mediated by the things they consume" (239). My use of "whatever" in this chapter is partly indebted to Gregory's phrase "the Kingdom of Whatever" (112), although I have taken it in a different direction.

4. In her review of Roger Scruton, *Face of God*, Judith Wolfe says: "The summit of our existence as subjects that live face to face is, for Scruton, our ability to give ourselves as a gift. And this he argues, may in the end be possible only in a world that is gift: 'Being, for the religious person, is a gift, not a fact'" (Review, 19).

bring out a few educational implications of these comments on vocation and discernment.

## VOCATION

In 2012 in my own church we have seen the launch of the National Vocations Framework, a process to help people discover discipleship.[5] This fresh initiative seeks to help believers to hear the call of Christ and to identify what this call might entail for them as individuals with regard to the life paths they adopt and the major decisions they make. Vocation is interpreted in a broad and inclusive way. Strong emphasis is placed on discernment. The aim of the process is to promote a culture of vocation, one which realizes that everyone is called to holiness, encourages reflection on vocation, and provides models and support for people discerning their own particular vocation.

As I understand the term, vocation gives me my sense of *where* God wants me to be, *what* God wants me to do, *how* God wants me to do it, and *who* God wants me to be. Vocation links identity, task (or mission), giftedness and giving; it is where knowing, desiring and doing come together. It requires me to be attentive to and discriminating about what is pushing and pulling me—the direction that my energies in life are going. For religious believers vocation is about God's call and our response. Its elements include, first, our *attraction* to a calling; second, our *fitness* for it; third, a sense of and a desire to address the *needs* of a group of people; and fourth, either an explicit or an implicit *recognition* or validation by authoritative representatives of the community (faith or civic). For Christians, their vocation is more about call, rather than choice; it is modeled on Christ; it constitutes a mode of discipleship; it changes one's life; therefore it must be taken seriously, with singleness of purpose and resolution; our vocation will influence the company we keep. As has often been claimed, vocation is where one's own gifts and the world's needs come together. At its heart is the belief that God calls me *through* others *for* others. Vocation challenges us to reflect upon and to bring together (or allow to be brought together in us) God's will, human freedom, our particular identity and gifts, the needs of others, awareness of the sources of motivation and commitment, the need for discernment and decision, and grace and life in Christ.

---

5. The National Vocations Framework was written by Dom Christopher Jamison OSB for the Catholic Bishops' Conference of England and Wales. See Bishops Conference, "National Vocations Framework."

Vocation opens the way to central forms of self-expression, authenticity, identity, and self-giving. Seen in this light, vocation is personal (in that it builds upon my own characteristics); it is a serious matter, because it governs or frames important elements of my life; it has a service orientation, rather than being merely self-indulgent; it is informed by self-knowledge and a realistic assessment both of the opportunities made available by the world and the challenges and needs posed by it. Creating a climate where vocation is taken seriously invites people to ask themselves such basic questions as who am I, who and what am I for, what really matters to me, what are my special gifts and responsibilities, what am I going to do with my life.

Let me identify four further features of vocation. First, the sense of being called is not just to a specific action or response to need (though that might trigger it); rather the call brings with it a way of putting our whole life into a narrative or story that removes from it any sense of fragmentation, dispersion or dissipation. It offers meaning to our life and it unifies its diverse elements. Second, the call offers us a way to be true to, to live in harmony with, what is, deep down, central to our nature; it helps us to be authentic and genuine, living according to the grain of what we should be, doing justice to the fact that we are made in the image of God. Third, not only does the call enable us to be true to who we really are, it also enables us to contribute positively and realistically to our context and to those in need in that context. Fourth, when responding to the call wholeheartedly, we might say obediently, when nothing obscures or hinders the passage from hearing to doing, we enjoy the assurance of resonance between ourselves and the source of our being, even in the midst of trials and setbacks, misunderstanding and malign forces.

For many of us, our call is heard, not with total clarity, or in a blinding light, or once and for all.[6] The voice we hear calling us will often seem, especially at first, unclear and elusive. I am referring here to our muffled hearing as to the source of the call, the nature and scope of the call, and the group that the call directs us to serve. The call will often feel uncomfortable at first, since it almost definitely entails being willing to change in some important part of our affections, purposes, values, behavior, or company. In speaking of the larger obligation that vocation presses upon us (understood as coming from a transcendent source, even though it will often be mediated by our multiple human relationships with their attendant obligations).

---

6. Melina reminds us that the call "is not heard only at one particular moment in time but is *progressively* drawn out as the believer becomes more like Christ" (*Epiphany of Love*, 95; emphasis added). Through the relation with God at its heart, and according to Emmanuel Mounier, Melina tells us, a vocation "allows the *gradual* integration of our actions and the unification of the person" (97; emphasis added).

A. J. Conyers refers to the self being "'laid hold of' by another, having a claim made upon his time, his future, his destiny, the shape of his life that originates from outside the self. It is the opposite of 'choice,' or of freedom in the sense of self-determination."[7] Yet in another way, obeying the call is the route towards a more real freedom, since it frees us from inner contradiction, from distractions, and from the call of the crowd. Conyers quotes P. T. Forsyth: "If within us we find nothing over us we succumb to what is around us."[8] Throughout his book on vocation Theobald stresses that the calling invites us to hear not only the obligation to follow, but alongside this also the benevolent reassurance—"you can." (This is God's "Yes, you can.")[9]

The sense of being called, of vocation, can come to us from many sources. It may come through reading Holy Scripture—or hearing it preached. It may come to us in the context of personal prayer. It may come to us in the context of our church community's worship. It may come from what we see and hear and at home, in the context of the family. I want to suggest that one of the tasks of a Christian school community is to foster a climate, to create an environment, where people can hear, welcome, appreciate, and embrace the particular call that God is sending to each of us, not only to discipleship in general, but to our special, personal, and unique way of living out this discipleship. Can schools enable people to ask seriously the important question: What am I going to do with my life? If they can, this is a task that can only be begun in a primary school; it needs to be continued in secondary school, and, for those who go to university, it should be further continued there too.

Some of us will find our way to God's will for our lives in a garden, on a mountain, by a seashore, in a forest, by a river, in the midst of a jungle, out in the desert, inside a cave, or as we gaze at the night sky.[10] Some of these jungles, deserts, or caves may be either literal or metaphorical. For some, the space in which discernment occurs may be one of stillness, peace, silence, and long listening. For many people, their sense of vocation comes to them through some unexpected personal encounter which alters the way they see things, which radically modifies their priorities, which makes them see themselves quite differently thereafter. For others, a sense of vocation is only arrived at after periods of hunger, disturbing anxiety, and painful wrestling. For all it will involve, at some point, a need for calm reflection and sober assessment, together with letting go, risk-taking, and trusting

---

7. Conyers, *Listening Heart*, 17.
8. P. T. Forsyth, *The Cure of Souls*, quoted in Conyers, *Listening Heart*, 171.
9. Theobald, *Vous avez dit vocation?*
10. With acknowledgment to Silf, *Landscapes of Prayer*.

vulnerability. We cannot plot in advance the precise path to discerning vocation, but we can ensure the question of vocation is posed, is kept open, is reflected upon, and is nurtured.

## DISCERNMENT

Let me mention some of the principal elements within acts of discernment. These include first, attending to, taking into account, and reviewing a mass of data; second, sifting, analyzing and weighing the relative significance of and "seeing through" this data; third, not being over influenced in the process by the loudest "voices"; fourth, reflecting with the aid of strong foundational principles and values that have been tested for their legitimacy, scope, sources, relevance, and applicability; fifth, operating from a stable, calm, unrushed position, in a spirit of freedom, with (relatively honest and clear) insight into one's own motives, the influences that are brought to bear on one, as well as limitations—limitations in one's capacities and knowledge and in what might be possible in a situation; sixth, reaching a decision as to what is needed and what action is to be taken. Discernment in this light is evidently a self-involving process, and it comes to fruition when one is ready to follow through a decision by action, aware of potential consequences for oneself and for others.

The discernment of vocation depends upon a number of factors. It needs an expansive imaginative sympathy; how else would the needs of those one might serve be sensitively identified? It requires the capacity to think, to question, to delve into issues and problems, and the ability to discriminate between reliable and unreliable explanations for why things are as they are; how else can we move beyond sentimental to serious responses? It relies on the formation of a character marked by habits of patience, perseverance, courage, resilience, and self-discipline, as well as capacities for sharing and cooperation; without such qualities, any vocation adopted would be likely to be feebly underpinned, lacking the necessary steel to endure or to be effective, merely individualistic and ephemeral dilettantism. In all this, with regard to vocation, the explanation of it, the modeling of it in action and creating the conditions in which others can discern their own vocation, personhood is prior to and the fundamental context for professional competence. When it comes to vocation (and discipleship in general) who we are is more important than what we can do.

Amadeo Cencini offers penetrating insights into a crucial yet neglected dimension of the process of discerning a vocation. Here I take liberties in a loose translation and summary of a few of the key points he makes with regard to an unpalatable aspect of self-knowledge. In each person there are both healthy desires and deep wounds. Each person has a fundamental incoherence at the heart of their being, their own principal defect, central conflict, major weakness, or inner vulnerability.[11] This inner conflict or weakness deforms their sense of identity, their vision of God, their perception of other people, and their ideas about life.[12] The process of growing into the image of God begins when one uncovers one's own particular demons.[13] Insofar as a person lacks the courage to name his central conflict, he will remain a slave.[14] Christian educators must continue to grow in self-knowledge themselves; otherwise they could never help others find their own way.[15] They must also help students, in the path towards mature self-knowledge, to become increasingly conscious of their behavior; habits and criteria for choices; their preferences, motivations, and reactions in the face of successes or setbacks; their friendships, sympathies, instinctive reactions, and attitudes; they must also teach students how to listen to the inner voice of conscience (a voice that not only exercises judgment, but which also must itself be subject to judgment).[16] Cencini connects such realistic yet searing self-knowledge to the ongoing task of integration of our drives, feelings, instincts, projects, dreams, and relationships around the living center that is Christ.[17] He also links realism about our weakness as we stand before the cross of Christ to our capacity for understanding and our openness in responding positively to the weakness of others.[18]

If someone wishes to discern his or her vocation, what might be some of the steps that need to be taken? Here I suggest ten considerations that might help the process of discernment. The order in which they are presented here is in no way intended to be normative; individuals may start from different considerations and pursue these in the order that seems appropriate for them. Those helping pupils and students to take the question of vocation seriously should be ready to guide those in their charge by facilitating reflection on each of these aspects of our experience; they will do this

---

11. Cencini, *Éduquer, former, accompagner*, 13, 15.
12. Cencini, *Éduquer, former, accompagner*, 66, 68, 72, 73.
13. Cencini, *Éduquer, former, accompagner*, 14.
14. Cencini, *Éduquer, former, accompagner*, 32.
15. Cencini, *Éduquer, former, accompagner*, 15.
16. Cencini, *Éduquer, former, accompagner*, 16–21.
17. Cencini, *Éduquer, former, accompagner*, 13, 88.
18. Cencini, *Éduquer, former, accompagner*, 99. Cencini quotes a message from John Paul II in 2003: "The human being only discovers his identity when he becomes the servant of his brother" (101).

more effectively if they have grown in mature self-knowledge themselves (though ultimately none of us is transparent to ourselves and we remain a mystery whose depths can never be fully plumbed).

First, attention might be given to our relationships. These give us a sense of belonging, of acceptance, of being at home; my relationships tell me who I am, and who matters to me. The company I keep affects what I see, what I care about, how I "receive" and respond to the world.

Second, there should be sober reflection on my gifts—the talents and areas of strength that seem part of who I am, alongside a clear awareness of my limitations, temperament and character.[19]

Third, I should take into account my desires, asking myself: What "turns me on"? What turns me off? What do I long for? What gives me a sense of fulfilment? Where is there harmony or congruence between what is expected of me and what I feel able to give?

Fourth, I should make explicit and subject to scrutiny my goals—my priorities and purposes: What do I want to do with my life? What do I want to give my life to (over the long term)? What brings everything together for me, giving my life its significance and savor?

Fifth, the wider context in which I find myself should be examined: What needs cry out for a response from me? Of course, not all needs can be met by me, but can I detect any match between my gifts, my sense of call and the needs of others that I might be able to meet? There should be serious investigation of the realities constituting and surrounding the needs if there is to be any prospect of realistically and effectively addressing them. What is learned through reflection on these five areas of questioning needs to be supplemented by attention to a further five steps in discernment.

Sixth, there should be a prudent weighing of the sources of guidance and advice available to me and thought given to who might validate or mandate any major decision that seems to be called for as a result of all these considerations. Although ultimately I am responsible for my own actions, rarely would it be the case that the judgments of others (judgments about my gifts and limitations and about the needs of the community) play no part in recognizing, supporting, and authorizing a vocation.

---

19. Aucante says, "Discerning the choice of a way of life begins with taking into account what we are before opening up to what we could become" (*Discernement selon Edith Stein*, 11). This means we should seek to be aware of our body, our thoughts, our feelings of joy, sorrow, anger, love, resistance, even our unconscious; all these should serve as messengers, but not as ultimate authorities, for us. What we might become, through the transforming grace of God, cannot be constrained by these human factors.

Seventh, all this needs to be informed by a life that is shaped and informed by personal prayer and participation in community worship and deep immersion in Holy Scripture.[20]

Eighth, it is vital that there is a serious counting of the cost of pursuing a particular vocation. This includes taking into account what has to be set aside or left behind, the training or preparation required, any necessary changes required in one's mode of life, together with the implications for others. There must be a realistic assessment of what is entailed by a decision that is being faced.

Ninth, as part of the process, it would be wise to speak with those who are already working in the field one is considering and to learn, from their experience and perspective, about what is involved.

Tenth, especially in the context of regular private prayer, one must ask oneself whether a sense of God's presence and calling remains.

An important caveat here is that, whether in the discernment of vocation we are reflecting on or witnessing to our own vocation, or assisting others as they seek to discern their vocation, we attend as best we can to the pedagogy of God, always conscious that we never establish more than a very weak appreciation of how this works. To speak of the pedagogy of God is to use a term that is relatively unfamiliar today, one that has been examined and discussed in a recent collection of essays.[21] Contributors to this book warn educators to be attentive to the role of the Holy Spirit in the process of transforming lives. The work of teachers is to prepare themselves and their pupils to be receptive, disposing them to be open to the work of the Holy Spirit.[22] To speak of the pedagogy of God is to remind oneself that God is the primary agent in the process of education and associated transformation—the foundation from which we build, the route by which we travel, and the goal at which we aim to arrive. In the introduction to *The Pedagogy of God*, Paul Watson points out that "only the divine action can touch the heart from the inside."[23] In this perspective, Petroc Willey alerts

---

20. Aucante comments: "In praying, we not only place ourselves before God, we also enter into communion with all those who have been—and are—on the road towards God" (*Discernement selon Edith Stein*, 53).

21. Farey et al., *Pedagogy of God*.

22. One becomes open to the Holy Spirit by being immersed in Holy Scripture and the teachings of the church, by participating in the liturgy and sacramental life, through the regular practice of personal prayer, and by being obedient to the practices prescribed by the church.

23. Paul Watson, in Farey et al., *Pedagogy of God*, 7.

readers to how revelation "'enlarges' persons so that they can participate in God's nature."[24]

If education contributes to the humanization of learners, attending to the pedagogy of God reframes that humanization so that it becomes part of divinization. The self-transcending aspect of education focuses on human growth, development, and activity, so that the outcome of education is the expansion, harnessing, and deployment of our powers. The pedagogy of God, on the other hand, stresses human receptivity in the face of God's giving; without this receptivity, the gift cannot be welcomed. As Philip Cary observes in his study of Augustine, "There is no knowledge of the other that is not ultimately a gracious gift of the other, which we must be glad to receive."[25]

In the end, Christian education is an invitation to share God's life, to welcome God's grace, to become more Christlike, to have one's selfhood redefined by the gospel, to have one's mind transformed. These are all aspects of the meaning of *theosis*, a process in which we move, with God's help, from our initial—and given—starting point, made in the image of God, to our final destination as reflecting our own unique likeness to God. In this process we are divinized, sharers by adoption in God's life, but without loss of our humanity. If the transmission of the gospel is "an event of the supernatural order, depending on the lively assistance of the Holy Spirit" as Avery Dulles claims,[26] we can extend this claim to include Christian education as part of the transmission of the gospel. Similarly, if "catechists are called to be privileged instruments through whom God continues his saving work today" and if "the success of their efforts will depend not on themselves alone but more crucially on the grace of God and the freely given response of the students,"[27] we can say the same for Christian educators more generally.

It is important to stress that, in a Christian perspective on education, the pedagogy of God does not dispense with human effort; rather, it builds on it and extends it. As St. Bernard of Clairvaux (1090–1153) once said, with reference to the way that the action of God and our own action should not be considered as separate, as if God did one part and quite separately we did our part, *sed opere individuo totum singuli peragunt*. That is, and translated very loosely, the whole job, the full work, is done hand in hand, simultaneously, in communion, and jointly; it is circumincession, a dancing

---

24. Willey, "Pedagogue and Teacher," 42.
25. Cary, *Outward Signs*, 150.
26. Dulles, *Evangelization for the Third Millennium*, 67.
27. Dulles, *Evangelization for the Third Millennium*, 113.

in tandem of the partners, not a dance by one partner, followed by a dance by another. To quote Bernard more extensively,

> What was begun by grace alone, is completed by grace and free choice together, in such a way that they contribute to each new achievement not singly but jointly; not by turns, but simultaneously. It is not as if grace did one half of the work and free choice the other; but each does the whole work, according to its own peculiar contribution. Grace does the whole work, and so does free choice—with this one qualification: that whereas the whole is done *in* free choice, so is the whole done *of* grace.[28]

This notion, that the divine and human agents are not competitors, was echoed a century later by St. Thomas Aquinas (1225–74):

> An effect that results from a natural cause and from the divine power is not attributed partly to God and partly to the natural agent, but it is completely from both according to different modes, just as the effect is entirely attributable to an instrument and also entirely to the principal agent.[29]

Education is thus simultaneously a human and a divine work. The task of educators is to awaken in students the power to wonder, imagine and question, to think, interpret, understand, evaluate, and appreciate, to receive and give, to live in God's presence—hearing and responding to Word and Spirit. These can all serve to equip us to learn how to love rightly, surely always *the* priority, not only for St. Augustine, but for all Christian educators.[30] But when we have done our part, there remains, and permanently so, the necessity of handing over our gifts and our work to the Spirit of God. As Ambrose Walsh so eloquently puts it: "It is a wonderful thing indeed, to integrate all our natural talents into our Christian calling but even more wonderful to be open to those supernatural gifts which the Spirit alone can give for the building up of the Church."[31]

---

28. Bernard of Clairvaux, *On Grace & Free Choice*, 106; emphasis in original.

29. Aquinas (*Summa contra gentiles* 3.70), quoted in Willey, "Pedagogue and Teacher," 43.

30. See Sullivan, "St Augustine, Maurice Blondel."

31. Ambrose Walsh, *Called and Sent*, in the collection of quotes in the anonymous "Living Spirit" column, *Tablet* (Jan. 28, 2012), 24.

## SOME IMPLICATIONS AND FURTHER REFLECTIONS

The kind of church that is likely to promote a culture of vocation, along the lines sketched out by Christopher Jamison, will be a learning community in which participation is invited, gifts are recognized, affirmed, and celebrated, responsibility is fostered, risk-taking is encouraged, and one where imagination and creativity are nurtured. It will be one in which the distributed intelligence and wisdom of God's people is acknowledged, the voices of all are heard, their experience is honored, the insights of local communities are heeded, and it will be one where critical understanding and questioning are treated as gifts for the enhancement of the common good. There is some way still to go in an *ecclesia semper reformanda* before such a culture begins to take hold. The same necessary features for a culture of vocation apply to schools; here too there is no room for complacency, despite some progress in the right direction.

There will be no capacity to give oneself, in responding to God's call, if there is no sense of gift and of gratitude for that gift. This means we must teach about the unmerited, endless generosity of God. There will be no capacity to take the question of vocation seriously if there is no sense of acceptance, of worth, of being loved, regardless of achievement. This has implications for how assessment and evaluation of progress need to be permeated by love in action. There will be no capacity for authentic response if there is no sense of freedom or scope for personal responsibility. This means that schools must ensure that pupils have opportunities to make decisions, to act in their own name, even to make mistakes and to learn from them. There will be no capacity to offer a free and willing Amen if one feels threatened, if there is the danger of being punished for raising unwelcome questions or for adopting a critical stance or if one feels exposed to risk by being different. This means risk-taking is to be encouraged, support provided, and diverse and flexible modes of accompaniment are developed.

I do not claim to have put flesh on all the required conditions for promoting a culture of vocation; I have merely offered a sketch of some of its constitutive elements. There is much that we do not know. To start with, God will always remain beyond our ken; we never have our understanding of God "taped," sorted, or settled. Then, we remain a mystery to ourselves, despite rare moments of insight, often granted to us by others who shock us by their observations of who we are and what we are like. As for other people, no matter how well we think we know them, they too escape our grasp; they have depths that we cannot reach. If we think of the church, she seems to be full of surprises for us, some welcome, others quite unwelcome.

As for the world, all attempts to predict the future, with the aid of all our scholarly tools and scientific technology, constantly are shown up to be inadequate. As embodied beings in time and space, our perspective, however attentive and disciplined we seek to be, remains limited and partial. If we were not open to surprise, we would be closed to grace. The more that we learn, the more we realize how puny is the scale of our knowledge. In addition to all those questions for which we have no answer, there are other questions which have not even occurred to us yet.

What does this unavoidable limitation on our knowledge add up to, with regard to Christian education and the discernment of vocation? It means that we will make mistakes, and that we often have to move forward in darkness rather than in the light, that we face ambiguity, confusion, contradictions. As a result, although we all need a degree of confidence, clarity and conviction, in order to function effectively in our secular and spiritual lives, too much certainty can open the door to cruelty, to others or to ourselves; at the same time, it can close us off from humility, openness to new evidence, alternative perspectives, new experiences; it can prevent us from recontextualizing and thus enriching the little that we do know.

Yet we are not alone; we belong to a community of learning, apprentices to Christ. There are guides along the way who can help (though relying on these guides cannot obviate the need for us to learn from our own experience and to experience in our own unique way God's ways with the world and God's plan for us). These guides can inspire, challenge, and support us in the movement from "whatever" to "Amen."

# 18

# Understanding and Overstanding
## *Religious Reading in Historical Perspective*

I WANT TO SUGGEST that we often use the word "understanding" when we mean "overstanding," and that this usage is linked to a range of approaches to reading in academic contexts, specifically a forgetting of assumptions and habits that were once integral to the reading practices sponsored and modeled by religious believers. It is only too easy to forget, as English scholar Alan Purves has argued, how central religious reading once was to the practice of reading in general. Purves claims that "it is in religious contexts that reading has been practiced by a large part of the population over the years. Church reading was the first introduction to reading for countless generations, and for many it is so still."[1] What I wish to bring out in this chapter is how religious approaches to reading differ, sometimes starkly, from the ways we usually read, and encourage others to read, especially the ways we do so as a central activity of the university. Insofar as schoolteachers internalize and become wedded to contemporary approaches to and assumptions about reading from their academic and professional formation at university, it is likely to be the case that they promote these in their work in schools throughout their career. My focus here will not be on reading in elementary and secondary schools, but in universities. However, I believe that the contrast we encounter when we consider some previous modes of reading should at least give Christian teachers at all levels of education pause for thought. In each of these work contexts they might even judge that, in some circumstances, they can alert students to the possibility of alternative ways to approach their reading.

---

1. Purves, *Web of Text*, 62.

In section 1 I indicate a more expansive appreciation than is common of what reading can do for readers. Then, in section 2, I draw upon Augustine and some medieval writers to illustrate this more expansive approach to reading, its links with religious commitment and its promotion of understanding. Finally, in section 3, I show how this contrasts with the attitudes built into more recent approaches to understanding, which I characterize as being better described as overstanding. I end with a very modest way of starting to get students to reflect on the multiple factors that bear upon our reading.

Let me clarify the specific focus and therefore also expose some of the limitations of this chapter. My intention is not to survey the theoretical literature about reading. This would have required attention to such writers as Cavallo and Chartier on the history of reading; or Jauss's reception aesthetics and literary hermeneutics; or Kivy's work on the performance of reading; or the seminal work of Rosenblatt on transactional theories of reading.[2] Rather, I seek to retrieve insights about reading drawn from some earlier theological and spiritual traditions, suggesting that these insights have applicability beyond their original settings and beyond the reading of religious texts. I hope, by contrasting a more full-blooded or holistic approach to reading, one that engages the reader more comprehensively and that makes greater demands on him or her, to show the limitations of a consumerist and instrumental approach to reading that encourages students to interrogate a text for useful data they can deploy without being changed in the process. Modes of reading other than the ones I draw attention to here are, in my view, both legitimate and necessary for university students and I continue to encourage their use. It is not my hope or expectation that all reading should display features of the more expanded interpretation of reading that was evident in the past; I am only advocating that some reading should do so. My focus is not on techniques of reading but on the continuing relevance of some past assumptions about its purpose and the activities and attitudes that surround and constitute it. My argument is that students—in engaging with some theological, spiritual, and religious texts, but also as they read historical, political, and literary texts—would benefit from receiving an opportunity to add to their repertoire of ways of reading the kinds of reading described here. By itself the more religious form of reading described here would be insufficient for a contemporary university's academic requirements in any particular academic discipline, including in theology. However, to fail to give students an opportunity to

---

2. Cavallo and Chartier, *History of Reading*; Rush, *Reception of Doctrine*; Kivy, *Performance of Reading*; Rosenblatt, *Reader, Text, Poem*.

experience what this kind of reading offers and demands would, in my view, sell them short and give them an impoverished appreciation of the range of reading open to them.

I make four assumptions for this chapter. Two are taken from Mark Pike and two from Chris Anderson. From Pike I accept the view that "reading is an essentially 'religious' activity, not in the sense that it is related to an established religion, but because it is value-laden and cannot be separated from the beliefs and values of readers and writers." I also take from Pike the judgment that "reader response theory . . . has demonstrated that what a person believes influences how they read (as well as what they read and why they read)."[3] I will argue that we would do well to acknowledge the force of these two points and apply them in teaching students how to read more deeply, self-reflectively and fruitfully. I concur with Chris Anderson that "all teachers at the university are teachers of reading," and I also agree with him that "reading requires community."[4] With regard to his first point, the universality of the task of teaching reading, I hope that, although my own teaching is based in a theology department, key aspects of eliciting better reading in that context have application in other disciplines. His second point, the role of community in creating the conditions for adequate reading, will not be developed here, except indirectly, and in two different respects. First, I argue that we should challenge students to move away from an individualist and consumerist approach to reading, where they seek to extract data for their own purposes and move them closer to ways of reading that require of them a degree of adjustment to and indeed submission (at least provisionally) to the journey expected by the text. Such "opening out" of the student is likely to be more conducive of community in that it breaks down some elements in our self-centeredness. Second, I give due attention, in the last part of the chapter, to the ecology of reading, the multiplicity of factors at work in influencing reading and their mutual interaction in classroom settings.

## READING AS A JOURNEY WHICH CHANGES US

I do not think many students expect their reading to change them or even to make demands on them. They look at it as an act of consumption, where they seek something which gives them the building blocks to address some assignment, which is itself a necessary hurdle along the way to accumulating

---

3. Pike, "From Beliefs to Skills," 284. See also Smith, "Poet, Child and Blackbird," on aesthetic reading, spiritual development, and challenging readers to change their lives.

4. Anderson, *Teaching as Believing*, 71.

a qualification. The act of reading is for a very limited purpose; once found and deployed, the information gathered can be jettisoned, having passed through the reader but without having changed her in any substantial way. The assumption is that the item of text being read is equally accessible to any reader of similar intelligence, regardless of that reader's basic convictions, character, lifestyle, or the company they keep. These elements in their life are considered private matters and quite irrelevant to what they can gain from their reading. It is not the business of the teacher to suggest there might be a connection between these aspects of their life and what understanding is made possible via reading.

An alternative view would be that reading is an exercise in change, that it is part of a personal journey which could be described as a pilgrimage, or as an ascent. It is not just like scanning a map; it goes beyond a passive observation of the words and thoughts of another. Serious reading prompts us to reach up to the thought of another, to clamber onto the path they offer us, to cross a threshold, to enter into an idea, a tradition, a form of conduct, or a way of life. This more expansive appreciation of reading combines inwardness, commitment and openness to transcendence. It engages the personal life of readers. It presses them to decide, to judge and in light of this to give themselves, to adhere to a concept, a skill, a virtue, a practice. In doing so, it reveals illusions which are to be left behind, it exposes bad practices which are to be given up and it paves the way to a receptive openness to change.

Let me suggest several phrases that religious readers in the past would have associated with the notion of reading: to remember rightly; to perceive accurately; to believe reliably; to respond promptly; to relate responsibly; to interpret justly; to love appropriately; to belong generously; to share joyfully; to surrender willingly; to pray fervently. At first sight, these phrases can strike us as having little to do with reading per se, decoding a text or finding information, for example. They appear to import all kinds of extraneous, unnecessary and, indeed, intrusive expectations. They link reading with habit, repetition and memory, with discipline and obedience, with conversion and transformation, with community and indwelling, with self-scrutiny, docility, humility and character, and with worship. This more full-blooded set of associations with the act of reading, though not restricted to Christians, is certainly very much in harmony with, even integral to, their tradition. This mentality is indirectly echoed, for example, in such biblical phrases as "the wisdom from above is first pure, then peaceable, gentle, willing to yield, full of mercy and good fruits, without a trace of partiality of hypocrisy" (Jas 3:17); and "if you continue in my Word, then you are truly my disciples; and you shall know the truth, and the truth will make you free" (John 8:32). The height of human wisdom is here a gift from above, rather than achieved through effort, virtuosity or technical expertise or dexterity; it embraces the whole person; character and insight are linked; it emerges not through being a rule unto oneself, but through being a willing disciple; it is not disconnected from the whole pattern of our choices and desires. Thus, where we read (our location), why we read (our purpose), how we read (the method we use), who we are that is reading (our identity and character), and who we are with when we are reading (the company we keep) all reciprocally interrelate and mutually influence each other.

Paul Griffiths distinguishes religious from consumerist reading, claiming that academic life encourages the latter, while neglecting the former. Religious reading depends on a certain kind of relationship between the reader and what is read, a relationship that allows the text to address, to question and to challenge the reader, and at the same time it adopts an attitude of reverence and obedience towards the text. Rather than standing in authority *over* the text, interrogating it with critical tools, deferring commitment, questioning its authenticity, the religious reader stands *under* or in the light of such a text. This kind of understanding entails a willingness to be vulnerable to the message contained in a text, submitting to its power, allowing it time to penetrate one's thinking and feeling and appreciating its resonance. By trusting its source, inhabiting its ambience and participating in the community which is the proper location for its interpretation, religious readers find themselves able to attain a depth of understanding that cannot be reached by consumerist reading and the detached use of critical methodologies. Religious reading, seen in this light, requires relations between readers and texts that are simultaneously "attitudinal, cognitive, and moral; [such relations] imply an ontology, an epistemology and an ethic."[5]

This is a view of reading that makes demands on us, rather than one where we make demands on the object of our reading. Rather than make the text answer our questions and somehow fit into the categories of our understanding, already arrived at in advance of the act of reading, the expectation was that readers entered into a moral relationship with what they read, one where readers are led rather than lead and where readers should conform themselves to the text as they would to the demands of a tutor. Of course, it is legitimate for us to make demands on what we read, but if the demands are always unilateral, from us to the material being read, we will miss out too much. We will be trying to stand over what we read, but in achieving such overstanding, we may fail to understand. In the study of religion for example, this distinction between understanding and overstanding can cast light on such questions as: Will we study religion on *our* terms or

---

5. Griffiths, *Religious Reading*, 41.

on *its* terms? Will we look *at* a religion or will we look *through* it at the world and at life? Would it be a fair analogy to ask: If you cannot climb a mountain without being physically fit, can you attain religious truth without developing spiritual capacities? This is not to suggest that religious truth is the fruit of human effort, but that our capacity to reach any worthwhile appreciation of such truth is obstructed hindered by lack of spiritual development. The more expansive approach to reading recalled here raises issues for our consideration, for example, our motivations, our intentions, our attitudes, our purposes, our readiness for, and our approach to reading.

A religious way of reading does not treat the individual as the basic unit; it gives priority to the religious community. It does not adopt a detached and distant perspective; it expects engagement, participation, and commitment. It does not divorce the personal qualities of the seeker from the public methods and outcomes of the search; it expects conversion and transformation of life as the price—and the key—for unlocking the doors to the treasures held within the tradition. Religious accounts of the world are learned in a social, linguistic, and institutional context[6] though this does not mean that there is a deterministic relation between relevant practice and religious accounts. There is an expectation in religious learning that the personal life of the student will be modified, redirected, and brought into line with the object of study. The will must be ordered and the appetites harnessed, away from self-centered gratification and toward God and other people.[7] The transformational practices enjoined on us as essential elements in religious reading give us a new identity, one that changes us intellectually as well as morally and spiritually.

Let me give an example of the difference between the understanding and the overstanding mentality. The religious thinker Friedrich von Hügel once described an experiment required of a prospective student by the Unitarian preacher James Martineau.[8] The student, already strongly analytical, sharply critical of religion and highly cerebral in his approach to his studies, was asked to spend two periods of six months with very different communities. The first was to be with uncultured, narrow-minded, but believing peasants in Westphalia. Then he was to spend six months with highly intelligent and skeptical medical students in Berlin. His reflection on how best to approach the study of religion was to be informed by his experience of how these two vastly different communities coped with their hopes and fears and how they responded to the successes and problems

---

6. Griffiths, *Religious Reading*, 13.
7. Griffiths, *Religious Reading*, 17.
8. Hügel, *Essays and Addresses* (1926), 12–29.

they encountered. The student took the view that the piety of the former, despite all its limitations and prejudices, took them further towards wisdom for a worthy life than the skepticism and freedom of the latter group. For all their shortcomings, the believing peasants acknowledged the givenness and objectivity of religious truth; they knew they stood (whether in darkness or in light) under its authority; they knew they should allow themselves to be conformed to the reality that stood over them, even if their progress was faltering and erratic. On the other hand, the medical students, in their intellectual pride and self-confidence, stood over a religion they cut even further down to the scale and meaning allowed it by their conceptual apparatus and methodology.

## AN EARLIER WAY OF READING

I once bought a poster which described a medieval allegory of the scribe's tools. The only attribution was to an anonymous medieval monastic sermon from Durham. On the poster the tools of a scribe were each viewed as spiritual aids for a Christian life.

> The parchment on which we write is pure conscience.
> The knife that scrapes it is the fear of God.
> The pumice that smoothes the skin is the discipline of heavenly desire.
> The chalk that whitens it signifies an unbroken meditation of holy thoughts.
> The ruler is the will of God.
> The straight edge is devotion to the holy task.
> The quill, its end split in two for writing, is the love of God and of our neighbor.
> The ink is humility itself.
> The illuminator's colors represent the multiform grace of heavenly wisdom.
> The writing desk is tranquility of heart.
> The exemplar from which a copy is made is the life of Christ.
> The writing place is contempt of worldly things, lifting us to a desire for heaven.

This allegory nicely illustrates some of the points made above about a more full-blooded set of associations linked with the act of reading and study. It clearly locates the path of learning with the path of discipleship. Augustine (of Hippo) similarly links the curriculum for study with the pilgrimage towards God. The academic and the spiritual, far from being separate, are closely integrated. John MacInnis shows how, in his *De Doctrina Christiana* (2.7.9–2.7.11), Augustine describes the various steps along which a pilgrim reader will travel: from fear to piety, to knowledge, to fortitude, to counsel, to purgation of the eyes of the heart, to single-mindedness, to wisdom. "For Augustine, attitudes of piety and docility are what we might call today preconditions for approaching sacred texts (3.1.1).... A personal posture of faith, which shows itself in prayer, is indispensable for approaching the inspired word."[9] In his *Confessions* (10.17–10.35), Augustine placed huge emphasis on the importance of memory within the act of reading. As Brian Stock, in his magisterial work *Augustine the Reader*, shows, Augustine unites study, remembering, and self-examination. One might contrast Augustine's approach to reading with contemporary surfing the internet or with forms of reading that resemble tourism. Tourists make short-term visits. They come as outsiders and remain outsiders by the time they leave. They pick and choose, according to their own idiosyncratic and spur-of-the-moment preferences, what to experience in the land they visit. They observe, rather than participate in, the events put on for their entertainment. There is all the difference in the world between aimless wandering and purposeful pilgrimage.

For many medieval readers "reading is an activity... [for] the authorial 'leading by the hand' of the reading soul unto the beatific vision."[10] Reading involved the whole person; it was founded on and framed by the activity of worship; it was set in a community context; it was carefully reinforced by diverse sensory cues, including posture and gesture.[11] It was an activity that entailed hearing as much as seeing, for most reading was done aloud, often in the company of others. We might call this acoustical reading.[12] The lips were used as well as the eyes and readers listened to the words pronounced, hearing, as Jean Leclercq says, the "voices of the pages," for "*legere* means at the same time *audire*": reading entailed hearing.[13] Reading, for the medievals, would be both anticipated and reinforced by preceding and succeeding activities intended as continuous with the reading itself and with the rest of the Christian life. Reading could be considered a kind of rehearsal of the enjoyment of the goods or realities it spoke about. To meditate in the act of reading implied, as Leclercq confirms, "thinking of a thing with the

9. MacInnis, "Theological Education as Formation," 386.

10. Candler, *Theology, Rhetoric, Manuduction*, 18.

11. For the role of gesture in learning to be members of the body of Christ, see Webb-Mitchell, *Christly Gestures*.

12. For the importance of the acoustical dimension in Christian communication, see Webb, *Divine Voice*.

13. Leclercq, *Love of Learning*, 19.

intent to do it; in other words, to prepare oneself for it, to prefigure it in the mind, to desire it, in a way, to do in advance, briefly, to practice it."[14] Reading was an act of the whole being: it took place "with the body, since the mouth pronounced it, with the memory which fixes it, with the intelligence which understands its meaning and with the will which desires to put it into practice."[15] A very common metaphor for reading was eating, sometimes described as mastication or rumination, for monasteries were dwelling places for mumblers and munchers of the word.[16]

One of the leading works on reading in the Middle Ages was Hugh of St. Victor's *Didascalicon*, written in the 1120s at the abbey of St. Victor near Paris. Hugh is a powerful representative of those many medieval writers who stressed the self-involving and transformational nature of reading in its role of relating us to God. Another example would be Bernard of Clairvaux.[17] For Hugh, learning, in which reading was a constitutive element, was an instrument in the restoration in us of divine wisdom. It orients us and moves us towards union with God. Learning and reading within this, combines intellectual, ethical, and spiritual dimensions. Both effort and love are required if we are to progress in learning and in virtue. "Through concern you look ahead; through alertness you pay close attention."[18] In linking self-discipline with progress in reading and learning, Hugh quotes Saint Jerome who pithily said "a fat belly does not produce a fine perception."[19] He acknowledges that reading is not always benign in its effects on us, for the spirit can be afflicted, as well as helped, by study: "Through its quality, if the material has been too obscure, and through its quantity, if there has been too much of it."[20] At its best, however, reading and study will enable us to equip ourselves to respond worthily to God, constructing a life of grateful fidelity out of the gifts and graces showered on us. In another of his works Hugh says, "You shall build a house for the Lord out of your own self. He himself will be the builder; your heart will be the place; your thoughts will supply the material."[21] This is reminiscent of the admonition of Gregory the Great: "We ought to transform what we read into our very selves, so that

---

14. Leclercq, *Love of Learning*, 20.
15. Leclercq, *Love of Learning*, 22.
16. Leclercq, *Love of Learning*, 90; Illich, *In Vineyard of Text*, 56.
17. See Sommerfeldt, *Bernard of Clairvaux*.
18. Hugh, *Didascalicon*, 100.
19. Hugh, *Didascalicon*, 100.
20. Hugh, *Didascalicon*, 130.
21. Hugh, *Didascalicon*, 171.

when our mind is stirred by what it hears, our life may concur by practicing what has been heard."²²

One of the different emphases between reading (and learning) in the Middle Ages and reading (and learning) in more recent times is a shift in the focus: instead of *sapientia* or wisdom and *intelligentia* or understanding being what is sought, it is *scientia* or knowledge that is pursued. This shift indicates a move from one form of study to a significantly different type. In seeking *sapientia* or *intelligentia* I stand *under* the material studied, accommodate myself obediently to its demands; I reach *up* to it as I seek to apprehend the world according to its categories. *Sapientia* or *intelligentia* is about understanding what comes to us from above us, from a higher level of being (and perfection). According to the medieval mentality, in pursuing *scientia* we investigate what is below us, a level of being that is inferior to us. Now what is studied is interrogated according to our categories, to satisfy our curiosity, in order to be amenable to our needs, to serve our purposes. Here we stand *over* the object of study. Understanding operates at a different level from overstanding. It calls upon some of the deeply personal and relatively passive qualities of the pilgrim seeker. To appreciate what comes to us from above requires waiting, patience, stillness, and silence. It might be more accurate to describe these qualities, when operating conjointly, as comprising an active receptivity, a level of heightened attentiveness and contemplative capacity which depend upon discipline and training. With understanding it is my personal life that is very much in the laboratory, under scrutiny. There is no sharp separation in me between my moral, spiritual, and intellectual dimensions. In the case of *scientia* I may be tempted to believe that my personal life is irrelevant to the progress of my studies, that it can be put aside when I am reading or investigating.

For the medievals, however, the goal of reading and study was wisdom and ultimately the beatific vision of God, gradually made possible via a growing capacity for spiritual apprehension, though this never occurs without God's grace, which precedes, accompanies, and brings to perfection our feeble efforts. Holiness was considered an integral element in wisdom the beatific vision, for faith in the truth and love of the good are united in God. Spiritual experience was not an optional extra but an essential feature of the most worthwhile studies. William of Auxerre, for example, who was writing in the early years of the thirteenth century, picked up the teaching in the Bible about the spiritual senses and developed this into a sophisticated analysis of how God uses our diverse capacities and desires to draw us to himself. The gifts of the Holy Spirit are, for William, as for so many

---

22. Hugh, *Didascalicon*, 220.

other medievals, derived from Isa 11:2–3: wisdom, understanding, counsel, fortitude, knowledge, piety, and fear of the Lord. These gifts lead us progressively from the exterior and active life (via fear, piety, knowledge, fortitude, and counsel) to the interior, contemplative life (understanding and wisdom). For William, if spiritual apprehension is ever to be developed in us, it will call upon the wide range of our knowing capacities, capacities that are deeply enhanced or hindered by our virtues (or lack of them), as well as by the nature of our desires (what they are targeted on and the purchase they have on our lives). Knowledge of what is above us requires that we ascend, that our nature is transcended, that our wayward nature is brought into order, that our energies are focused, that we open ourselves to be made, by God, more similar to the divine nature.

This is a view of learning in which the intellectual, the moral, the aesthetic and the spiritual are shown to interact reciprocally. In a recent major study of the spiritual senses in the theology of William of Auxerre, Coolman shows how, for William, certain senses had to be developed and heightened in us if we are to have a chance to appreciate the nature of the divine. Human beings are created with the seeds of qualities that correspond with divine characteristics. If we are to perceive God's fullness (*plenitudine*), beauty (*pulchritude*), symphony (*simphonia*), good aroma (*bono odore*), pleasantness (*suavitas*) and sweetness (*dulcedo*), then we must learn how to delight in God through spiritual sight (*visus*), hearing (*auditus*), smell (*odoratus*), taste (*gustus*), and touch (*tactus*).[23] Some of these phrases, such as symphony and good aroma, might strike us as strange, perhaps too earthy, and too literal, in relation to God. But I think that William, like so many of his contemporaries, was being realistic in believing that it was through harnessing, coordinating, disciplining and directing our God-given qualities and capacities that we would learn to read rightly not only the book of Scripture, but also the book of life as experienced in the world. For William there was an essential resonance between what we have received and the one who gave these gifts to us. Wisdom and the vision of God, though coming to us as a gift that we could not merit, nevertheless came to us via the gifts we had already received, the built-in capacity to respond to God's call through the development of spiritual senses.

In all this, William expected a conjoining of faith with love, facilitated by an employment of our spiritual senses. "Charity desires, hungers for, pursues, effects, maintains, and augments that delight which occurs in faith's apprehension," while "faith cognizes, estimates, apprehends—in short, faith is *visus* [sight]. Charity desires, pursues, possesses, conjoins,

---

23. Coolman, *Knowing God by Experience*, 29.

rests—in short, charity is *tactus* [touch]."²⁴ We have learned to be cautious about some forms of engaging the emotions in the process of religious communication, lest these slip into manipulation and reduce the freedom (and thus fail to take seriously the dignity) of the learner. However, for William, there is no sharp separation between the intellect, the will, and the spiritual senses: they each have a part to play; they belong together, rather than being in conflict; each has a legitimate role in the path towards knowing God better. "Spiritual experience does not abandon doctrinal formulation; prior forms of knowing are not left behind by, or radically dissociated from, later forms. . . . *Scientia-cognoscere* structures and informs *sapientia-sentire*, while *sapientia-sentire* subsumes and consummates *scientia-cognoscere*."²⁵ To put this in another way, the rigorous use of reason will guide our search, so that our findings are not fanciful, the result of wish-fulfilment, but warranted by the evidence. At the same time, the deployment and development of our other capacities that can assist cognition, our virtues, our desires, and our spiritual senses, can only enhance our use of reason, ensure it is an act of the whole person, press us to let our knowledge make a real difference in our lives, and open us up to respond to and to embrace the call and grace of God.

## BEYOND ANEMIC READING?

What I have described in section 2 is a more full-blooded, a more integrated approach to study, than we are accustomed to now. It reminds us that how we read, and what we write for others to read, is inextricably linked to the kind of people that we are. Too often, for the academic reader, "there is no moral relation between book and reader."²⁶ Yet sacred Scripture (for instance, 2 Pet 1:5–7) not only links knowledge to faith and virtue, as displayed in self-control, steadfastness, godliness, and love, but also subordinates knowledge to these qualities. Such a view implies that "the intellect, the emotions, the will, the spirit and the body are all intricately connected and must all be continually purified."²⁷

In a recent study of how theology was once taught in this more holistic way, as a pilgrimage towards God, one commentator says, "Reading is . . . the activity of rightly ordering our desire towards its proper object."²⁸ Such

24. Coolman, *Knowing God by Experience*, 149, 152.
25. Coolman, *Knowing God by Experience*, 5.
26. Griffiths, "Reading as a Spiritual Discipline," 38.
27. Poplin, "Radical Call to Service," 169.
28. Candler, *Theology, Rhetoric, Manuduction*, 45.

a statement is counterintuitive in many educational contexts today, when skills and competencies are talked of as if they could be detached from the memories, motivations, character and relationships of learners, rather like software can be easily transferable between different kinds of hardware, unaffected by the host machine. A medieval reader's memory was trained in a liturgical setting, so that texts that were read were inextricably linked for readers with an "entire network of bodily movements, sounds, smells with which these readings were associated, as well as the time of day and season in which they were read."[29] This is so different than our practice of private and silent reading, carried out as and when we please, and something quite separate for us from any fixed associations of location, surrounding activity, particular company, or directed toward an enduring overriding purpose.

Our reading for study is expected to display objectivity, disinterest, and detachment. It critiques, questions, and interrogates the texts under review. It judges them by our criteria of relevance. Historical perspective and consciousness are often determinative of our interpretation. As David Williams says about the dominance of historical consciousness accompanying our reading, "We are no more the intended audience of the Bible than of Herodotus."[30] The whole notion of attempting to read a text in accordance with the way it has been read throughout a tradition seems to strike right at the heart of the unfettered freedom of the reader. Of course, there is nothing wrong with reading that is influenced by our current preoccupations and interests, so long as we are not blinded by these to other possible readings and interpretations, ones that differ radically from, perhaps which challenge and even contradict them.

What are the implications for Christian educators of my brief foray into past ways of approaching reading? My aim here is very modest. I believe that it is not our business to lament a lost past; nor is it helpful to lambast a deficient present. What I think we can do is to show our students that the assumptions we bring to reading can make a significant difference to what we get out of it. We can propose to them that it is legitimate to consider a richer, more full-blooded and more holistic way of seeing their reading and their studies, as illustrated by some examples from the past. We can invite them to reflect on their own life and how the multiple dimensions of this might be influencing their reading, not only of texts in the traditional sense, of but also of their "reading," reception, or interpretation of all that happens to them and of all whom they meet. If it is true that "the inhabitants of a tradition enter its stories, enact its rituals, play its roles, explore its visions, try

---

29. Candler, *Theology, Rhetoric, Manuduction*, 78.
30. D. Williams, *Receiving the Bible*, 53.

its arguments, feel its sensibilities,"[31] then standing at a distance, refusing to try out its perspectives, merely looking at a tradition, rather than through its spectacles, not allowing one's pattern of life to be challenged by it—all this will prevent our being able to read very deeply what it might have to offer us. It would be standing over what we study, but not standing within it. Such a stance might well prevent us reaching a worthwhile understanding.

In my experience of working with university students in recent years, I have begun the process of trying to help them to move from overstanding to understanding by inviting them to consider the factors that might be influencing their "reading," interpreting reading very broadly. I simply suggest the following ten clusters of factors as worthy of consideration.

First, their experiences, memories, and assumptions: What is the baggage (to use a negative term) or the equipment (for a more positive term) that they bring to the object of study? In some modules (both undergraduate and at master's level) I invite students to reflect on how their past experience, whether in academic studies or their life experience more broadly, can either orient them towards or perhaps makes them resistant to what we are going to study. I help them to see that they do not arrive in the class as a blank, or without expectations or preliminary notions about the topic or the text. Chris Anderson describes how he once conveyed to his students that "we all bring things to the text" by putting on his alb and stole in the classroom as he started to teach a class. In commenting on this activity of self-consciously dressing up in front of his students, Anderson quotes Northrop Frye that we live within "a body of assumptions and beliefs developed from our existential concerns."[32]

Second, their knowledge, maturity, and intellectual capacity: rather than ask students to analyze these, I usually seek to get an initial sense of these for myself as teacher, through preliminary checking of what is known at the start of a course, although I invite them to recognize that each of us will bring a different and an uneven personal development to a task; we can be mature and confident in some respects, yet less so in others.

Third, their hopes and fears (and the state of their feelings more generally): students are invited at the start of a module to acknowledge, at least for themselves, even if this is not disclosed, that we can easily be preoccupied with concerns outside of class that distract us from attending fully in the sessions, and that our hopes and fears for this module and the tasks associated with it could be well founded or based on misunderstandings about what is required. Either way, they fairly easily accept that our energies

---

31. D. Brown, *Boundaries of Our Habitations*, 86.
32. Anderson, *Teaching as Believing*, 27.

for the forthcoming tasks can be reinforced and focused or dissipated and dispersed because of our personal emotional "climate"—and that this may not be under our control. Cumulatively, consideration of these factors assists the students in becoming reflexive in their self-understanding and more aware of how they are relating to the reading to be tackled.

Fourth, their purposes and priorities (short and long term): students are invited to connect the questions of the course with the questions of their lives and to see how strong links between these are likely to help their motivation in coping with the demands of the course.

Fifth, although I must be careful not to intrude into their privacy, or appear judgmental or puritanical about their lifestyle, I point out that what they are doing outside of class is likely to be as influential a factor in their progress as the kinds of learning they are engaged in with faculty at this time. Arriving in class after a late night's heavy drinking or partying might make participation in class today or concentration on required reading in the library difficult.

Sixth, who they are with (the company they keep in and outside of class): if we all need a plausibility structure, to borrow a phrase from sociologist of religion Peter Berger, to support us in our various types of believing, then students should be conscious of how their pattern of friendships, affiliations, and relationships both helps and hinders their work in class and their capacity to meet the demands of the course. Cumulatively, consideration of these factors suggests to the students that what is done in class is only the tip of the iceberg of their presence and participation: what appears on the surface is sustained by much more that lies beneath.

Seventh, their attitudes towards and relationship with the "text" or speaker: in some cases students have encountered a lecturer in an earlier part of their studies, or they have already engaged with a text at a different level or for a different purpose than the one that pertains now. If the encounter with lecturer or text is new, it will still be mediated by initial impressions that "frame" the engagement, for example, by the age, appearance, clothing, voice, and bearing of the speaker; or by the appearance, font size, packaging, and presentation of a text. Rather than focus on this at the start of a piece of work, I sometimes invite students to reflect at the end of a piece of work on how their relationship to speaker or text has changed in the period of study and to ask themselves to what degree initial impressions and expectations were met or modified in light of experience and what they would say to incoming students faced with the same speaker or text.

Eighth, the clarity and quality of the "text": obviously, it must be acknowledged that this varies enormously; not all texts will prove accessible, interesting, or relevant to any particular group of students. What "gets through" to one student might not to another. To consider this factor is to recognize that not all progress or setbacks in our "reading" can be attributed to the subjective conditions of the learner.

Ninth, chance and unforeseen circumstances and connections: these can make a significant difference to how individual students or even a whole class receive a text. A personal tragedy, a political crisis, a popular song in the charts, and a host of trivial and serious life experiences can trigger associations between student and text that could not have been foreseen by them or by their teacher. Rosenblatt puts it thus: "The same text will have a different meaning and value to us at different times or under different circumstances because some state of mind, a worry, a temperamental bias, or a contemporary social crisis may make us especially receptive or especially impervious to what the work offers."[33] To be inattentive to the operation of serendipity and calamity in our responses to texts and the resonances they might have for us would be to treat teaching and learning as a process that is logical, automatic, and predictable, whereas in practice it is often wonderful, dramatic, and escapes our most careful attempts to chart its progress.

Cumulatively, consideration of these factors brings home to students the need for an appreciation of the complexity of (and mutual interaction between) the tasks of learning and need for attaining some meta-cognitive perspective on their progress. Crude judgments, such as "This [activity] is stupid," "I can't do this," or "This text is impossible" are less likely to be made; while a comment such as "This is what I think is happening that is affecting my learning (positively and negatively)" is more likely.

Tenth, I suggest to students that our character, with its moral and spiritual dimensions, can make a difference to the effectiveness of our studies. Qualities such as persistence, readiness to accept correction, humility, patience, courage, willingness to co-operate, self-discipline, and commitment can create the conditions for successful study. By bringing together the character of the student with the "character" of a text, I try to encourage students to question how what they are saying, assuming, valuing, privileging, neglecting, downgrading, and committed to relates to what the text is advocating, displaying, revealing, ignoring, critiquing, and taking for granted. By the time they have got to my tenth factor influencing reading, they are beginning to be open to the possibility of expanding their appreciation of what real reading might require of them. Even if they do not wish to take that journey very far, they are less likely to overrate the quality or to exaggerate the value of the reading they have done, and they are more willing to see the potential connections between their personal and their academic

---

33. Louise Rosenblatt, quoted in Pike, "Bible and Reader's Response," 44.

lives. This is not to be inside the world of faith, but it might encourage them to cross the threshold which divides overstanding from understanding.

# 19

# Living Tradition and Learning Agency

*Interpreting the "Score"*
*and Personal Rendition*

## INTRODUCTION

In the summer of 2013 I co-edited *Education in a Catholic Perspective*.[1] In a chapter of that book, I explored some of the tensions that inevitably arise between the attempts of institutions to form their members and the needs of individuals who do not seem to fit easily into that formational process, bringing out the balancing acts required for the healthy flourishing of both the institution and all the individuals involved.[2] Here I want to take further an implication of that chapter, one which was not explicitly treated there: namely that, in doing justice to the living tradition mediated by Catholic schools, there is also the task of facilitating the development of the agency of pupils and students.

This task has three aspects. First, one needs to foster safe pedagogical spaces for learners (and teachers) who have doubts and difficulties with the faith tradition's official line. Second, teachers in Catholic schools and in the Catholic Church must respond to the reality that learners are assembling their religious identity and spiritual capital as *bricoleurs*—drawing upon the faith tradition but also from other aspects of their experience—and in ways that may be unorthodox, incomplete, idiosyncratic, and not fully coherent. Third, it must be acknowledged that, though there is in some senses an objective "package" or tradition to pass on and to receive (one that precedes

---

1. McKinney and Sullivan, *Education in a Catholic Perspective*.
2. Sullivan, "Individual and Institution."

and outlasts us as individuals), attention must also be given to personal appropriation, ownership, engagement, and responses that are mediated by personal experience, gifts, needs, blind spots, and challenges.

Put differently, Catholic education (and other forms of faith education) involves discipline, training, and formation—but it must also provide unforced, free spaces for connections to be made by learners, so that ideas and practices presented to them by teachers can become internalized and embedded within the context of the complexity and unfolding nature of their lives, in ways that they control (even if inaccurately or inadequately in the eyes of teachers and church leaders) and in ways that allow for creativity in application. The dialectic between doing justice to the "score" of the tradition and empowering personal rendition of it is central to the task of promoting real agency among learners—both in the church and in the school. Responsible discipleship depends on real agency as much as is the case with ownership of learning in school. Teachers seeking to invite serious engagement with the faith tradition should be concerned to foster not only resemblances between members of the "household of faith" (what they share in common), but they should also be open to, patient with, and positive about the fragile emergence of the personal "signature" of each student.

I have written elsewhere about the constitutive elements of Catholic education, about formation and about living tradition.[3] Here my focus is on the fostering of a learning space that supports the development of agency on the part of students in Catholic schools. I would hope that, despite the specificity of the main context I have in mind, there would be some degree of transferability—with regard to the relevance of the principles and issues raised—to other contexts for education in matters of faith for Catholics, other Christians, and people of other faiths. In the first section, I develop further my initial comments about learning and agency. In the second and third sections I draw upon two recent philosophers of education who have commented insightfully on different aspects of the issue being explored here, these being Graham McDonough (from Canada) and Pádraig Hogan (from Ireland). The fourth section outlines the principal risks and benefits one might expect to incur by giving salience to learning agency as advocated by McDonough, Hogan, and others. Finally, in the fifth section I underline the importance, both for their educational and their religious development, of eliciting an original response from those we teach.

---

3. Sullivan: *Catholic Education*; "From Formation to the Frontiers"; "Text and Context."

## LEARNING AND AGENCY

People engage in learning to cast light on their own circumstances, possibilities, needs, and limitations and those of others, and in order to understand and better appreciate the wonder and complexity of the world. Teachers hope that, in promoting learning, they serve to activate, focus, train, direct, discipline, and liberate the powers of students in service of a flourishing life and community and, for Christians, in service of God's kingdom. Such learning is necessarily a shared engagement more than it is an individual achievement. It always has the hallmark of provisionality, since learning can never be more than precarious, finite, limited, fallible, and incomplete. Despite much of the language of curriculum objectives and learning outcomes in educational literature, learning rarely leads to mastery, possession, finality, certainty, or security.

The verbs that characterize the teacher's actions can sometimes seem to students to include some or all of the following: impose, force, control, possess, intrude, drive, capture, deliver to, or transfer. In contrast, if learning agency is to be sought after, more appropriate verbs would be some or all of the following: receive, accept, include, invite, elicit attention, nurture, affirm, encourage, liberate, give space to, inspire, enthuse, stimulate, animate, hear into speech, provoke thought, accompany. These are verbs that bear upon and exemplify the intention of promoting active participation and ownership by learners of what they encounter in classrooms.

This is not to deny the need for structure, limits, rules, prescriptions, and the holding of students to certain standards of reasoning and the presentation of their work. Nor it is to ignore the asymmetrical nature of the teacher's relationship to students. Nor is it to assume that the obstacle to the emergence of agency among students is necessarily the behavior of heavy-handed teachers, for important inhibitors of the emergence of agency among learners can be other students. Furthermore, in suggesting that there should always be room for the questioning and critique of tradition, it is also important to ensure that the assumptions behind the questions and critique are themselves brought to light and made subject to scrutiny and testing.

As teachers seek to make the "text" speak to these students here and now, these students too have to speak from where they are. "Text" here includes any body of knowledge, set of skills, connected set of practices, or living tradition that the educational institution seeks to invite students to engage with. If learners are to be spoken to, addressed in such a way as to invite engagement and participation, then they also need to be heard. The teacher has to do justice both to the "text" they are mandated to present and to the students within this context—an undertaking that requires learning spaces that are both structured and sensitive, taking into account the age, maturity, experience, situation, concerns, and questions of learners. The French philosopher Louis Lavelle appositely and wisely offers three observations relevant for teachers and would-be spiritual guides here:

> Your desire to win me over to your point of view puts me on my guard, and stimulates opposition. . . . Communion is possible the moment the idea of conquest has been abandoned. The greatest good that we can do for other men is not the gift of a treasure of our own, but the revelation of something which was theirs already.[4]

These insights get to the heart of many pedagogical encounters by being sensitive to the natural resistances of students to any attempt to take away their freedom, the positive space that opens up when the dignity and freedom of students is respected, and the self-effacing nature of teaching that focuses on the giftedness of learners. They are reflected in the work of Brazilian adult educator Paulo Freire, who stressed so strongly the need to respect the agency of learners, rather than seeking to mold them into some predetermined shape of who they should be. For Freire the educational goal is an active knower, not the mind as passive repository of information transmitted by authorities.[5] In one of his later works he claims:

> True discipline does not exist in the muteness of those who have been silenced but in the stirrings of who have been challenged, in the doubt of those who have been prodded, and in the hopes of those who have been awakened.[6]

And he goes on to explain how he envisages his task as a teacher: "My role is essentially one of inciting the student to produce his or her own comprehension of the object [of our joint study], using the material I have offered."[7] Julián Carrón, in his synthesis of and commentary on the writings of Christian educator Luigi Giussani, makes a similar point: "The student must verify the traditional contents being offered to him, which can be done only if *he himself takes the initiative*: no one else can do it for him."[8] Carrón continues by directly quoting Giussani: "Precisely because of his discretion and respect for the student, in a certain sense the role of the

---

4. Lavelle, *Dilemma of Narcissus*, 163–64, 167.
5. Freire, *Pedagogy of the Oppressed*.
6. Freire, *Pedagogy of Freedom*, 86.
7. Freire, *Pedagogy of Freedom*, 106.
8. Carrón, *Disarming Beauty*, 154; emphasis in original.

educator is to step back behind the overshadowing figure of the one Truth by which he is inspired."[9] Students are to be encouraged (according to their level of maturity and capacity) to assume responsibility for what they take on board from their educational encounters. As Carrón points out: "Christ did not become incarnate to spare us the work of our reason, our freedom, or our engagement, but to make it possible."[10]

One reason for my emphasis on learning agency is that I believe it can help students (and aspiring disciples more generally) in moving from secondhand faith to firsthand faith. Inevitably, in the journey of faith one begins with something handed down from others, some expressions and practices that witness to someone else's faith, long before there is any chance of coming to it of our own accord. This is part of the human condition. However, it is important to avoid suggesting that faith can be presented safely in a prefabricated version, conveyed on an assembly line. Christian teachers, in church and in school, want people to hear God speak to them now. All their teaching and "tools" are intended to facilitate a living, personal, present, spontaneous and direct relationship with God. By its nature this has to be unique and individual in character, even though it is also externally shaped and communally shared. Learners receive from others but then they have to reauthorize this faith as they internalize and appropriate or critique or modify it so that what they learn becomes their own. They must construe its significance for themselves. It must speak to their condition; it must address their context; it must make sense of their experience; it must answer their questions. In response to teaching and to the offer of formation, as they learn how Christian (or other religious) language is spoken, at some point in their language and living they need to incarnate this, to embed this in the particular circumstances of their life, to take it on as a second but natural language with all the freedom, idiosyncrasies, peculiar blend of rule following and rule breaking that accompanies fluency in any language.

While I may develop my own voice through imitation of and response to the voices of others, if each of us is to speak authentically this entails that we go beyond mere reiteration of their voices and that we create a new performance, guided by the grammar of the tradition, but not prevented by this from injecting something creative and fresh into the "conversation." Spiritual maturity is arrived at only in the light of acts of initiative and responsibility and not merely by following instructions. Such acts require space, choice, alternatives, freedom, even temptation. They involve experiment, struggle, and mistakes. As we encounter unmapped territory (unfamiliar at

---

9. Giussani, *Risk of Education*, 64, quoted in Carrón, *Disarming Beauty*, 155.
10. Carrón, *Disarming Beauty*, 202.

least to us, if not to others), and if we are to develop our capacity for judgment, we need opportunities for rehearsal and we depend on the patience and trust of others, as well as affirmation, healing, support, and healing.

Emphasizing the agency of the learner as crucial in education is not new. In a critical retrieval of the educational writing of twentieth-century French philosopher Jacques Maritain, Luz Ibarra shows that he reiterated as central to Thomas Aquinas's view of teaching that the learner is the primary agent of the educational act,[11] a view that was also held several centuries earlier by Augustine. Ibarra, in summarizing Maritain, says that teachers must prepare the human mind to think for itself, by appealing to the child's/adult's power of understanding.[12] She laments that "religious education has not made an appeal to the freedom of the individual."[13]

This judgment is echoed by a scholar who has conducted an ethnographic study of several Catholic secondary schools in the UK, Ann Casson. Through her close observations of what goes on in practice, Casson demonstrates that:

> Religious identity is not something that is solely transmitted, passively received, or handed down intact through the generations; young people play an active role in constructing their identity, whether religious, personal or national.[14]

Deploying the term *bricolage*, borrowed from the sociologist of religion Danièle Hervieu-Léger, Casson indicates how young people are constructing their own religious identity, from the materials available to them, but not necessarily in ways expected (or desired) by their teachers or the church.[15] Casson's work is significant because it shows the folly of any policy for religious education in such schools which fails to take note of the kinds of ways students interpret what the school (and the church) offers and which also fails to do justice to the plurality of views actually present in Catholicism. She claims that

> the Catholicism portrayed and encountered in RE lessons was "artificially monolithic"; the RE curriculum did not for example include reference to Catholic groups supporting the ordination

---

11. Ibarra, *Maritain, Religion, and Education*, 98n125.
12. Ibarra, *Maritain, Religion, and Education*, 109.
13. Ibarra, *Maritain, Religion, and Education*, 165.
14. Casson, *Fragmented Catholicity and Social Cohesion*, 49.
15. Casson, *Fragmented Catholicity and Social Cohesion*, 50.

of women priests, or Catholic organizations which were supportive of divorcees or homosexual rights.[16]

This particular issue is taken up in the following section.

## MCDONOUGH ON DISSENT

Canadian philosopher of education Graham McDonough has recently written a substantial, carefully argued, and deeply significant book that confronts in a critical yet sympathetic manner a major weakness in the theory of Catholic education: its too ready assumption of the appropriateness, both in terms of ethics and of efficacy, of a monolithic transmission model of Catholic faith and tradition. He argues that this assumption is unrealistic, in that it ignores the existence of diversity in beliefs and values among the Catholic faithful, a diversity amply demonstrated by Casson's research (referred to briefly in the previous section), that it is damaging, in that it imposes on some students and staff unreasonable demands and expectations and that it undermines the pedagogical relationship between teachers and students. Furthermore, he makes a very cogent argument that such an approach is corrosive of mature membership in the church, stunts the growth of responsible participation as ecclesial members, and fails to address the needs of those who question aspects of the tradition, either by pretending that such doubts do not exist or by treating those who harbor such doubts and difficulties as presenting threats to the faith from which school should be quarantined.

McDonough claims that students are presented with an

> apparent false choice between complete adherence to the prevailing Catholicism, complete abandonment of it, or, . . . existence uneasily at odds with prevailing norms.[17]

> If dissidents of all sorts perceive that the Church cannot receive disagreement, and that the institutions of Catholic education are unable to assist them academically in working out their disagreements . . . many people . . . simply resign themselves to abandoning Catholicism before they have an opportunity to work out their disagreements in greater depth.[18]

---

16. Casson, *Fragmented Catholicity and Social Cohesion*, 155.
17. McDonough, *Beyond Obedience and Abandonment*, 6.
18. McDonough, *Beyond Obedience and Abandonment*, 10.

This is a false choice, since it is clear that a significant number of Catholics, including many who continue to attend church and receive the sacraments regularly, differ from official teaching on a wide range of issues. These include people who have taken the trouble to inform themselves properly about such church teaching, who differ from it, and do so with a clear conscience. The diversity cannot be attributed to bad faith, ignorance, inadequate formation, or colonization by secular culture, even though these factors may also play a part in some cases. It is selling students short to imply that there is no middle way between total acceptance of "the whole package" as handed down by authority and complete abandonment of it—and for two reasons.

First, it flies in the face of ecclesial realities; in other words, it is simply untrue, in that many people do live somewhere in the spectrum between these alternatives. Second, it implies that the tradition is fixed, has reached completion, and has no need to, nor any capacity to, develop further. Short of the *eschaton*, such an implication would be a form of idolatry, in denial of the truth that the church is always in need of reform. Furthermore, by preventing the airing, sharing, and discussion of doubts and difficulties in an educational (or ecclesial) setting, it would fail to model how faith can legitimately be questioned and critiqued because one cares about it, wants to be serious about it, needs to probe it, not least in order to develop a defense of it in the face of external criticisms; otherwise there is little chance that such faith could ever be owned responsibly, lived honestly, or communicated effectively.

Given the prevailing failure in many Catholic schools to allow an appropriate pedagogical space for the exploration of doubts and difficulties with regard to faith, it is not surprising that religious education teachers in particular find themselves in a challenging situation. They have to negotiate between competing responsibilities: on the one hand, they are expected to maintain "the norms of an authoritarian institution"; on the other hand, they are tasked with "attending to the students' individual pedagogical needs."[19] McDonough sets out the problem clearly thus:

> If the school does its job of "teaching" (as in "presenting") what the Church directs but the students do not accept its validity, has the school done its job to meet the needs of these students? Likewise, if the school eschews any care for what the Church teaches and for expedient reasons of good relations with students and parents adapts and alters Catholicism to such a

---

19. McDonough, *Beyond Obedience and Abandonment*, 14.

degree that it no longer accurately represents the Magisterium, is it doing its job to meet the needs of the Church?[20]

One might ask here: What kind of picture is envisaged of the student as a member of the church? Is it as a captive audience or as raw material for producing a faithful person? Or is it as an ecclesial citizen with his or her own critically functioning conscience? McDonough is right in diagnosing that "one of the great challenges Catholic curricular theory faces is to present normative Church teaching in a way that respects the learner's religious freedom,"[21] to which one might add, in such a manner as to take into account her essential agency in learning. Further on in the book, McDonough comments:

> Independently of the *content* of students' opinions, the pedagogical imperative is developing students' skills in assembling, judging, and presenting rational evidence for the perspectives that they have developed.[22]

In developing the challenge, he asks: "How might a Catholic person challenge his or her Church without (being accused of) anti-Catholicism, apostasy, heresy, or de-Catholicizing the institution?"[23]

Unless this is possible, for students and for teachers, one runs the risk that an unfortunate impression is given that "Church teaching is not a dialogue in which one might participate but a monologue to which one must assimilate."[24] On the contrary, as he points out:

> Engaging with dissent in a way that develops a student's agency as a dissident within the Church is a way of reaching out to a fellow Catholic with the intent of helping them to re-imagine their place in the Church.[25]

---

20. McDonough, *Beyond Obedience and Abandonment*, 113–14.
21. McDonough, *Beyond Obedience and Abandonment*, 127.
22. McDonough, *Beyond Obedience and Abandonment*, 178; emphasis in original.
23. McDonough, *Beyond Obedience and Abandonment*, 123.
24. McDonough, *Beyond Obedience and Abandonment*, 195.
25. McDonough, *Beyond Obedience and Abandonment*, 221. Compare David Lose's reference to Ricoeur on distanciation as a necessary step towards appropriation: "Philosopher Paul Ricoeur . . . describes the process of participation and distanciation that leads to genuine appropriation. . . . Ricoeur proposes that one needs both an immersion into the existential import of the topic (participation) as well as the critical space in which to question, wonder about, even reject the conclusions offered (distanciation) in order genuinely to actualize and internalize the truths offered (appropriation). (Lose, "How Do We Make Space," 24).

## HOGAN ON EDUCATION AND LEARNING

McDonough has identified a problematic area of weakness in the current theory of Catholic education. While he does not make this explicit, his argument depends on an understanding of education that envisages it as a substantive or sui generis activity, as opposed to a subordinate one, subordinate in the sense that its purpose is to meet the preset ends of some external body or community, for example, the church, the government, the political party, or business and multinational companies. He hints at this in his comment that

> other Catholic agencies such as hospitals, homeless shelters, and soup kitchens do quite well to work *from* a religious orientation of providing service to all in society, but without an expectation that the objects of their care are or will become Catholic persons, and without that fact being a threat to the institution's Catholic identity.[26]

While one should expect Catholic teaching and tradition to receive explicit, substantive, comprehensive and coherent treatment in a Catholic school, and the church to be salient in its life and work, such salience should not override the principal role of the school as an *educational* community, one whose primary concern is to promote learning by students, however much it is in dialogue with its partners, the parents, the church, and the wider community. The second philosopher of education I draw upon here, Pádraig Hogan, supplies an explicit examination of what McDonough leaves implicit.[27] In doing so he provides support for McDonough and for prioritizing the agency of learners over the preservation of tradition, believing that not only would students benefit from such an emphasis, so too would the tradition.

Hogan's argument could be summarized in six steps. First, when education is considered as a form of custodianship, the preservation and passing on of a culture or tradition (whether religious, political, economic, or social), schooling slips into being more concerned with the interests of what is being preserved and passed on than with the needs of those being educated. The students are being prepared and equipped to join, to maintain, and to contribute to a preexisting set of cultural, religious, or other arrangements and patterns of behavior. Hogan explains that "custodianship here means a schooling of mind and heart that was often as restrictive as it was

---

26. McDonough, *Beyond Obedience and Abandonment*, 22; emphasis in original.
27. Hogan: *Custody and Courtship of Experience*; *New Significance of Learning*.

enabling."[28] Such custodianship can be attempted by diverse bodies: "Where ecclesiastical authorities lost control of schooling, that control passed not to schools themselves but to newly powerful secular interests, often of a utilitarian, or nationalist, or commercial tenor."[29]

Second, instead of seeing themselves as taking students into custody (obviously intended to be of benefit to them in this way), teachers should approach their work as a form of courtship, of wooing or eliciting and activating the sensibilities and capacities of students. This wooing of students is "not so much of their affections, as of their best imaginative efforts."[30] In this special form of courtship, teachers confront and engage the students' "sensibilities . . . enthusiasms, aversions, inclinations, resistances, tolerances, prejudices, susceptibilities, credulities, etc."[31] Hogan now prefers the word "heartwork" to "courtship" but is still keen to retain the connotations of mutuality that are more evident in the term "courtship." I am not sure "heartwork" is quite the right term here; it might be better simply to use the expression "teachers invite students to engage with" whatever is the object of study.

Third, this does more justice than a transmission model of teaching to the essentially *joint* nature of teaching and learning, one where there is always interplay or mutual exchange between teachers and learners (and also between a tradition and its members). With regard to the transmission model, Hogan notes that "such commonplace usage casts teachers mainly in the active role of instructors and students mainly in the role of receivers."[32] In contrast, Hogan advocates an approach in which

> the student is seen not as material to be molded to the teacher's design, nor as a mind to be furnished with a preferred body of teachings and outlooks. Rather, the student is acknowledged as a new participant in the venture of learning.[33]

Fourth, teachers should beware of adopting any proprietorial designs on their students; education is not about possessing learners but about liberating them in service of learning. As with other professions, education has a central purpose that is not compatible with proprietary aims. In social work, counseling, medicine, and law, the primary purpose in each case,

28. Hogan, *New Significance of Learning*, 4.
29. Hogan, *New Significance of Learning*, 5.
30. Hogan, *New Significance of Learning*, 57.
31. Hogan, *New Significance of Learning*, 57.
32. Hogan, *New Significance of Learning*, 58.
33. Hogan, *New Significance of Learning*, 75.

regardless of the personal hopes held by practitioners, is enabling people to cope with particular kinds of difficulties, self-understanding, health, and justice, respectively. So too in education, Hogan observes:

> I've put a foot wrong if my approach presumes some proprietorial claim on the minds and hearts of students. . . . The explicit disavowal of such proprietorial claims is a "must" for professional discipline in teaching.[34]

Fifth, he finds helpful Alasdair MacIntyre's treatment of the centrality of traditions to the development of rationality, morality, and practices,[35] and he appreciates MacIntyre's recognition of such traditions as ongoing arguments about the goods at their heart;[36] but he also judges that MacIntyre's stance towards the role of tradition is too partisan and adversarial. In contrast he prefers Gadamer's emphasis on tradition as a conversation partner,[37] finding this does more justice to the mutual exchange at the heart of educational encounters.[38] Gadamer refers to a "fusion of horizons" made possible in an encounter with tradition: "On the one hand, the horizon of understanding the individual brings with him or her to the encounter, and, on the other, the horizon of meaning that addresses the individual in this encounter."[39] Hogan prefers the word "frisson" to "fusion" because, as he points out,

> what Gadamer has in mind is not a melting together in which all tensions are laid to rest, but an attentive to-and-fro between the learner and the different-ness of that which addresses him or her. It is an interplay in which tensions are uncovered and brought to the fore rather than glossed or passed over.

Such uncovering of tensions within the tradition can serve simultaneously to invite the agency of learners to participate in a shared journey of exploration and to contribute to the development (and perhaps also even the healing) of the tradition.

Finally, Hogan stresses that treating the sphere of education as having its own particular character and role, one that differs from the religious, political, and economic, and so forth, without necessarily being in conflict with them, gives priority to, and in practice is more enabling of, the development

---

34. Hogan, *New Significance of Learning*, 66.
35. MacIntyre: *After Virtue*; *Whose Justice? Which Rationality?*
36. Hogan, *New Significance of Learning*, 11–13.
37. Gadamer, *Truth and Method*.
38. Hogan, *New Significance of Learning*, 121, 132.
39. Hogan, *New Significance of Learning*, 118.

of agency in learners. It follows from this sui generis nature of education that "religious traditions are to be encountered on different grounds in public educational settings than they are in homes, Sunday schools and other places of upbringing; or in churches, mosques, synagogues and other places of worship."[40] Such different grounds are intended, through their exploratory and interrogative modes of engagement, to complement and to illuminate, not to contradict or to reject, religious commitment.

## RISKS AND BENEFITS OF PROMOTING AGENCY

What are the risks that might be incurred by so stressing the importance of developing the agency of learners in the context of teaching about matters of faith, along the lines suggested by McDonough and Hogan, thus giving space to the expression of dissent and seeking to woo the emotional and intellectual sensibilities of students? These risks need to be considered and taken into account, if the teaching style one adopts is to be responsible, not least because those who prefer a more custodial approach to education (to use Hogan's term) may well be influenced by one or more of the following objections.

First, by appearing to privilege the learner over the tradition, the student might fall into the trap of picking and mixing from what is offered, develop a deficient or distorted interpretation of its "score," and arrive at a version of it that lacks coherence and integrity.

Second, and following on from the first risk, in adding to the plurality of versions of the "score," there could be a reduced capacity among God's people to present the harmonious symphony of God's truth, which might now come across as cacophonous and confusing.

Third, giving priority to the agency of learners may lead to a situation where undue influence is exerted, consciously or unconsciously, by "external" cultures and ideologies that are hostile to faith.

Fourth, the "courtship" approach may contribute to students having insufficient respect for authority (as understood by church or school leaders).

Fifth, this might lead to an ensuing risk to the personal salvation of students if they fail to allow their nascent faith to be appropriately nourished, guided, deepened, and illuminated by divine teaching, spiritual practices, and a suitably disciplined moral life.

Sixth, communion within the church might be undermined because less is held in common by its members and therefore there is an erosion of

---

40. Hogan, *New Significance of Learning*, 168.

the processes of bonding, binding, and reinforcing of faith that can come about from the example of (and by being immersed in) a church with clear identity, explicit boundaries, and significant commonality of practice and experience.

Seventh, it might be argued that by giving space to dissent, in the ways suggested by McDonough, and by following Hogan in treating educational activities as substantively sui generis—rather than as mere delivery methods for externally decided ends—teachers might reinforce in students a tendency to pride, egoism, and undue reliance on self. They might thereby encourage in learners a reluctance to accept any teaching which they find uncomfortable, leading to an inappropriately selective and secular filtering out of Catholicism, where the demands of religious faith are muted, less intrusive or even obscured. In such a situation, teachers might find themselves colluding with students' desire to prevent important aspects of their lives from being addressed and converted.

While I would not give equal weight to each of these concerns, and despite my view that, even taken together, they should not count against the imperative, for the sake both of the church's living tradition and of the individuals involved, of promoting agency among learners, neither do I think that they should be lightly dismissed. Teachers should be vigilant in their efforts to guard against these possible side effects of facilitating agency in learners.

To downplay agency in learners, however, might be to assume too readily that there are only gifts and treasures within the faith tradition and not to acknowledge that there are also distortions and damaging features, or, to use the terminology of philosopher of education Jane Roland Martin, to fail to distinguish the "assets" from the "liabilities" that reside in tradition.[41] This might deprive learners of growing in the capacity for discerning, along with others, which features of the tradition fall into which category.

What are the possible benefits from prioritizing agency, as recommended by McDonough, Hogan, and others? While the seven potential gains I comment on here cannot be guaranteed as outcomes, I believe that their promise far outweighs the various risks just outlined and that they are worth striving for with energy, expertise, and enthusiasm.

First, prioritizing agency increases the chances that a mature conscience will be developed and actively deployed by learners. Compared with a reliance on a more passive reception by learners of the voice of authority, the greater degree of engagement, participation and contribution made by learners if their agency is invited, nurtured, and affirmed is likely to lead

---

41. J. Martin, *Education Reconfigured*, 10, 128.

them to have a more vibrant and personal sense of ownership and responsibility for the moral values they live from. The exercise of conscience rests on a sound foundation, one that has been internalized and accepted as one's own, not merely handed down "from above," received secondhand, or borrowed from others. This was a point about which, as a Catholic, John Henry Newman in the nineteenth century was very sensitive—as is illustrated by his claim that, "in religious inquiry, each of us can speak only for himself, and for himself he has a right to speak."[42] Apart from his celebrated toast to conscience in the nineteenth century,[43] the overriding authority of conscience continues to be central to Catholic teaching, as is indicated in the quotation below from a theologian who later became a church leader at the highest level:

> Over the Pope as expression of the binding claim of ecclesiastical authority, there stands one's own conscience which must be obeyed before all else, even if necessary against the requirement of ecclesiastical authority. This emphasis on the individual, whose conscience confronts him with a supreme and ultimate tribunal, and one which in the last resort is beyond the claim of external social groups, even the official Church, also establishes a principle in opposition to increasing totalitarianism.[44]

While conscience must be informed, needs to be guided by others, and can be erroneous, it remains essential for the moral life and relies on acts of personal judgment and the exercise of responsibility for one's decisions and actions. Such a sense of judgment and mature responsibility cannot be arrived at without early and continuous opportunities to be agents in one's learning, in school, as well as in life generally. Teachers' appeals to agency in their students invite commitment on their part, whereas pressing for compliance is more likely to inhibit the development of conscience and of commitment.

A second likely benefit of promoting agency is that such agency reduces the frequency with which untapped potential lies dormant in learners. If one accepts Jane Roland Martin's argument that enhanced learning by individuals (prompted by their encounter with a culture or tradition) also contributes to the development of that tradition,[45] then increasing students' agency and thereby activating their potential should feed into the tradition, bringing to the surface its untapped potential, and it should

42. Newman, *Essay in Aid of Grammar*, 300.
43. Newman, "Letter to Duke of Norfolk," 261.
44. Ratzinger, "Chapter 1," 5:134.
45. J. Martin, *Education Reconfigured*, ch. 1.

enhance the possibility that the tradition will be rejuvenated, reinterpreted, reconfigured, reoriented, and more creatively applied. In this way, the tradition will be able to draw more fully than it otherwise might on the constructive contribution of students in schools but also as they take their place in the world as adults.

Third, because side effects of promoting real agency might be expected to include greater participation, more confidence in taking the initiative, a deeper sense of ownership of learning, together with a more robust capacity to go on learning, students should be better equipped to cope flexibly and creatively with changing circumstances and unforeseen challenges. Where students remain members of the tradition, this capacity to adapt flexibly should benefit the tradition as well as the individual. The enhanced agency of learners enriches the human resources and gifts of imagination, initiative, and creativity available for the church's life and work.

Fourth, students who have been encouraged to become more actively engaged in and to exercise more initiative in and control over their learning are less likely to be at the mercy of the diverse range of hidden persuaders (and abusers) who might seek to enlist their loyalty or allegiance; they will be more ready to test for the veracity of the claims of others and to be vigilant as to their motives. Where educational spaces are ones that resist colonization and conquest, and where education is treated as a substantive sui generis activity instead of being subordinate to and derivative of externally driven aims (whether of church, government or other bodies), then educational encounters and conversations are likely to be both more positively received and more fruitful in outcomes.

Fifth, when teachers promote the agency of students they facilitate a more adept integration by students of faith, life, and culture (a central goal of Catholic education), prompting learners to draw upon all of their experiences from home, friendships, school, church, and the culture in which they find themselves.

Sixth, in drawing out and encouraging the articulation of the perspectives, questions, criticisms, concerns, gifts, capacities, and initiatives of young people, and through inviting greater participation by them in their learning, two simultaneous gains may be achieved: one is an atmosphere of greater honesty about the very real differences among believers as to how faith is understood and lived out; and the other is a more accurate reflection of the glorious diversity of God's people, for example, with regard to worship and expressions of faith and in ways of living.

Finally, one might claim that, for each individual, revelation, whatever the external prompt, source, medium, or trigger for receiving this might be—Bible, church teaching, private prayer, liturgy, spiritual practices, a life of loving service—takes place within, and has to relate to, the experience of each person. Thus, promoting the agency of learners enhances their capacity for real rather than notional apprehension and reception of revelation, for the emergence of faith that is firsthand, one's own, instead of a borrowed, secondhand faith. Christian faith tells us that God is present to us, regardless of whether we, as teachers and learners, advert to that presence. It also tells us that no one, including the church, can claim to monopolize, direct or control God's action in the world.[46] A failure to give sufficient priority to the development of agency in learners, if motivated by a desire to ensure that the tradition is conveyed in a comprehensive and orthodox manner, runs the danger that it might preserve sacred (but dead) relics instead of promoting the risk-laden life that draws on a living legacy.

## ORIGINAL RESPONSE

To bring this chapter to a conclusion, a few brief comments on originality, responsible ownership and the correlative links between obedience and freedom are in order because they bring out key features of the nature of the learning agency that has been argued for as an educational priority. With regard to originality, discipleship (understood in its broadest sense, not just with regard to Christ), entails a complex interaction between imitation and originality, of docility and creativity. Just as Christ saves me in a unique way (in relation to my unique combination of needs, strengths, sins, gifts, blind spots, situation), so my response must also be unique and particular, with my own input providing some element of originality—making something of what I have been given, doing something special and creative with my inheritance.[47]

Teaching Christian faith, whether in church or in school, is always with a view to inviting those being addressed to transcend passive acceptance by responding with an element of originality, allowing transformation in themselves but also in the tradition. Hogan claims that, if his heartwork perspective is adopted, this entails "a major shift of emphasis from an order of compliance to an order of originality."[48] Maritain prayed, "Let Divine Love Who calls each being by his own name mould you and make of you a person, a true original, not a copy."[49] "The saint has always been an origi-

---

46. Moog, *À quoi sert l'école catholique*, 70.
47. See, for example, Jesus's parable of the talents in Matt 25:14–30; Luke 19:12–27.
48. Hogan, *New Significance of Learning*, 67.
49. Maritain, *Education at the Crossroads*, 36.

nal, never an imitation," says moral theologian James Keenan,[50] a comment echoed by moral philosopher Jennifer Herdt, who claims, of exemplars of Christian faith, that "all are understood as having imitated Christ, but they are nevertheless a far cry from carbon copies of one another."[51]

In a recent article, two commentators reflect on originality as a crucial element in the response that both the church and the school should be looking for and they comment on how this relates to imitation. I quote them extensively to illustrate this point.

> The saints are all originals; they became virtuous and morally excellent in their own ways, and so too must all moral agents become virtuous and morally excellent in their own ways. They must become authentically, virtuously, and morally themselves, not simply clones of Augustine or Thérèse or Maria Goretti.[52]

> To become authentic and authentically virtuous, children must develop into *their* authenticity, *their* virtue and *their* adulthood. . . . They can be shaped by imitating past models but finished only by a fresh articulation. The dynamic of virtues begins with imitation of role models but concludes with authentic morality through personal decision and responsibility.[53]

As for responsible ownership of one's learning, Peter Abelard taught in the twelfth century that by doubting we are brought to inquiry and by inquiry to truth.[54] It is not sufficient for teachers to convey to students what they believe is the truth; students have to be helped to engage with the material in such a way that the outcome of the engagement is a cognitive position that they own for themselves, even if, by some criteria, that position is "wrong" in some respects. I do not want to set up as stark alternatives what might be labeled as "look-it-up Catholicism" and "think-for-yourself Catholicism," since neither of these on its own can be satisfactory as a solution for individual believers, nor can they be so for the church.[55] In referring to problems in instructing the modern conscience, Michael Lacey contrasts an important difference between secular and ecclesial approaches:

> In the secular world . . . the shared aim of teacher and pupils alike is for the teacher to pass along some degree of mastery and

50. Keenan, "Proposing Cardinal Virtues," 713.
51. Herdt, *Putting on Virtue*, 8.
52. Lawler and Salzman, "Virtue Ethics," 449.
53. Lawler and Salzman, "Virtue Ethics," 450; emphasis in original.
54. Abelard, *Sic et Non*, prologue.
55. Lacey, "Problem of Authority," 4.

step aside.... One graduates and comes to share with teachers the status of adulthood and its responsibilities. In the ecclesial setting [however] ... it seems one does not really grow up and move on to independence, but as part of God's plan is expected to remain forever in a state of tutelage.[56]

## CONCLUSION

The argument of this chapter has been that education should aim for agency on the part of learners, holding in view a long-term hope that they will move from initial dependence to a mature interdependence, owning who they are becoming and taking responsibility for their commitments. If this view of education is accepted, then tutelage can at best be a temporary state, or, to use Hogan's term, any temptation to exercise a proprietary role over students must be resisted, both by teachers themselves, but also by students as they get older.

One way that tutelage and its associated custodial role can be recognized is when teachers, in the school and in the church, "present answers to questions that have not arisen in students' minds yet at the same time fail to face the questions they do raise." The Czech priest, philosopher, and psychotherapist Tomáš Halík suggests that "answers without questions are like trees without roots."[57] He says:

> Insofar as we preserve our *originality* imprinted and stored by God—and we do not become a copy of others: a *forgery*—each of us will proclaim through our unmistakable uniqueness something new and truthful about God and His inexhaustible mystery.[58]

Then, drawing upon theologian Joseph Moignt, Halík proclaims that "the interval between losing the 'God of the fathers' and finding *the faith of the sons* (no longer an 'inherited religion' but a free response to the way the Spirit blows today) is not to be feared,"[59] because, in a generously inclusive approach to the plurality of ways that people come to find God, one might speak of these as "different keys to opening the same room with many doors;

---

56. Lacey, "Problem of Authority," 7.
57. Halík, *Patience with God*, 7.
58. Halík, *Patience with God*, 48; emphasis in original.
59. Halík, *Patience with God*, 50; emphasis in original.

maybe we will tend to use the one that is closer to our style of thinking and vocabulary."[60]

Finally, it is important to hold onto the integral relationship between, on the one hand, the obedience that is part of formation in the ways of thinking, living, and belonging to a tradition, formation that preserves the continuity of that tradition across time, and, on the other hand, the freedom that is both the sought-after goal of both education and discipleship and at the same time an essential condition for the development of mature judgment, commitment, and responsibility. The key feature of obedience is deep listening (with one's whole self) to the other; this requires self-giving. To give oneself, one must have a self to offer. The best form of authority is given freely, authorized by those who accept it in a free act; and for this they must have agency. Obedience and freedom are correlative states, not contradictory ones. For

> just as great works of art evidence simultaneously a creativity (freedom) and a lawful orderliness (obedience to some harmonizing idea), so also the Christian's life is both a submission to God's "idea" for his or her life (thus obedient) and also a creative embodiment of the Spirit's prompting (and thus free).[61]

Furthermore,

> To interpret is not to change [God's] Word, but it is to "play" it with all one's person, like a musical score. This musical score is the same for everyone, and it must be played faithfully, but each must play it with what he or she is, and make it a wholly personal rendition. When, through the intimate relationship with God in our heart, we come to know God's "score," we can play it in our lives.[62]

In all of this there is no sharp separation between the workings of nature and those of grace. As St. Bernard of Clairvaux put it:

> What was begun by grace alone, is completed by grace and free choice together, in such a way that they contribute to each new achievement not singly but jointly; not by turns, but simultaneously. It is not as if grace did one half of the work and free choice the other; but each does the whole work, according to its own peculiar contribution. Grace does the whole work, and so does

---

60. Halík, *Night of the Confessor*, 84–85.
61. Steck, Review of *Dramatic Encounter*, 158.
62. Linnig, "Pedagogy of God," 161.

free choice—with this one qualification: that whereas the whole is done *in* free choice, so is the whole done *of* grace.[63]

Parents and teachers would do well to remember the lines of Kahlil Gibran in *The Prophet*:

> Your children are not your children.
> They are the sons and daughters of Life's longing for itself.
> They come through you but not from you,
> And though they are with you yet they belong not to you.
> You may give them your love but not your thoughts,
> For they have their own thoughts.
> You may house their bodies but not their souls,
> For their souls dwell in the house of to-morrow, which you cannot visit, not even in your dreams.
> You may strive to be like them, but seek not to make them like you
> For life goes not backward nor tarries with yesterday.
> You are bows from which your children as living arrows are sent forth.[64]
>
> The archer sees the mark upon the path of the infinite, and He bends you with His might that His arrows may go swift and far.
> Let your bending in the Archer's hand be for gladness;
> For even as He loves the arrow that flies, so He loves also the bow that is stable.[65]

---

63. Bernard of Clairvaux, *On Grace & Free Choice*, 106; emphasis in original.
64. Gibran, *Prophet*, 20.
65. Gibran, *Prophet*, 23.

# PART FIVE
# Connecting Tradition to Culture

## INTRODUCTION

*Gaudium et Spes,* an important document from the Second Vatican Council (1962–65), speaks of the "duty of scrutinizing the signs of the times and of interpreting them in the light of the Gospel."[1] The signs of the times—those changes in society and culture that hold a deeper meaning that can be discerned in the light of careful reading of Scripture, prayer, and openness to the Holy Spirit—should be distinguished from the spirit of the age: the common assumptions, fashionable trends, and popular opinions that permeate society, the seductions of advertising, and the siren calls of those agencies which invite us down the route of a narrow self-indulgence. As a steward of a living tradition, the Christian educator strives to make faith available, visible, audible, intelligible, credible, attractive, and robust in the face of life's difficulties, and in response to corrosive alternatives which are proposed by contemporary culture. The Dominican Timothy Radcliffe proposed as a mission for the Catholic weekly journal *The Tablet* the following: "We are called to live the tension between the convictions of the Church and the questions of the world. *The Tablet's* mission is to live this tension fruitfully, for and with its readers."[2] Christian educators could well adopt Radcliffe's first sentence as their own task as they seek to bring about dialogue between their living tradition and the culture of their times: "We are called to live the tension between the convictions of the Church and the questions of our

---

1. Paul VI, *Gaudium et Spes,* §4.
2. Fergusson, "Listening Cardinal," 5.

world." This task entails engaging with the language, concerns, sensitivities, and modes of thought of the culture of our time and place.

The challenge entailed in connecting a faith tradition to culture is sometimes referred to as inculturation—the task of showing how the gospel relates to a particular time, place, and cultural setting. This is a two-way process. Just as the gospel casts new light on each human situation, in turn that situation can bring different dimensions of the gospel into salience. Throughout history, each generation has had to read, receive, and respond to the gospel in ways made possible by, but also in ways that are restricted by, the patterns of perception and behavior associated with life in the world. The gospel always has to take roots, to touch down in flesh-and-blood people, in very particular circumstances. Inevitably, in doing so, it changes color, depending on what is already lighting up the lives of the people and what is darkening them.

The process of inculturation—relating the gospel to the changing contexts, questions, assumptions, thought forms of society—is an ongoing requirement and task of anyone involved in Christian preaching and teaching. Ideas and ways of life take their form and are understood in relation to surrounding ideas and practices (borrowing from, reacting against and building on these). Christianity—how it is understood and communicated—and thus Christian education—always exists in creative tension with the surrounding world. As the questions, concerns, possibilities, and problems aroused by the world change, so too must Christians rethink and reexpress their faith—and its relationship to the world.

In an encounter with Christian faith, the culture will find itself challenged and be pressed to see itself in a new light. At the same time, when Christians encounter another culture, they will find their faith challenged, and they will find it necessary to reinterpret this faith and see it differently. Modifications in self-understanding are likely to be necessary on both sides as bridges are built between the heritage of Christian faith and the value systems, symbols, and cultures of learners. Incarnating the faith in a particular context will entail engagement by Christians with the language, perceptions, priorities, preoccupations and practices of the people therein. Such engagement facilitates the reception and appropriation of Christian faith in terms understandable to the receiving culture. In turn however, all cultures need to be evangelized, brought into the light of the cross. The discerning Christian educator needs to take into account those features of our culture that we experience (or should perceive) as challenges, threats, and temptations—as well as features we judge to be allies, sympathetic, in harmony with or supportive of our faith.

However, part of the difficulty here is recognizing that, before we begin the task of such cultural discernment, we have already been—to some degree at least—colonized by the culture within which we live. It has seeped into our practices, shaped our preferences, and framed our outlook on life. We do not start from a pure or uncontaminated position. Thus, as the Jesuit theologian Joseph Mattam points out:

> Before we can effect any meaningful inculturation of the gospel, we must first undergo a de-culturation that frees us from a particular outlook of the world, and a re-culturation, a re-entry into the outlook of Jesus. The world's outlook evaluates and understands by equating the person with possessions, positions, achievements, actions, linguistic or religious or cultural groups. Inculturation of Christianity is an ongoing process of reciprocal and critical interaction and assimilation between culture and Christian life.[3]

This preformation or inevitable assimilation of the perspectives and values of the culture we are born into is an unavoidable feature of the human condition, in any age. However, there are some factors worth taking note of that seem to be operating as part of the background to the relationship between Christians and secular society in our own age. There is operating, beneath the surface, an implicit rationalization of the way that many Christians have accommodated the requirements of liberal secular democracy. Relevant factors seem to include guilt about past Christian dominance and abuse of power; a desire to be as inclusive as possible; an appreciation that God is at work beyond the church and within the secular; a fear that being too "in your face" will be counterproductive in eliciting a very negative rejection of Christianity; false readings of what people of other faiths might want of Christians; and a tendency towards adopting a self-denying, self-emptying, and service mode of Christianity, rather than seeking privilege and power. One could add to these, as particularly relevant for Christian educators, the marginalization of Christian faith from academic and professional development and socialization, which contributes (along with other factors) to the privatization of faith; effective lobbying by secularists to eradicate or minimize Christian influence, and a fatal separation of worship and intellectual endeavor.

Each of the four chapters in part 5 casts some light on an aspect of the Christian educator's task in connecting tradition to contemporary culture. In chapter 20, after sketching a range of responses to Christianity within an increasingly secular society, and, reciprocally, how Christians typically have

---

3. Mattam, "Inculturated Evangelization & Conversion," 229.

responded to that society, I provide a critical retrieval of two significant but contrasting responses by Catholic thinkers to a secularizing landscape, those offered by Romano Guardini and Ivan Illich, each of whom sought to present a blend of the pastoral and prophetic in their interpretation of and engagement with twentieth-century culture. Affirmation of the positive features of society and criticism of its negative features need to be held in creative tension, but there is no magic formula for how to manage this task.

In chapter 21, I explore how the metaphor of translation casts light on the delicate balancing acts that accompany the task of Catholic education—indeed of any faith-based education. Translators seek to represent faithfully the text and tradition that they convey in a different language. At the same time, they hope to make that text and tradition meaningful and "alive" for their readers or hearers. Christian educators face the same twin task, of faithful representation and of creative interpretation. Translators and educators always run the risks of betrayal, of falling short, either in the task of faithful representation or in the imperative to render what is passed on as relevant, attractive, and transformational.

Chapter 22 addresses two dimensions of being open to others, both of which are then related to inculturation, a task shared by the church and her schools and universities. First, the micro-level of personal communication with other individuals is considered, along with the qualities and virtues that enhance such communication. Second, the focus switches to the broader level of an intelligent and sensitive engagement with the media of communication deployed within contemporary culture. In the final section there is an indication of the bearing on inculturation and the relevance for Christian educators of both effective personal communicative relationships and a critical discernment of culture and its media of communication.

To counteract any impression that might be given by some of the preceding chapters—that the church has a benign and always positive influence to bring to bear on society, while having little to learn from the secular world—in chapter 23 I explore some of the dysfunctionality often found in the church, features of its life and teaching that can stand in the way of an effective communication of the gospel, and then I identify some ways in which the church needs to learn from the world if her voice—as heard by the world—is to sound credible and winsome. My own (Roman Catholic) church certainly also needs to open herself more fully to the gifts and insights of Christians in other parts of the wider family of faith and also to the spiritual wisdom developed in other faith traditions. The current synodal movement within Catholicism could legitimately be described as being, at least in part, an appropriation of the Baptist insight that "when all exercise their gifts and callings, when every voice is heard and weighed, when no one is silenced or privileged, the Spirit leads communities to read wisely and to practice faithfully the direction of the gospel."[4] Although it is too soon to know if the synodal movement will yield the fruits it promises, I am hopeful that this will be the case. Whether or not it does, it remains true that the church's witness to the world—and therefore its communication with the wider culture—needs to grow out of and be founded on a healthy internal ecclesial life.

---

4. Steve Harmon, quoted in Medley, "Stewards, Interrogators, and Inventors," 86n70.

# 20

# Catholic Pastoral and Prophetic Responses to a Secularizing Landscape

AFTER AN INITIAL SKETCH of responses to Christianity in our culture and of responses to this culture by Christians, I focus on two exemplars of Catholic responses to secularization, very different in tone, style, and emphasis: Romano Guardini (1885–1968) and Ivan Illich (1926–2002). Although each of these priests could justifiably be described as offering both a pastoral and a prophetic approach in their dealings with individuals and through their critique of society, Guardini tended towards a more pastoral emphasis, while Illich's stance was more prophetic. Both offered an analysis and a critique of developments in the society and culture of their time. While their insights, even when combined, do not suffice on their own as comprising a comprehensive Catholic response to a secularizing landscape for our time, they provide an indication of some key features needed as part of such a response.

The work of both Guardini and Illich has been taken up, not only by Christians outside Catholicism, but also by people of other faiths and by those who claim no religious affiliation. Guardini's writings on literature, as well as those on the challenges for modern culture posed by technology, have a wider appeal than merely to his fellow Catholics and to other Christians. Many of Illich's writings were addressed to—and received widespread commentary from—a secular readership. However, my retrieval of central aspects of the work of Guardini and Illich is intended to bring out some of the richness of the resources inherent in Catholicism, resources that can help Catholics to engage discerningly, constructively, and effectively with an increasingly secularizing landscape.

# FACING THE CHALLENGE OF SECULARIZATION

Secularization can refer to the process where there occurs a transfer of control or influence over key features and functions of society—for example, education, health, social welfare, politics, and morality—from the church to secular bodies. It can also refer to a situation in which there is a notable decline in numbers of those espousing and practicing religious belief and the rise in numbers of those claiming allegiance to no religion. While lamented by some Christians, neither of these two signs of secularity necessarily imply any serious undermining of the mission and role of the church; indeed, the loss of ecclesial power and the turning away from church attendance may allow for a more authentic expression of the church's nature and indicate a smaller but more sincere committed church membership than is the case when affiliation to a church was a cultural necessity. Charles Taylor suggests a third sense of the emergence of secularity, one that is more challenging for—and potentially corrosive of—Christian self-confidence: "a move from a society where belief in God is unchallenged and indeed, unproblematic, to one in which it is understood to be one option among others,"[1] contested and questioned, if not resisted and resented by major cultural agencies and forces. In such a society it becomes harder (though, of course, not impossible) to admit to Christian faith and to express such faith openly. Without a doubt, secularization—in all three senses just described—also affects faiths other than Christianity, though in different ways, according to the relative weight that adherents of these faiths attribute to such features as their scriptures and doctrines, their structures of authority, and their understanding of community and tradition. How it does so is beyond the scope of this article.

The process of secularization might overlap with, or even lead to secularism—a worldview that seeks to deny any public authority or privilege to religious belief, either of individuals or of religious institutions—but that is not an inevitable or necessary outcome of secularization. A highly secularized society might still constitute a benign and hospitable space for Christians and people of other faiths, depending on the nature of the secularist elements within it and depending on the authority that society grants to those elements. Generally, however, secularization tends to erode our connections with history, culture, and community, because of the habits of thought and lifestyle that accompany secularizing processes.

Christian faith has met with a range of responses within different cultures and societies. Some people have expressed great hostility to the

---

1. Taylor, *Secular Age*, 3.

church because of experiences of abuse, authoritarianism, or unloving behavior by church leaders or by the Christians they have come across. Some have displayed great ignorance about the faith, while others, even if they possess some knowledge about it, remain indifferent, seeing it as irrelevant to their concerns in life. Others again seem to be highly selective in apparently adopting some kind of partial, but incomplete, and thus distorted acceptance of the faith. They borrow some Christian values, but do so blindly, unaware of their source or their true nature.

Even after acknowledging the very real opposition to Christianity that does exist in various sectors of society, it could well be argued that the more damaging factor for the church is the weakness of Christians' positive presentation of and practical witnessing to the faith when they do have the opportunity for this. It could be argued that Christians have not offered in the past, and are still not offering, a serious, cogent, and winsome counterculture and alternative vision for humanity in the church and in church-sponsored bodies, including her schools and higher educational institutions.

A recent commentator on the situation of the church in modern society deploys two striking images to emphasize the challenge to be faced. First, he likens today's believers to "hostesses or stewards on airplanes who explain safety rules before take-off, without being heard by anyone." Then he refers to the risk that Christians might be perceived as "custodians of a museum, constantly confronted with beautiful realities, whose salvific content has, however, been forgotten."[2] These two images might prompt Christians to reflect on how they are being received by society and why they are being received as they are.

Just as one can discern a range of responses to Christian faith in modern culture, so too there is a range of responses by Christians to a secularizing landscape. Some seek to combat and reconquer the world and to reestablish Christendom. Others prefer the path of withdrawal from society, in order to be uncontaminated by its evils. A third category, while claiming to hold onto their faith, are willing to be accommodating to cultural norms, and in doing so, often end up self-secularizing. A fourth response is to use secular "tools" to modernize the church or in an attempt to communicate her message more effectively, for example, through better management techniques to improve leadership, or by deploying sociological data to inform decision-making and to analyze what is going on "on the ground," or via the use of new media in order to communicate the faith in ways recognizable to digital natives. Alternatively, a fifth approach has its focus on dialogue and

---

2. Maspero, *After the Pandemic*, 56.

encounter, in an attempt to reach out, in a reconciling manner, to the disaffected, the wounded, those with alternative worldviews, and those who are searching for meaning and purpose in life.

With a sharper edge and tone of voice than the culture of dialogue and encounter, sixth, there are those who call for a more militantly prophetic emphasis, where the current idols before which many people worship (or give their allegiance) are confronted and critiqued. For Searle, "The prophet sees the present in the light of eternity and is able to perceive God's redemptive purposes in the world.... The truly prophetic figure is someone who is aware of the spiritual forces acting in history and knows all the possibilities contained within the infinite sphere of the effective action of God for whom all things are possible."[3] In reading the signs of the times and finding where God is pointing us to, Searle asserts that prophecy can involve lamentation, exhortation, and protest about the present situation followed by ending the tendency for Christians to retreat into religious clubs,[4] and, instead, offering a courageous and confident response of confrontation, outreach, and demonstrating an alternative lifestyle.

Closely linked to the call for a more prophetic stance towards the world, there is the powerful cultural commentary given by Phil Davignon. Davignon interrogates the practical atheism he sees as pervasive in society, including among many of those who claim to be Christians. By practical atheism, he means living as if God does not exist. Davignon proposes that "culture is not only transmitted through liturgies that directly shape people's desires, imagination, and identity, but also within more mundane social practices that quietly form enduring dispositions (virtues or vices). Even if these dispositions do not directly shape one's ultimate desires, they still incline people to think, feel, and act in ways that are either hospitable or inhospitable to the Christian life."[5]

If culture is most powerfully transmitted implicitly, via "taken-for-granted habits, routines and practices," for example, in the family, in education, in the world of work, and in a consumerist lifestyle, and if these contexts are organized according to secular assumptions and values, rather than in the light of the gospel, these domains of life "foster habits and dispositions that undermine people's ability to fully embody the Christian faith in their daily lives."[6] Davignon poses an important question for Christians of

---

3. Searle, *Theology After Christendom*, 27.
4. Searle, *Theology After Christendom*, 28.
5. Davignon, *Practicing Christians, Practical Atheists*, xvi.
6. Davignon, *Practicing Christians, Practical Atheists*, xvii.

any church to ponder: "Do congregations offer the kind of formation that could offset the secularizing effects of modern culture?"[7]

James Davison Hunter calls for Christians to exercise a faithful presence in the world, while at the same time not being *of* the world.[8] Sherry Weddell sees the need to rejuvenate and to revitalize the faith community.[9] From an Eastern Orthodox perspective, Evi Voulgaraki-Pissina believes that, in order to foster Christian witness amid the desert of postmodern cities, what is required is a rediscovery of theology. She claims that "we need to apply ourselves, with devotion, diligence, and love, to studying the riches of our tradition" in order to present to the world "a moving, flexible, living faith."[10]

As a final example, Carmody Grey and Oliver Dürr advise Christians, faced with a society that scarcely knows Christianity at all, to focus on the nature and needs of humanity, rather than to rely on traditional religious language.

> If we seek to locate and articulate, in order to reflectively engage, the horizons within which contemporary northern Europeans generally live, the goods that orient people's lives, and the ideas and values that move and motivate them, we need to talk not about "religion" and the lack of it, but about the idea of the human. Within the concept of the human is nested today the sense of orientation, meaning, goodness and importance that notions of "religion" used to express.[11]

In giving attention to the nature and needs of the human person, Christians should ask, in common with other questioners from diverse worldviews: "What fulfils her; what hurts her; what renders her life meaningful, worthwhile, or not; what makes it possible for her, despite everything, to go on."[12] This constitutes a call for a renewed form of Christian humanism, one that equips members of the church to engage constructively and winsomely with contemporary culture.[13]

These diverse responses are not necessarily alternatives; some can be and have been combined. Nor do they exhaust the possibilities for ways to respond to secularization. In what follows I explore in more depth the

---

7. Davignon, *Practicing Christians, Practical Atheists*, 89.
8. Hunter, *To Change the World*.
9. Weddell, *Forming Intentional Disciples*.
10. Voulgaraki-Pissina, "Theology, Witness, and Spirituality," 6.
11. Grey and Dürr, "On Changing the Subject," 1.
12. Grey and Dürr, "On Changing the Subject," 15.
13. Sullivan, "Catholics, Culture."

responses of two Catholic priests to a world they saw as increasingly being secularized. Guardini is better known within the church, while Illich is better known outside it.

## ROMANO GUARDINI

Ordained in 1910 and having completed two theses on Bonaventure in 1915 and 1922, Romano Guardini served as professor in philosophy of religion and Catholic worldview at the University of Berlin from 1923 until 1939. He exercised throughout this period a leadership role in Quickborn, a German Catholic youth movement. After the Second World War he again taught as professor of philosophy of religion and Christian worldview, first at the University of Tübingen (1945–48) and from 1948 to 1962 at the University of Munich. Pastoral in tone, emphasis, and ethos, he set about equipping people to engage in the life of faith, constantly providing formation and encouragement, especially to young Catholics, displaying sensitivity and gentleness. From a young age, he formed study circles with friends. Later he fostered similar networks for students and young people more generally, where they discussed literature, theater, and art as well as matters of faith. He also led retreats and pilgrimages and organized social events for the young he was nurturing. Active in pastoral ministry, he never restricted his time and energy to the academy. A regular preacher, he took seriously new communication media, such as films, radio, and television. A telling glimpse of how he saw himself is given by Jane Lee-Barker when she quotes Guardini: "I found myself the type of brotherly priest who does not act out of his official position but carries the priesthood in himself as a pastoral force; who does not confront the faithful as the owner of authority but stands next to them . . . [and] joins them in their searching and asking in order to arrive with them at common results."[14]

Not only was he fluent in German and Italian, languages spoken at home, he also learned Latin, Greek, French, and English. Before studying theology he had tried chemistry and economics. He wrote books about Dante Alighieri, Michel de Montaigne, Blaise Pascal, Fyodor Dostoyevsky and Friedrich Hölderlin, Rainer Maria Rilke, Socrates, Augustine and Søren Kierkegaard. His writing was a blend of personalism, existentialism, scriptural reflections, explorations of the liturgy, interpretations of literature, cultural commentary, and opening up mystical dimensions. He made important contributions to the renewal of church thinking on the liturgy, Christology, the church, and theological anthropology—all of which

14. Lee-Barker, *God's World*, 36.

contributed to how he revealed aspects of a Catholic worldview. The many questions he addressed included: What difference does having Christian faith make as we engage with the world? What does it mean to live from the church? What is the relation between faith and culture? As a recent commentator on the thought of Guardini has observed, his books "transcend the boundaries between theology, philosophy, literary criticism, and human biography and they touch on psychology, sociology, and numerous other areas."[15]

This rich intellectual hinterland, combined with his warm and pastoral concern, his essential humility, and his facility in making connections between contemporary culture and the living tradition of Catholicism marked him out as a distinctive voice and as an attractive representative of the faith. One admirer, referring to Guardini as a sapiential theologian, claims that "a writer such as Guardini stands as a prophetic alternative to those theologians who have allowed their work to become so academically rarified that they cannot speak beyond the narrow limits of their academic specialty."[16] It was his close attention to the real-life contexts and experiences of those he hoped to reach that shaped how he communicated the faith. He acknowledged the diverse ways that people come to and experience faith in different ways according to their circumstances. "The structure of faith will be one thing for those who educate, teach, heal, assist, and serve, and something different for those who fight, conquer, reign, etc."[17] We can extend this to those who clean, care, produce, sell, advertise, suffer, endure illness, experience betrayal or abuse. He goes on to refer to the different perspectives caused by gender, age, intellectual capacity, social location, and roles at work.

Admired by several popes, including John Paul II, Benedict XVI, and Francis, Guardini influenced deeply Hannah Arendt, Karl Rahner, Josef Pieper, and Hans Urs von Balthasar. Robert Krieg describes Guardini as a forerunner of Vatican II, claiming that "he played a major role in leading Catholicism from Pius IX to John XXIII, from the knowing stance of the First Vatican Council to the listening stance of the Second Vatican Council."[18] In an earlier work Krieg summarizes the difference in tone and purpose between the First and Second Vatican Councils: "The church of Vatican I saw itself as a fortress or bastion of truth against the errors of the Enlightenment; in contrast, the church of Vatican II sees itself as a pilgrim

---

15. Lee-Barker, *God's World*, 7.
16. Cunningham, "Romano Guardini as Sapiential Theologian," 70.
17. Guardini, *Living the Drama of Faith*, 88.
18. Krieg, *Romano Guardini: Precursor of Vatican II*, 22.

people on its way, in dialogue with other peoples, to the reign of God," and he attributes a major part in this shift to Guardini.[19]

For those Catholics who view Vatican II unfavorably, and who accept the assessment that Guardini can accurately be interpreted as a precursor of that council, then Guardini might be considered to have contributed to the damage they believe was caused by it. For example, with regard to liturgical changes, his emphasis on the meal (rather than sacrifice) as being the essence of the Mass will be a bone of contention for some. His flexibility and his avoidance of being easily classified make him vulnerable to accusations of vagueness, especially with regard to doctrine. His tendency to avoid using Thomist language and to be closer to the Augustinian tradition made him suspect for some readers, especially in the half century between the crushing of modernism and the years of the Second Vatican Council, when Thomism prevailed as the normative form of describing and explaining the faith. He might also be accused (from different quarters) of being an impractical Romantic, of addressing only people who were highly educated, rather than ordinary people, and of being inattentive to developments outside Europe. In light of later technological developments that occurred after his death, he may seem insufficiently aware of the colonizing and unhealthy effects of these developments on human lives. And, although he was in favor of members of the church engaging in dialogue with the modern world, many of his writings might come across today to readers outside of the Christian faith as conservative and exclusivist in their claims. Despite these potential shortcomings, as seen from various perspectives, Guardini represents a fertile example of how a person of his time, steeped in the Catholic faith, reached out to the people of his culture in a manner that bridged the gap that often opens up between life, faith, and culture.

For the purposes of this chapter, among the many themes explored in his writings by Guardini, I shall attend to only four: his treatment of a Catholic worldview; the importance he attributed to liturgy in founding and shaping that worldview; belief in providence as a constitutive element within a Catholic worldview; and the cultural critique he brought to bear as a consequence of reading the world in the light of that worldview.

## Worldview

To hold a worldview, according to Guardini, is a matter of seeing the totality of things and the character of the world that is given to us, perceiving its inner unity, able to contemplate it, to assess its value and relation to us, and

---

19. Krieg, *Romano Guardini: Proclaiming the Sacred*, 25.

taking up a stance toward the world.[20] Having a worldview goes beyond the possession of knowledge to include accepting that one has a task to accomplish in response to this world.[21] He believed that both the world within a person and the world that surrounds that person come from God. "The task of human beings is to walk towards God and to take the world with them."[22] A proper appreciation of and response to the world requires from us both distance—in order to maintain perspective on it and also a degree of liberty from it—and a love that is open to all being.[23] To embrace a Catholic worldview means taking seriously divine revelation in all its content and in all its implications for how we live.[24] That, in turn, calls believers to accept their need to live their lives nurtured and guided by the church, which is the historic depository of how Christ sees the world. Life within the church, with all its dimensions such as dogma and liturgy, has implications for what we can come to know and how we should think and act.[25]

In addition to learning from a Catholic worldview, Guardini also advised his audiences to be willing to learn from today's world (despite its defects)—because God is its Creator, the source of all truth, beauty, and goodness, and because God both loves the world God has created and, through his Holy Spirit, is active within it. Catholics are therefore called to engage with the culture around them, not to shun it, but nor are they to allow themselves to be colonized by it. That engagement has to be discerning, appreciative yet also critical.

## Liturgy

The foundation for an authentic way of life is given in the liturgy, according to Guardini. We begin with what is given by Christ and continued in the liturgy. To become immersed in the liturgy shapes our outlook and our desires and it orients us towards a Christlike mode of reading and responding to the world. In order to live charitably in the world we must first embrace the identity given to us in the Eucharist. For Guardini there is a direct link between the proper celebration of liturgy and the authentic renewal of culture.

20. Guardini, *Vision catholique du monde*, 32–33.
21. Guardini, *Vision catholique du monde*, 40.
22. Guardini, *Vision catholique du monde*, 46.
23. Guardini, *Vision catholique du monde*, 51.
24. Guardini, *Vision catholique du monde*, 68.
25. Guardini, *Vision catholique du monde*, 71.

Among the strengths of the liturgy, for Guardini, are its corporeal and communal dimensions: it deploys the body through various liturgical gestures and it bonds us into a community and thus releases us from the insistent individualism which is a feature of contemporary culture. In place of the constant busyness and shallow self-expression of much of modern life, the liturgy promotes stillness, reserve, and repose.[26] Yet this does not constitute an escape from caring for and exercising responsibility within the world; rather what happens in the liturgy is meant to be connected to and carried forward into the "problems and tasks of public and family life, and with those of Christian charity and of vocational occupations."[27] Another strength is the way, across its various seasons throughout the year, the liturgy "embraces, as far as possible, the whole of Divine teaching,"[28] in contrast to partial and incomplete readings of that teaching. With Christ at the heart of its focus and the Holy Spirit as its animating force, the liturgy incorporates us into Christ and gives us a share in the divine life. The cost of opening ourselves up to these benefits is the renunciation of self-determinism and of spiritual isolation; we humbly submit to the body being built up in liturgical celebration, rather than going our own way. As Guardini puts it, "The liturgy is a school of religious training and development to the Catholic who rightly understands it [and also of] cultural formation."[29]

It achieves this because it puts worship first, an acknowledgment of our dependency on our Creator, and because it addresses our deepest needs, which go far beyond the desire for material satisfaction as promised by the prevailing mechanized worldview and technocratic mentality. Liturgy, for Guardini, is the context in which we discover the true freedom granted by living in conformity with our God-given nature. It connects us to ultimate and life-giving truth. As Roland Millare explains, "Adoration is a concrete recognition on the part of the human person that he is not self-sufficient or autonomous. Adoration is a humble act that recognizes God as the source of all existence."[30] Only when we are in right relationship with God can all our other relationships become properly ordered and sustained.

---

26. Guardini, *Spirit of the Liturgy*, 14.
27. Guardini, *Spirit of the Liturgy*, 19.
28. Guardini, *Spirit of the Liturgy*, 24.
29. Guardini, *Spirit of the Liturgy*, 47.
30. Millare, "Hermeneutic of Continuity," 530.

## Providence

Jane Lee-Barker argues that providence is a pervading theme running through all of Guardini's writings. Divine Providence is "that order which exists between God and those who give themselves to him in true faith. To the extent that man recognizes God as his Father, that he places his trust in him and makes the kingdom the primary concern of his heart, to precisely that extent, a new order of being enfolds about him, one in which 'for those who love God all things work together unto good' (Rom. 8:28)."[31]

Building on Matt 6:25–34, calling us to trust in God's care for each of us, Guardini, while endorsing the need to trust that God is present to us and caring for us at each moment of our lives, does not imply mere passivity on the part of God's people. Rather he suggests that we open ourselves to God's grace so that we can cooperate with this in acting with initiative and responsibility in the world. As Lee-Barker says, "In God's created and very sacred world, people are given the opportunity for discernment, decision, and action in relationship with God who guides but does not force, coerce, or thrust 'fate' upon them."[32] A little further on, she continues, "Providence in Guardini's view is not a finished act or plan which God imposes on the world. Being open-ended it allows for the possibility of human involvement in its completion.... One must be transformed by the grace of God in order to contribute to a transformed world."[33]

Thus providence is not only a gift and help to us but also a task and a demand, a call to display a godly care for creation. But that is only possible if we are truly participating in the life of God, mediated to us through the church, receiving the sacraments, intentionally developing a personal relationship with Jesus Christ, and actively opening oneself to the work of the Holy Spirit. As Lee-Barker describes Guardini's teaching on providence, "Providence ... is the process of a person, becoming redeemed, in a world also in the process of being redeemed. The human person can contribute to this process by allowing God to be active in his or her life, making the person more Godly and enabling the person to be a door for God in the world. Guardini will argue that Godly people can help the world to be a Godly world."[34] The possibility and privilege of each person having the capacity to

---

31. Romano Guardini, quoted in Lee-Barker, *God's World*, 31–32.
32. Lee-Barker, *God's World*, xiii.
33. Lee-Barker, *God's World*, 5.
34. Lee-Barker, *God's World*, 95.

act as a door through which God can enter the world is a motif that recurs several times in Guardini.[35]

One further point might be made here about Guardini's teaching on providence. This is that an appreciation of providence emerges from, relies upon and has implications for communal life. There are two aspects here. First, a person learns how to understand God's purposes only in the context of community—with that community itself being informed by the liturgy. Second, the faith that is supported by a strong sense of providence not only calls for a vibrant personal relationship between believers and God, but also requires that they involve themselves, insofar as it lies in their capacity, in the right ordering and developing of the world.

## Cultural Critique and Technocratic Mentality

Once one has appreciated Guardini's take on what is entailed in possessing a Catholic worldview, the centrality of the liturgy in shaping and orienting that worldview, and his emphasis on providence, it follows that one recognizes how the ethos of modern culture is governed by an entirely different set of values, purposes, and priorities.

Whereas "the *ethos* of modern culture is governed by a mechanistic and utilitarian *logos,* the *ethos* of an authentic Christian culture is underpinned by a Eucharistic *logos* oriented towards self-giving love."[36] For Guardini, "The technological mind sees nature as an insensate order, as a cold body of facts, as a mere 'given,' as an object of utility, as raw material to be hammered into useful shape."[37] Guardini urges that Christians turn from the *logos* of *techne* to the *logos* of the liturgy. In his view, a culture which prioritizes *techne* is one that is concerned with the exercise of power and domination; it is means oriented, without adequate attention to the ends being pursued; it lacks ethical depth; in its focus on what technology makes possible, it is so present oriented that it neglects the wisdom of historical traditions; it limits itself to an anthropocentric and immanent perspective; and it fails to be open to the transcendent or to revelation.[38] As Millare observes, "Another name for this separation of culture from revelation is secularization."[39]

---

35. Lee-Barker, *God's World*, 12, 22, 87.
36. Millare, "Primacy of Logos," 974.
37. Guardini, *End of the Modern World*, 55.
38. Sullivan, "Transcending the Technocratic Mentality."
39. Millare, "Primacy of Logos," 976.

A purely secular society, one which is not illuminated by revelation, in Guardini's view, misreads human nature, with serious consequences. It assumes that material needs are preeminent in human decision-making, while either neglecting or at least underestimating humanity's spiritual needs and nature. As Tracey Rowland points out, "Guardini argued that advanced industrial society created false consumer needs that integrated individuals into a system of media-driven mass consumption." The bourgeois temperament that emerges in this context is "calculating, pragmatic, focused on efficiency and predictable outcomes. It discourages moral heroism as unreasonable.... It both levels and narrows horizons."[40]

Another manifestation of a secular landscape is the denial of the important role played by asceticism in granting men and women freedom from being controlled by their desires and passions and in freeing them for a higher form of life. Without the self-giving (and therefore, also, when necessary, self-sacrificing) love called for by Christian faith, humanity loses self-control.

> Man has extensively mastered the immediate forces of nature, but he has not mastered the mediate forces because he has not yet brought under his control his own native powers. Man today has power over things, but ... he does not yet have power over his own power.[41]

> Only the freedom won through self-mastery can address itself with earnestness and gravity to those decisions which will affect all reality.[42]

> As long as men are unable to control themselves from within, they will inevitably be "organized" by forces from without.[43]

On this point Guardini was to be echoed in a later generation by Ivan Illich, who also stressed the need for humanity to learn to live within limits and with self—restraint.

In his critique of culture, Guardini also exposed two erroneous understandings of the human person. One was to overemphasize autonomy and to reduce people to isolated monads who failed to appreciate their inescapable interdependence. This was corrosive of an attitude of solidarity with other people. Liberal capitalism was particularly prone to this misreading of

---

40. Rowland, *Beyond Kant and Nietzsche*, 128.
41. Guardini, *End of the Modern World*, 90.
42. Guardini, *End of the Modern World*, 93.
43. Guardini, *End of the Modern World*, 113n5.

our nature, encouraging a selfish and even ruthless competition for goods while neglecting the common good. The alternative extreme, preferred by both communist and fascist collectivism, led to "mass man," subordinated and sacrificed individuals to the needs of the party or the state, and failed to preserve a space for the uniqueness, mystery, and essential incommunicability of each person. A liturgically shaped outlook, as advocated by Guardini, would allow for a better balance between individual dignity and freedom on the one hand, and, on the other hand, commitment to the common good.

Although Guardini died before some of the most recent developments in technology had surfaced, he had exposed the direction of travel, sounded alarm bells, and proposed a path towards a more humane and healthy alternative. His insights have been taken up by Pope Francis in *Evangelii Gaudium* and in *Laudato Si*, as has been noted by Massimo Borghesi.[44] Guardini's project of addressing contemporary culture from a Catholic worldview was to be taken up in the final third of the twentieth century and into the beginning of the twenty-first century, although in ways that sound strikingly different.

## IVAN ILLICH

In many respects, Ivan Illich seems surprisingly similar to Guardini with regard to the importance he attributes to the church, liturgy, personal responsibility, cultural critique, and historical perspective. Yet he also comes across as displaying strikingly different emphases on each of these and adopting a radically different tone of voice. He was an eclectic and idiosyncratic thinker, who stood outside current terms of debate and therefore saw issues afresh, opening up new possibilities. He took pains to attend to and redefine the categories within which our conversations usually take place. Disconcerting in his exposure of many prevailing assumptions and discomforting in the starkness, scope, and radical nature of his arguments, he could be scathing and satirical, but also poetic and prophetic. Scholastic and erudite, often aphoristic in style and offering a kaleidoscope of images and metaphors to jolt his readers and audiences into fresh perspectives, Illich could be described as an ascetic anarchist, a restrained revolutionary, simultaneously humble yet bold, reticent yet given to sweeping assertions.

He was a controversial figure for a number of reasons: his readiness to critique the institutional church, a stance that—when he began to do this—seemed to put him beyond the pale; his frequent scathing language

44. Borghesi, *Mind of Pope Francis*, 103, 105, 138, 139.

about viewpoints he castigated; his tendency to offer sweeping generalizations and to pontificate about professions about which he had only a relatively superficial knowledge; his inclination to view medieval Christianity too benignly as an ideal expression of faith; and his image in his later years as a jet-setting and deliberately provocative intellectual celebrity. Despite all this, Illich does exemplify how Catholics can, drawing upon their faith and its intellectual and spiritual traditions, engage with their culture in a manner that is challenging, fertile, and with something pertinent to say to many aspects of secular life.

For Illich, what is important is poverty, powerlessness, spontaneity, and freedom in exercising initiative. Rather than planning or control, he stressed the need for openness to the surprising and what comes to us as gratuitous. He deployed historical perspective to provide a necessary and essential vantage point from which to help us gain some degree of distance from our current assumptions and concerns, our ways of thinking and acting in which we are so submerged that we are often imprisoned by them. He was both radical and conservative, orthodox yet also iconoclastic. His understanding and expression of faith was seen by some as subversive of many church policies.

He was influenced by Hans Urs von Balthasar, Erich Pryzwara, Romano Guardini, Jean Daniélou, and particularly by Jacques Maritain. Among other influential figures, he was close to Archbishop Helder Camara and Erich Fromm. He taught in several German universities and also in several American ones. Alert to contemporary cultural developments and interpreting these in light of Christian tradition, he addressed a wide range of audiences and readers: architects, educators, policymakers, medical personnel, Lutheran bishops, economists, and many others. Although his sensitivity to the issues facing these different groups was remarkable, it was inevitable that in some cases his grasp of the specificities and detail in each case could sometimes be rather broad brush and possibly lacking in depth of penetration. Intending to be a gadfly, exposing assumptions with a view to provoking fresh thinking, he wanted to undertake an archaeology of modern "certainties," those ideas and feelings that seem too obvious and too "natural" ever to be put into question; and he had come to see the twelfth century as one of the great seedtimes of these certainties.[45] Among such certainties he considered that contemporary ideas of conscience, citizenship, technology, text, individuality, and marriage all began to emerge in that era. "Certainties are those things that we can't think *about* because they

---

45. Cayley, *Rivers North*, 19.

are what we think *with*—they are what lie, Illich says, 'beyond the horizon of our attention.'"[46]

After initial and highly successful pastoral work, especially with a Puerto Rican community in New York, in 1956 Illich had been recommended by Cardinal Spellman for the post of vice-rector of the University of Puerto Rico, after which he went on to be director of the Center for Intercultural Formation in Cuernavaca from 1960 to 1967. This center was "an experimental micro-cosmos with powerful transformative characters in interaction with a very conservative Mexican Catholic hierarchy associated with the powerful."[47] The tensions arising between the conservative expectations of church leaders and Illich's own creative and prophetic thinking led him eventually to remove himself as an official spokesperson for the church in order to give himself the freedom to forge ahead with his own vision of a radical role for the Christian in the world. This vision led him not only to call into question the comfortable assumptions held by many in the church (assumptions that made them complicit in a colonialist and paternalistic mentality), but also to offer a reading of trends in the secular world that needed to be resisted. Colin Miller claims that "one of Illich's great contributions is to give a non-Marxist account of the relation between our material culture and our intellectual habits."[48] However, despite the fact that a glance at Illich's many publications after he had left the service of the church may seem to justify describing him as a social critic, one who wrote from a rather idiosyncratic historical perspective, his close friend and collaborator Lee Hoinacki suggests that, rather than be considered as a social critic, philosopher, or historian, Illich should be understood instead as an apophatic theologian.[49] This theology running through and underpinning the whole corpus of his writings might be implicit, rather than spelled out, but it was never absent.

Because of his early formation in scholastic theology and then his particular interest in the work of Hugh of St. Victor—and twelfth-century life and thought more generally—a marked feature of Illich's writing and lectures was the historical perspective he brought to bear on twentieth-century practices, institutions, and assumptions.[50] He sought distance from the present to enable him to see it with a mind strongly informed by and familiar with quite different ways of living and thinking. "I plead for a historical

---

46. Cayley, *Ivan Illich*, 13; emphasis in original.
47. Bruno-Jofré and Zaldívar, *Ivan Illich Fifty Years Later*, 47.
48. Colin Miller, "Ivan Illich, Catholic Theologian," 91.
49. Hoinacki, "Trajectory of Ivan Illich."
50. Illich, *In Vineyard of Text*.

perspective on precisely those assumptions that are accepted as verities or 'practical certainties' as long as their sociogenesis remains unexamined."[51] Elsewhere he explained his use of history: "I study history to become sensitive to those modern assumptions which, by going unexamined, have turned into our epoch-specific, *a priori* forms of perception."[52] His purpose was to loosen the grip of what is normally taken for granted and to open up the possibility of imagining a different future.

In what follows I will focus on four themes from Illich's writings and lectures. The first of these is his sense of the church. Under this heading I will refer to his comments on mission, renunciation of power and on tradition as a source for renewal. Then I attend to his cultural critique of leading professions and their implicit curriculum, by using the example of schooling as promoting an unhealthy dependency. His criticisms of schooling were intended to show the need to promote self-sufficiency, initiative, and personal responsibility among learners. Third, Illich developed an unusual and original theory that modernity can be seen as the perversion of Christianity, with modern institutions and professions operating as replacements and distortions of church and ministry. Finally, I draw attention to his desire to model and be an advocate for friendship as a counter to the negativity and damage caused by contemporary culture, envisaging friendship as a matrix for mutual and authentic learning and for healing the world.

## The Church

Although Illich was always a devout Catholic, fully subscribed to church doctrine and moral teaching, loving the liturgy and reading the world in the light of revelation and the formation in faith he had received in his childhood, his youth, and the seminary, his relationship with some of the institutional aspects of the church was not always smooth. He was critical of the church as an institution, its bureaucracy, its political role in Latin America, the seminaries, and the role of the priests and of celibacy.[53] Although not involved in social action or in liberation theology, he did have a great interest in—and made significant contributions to—the pastoral preparation of religious and laypeople.[54] However, he came to believe that, as an institution, the church, in some of its stances, actually operated in a way that

---

51. Illich, *In Mirror of Past*, 9.

52. Cayley, *Ivan Illich*, 291.

53. Bruno-Jofré and Zaldívar, *Ivan Illich Fifty Years Later*, xvi; Bruno-Jofré and Zaldívar, "Monsignor Ivan Illich's Critique."

54. Bruno-Jofré and Zaldívar, *Ivan Illich Fifty Years Later*, 59, 62.

undermined the gospel. Therefore, in 1969 he resigned from church service and renounced his priestly titles, benefits, and privileges, left ecclesiastical structures and roles, yet never left the church.

For him, whether in his time working for the church or in the secular world, the church should act as a leaven which penetrates and lifts up the world with which it engages. "To separate the leaven from the flour means uselessness for both. If Catholics ever lose their concern for those who do not have God, they lose also their charity."[55] If his earlier years were spent in pastoral service and the final three decades of his life were committed to a more prophetic role, in both cases one can claim that he acted as a leaven, mingling with, reaching out to, immersing himself in diverse groups of people in multiple contexts, always seeking to give himself away to them and thereby enhancing their activities.

This chimes with how he described the role of the missionary in 1961: "The missioner is he who leaves his own to bring the Gospel to those who are not his own, thus becoming one of them while at the same time continuing to be what he is."[56] "Mission . . . requires an ability to bracket and relativize one's own culture in order to hear what the Gospel says when it speaks in the voice of another culture."[57] This willingness to let go of one's own inheritance and to be open to the perceptions and needs of those one hopes to serve was a manifestation of spiritual poverty, "willingness to be without what we like."[58] "Just as spiritual poverty implies not the absence of likes, but freedom from them; so the attitude of the missioner carries him not to the denial of his background but to communication with that of another."[59] Without such spiritual poverty, he believed that missionaries were in danger of unwittingly importing a foreign culture, an alien gospel, a misguided pastoral approach, all of which functioned as favoring an unhealthy Western capitalism (to which the church was only too accommodating). Not only that, but the drive to send thousands of missionaries from North America and Europe to South America ran the risk of obscuring the need for radical reforms in how the church conducted herself.

> If North America and Europe send enough priests to fill the vacant parishes, there is no need to consider laymen to fulfil most evangelical tasks; no need to re-examine the structure of the parish, the function of the priest, the Sunday obligation and

---

55. Illich, *Powerless Church*, 11.
56. Illich, *Powerless Church*, 51.
57. Cayley, *Rivers North*, 20.
58. Illich, *Powerless Church*, 53.
59. Illich, *Powerless Church*, 53.

clerical sermon; no need for exploring the use of the married diaconate, new forms of celebration of the Word and Eucharist and intimate familial celebrations of conversion to the Gospel in the milieu of the home.[60]

Rather than the temptation to hold onto power and privilege, for Illich the church needed to accept that the renunciation of power is a precondition of love and a necessary corollary of accepting the cross as the sign of the Christian. He warned that "the Church's community-creating functions break down when supported by symbols whose driving force lies in an authority structure."[61]

Despite his urging the church to be ready to renounce power and privilege, Illich had a nuanced appreciation for the role of tradition and how Christians should be ready both to embrace and deploy this, as well as to discern when to either sit loosely to it or to dare to develop it in new directions. On the one hand, sharing in "the sense of the Church" occurs when a person is "rooted in the living authority of the Church, lives the imaginative inventiveness of the faith, and expresses himself in terms of the gifts of the Spirit. This 'sense' is the result of reading the sources of authentic Christian tradition, of participation in the prayerful celebration of the liturgy, of a distinct way of life."[62] On the other hand, one must not turn the church into an idol. This would be to abdicate personal responsibility. "Each Christian must struggle to establish and maintain a delicate balance between independence of the Church and dependence on the Church."[63] For Illich, tradition does not prevent or oppose change; rather it orients and anchors it. This is possible because "freedom to innovate and rootedness in tradition are different sides of the same coin. Without rootedness, innovation is promiscuous and unguided. . . . Without the innovation, . . . rootedness in tradition lapses into arid habit. . . . Grounding without freedom is bondage, ungrounded freedom only permissiveness. . . . [A] wholeness can only be sustained when the opposites that compose the whole are each given their due."[64] Illich modeled a deliberately cultivated, careful, and self-disciplined freedom within and for the church at the same time as drawing from her the depth and enduring motivation of his life.

60. Illich, *Powerless Church*, 95.
61. Illich, *Powerless Church*, 111.
62. Illich, *Powerless Church*, 117.
63. Illich, *Powerless Church*, 140.
64. Cayley, *Ivan Illich*, 464.

## Education as Example of the Promotion of Unhealthy Dependency

Illich controversially lambasted a range of modern professions and cultural trends. Among these he offered a searing critique of medicine. This is illustrated in the following quotation: "A professional and physician-based health care system which has grown beyond tolerable bounds is sickening for three reasons: it must produce clinical damages which outweigh its potential benefits; it cannot but obscure the political conditions which render society unhealthy; and it tends to expropriate the power of the individual to heal himself and to shape his or her environment."[65]

This sentence encapsulates claims that he also addressed to other aspects of modern life: something originally worthwhile and benevolent has grown unwieldy through exponential growth; the profession "managing" particular services holds a monopoly, thereby denying others an opportunity to contribute; there are damaging side effects of the profession's practices that are too easily ignored; the very need felt by the general public for the services of this profession prevent them from recognizing wider social conditions that should be addressed; and unwarranted dependence on these services encourages excessive passivity and undermines initiative and the development of a mature responsibility in the population.

Although Illich's book on medicine stirred up lively arguments, it was his writings on education that really brought him fame and notoriety. Just as people put too much trust, he asserted, in the medical profession, so too they relied too much on institutions set up to provide education. In *Deschooling Society* and in other writings of the 1970s and 1980s, Illich was critical of how the nation-state had secured a monopoly of education through its schools. He exposed what he saw as a malign hidden curriculum that was being promoted in schools. He denounced one outcome of this state monopoly as leading to the conflation in people's minds between schooling and the broader endeavor of education. "Work, leisure, politics, city living, and even family life, depend on schools for the habits and knowledge they presuppose, instead of becoming themselves the means of education."[66] He shrewdly noted that most people acquire most of their learning outside of school, as a side effect of their informal engagement in ordinary life activities and relationships. "The child grows up in a world of things, surrounded by people who serve as models for skills and values. He finds peers who challenge him to argue, to compete, to cooperate, and

---

65. Illich, *Medical Nemesis*, 11.
66. Cayley, *Ivan Illich*, 19.

to understand; and if the child is lucky, he is exposed to confrontation or criticism by an experienced elder who really cares. Things, models, peers, and elders are four resources for education."[67]

His critique of the education system was hard hitting, and to many, it seemed unduly harsh. He claimed that "education serves the dominant minority as a justification for the privilege they hold and claim."[68] In one lecture he went so far as to assert, "The school system is a worldwide soulshredder that junks the majority and hardens an elite to govern it."[69] He compared the certificates that pupils received at the end of schooling with those given out by those selling indulgences in the later Middle Ages, implying that both were meaningless and without value. Too many people acted as if they held a religious faith in the power of education to fit them for the world. "The first thing the child learns from the hidden curriculum of schooling is an age-old adage of faith corrupted by inquisition,—*extra scholam nulla est salus*—outside this rite, no salvation."[70]

At the heart of his critique of schooling was his concern for individual imagination and personal freedom, initiative, creativity and responsibility. Enforced instruction stifles the will to learn independently. "By making men abdicate the responsibility for their own growth, school leads many to a kind of spiritual suicide."[71] His views here are an outgrowth of his concern that the church, like schooling, fosters dependence, passivity, immaturity, and a lack of authentic ownership of one's own faith formation. In such cases, learning, whether sacred or secular, in the church or in schools, fails to lead to a transformation of consciousness. He wanted to make *the expansion of freedom*, rather than the growth of services, the criterion of social progress; he hoped to "uncover and encourage the abilities, intuitions, and encounters that are smothered by the blanket of professional care."[72]

## Modernity and the Perversion of Christianity

Some might claim that Christianity has been left behind by the gains of modernity and is now merely of historical interest. Perhaps it only ever constituted a stage in human development, and we have learned how to advance beyond Christianity's superstitions, misogyny, indoctrination, and

67. Illich, *In Mirror of Past*, 98.
68. Illich, "Lima Discourse," 85.
69. Illich, "Educational Enterprise," 2.
70. Illich, "Lima Discourse," 86.
71. Illich, *In Mirror of Past*, 80.
72. Cayley, *Rivers North*, 38.

restrictions on freedom. Its shortcomings have been exposed, and we exist in a much more enlightened age. Others might claim that, although Christianity did pave the way for the emergence of modernity, we can now safely liberate ourselves from its metaphysical, mystical, and ecclesiastical dimensions, while borrowing (selectively) from some of its moral teachings. Illich, however, argued that modernity is neither the fulfilment nor the antithesis of Christianity, but its *perversion*. Furthermore, he believed, this perversion of the faith has come about not through the evil machinations of people in modern times who misinterpreted and distorted what was once pure and authentic in the church's teaching and practice, but that the church herself modeled the perversion and distortion, instead of exemplifying what should have been at the very heart of the church's life and modus operandi.

I have already pointed to Illich's commitment to the church and what he saw as central to her life: mission, renunciation of power, and living tradition. The problem, as he saw it, was the misguided tendency—one which had been a constant temptation since the fourth century, when, in rapid succession, Christianity went from being proscribed and persecuted, to toleration (in AD 313), and then to being prescribed as the official religion of the Roman Empire (in AD 383)—to try to preserve, guarantee, and enforce the faith, to circumscribe its teachings and life with regulations and power. When this happens, the gospel has been corrupted and what should be the best becomes the worst. "I can't do without tradition, but I have to recognize that its institutionalization is the root of an evil."[73]

Illich distinguished two forms of the church—as *she* and as *it*. The first is "the living embodiment of Christian community" while the second is "a self-serving, worldly power."[74] And, acting as a self-serving power, the church was always tempted to adopt the methods and tools of other worldly powers. In doing so, she betrayed the very gospel she was meant to serve and demonstrated that she did not fully believe in or trust this gospel or the Holy Spirit to bring about God's will. This betrayal, and the ensuing perversion of the faith, not only began with the church, but spread to later institutions, agencies, and professions. Thus, he claimed, "It was the Church that first gave its clerisy legal jurisdiction over souls and made the faithful dependent on clerical services. It was the Church that made learning a consequence of authoritative teaching, that made standing in the faith a result of correct answers to catechisms and inquisitions, and that made salvation a question of compulsory attendance at various rituals."[75]

73. Cayley, *Rivers North*, xv.
74. Cayley, *Rivers North*, 4.
75. Cayley, *Rivers North*, 12.

At the heart of Christian faith lies the freedom to accept God's invitation to share in his life, as taught by Jesus. The use of force, whether hard or soft power, is corrosive of the free response of the human spirit to the Holy Spirit. For Illich, the church, which he loved, also exasperated him by the tendency to use compulsion, to confuse conformity with true commitment, and by the abuse of authority. "The Church identified salvation with attendance at services, submission to prescribed rituals, and obedience to Church rules."[76] As a result, Illich noted, the church "contains the Gospel in both senses of the term—it preserves and protects it, but it also holds it in, containing its power and shielding society from its effect."[77] In his wide-ranging critique of the institutions, agencies, and professions of modernity, Illich claimed that his contemporaries were practicing a perverted and degenerated form of Christianity; they did so because they participated in institutions that had learned only too well from the church's example and that still bore the church's genetic imprint.

## Friendship

In contrast to his prophetic and critical commentary on the church and on modern institutions and professions, Illich showed a softer and more pastoral side when he both spoke about and demonstrated in his own life the enduring benefits and potential of friendships. Friendship offers each of us a mode of belonging quite different than that of the family or the nation, more expansive and liberating than the former and less fraught with the power to swallow up our individuality than the latter. "For me friendship has been the source, condition, and context for the possible coming about of commitment and like-mindedness."[78] In response to the question "How can one live gratuitously in a world like this?," Illich simply and succinctly replies: "Friends."[79] It is clear from many of his comments that Illich had a deep appreciation of the potential of friendship to open up paths towards more humane ways of living. Friendship requires and calls forth attention, responsiveness, celebration, renunciation and self-limitation, presence, fidelity, self-discovery; it generates community.[80]

For Illich, the effective and winsome communication of faith depends on it emerging from a communitarian and fraternal mode of living.

76. Cayley, *Ivan Illich*, 386.
77. Cayley, *Ivan Illich*, 391–92.
78. Cayley, *Rivers North*, 147.
79. Cayley, *Rivers North*, 228.
80. Sullivan, "Friendship and Spiritual Learning."

Compulsion and speaking from a position of power stifle the human spirit and obscure openness to the working of the Holy Spirit. Even the search for truth, he believed, presupposes an ambience of friendship rather than a lonely and insistent individualism, however dogged and persistent this may be. Deeply committed human bonds are needed to sustain a common investigation into the issues facing humanity. "The vocation by which I try to live today I would call that of a friend rather than the prophet. . . . This is the way in which hope for a new society can spread. And the practice of [friendship] is not really through words but through little acts of foolish renunciation."[81]

# CONCLUSION

Both Guardini and Illich offer resources for contemporary Christians to draw upon in responding to a secularizing landscape. If both provided a critique of contemporary culture and the forces that threaten to destroy our humanity, each gave emphasis to different aspects of a remedy. Guardini stressed the need to develop a Catholic worldview, to draw life and orientation from the liturgy, and to trust in providence. Illich not only highlighted the vital importance of mission, renunciation of power, and tradition as a source for renewal, but he challenged the church to recognize her own contribution to the distortions of modernity and to look to friendship rather than control as a counter to the defects of contemporary culture.

Thinking and speaking about God and God's relation to us cannot be restricted to church settings. In order to speak with credibility and confidence of God in multiple contexts, Christian theologians need to be learning from and contributing to dialogue with people from many different disciplines. One of the reasons that both Guardini and Illich exerted such influence—and showed the way for others to do so today—is that, building on the foundation it had given them, they took their Catholic faith out into the world, beyond the borders of the church, and engaged with discernment the culture of their time. Can the church offer an alternative today to the state, the university, the media, the market and to technological progress when it comes to giving people inspiration and guidance for why and how to live?

81. Cayley, *Rivers North*, 170.

# 21

# Catholic Education as Ongoing Translation

BRENDAN CARMODY HAS RECENTLY made a valuable contribution to the development of a contemporary Catholic philosophy of education.[1] In part 1 of this chapter, I comment on and respond to Carmody's analysis. In part 2, I pick out two features of this particular moment in time, features that prompt fresh reflection on what is at stake in articulating a Catholic philosophy of education. These two features are the fiftieth anniversary of the beginning of Vatican II (1962–65) and the introduction in 2011 of the new translation of the missal, a process that focuses attention once again on the salient role of Latin in the life of the church. In part 3, I explore how the metaphor of translation casts light on the delicate balancing acts that accompany the task of Catholic education. Translators seek to represent faithfully the text they convey in a different language. At the same time, they hope to make that text meaningful and "alive" for their readers or hearers. Catholic educators face the same twin task of faithful representation and of creative interpretation. Translators and educators always run the risks of betrayal, of falling short, either in the task of faithful representation or in the imperative to render what is passed on as relevant, attractive, and transformational.

## RESPONDING TO CARMODY

Carmody offers a critical retrieval of the relevance for education of the thought of his fellow Jesuit Bernard Lonergan (1904–84), in particular,

1. Carmody, "Contemporary Catholic Philosophy."

Lonergan's analysis of self-transcendence. His article is based on substantial, broad, and sound scholarship; it is written clearly and cogently; and he makes many fine points which deserve to be considered carefully by those concerned to promote an understanding of the nature and scope of education in a Catholic perspective. Lonergan begins, not with theory, nor with transcendence, but with empirically based philosophy and with immanence, focusing on the developing person and levels of consciousness. What Lonergan refers to as "conversion" (in its various modes as intellectual, moral, and spiritual), a word with religious freight, might be termed by others, more neutrally, as "growth." Carmody shows how working from "below upwards" opens the way to a vision of education that links to the more traditional "from above downwards."[2]

## The Inner Word and the External Word

Another way of saying this is that Lonergan and Carmody do justice to the inner word by which God addresses us in our very nature, an inner word that can be connected to the outer word God sends through Holy Scripture, revelation more generally and through the living tradition of the church. As Karl Rahner says, "It is only the inner grace that makes it possible for [us] to hear the external word of God *as* the word of God."[3] If, with regard to the external word, we listen to others and to what is going on outside of us, with the inner word we listen to ourselves and what God is telling us from inside. Himes explains how "the external word gives shape and direction to the inner longing of the human person for life and purpose and hope and forgiveness." This is where the self-transcendence analyzed by Carmody is put into dialogue with revelation. Himes brings out the mutual implication between inner and outer word when he says, "Without the external word, the internal word remains implicit and without focus; it is unnamed. Without the internal word, the preaching and teaching of the faith remains, at most, the imparting of more or less interesting information."[4]

One of the strengths of the Carmody-Lonergan approach is that it is concerned to foster personal integration. Another is that such an approach offers mutual ground where sacred and secular perspectives can meet. Furthermore, Carmody effectively brings out some of the implications of Lonergan's treatment of self-transcendence for such key concepts in Catholic

2. Carmody, "Contemporary Catholic Philosophy," 110.
3. Karl Rahner, quoted in Himes, "Communicating the Faith," 122; emphasis in original.
4. Himes, "Communicating the Faith," 123.

education as person, mission, and community, as well as indicating how Lonergan's turn to the subject needs to be reinforced by attention to the sociopolitical dimension of human life. These are all valuable "ingredients" or elements in an appreciation of the purposes guiding the human endeavor of education.

However, let me make two cautionary comments. The first of these is about the subtle yet important distinction between a Catholic philosophy of education and a philosophy of Catholic education. Failure to take note of this distinction can lead to a blurring of the difference between secular and sacred in the context of education. The second, which builds on this distinction, reminds us of the need to continue to attend to the "outer word" of God, even in the midst of attending to God's inner word. Failure to be vigilant about this can lead to an unbalanced and incomplete approach to education.

## A Catholic Philosophy of Education and a Philosophy of Catholic Education

First, although Carmody does not make this mistake, there is some confusion as to whether "a Catholic philosophy of education" is exactly the same as "a philosophy of Catholic education." It often seems as if these terms are treated as alternative names for the same thing, when there is an important distinction to be made between them, despite the significant areas of overlap between them and much common ground that they share.

I understand the first of these two phrases to refer to the purposes, principles and constitutive features that jointly would have to be present if an activity is to count as educational. Here I have in mind, among other features, a concern to develop rationality, autonomy, and the capacity for critical questioning. Without these qualities, learners might be treated as means and not as ends; and without these qualities they could not become moral agents, capable of taking decisions and directing their lives. I would expect education to foster relationships where dignity and mutual respect are held as vital. Without these qualities, the learning of skills and knowledge might lead to selfish dominance over others. I would expect educators to encourage students to be confident in the self-expression and responsible ownership of their gifts and the harnessing of these in service of important needs in the world, eliciting and nurturing wonder at the world and those who inhabit it. Without such qualities, there would be an inadequate human foundation for individual vocation to be heard and embraced.

Teachers should also strive to promote among learners both the desire and the capacity to go on learning from life's experiences. Otherwise they would be restricted to the knowledge gained in formal education, knowledge that would be soon become outdated and superseded. I would expect educators to equip young people with a confident sense of their own identity and perspective and a generous receptivity and responsiveness to others. These are principles and practices that a Catholic would expect to be operating in education, any kind of education. However, these purposes, principles and features of education can be arrived at via routes other than Catholic faith, even by people who reject Catholic Christianity. They are not only compatible with Catholic faith; they seem demanded of education from a Catholic perspective. To the extent that they were missing, the education provided would be less than optimally educational. By themselves, however, these principles would not necessarily lead to a fully Catholic education.

I understand the phrase "a philosophy of Catholic education" to refer to the principles and practices that would have to be evident if an activity is to count as Catholic education. While this would certainly include all the principles mentioned in the preceding paragraph, it would go beyond these to ensure that explicit, substantial, systematic, and ongoing attention is paid to key elements of Catholicism's living tradition.[5] Personal prayer, community worship, sacraments, the liturgical cycle, the teaching (doctrinal, moral, spiritual, social) of the church—all these would be evident in a fully Catholic education, one that is informed by a Catholic understanding of creation, anthropology, Christology, and ecclesiology.

Connected to this point, a second cautionary response to Carmody's deployment of Lonergan might be put like this. The focus on self-transcendence allows attention to be given to the "inner word" spoken to us by God, revealed to us by intelligent reading of our personal experience. This can provide a necessary counterbalance to earlier overemphases on God's "outer word," a word revealed to us "externally" through sacred Scripture and the teaching and tradition of the church. Such an "external" word could, in certain presentations, seem disconnected from our inner lives, nature, and needs—and thereby it could seem so foreign as to appear alien. However, the way of immanence does need to operate hand in hand with the way of transcendence, if justice is to be done to the pedagogy of God.

---

5. For treatments of aspects of this, see Sullivan: *Catholic Education*; "Faith Schools"; "Philosophy of Catholic Education"; "Text and Context"; McKinney and Sullivan, *Education in a Catholic Perspective*.

PART FIVE | CONNECTING TRADITION TO CULTURE

## The Pedagogy of God

To speak of the pedagogy of God is to use a term that is relatively unfamiliar today, one that has been examined and discussed in a recent collection of essays.[6] The contributors to *The Pedagogy of God* remind readers of the need for educators to be attentive to the role of the Holy Spirit in the process of transforming lives.[7] The work of teachers is to prepare themselves and their pupils to be receptive, disposing them to be open to the work of the Holy Spirit. One possible interpretation of what the authors of *Pedagogy of God* have in mind as ways to foster being open to the Holy Spirit might be put thus: one becomes open to the Holy Spirit by being immersed in Holy Scripture and the teachings of the magisterium, by participating in the liturgy and sacramental life, by the regular practice of personal prayer, and by being obedient to the practices prescribed the church.

To speak of the pedagogy of God is to remind oneself that God is the primary agent in the process of education and associated transformation—the foundation from which we build, the route by which we travel, and the goal at which we aim to arrive. In the introduction to *The Pedagogy of God*, Paul Watson points out that "only the divine action can touch the heart from the inside."[8] In this perspective, Petroc Willey alerts readers to how revelation "enlarges persons so that they can participate in God's nature."[9] The role of the teacher who seeks to accommodate herself to God's pedagogy with regard to the student is "to support the filial relationship with the father."[10] The systematic and progressive presentation of revelation, as mediated through the church by the teacher, is intended to lead to the Christian maturity spoken of in Eph 4:13, "mature with the fullness of Christ." Salvation history is to be told so that "each person, with his own unique 'life story,' may find his identity within the context of this overarching story."[11]

If, on the one hand, the emphasis on self-transcendence, as expounded by Lonergan and by Carmody, ensures that the individuality of each person is engaged in education, that education serves to promote the gradual process and unending task of personal integration, and that education contributes to the humanization of learners, then on the other hand,

---

6. Farey et al., *Pedagogy of God*.
7. On this role, see also Zuck, *Spirit-Filled Teaching*; M. Anthony, "Pneumatology and Christian Education."
8. Paul Watson, in Farey et al., *Pedagogy of God*, 7.
9. Willey, "Pedagogue and Teacher," 42.
10. Willey, "Pedagogue and Teacher," 53.
11. Willey, "Pedagogy of God," 67.

attending to the pedagogy of God reframes that humanization so that it becomes part of divinization. Self-transcendence stresses our growth, development, and activity, so that the outcome of education is the expansion, harnessing, and deployment of our powers. The pedagogy of God stresses our receptivity; without this receptivity, the gift cannot be welcomed. As Philip Cary observes in his study of Augustine, "There is no knowledge of the other that is not ultimately a gracious gift of the other, which we must be glad to receive."[12]

In the end, Catholic education is an invitation to share God's life, to welcome God's grace, to become more Christlike, to have one's selfhood redefined by the gospel, to have one's mind transformed. These are all aspects of the meaning of *theosis*, a process in which we move, with God's help, from our initial—and given—starting point, made in the image of God, to our final destination as reflecting our own unique likeness to God. In this process we are divinized, sharers by adoption in God's life, but without loss of our humanity. If the transmission of the gospel is "an event of the supernatural order, depending on the lively assistance of the Holy Spirit," as Avery Dulles claims, we can extend this claim to include Catholic education as part of the transmission of the gospel.[13] Similarly, if "catechists are called to be privileged instruments through whom God continues his saving work today" and if "the success of their efforts will depend not on themselves alone but more crucially on the grace of God and the freely given response of the students," we can say the same for Catholic educators more generally.[14]

It is important to stress that, in a Catholic perspective on education, the pedagogy of God does not dispense with human effort; rather, it builds on it and extends it. As St. Bernard of Clairvaux (1090–1153) once said, with reference to the way that the action of God and our own action should not be considered as separate, as if God did one part and quite separately we did our part, *sed opere individuo totum singuli peragunt*. That is, and translated very loosely, the whole job, the full work, is done hand in hand, simultaneously, in communion, jointly; it is circumincession, a dancing in tandem of the partners, not a dance by one partner, followed by a dance by another. To quote Bernard more extensively,

> What was begun by grace alone, is completed by grace and free choice together, in such a way that they contribute to each new achievement not singly but jointly; not by turns, but simultaneously. It is not as if grace did one half of the work and free choice

---

12. Cary, *Outward Signs*, 150.
13. Dulles, *Evangelization for the Third Millennium*, 67.
14. Dulles, *Evangelization for the Third Millennium*, 113.

the other; but each does the whole work, according to its own peculiar contribution. Grace does the whole work, and so does free choice—with this one qualification: that whereas the whole is done *in* free choice, so is the whole done *of* grace.[15]

This notion, that the divine and human agents are not competitors, was echoed a century later by St. Thomas Aquinas (1225–74):

> An effect that results from a natural cause and from the divine power is not attributed partly to God and partly to the natural agent, but it is completely from both according to different modes, just as the effect is entirely attributable to an instrument and also entirely to the principal agent.[16]

Education is simultaneously a human and a divine work. I am tempted to say that a Catholic philosophy of education emphasizes the human aspects of this work, aspects that can be shared by many other educators who do not accept the Catholic faith, while a philosophy of Catholic education attempts to take account of the divine dimension, without any loss of the human. However, I suspect this may be to seek a distinction which in educational practice is hard to maintain, even if conceptually it can be upheld. It is also a distinction that may mislead some to think there can be a human experience that is not already graced. The task of educators is to awaken in students the power to wonder, imagine and question, to think, interpret, understand, evaluate, and appreciate, to receive and give, to live in God's presence—hearing and responding to Word and Spirit. These can all serve to equip us to learn how to love rightly, always *the* priority for St. Augustine.[17] Catholic teachers should also help their students to develop a sense of the faith and a capacity to receive it, to penetrate it, to adhere to it and to apply it in their lives. I have argued elsewhere that education and evangelization have much in common and can work in harmony.[18]

## A MOMENT IN TIME

Over the centuries there have been many contributors to the developing tradition of Catholic education. Lonergan himself built upon two preeminent thinkers as he constructed his own particular approach: Thomas Aquinas

---

15. Bernard of Clairvaux, *On Grace & Free Choice*, 106; emphasis in original.
16. Aquinas, *Summa contra gentiles*, 3.70, quoted in Willey, "Pedagogue and Teacher," 43.
17. Sullivan, "St Augustine, Maurice Blondel."
18. Sullivan, "Education and Evangelization."

and John Henry Newman (1801–90). In addition to these, and apart from Augustine, perhaps the greatest source that could be drawn upon, there is much valuable guidance for building a philosophy of Catholic education (and a Catholic philosophy of education) in the writings of Hugh of St. Victor (1096–1141), who extended Augustinian thought in creative ways in the twelfth century; Giambattista Vico (1668–1744); and, in more recent times, Edith Stein (1891–1942); Maurice Blondel (1861–1949); Christopher Dawson (1889–1970); Gabriel Marcel (1883–1973); and Jacques Maritain (1882–1973).[19]

Each of these profound thinkers offers rich resources for reflecting on the human and divine dimensions of education. But in each case, in order to fully appreciate their thinking, one has to take into account the context in which their work was developed, the issues that seemed salient at the time, the conceptual resources and vocabulary available to them, and the threats to education and to faith that loomed large for them.

Catholic Christianity is essentially a faith that is built upon historical foundations; it is deeply marked by historical developments; and historical consciousness is integral to a Catholic outlook. The permanent nature and ongoing relevance of Catholic faith is always and inevitably mediated by historical developments, in both promulgation and reception. Despite all the continuities in human nature and in the church's basic mission, each age has to face its own challenges and opportunities; each is gifted with

---

19. Edith Stein taught and wrote about such topics as interiority, the spiritual dimension of life, education in service of freedom and personhood, vocation, formation and values, and the art of the educator as a holy office. For two penetrating analyses of her writings and work, see Rus: *Intériorité de la personne*; *Art d'éduquer selon Edith Stein*. Maurice Blondel had an impressive record as a highly effective and deeply influential teacher. He devoted his life to opening up a space for religious faith, specifically Catholicism, in a hostile, secular academy. For two essays that present key features of his thought as applied to Catholic education, see ch. 4 of this book and Sullivan, "St Augustine, Maurice Blondel." Christopher Dawson's work, especially with regard to the relation between faith and culture, and between the material and the spiritual, has massive significance for Catholic educators. For a volume about his life and thought, see Birzer, *Sanctifying the World*. For an essay about his relevance to Catholic education, see Sullivan, "Church and World." Dawson devoted a monograph to education, developing a strongly Catholic perspective: *Crisis of Western Education*. Gabriel Marcel provides valuable reflections on the human person, on the nature of knowledge, on contemporary culture, and most importantly of all, on relationships and availability, all of which have a bearing on Catholic education. To access his thought, see Marcel, *Gabriel Marcel Reader*. Maritain has written much that is worth pondering by Catholic educators, for example, with regard to how personhood and individuality, integral humanism, the material and the spiritual, and knowledge that is connatural all have educational implications. For an entry into his thought, offering extracts of his writings together with commentary, see Mougniotte, *Maritain et l'éducation*.

particular insights, while operating with its own blind spots; each has to address a uniquely complex configuration of tasks. Although it may be true that, for people of all ages, what is offered to them in Catholic education has similar features—"a story to enter"; "a language to speak"; "a group to which to belong"; "a way to pray"; "a work to undertake"; "a face of God to see"[20]—what can differ significantly is what surfaces as salient at particular moments as a threatening iceberg to avoid or as a helpful tide on which one might harness one's energies.

## The Second Vatican Council

At this moment in time the church marks the fiftieth anniversary of the opening of the Second Vatican Council in 1962. That council is still being wrestled with, both by those who experienced it as a deep caesura in the life of the church, as discontinuous (for better or worse, according to one's perspective) with what preceded it, and by those who recognize underlying continuities between what led up to it and what followed in its aftermath, those who see the *aggiornamento* (or bringing up to date) aspects of renewal as being rooted in and emerging from *ressourcement* (or return to and drawing out riches from earlier traditions). This is not the place to weigh up the arguments pro and contra the hermeneutics of rupture or of continuity, with regard to changes at Vatican II, though these arguments persist, with painful effects and unseemly polarization in the life of the church. Such an anniversary, however, should prompt fresh reflection on the basic principles that govern the enterprise of Catholic education. Furthermore, the introduction in 2011 of the new translation of the missal, a highly controversial process that will take some time to be accommodated in the life of the church, provides an echo of at least one major change made in the aftermath of Vatican II and raises questions about the nature and role of translation as a way of understanding what is at the heart of Catholic education.

One of the most obvious changes brought about by Vatican II was the move from Latin to the vernacular as the language of the Mass. This was experienced by many as bringing the world of the church closer to the everyday world. Of course, what some felt was a progressive move, an evidently more relevant and down-to-earth church, others came to judge as a loss of the transcendent, obscured by too heavy an emphasis on the immanent dimension of faith. For centuries Latin had been the universal language for liturgy, for seminary instruction, and for official documentation in the

---

20. Brien and Hack, "Charism," headings, 6–9.

Catholic Church. It had not always been so, for in earlier centuries Greek, Coptic, Arabic, and even Gothic had been the language used in the liturgy.

The move in the early church from Greek to Latin as the principal language for liturgy in some ways paralleled the move in the late 1960s and early 1970s from Latin to the vernacular, in that it was a move from a sacred and revered language to the "simple language of daily Roman speech."[21] The historian of language Nicholas Ostler describes Latin, at the time when it began to be used in the liturgy, as "ground-level speech."[22] "Christian Latin was the Latin of the street . . . [and] was happy to identify itself with common speech patterns."[23] Furthermore, he observes, "A general feature of Latin as used by Christians was its aggressively vulgar, plebeian, tone."[24]

However, this has been forgotten. Latin became linked with unity and immutability in belief; the eternal nature of tradition; universality of communion; resistance to fragmentation, schism, and nationalization; preservation of the sacred mysteries and the dignity reserved for the language of worship; together with assertion of authority in the church and maintenance of a differentiation of roles between clergy and laity. An interesting point to note, especially relevant to the deployment (in part 3, below) of the metaphor of translation as applied to Catholic education is that, after Latin lost its cultural dominance, "new ideas were henceforth to be translated into Latin, rather than conceived in it."[25] This has implications for ongoing translation and inculturation of the gospel, openness to the promptings of the Holy Spirit and the rejuvenation of tradition. To be Catholic is to have universal application and an unending reach; it is to be open, not closed; on the move, not static; constantly expanding in inclusiveness, not hardening through exclusivity; it is to seek to bring all people into its fold and to relate the gospel to all areas of knowledge; it is to be creative, not just repetitive of the past, even while trying to be faithful to that past.

If Wittgenstein is right in claiming that the limits of my language are the limits of my world,[26] then if a language, such as Latin, has lost its capacity to foster creativity and to give birth to new thinking, it will not be the best vehicle for conveying or facilitating the expression of the creative aspect of education, even if it still serves to ensure links with the tradition's past. Unfortunately, the link with the past can exert too much influence

---

21. Ostler, *Ad Infinitum*, 115.
22. Ostler, *Ad Infinitum*, 124.
23. Ostler, *Ad Infinitum*, 118, 119.
24. Ostler, *Ad Infinitum*, 117.
25. Ostler, *Ad Infinitum*, 317.
26. Wittgenstein, *Tractatus Logico-Philosophicus* 5.6.

in the delicate balancing act that education, and any act of translation, seeks to maintain. Thus, Latin in the liturgy "acquired a patina of archaism that ended by placing it outside time and withdrawing it from common intelligibility."[27] Its fixed and immutable nature became a feature that was considered to be a strength. Vernacular translations of the Bible in the past have been treated as opening the door to heresy. While Latin was associated with permanence, the vernacular was, through its openness to change, linked with instability. "Latin was seen as a means for defending the Church's authority and control over the faithful."[28] Wacquet quotes Chateaubriand: "We believe that an ancient and mysterious language, a language that has ceased to change over the centuries, is pretty well suited to the worship of the eternal, incomprehensible and immutable being."[29] Well into the twentieth century there was a fear that, once exceptions were made in the mandatory use of Latin, such a break with tradition would be the start of "a series of variations that would never stop."[30]

With the new translation of the missal, arguments over the place of Latin in the life of the church, which not long ago might have seemed merely of historical interest, have resurfaced, and with bitterness in some quarters, since there is both a suspicion that fidelity to Latin has once again become a sign of orthodoxy and a fear that other priorities, such as relating faith to the culture of our time, have been sacrificed in order to preserve the policing role of Latin with regard to liturgical developments. Whether or not such fears are justified, there is some value in exploring the metaphor of translation as illuminating key features of the task of Catholic educators.

## TRANSLATING THE TRADITION

Considering Catholic education in the light of and as a form of translation brings to the surface the tension between two priorities that can seem hard to reconcile: on the one hand, fidelity to the truth conveyed by the "text" of the tradition (understanding "text" to include Scripture, liturgy, doctrinal teaching, the witness of the saints, and the complex totality that comprises living tradition); on the other hand, offering an attractive, credible, and transformational encounter with the gospel and the tradition for people in contemporary culture. When he was a cardinal, the current Pope Benedict XVI spoke of the need for preachers and catechists to translate the church's

27. Wacquet, *Latin*, 42.
28. Wacquet, *Latin*, 47.
29. Wacquet, *Latin*, 63–64.
30. Wacquet, *Latin*, 68, quoting a 1925 Catholic dictionary article.

decisions "into a language which relates to people and to their respective cultural environments."[31] He was referring in this instance to explaining the church's refusal to give communion to divorced and remarried Catholics. He was concerned that "if at times in the past, love shone forth too little in the explanation of truth, so today the danger is great that in the name of love, truth is either to be silenced or compromised." While this particular aspect of the church's teaching remains neuralgic at best (and even repugnant) for many Catholics, it certainly is the case that in acts of communication there can be a tension between speaking the truth (as we see it) and loving the other person.

Joanna Waller brings out another aspect of translation when she says that

> the aim of a translation, more than producing any "literal" equivalence, is to create the same effect in the mind of the reader (obviously according to the translator's interpretation) as the original text wanted to create ... a good translation must generate the same effect aimed at by the original.[32]

Then, in relation to the new translation of the missal, she adds,

> Thus in translating the liturgical texts, our esteemed experts should be considering, not just a faithful rendering of the original Latin into the vernacular, but also the effect this will invoke in the congregation of a Sunday Mass in rural Herefordshire, inner-city Chicago, a base community in Brazil or the Alaskan oilfields—anywhere a Catholic group gathers to celebrate the most important day of the week.

Translation then serves the purpose of seeking to make a text come alive so that it can be internalized, owned, and acted upon by a new target group. While it must not betray the source from which it draws, the task of making a translation come alive for others, often in a very different setting from that in which the source document originated, calls for a degree of liberty, initiative, and creativity, if it is to engage new readers and hearers. Indeed, any translation carried out without careful attention to the nature, needs, and concerns of readers is likely to be less effective and to invite misreading.

A basic principle of communication, derived from ancient rhetoric, is that there needs to be a match between the *logos* of the message (the content and reasoning it contains) and the *pathos* of the recipients (their felt needs,

---

31. Joseph Ratzinger, quoted in *Tablet*, "Defence of Communion Ban."
32. Waller, "Gained in Translation," 5.

their hopes and fears, their priorities and concerns). There also needs to be a match between *logos, pathos,* and the *ethos* of the communicators (their credibility, trustworthiness, reliability and the care they display for those they seek to convince). Thus, in communicating Catholic faith, educators must ensure that they have translated it first for themselves, so that it has been not only heard by them, but accepted into their hearts and so that it permeates their lifestyles before being communicated in words. Otherwise it will not "ring true," their words will not resonate with their character; however accurate or orthodox their teaching, it will emerge in the wrong tone of voice.

Here I draw on three commentators on translation, the first two being philosophers and the third a professional translator, indicating the bearing of their insights for understanding what is at stake in Catholic education.

Merold Westphal, drawing on Gadamer, brings out the links between translation and performance. "To perform . . . is to translate. It is to (try to) make [a text] understandable in a semantic context different from that of the author or composer."[33] Catholic educators are also performers and thus translators, hoping to make the living tradition understandable in the context of their students. This means they have to interpret the "script" or the "score" in the process of their "performance." Westphal points out an interesting feature of such performances.

> Not only do different performers who are historically contemporary give *different* interpretations of the *same* work, but also performers continually tell us that no two performances of their own are the same. . . . It is because every performance is a different interpretation of the same thing and thereby a unique event that interpretation can never be merely reproductive.[34]

In the same way, many teachers will confirm that this applies to their own "performances" in the classroom. There can be no definitive interpretation of a given work (for Christians, with the sole exception of the life of Jesus Christ), whether this be music, drama, or the task of Catholic education. There is always scope for a new approach, a fresh interpretation, in our representation and translation of the tradition. While some "translations" will fall short, be inaccurate, incomplete, or misleading, others can accurately reproduce the "text"—as Westphal says—"play all the right notes in all the right rhythms, . . . or say all the right words in the right order—but in such a poor way that we call the interpretation right but regrettable."[35]

33. Westphal, *Whose Community? Which Interpretation?*, 98.
34. Westphal, *Whose Community? Which Interpretation?*, 103; emphasis in original.
35. Westphal, *Whose Community? Which Interpretation?*, 105.

In the context of Catholic education, we might say that the "seed" has been scattered, but without loving attention to the "soil" it was meant to "fertilize." Even in the case of the very best performances, interpretations or translations, we note that each will be "*different* from the others although they are presentations of the *same* work."[36] Of course, if an interpretation "is not to be arbitrarily subjective, it will have to submit to the constraint of the script, the score, the text. This is the reproductive moment."[37] But the effective performance of a text (and this is true for the faithful translation of Catholic tradition) goes beyond the reproductive to include the productive or creative dimension. This means that "there will be a variety of 'correct' interpretations that differ from one another."[38] With regard to Catholic education, the goal is learning to love rightly and holy living; the means is a translation of the tradition. Catholic educators hold in view (and in their hearts) not only what it is that they are conveying, but above all what they want to achieve, the intended effect of their translating efforts, a transformation of life into Christ.

In his introduction to Paul Ricoeur's little book *On Translation*, Richard Kearney tells us that the endlessly unfinished nature of translation "is a signal not of failure but of hope."[39] This is because there is an ongoing fertility to the best of texts; they contain within them resources for constantly new interpretations and translations. As they are brought to bear in new circumstances, with new questions and concerns, they continue to offer valuable insights, partly from being reproduced, but also partly in being freshly "translated." In each culture one comes across both opportunities and constraints in the task of conveying a tradition. Catholic educators need discernment in identifying the ways in which a culture presents both obstacles and aids to their task. There can be no interpretation of faith that is entirely culture-free and one implication of this is that there can be "no absolute criterion for good translation."[40] Translation can offer equivalence without being identical to its source text. There will always be the risks of both "serving and betraying" the tradition.[41] This danger should make us vigilant but not paranoiac about our efforts, given the realities of sin (in ourselves, in learners, and in the tradition), of grace and of free will.

---

36. Westphal, *Whose Community? Which Interpretation?*, 105; emphasis in original.
37. Westphal, *Whose Community? Which Interpretation?*, 105.
38. Westphal, *Whose Community? Which Interpretation?*, 105.
39. Richard Kearney, in Ricoeur, *On Translation*, xx.
40. Ricoeur, *On Translation*, 22.
41. Ricoeur, *On Translation*, 23.

One final point from Ricoeur is relevant here: in the practice of translation we do not move "from the word to sentence to text to cultural group," but the other way round.[42] A text emerges from a culture and context; translators seek to make that text meaningful for a different culture and context; the words are means or tools to that end of conveying significance; they are not to become idols or obstacles to mediating meaning. When applied to the human and divine endeavor of Catholic education, I take this to mean that it is vital that teachers always keep in view the bigger picture, the whole story of salvation history and the long-term goals of their work, even in the midst of specific and particular aspects of their work of translating, aspects and topics that make proper sense only within the totality of the tradition.[43]

Edith Grossman expresses the same point in the following way: "Words do not *mean* in isolation. Words *mean* as indispensable parts of a contextual whole that includes the emotional tone and impact, the literary antecedents, the connotative nimbus as well as the denotations of each statement."[44] She also echoes Westphal on there not being a final definitive performance or translation when she says "In translation, the ongoing, absolutely utopian ideal is fidelity. But fidelity should never be confused with literalness."[45]

She helpfully reminds us of two further aspects of translation. First, she points out that, in translation, "the work becomes the translator's (while simultaneously and mysteriously somehow remaining the work of the original author) as we transmute it into a second language."[46] It cannot be emphasized too much that teachers need familiarity and confidence in the tradition that they are charged with translating if they are to show finesse in building bridges between the text and learners. Internalization of the tradition by teachers must be ongoing; the depth of penetration needed for creative fidelity can only be achieved if teachers continue to grow in their knowledge, practice, and love of the faith. Just as in "the beat of a line, it is incumbent on me as the translator to hear that beat and transfer an equivalent pulse in to the lines," the Catholic teacher needs a parallel sensitivity

---

42. Ricoeur, *On Translation*, 31.

43. In order to assist teachers to keep in view the bigger picture to which their work contributes, many Catholic schools in the UK facilitate regular (usually annual) days of continuing professional development that provide opportunities to revisit and reflect upon the mission of the school, in a way that combines academic, professional, and spiritual dimensions. Often there are elements that would fit well in a retreat, with prayer and liturgy, a rearticulation of the key principles of Catholic education, and attention given to the sense of personal vocation of those who work in Catholic schools.

44. Grossman, *Why Translation Matters*, 71; emphasis in original.

45. Grossman, *Why Translation Matters*, 67.

46. Grossman, *Why Translation Matters*, 8.

to the language of the faith, its "pauses, its convolutions of meaning, its cadences, its musicality."[47]

Second, in the unlikely event that we might forget, she admits that readers are "individuals who respond to texts in idiosyncratic, eccentric, and thoroughly unpredictable ways."[48] As teachers, we do not know everything that is going in our students' lives, the connections they will make for themselves between our teaching and their situation, we are unaware of many of the factors at work that influence what resonates with them and what baffles them. The freedom of learners, in the light of their own (often unrecognized) priorities, to filter the communicative efforts of teachers is part of the mystery of teaching, a process that can never be reduced to the merely mechanical. Himes is right to remind us that "the teacher can never know when the internally spoken word of God is, as it were, aligned with the externally spoken word."[49]

The theologian Ormond Rush provides a penetrating analysis of the interaction that goes on between traditions and those who receive them. An implication of his study is that not only are receivers shaped (with varying degrees of success) by the tradition into which they are inducted, but it is also true that "traditions are the products of a constant process of reception."[50] He claims that

> each reception brings to the fore elements that others may leave in the background; each reception, in its particular selection, is a distinctive configuration of the Christian religion. No one reception exhausts the full meaning of what was originally given and originally received in revelation: the Christ event.[51]

The treasures of tradition will not only be appreciated differently, according to the context and experience of those who receive them as "tailor made" for them, but they will even be added to through what recipients bring to their encounter with the teachings, practices, and life of the tradition. Thus, "Rahner says [that] every believer creates a concrete catechism, which is necessarily a selection of beliefs for this or that concrete situation in daily life"[52] This, we might say, is a necessary part of incarnating the faith, embedding it in real lives.

---

47. Grossman, *Why Translation Matters*, 97, 99.
48. Grossman, *Why Translation Matters*, 23.
49. Himes, "Communicating the Faith," 123.
50. Rush, *Eyes of Faith*, 107.
51. Rush, *Eyes of Faith*, 161.
52. Rush, *Eyes of Faith*, 222.

Given the shadow side of institutional dynamics, where attachment to power and influence can desensitize those in authority, it behooves the church and Catholic educational communities to attend carefully to how people are receiving the messages directed at them. This means taking pains to listen to as many voices as possible in the process of making a translation of the tradition and striving to avoid premature closure in this respect. For "if their perspective is sought, the inactive, the lapsed, the disaffected, and the marginalized may bring to the discourse of faith questions from the margins which are for the good of the church."[53] Not only is the word coming from the past to be translated, but so also is the word emanating from contemporary circumstances (where the Holy Spirit is alive and active). As Rush says, "Listening to God speaking in the present enables the church to recognize and to faithfully interpret what the same God has spoken in the past—and vice versa."[54] If the translations made by Catholic educators are to be faithful to the tradition that has been passed down to them as well as life giving for those they seek to serve, then the task of translation must be ongoing.

---

53. Rush, *Eyes of Faith*, 260.
54. Rush, *Eyes of Faith*, 295.

# 22

# Communication, Media, and Inculturation

IT IS ONE THING to believe that by being fully open to God's self-communication we make possible the emergence and flourishing of our own authentic identity; that is hard enough. To accept the risk of letting down the barriers we hold up against God and to trust that God both has benign intentions for, as well as supreme knowledge of, who we are and who we can become, with the help of grace, already seems highly risky. Somehow, it seems even more difficult and rash to be fully open to other people, whose goodwill towards us and whose capacity to understand us, we often have good reason to doubt. Yet, this is our calling: to meet God in, through and with the other person. For us to hear and respond to this call—and thus to enter into communion with others—requires us to engage in serious communication with a view to being really present to one another. If education is to promote our humanity, and if becoming more human is the necessary path towards participating in the life of God, then a major task of educators is to facilitate, to encourage, and to model the capacity to communicate with others. In this chapter I draw attention to some aspects of this task by bringing out its demands, complexities, and challenges. In part 1 the focus will be on personal communication and its requirements. In part 2 a feature of the wider culture is brought into view, one that deserves more attention than it has so far received from faith educators, despite the efforts half a century ago of that far-sighted commentator Marshall McLuhan: the impact of new media of communication.[1] Finally, and briefly, in part 3 it is suggested that the educational task of inculturation—relating the gospel to a particular culture—a task which is shared between the church and her schools and

---

1. McLuhan: *Understanding Media*; *Medium and the Light*.

universities—has to be both sensitive to the personal dimensions of communication and alert to the significance and implications of the media used in communication.

Kevin Trowbridge distinguishes communication from media in terms that are pertinent to my areas of focus in parts 1 and 2 of this chapter. "*Communication* is the relational process of creating meaning while *media* refers to the channels through which messages pass from one communicator to another. . . . Meaning is created through a relational process that involves the interaction between communicators, messages, and channels."[2] Thus, in the first section I will concentrate on the human interactions, the "software" of human qualities, virtues, and capacities that is at the heart of communicative relationships, while in the second I attend to the bearing of the "hardware" of the media employed in contemporary culture on human perspectives and interaction. In the light of parts 1 and 2, I end, in part 3, by proposing that inculturation of the gospel depends on both the fostering of effective communicative relationships at the personal level and the critical discernment of a culture, especially being alert to its media of communication.

## COMMUNICATION BETWEEN PERSONS

Two dangers come to mind when we reflect on interpersonal communication. There is the raw truth of what is inside us and needs to come out. This will be deeply personal and subjective. It may be one sided. It may be vehemently expressed. It may emerge from pain. It has immediacy and vigor. It comes from below. Its claim is to be authentic, true to self, rather than applicable to all. In contrast, there is a carefully honed, precise expression of truth which has been "validated" by some tradition as authoritative. This will be more objective than subjective, more universal in scope than particular to individual cases. It comes from above or outside us and claims to be transferable between people.

Both these types of truth can play a valuable part in communication, and both are valid and necessary, but each, taken on its own, is insufficient, because what is lacking in each is the complex and demanding task of entering into the experience and perspective of the other. This is a failure in relationship. In the first case, the person uttering a truth is insufficiently free at that moment from their pain (interpreted broadly) to attend to, to hear and to take fully into account other person(s), their needs and perspectives. At its best, such raw expression conveys a real authenticity, it calls for

---

2. Trowbridge, "Communication and Media," 325, 327.

attention, and it invites some reciprocity in response, preferably one that is restrained, sensitive, and appreciative. At its worst, it can slip into mere self-indulgence, being both aggressive and defensive at the same time, lashing out in an undiscriminating manner. In the second case, because of their relatively detached and measured language, the person uttering a truth can seem to be insufficiently invested in, or affected by, the truth they utter; they can seem safely "above the fray" rather than in the midst of the mess of life. They can appear insufficiently in touch with or sympathetic to those they speak to; if so, they fail to elicit a hearing. Their language comes across as abstract, and it lacks concreteness or a "down-to-earth" quality.

We must find ways to reconcile these two sources of truth and to bring them into dialogue because to leave them apart is damaging, damaging to individuals, damaging to traditions, damaging to communion between people, and damaging in that such separation blocks off avenues to a fuller appreciation and understanding of truth. To rely only on the first would leave people trapped by the limitations of their own experience and it would narrow their worlds unduly. To rely only on the second would be to inhibit serious personal engagement with the resources that traditions have to offer, it would prevent ownership and invite inauthenticity, it would undermine the capacity (and the need) for traditions and "validated" truth claims to be tested by the reality of people's experiences, to learn from this, and to be open to further development.

Disagreement sometimes will be inevitable, but such disagreement does not have to be taken to be deliberately destructive; it can be constructive both in its intention and in its effects. Disagreement is often taken by leaders to be a sign of disloyalty, instead of as a different understanding of what loyalty requires of us. The expression of disagreement usually calls for courage in overcoming fear of disapproval or of upsetting others. If the disagreement is to be constructive, care must be taken that it is not expressed aggressively. Here the tone of voice, as well as the language used, matters. Furthermore, if the disagreement is to be constructive, then the aim should be to assist in the process of finding a better way forward. Thus, commitment to a cause, about which one cares, is to be combined with civility; the critique offered is concerned with reconciliation rather than victory of one side over another.

The German philosopher Jürgen Habermas has drawn attention to the conditions necessary for communication to have a chance to flourish: one must believe that genuine consensus is possible; there should be equality among participants, together with freedom from constraint; there should be no premature closure of discussion topics or outcomes; all participants should have voice, respect, and attention.[3] Nicholas Burbules points out the key communicative virtues, which include tolerance, patience, openness to give and receive criticism, readiness to admit one may be mistaken, a desire to reinterpret or translate one's own concerns so that they will be comprehensible to others, self-imposition of restraint in order that others may speak, and willingness to listen thoughtfully and attentively.[4]

Many elements play a part in the communicative relationship: presence and posture, tone of voice, rhythm and repetition, pace and pausing, cadence and gesture. Communication requires language (or media), together with relationship; it is supported or obscured by the exercise of the art and the power as well as by the intentions and clarity of the communicator in addition to the capacity and receptivity of those one wishes to reach. Communication is not a matter of merely broadcasting a message, but of bringing people together. This is best done as a joint activity, with shared effort and with reciprocal exchange. It is important to be alert to the gaps that can occur in attempts to communicate. There can be slippage between what one means to say, the degree to which one manages to say what one means, what the other person thinks should have been said, what the other person thinks was said, what the other person thinks was meant, and how others interpret what others tell them was said. Words can change their significance for us according to several factors that exert an influence on their reception: what other words are used alongside them; who is saying them; our relationship to the person saying the words to us; where they are said (in what context); who else is present when they are said; our knowledge of the topic; whether we have prepared ourselves appropriately; and what else is going on in our lives at the time.

Various obstacles to dialogue can interrupt or distort communication: perhaps fear of disapproval or of reprisal, or insufficient trust in the other person's goodness and sincerity, or lack of confidence in the validity of one's own experience and insights, or, in contrast, too much confidence in one's own perspective and convictions. Other obstacles might be flattery, gossip, lies and slander, twisting of words, misrepresentation, and selective deployment of truth or evasion. Excessive reticence might lead one to fail to speak when this is required, while excessive boldness might tempt one to jump in too quickly to have one's say without consideration of the consequences or likely impact. Another factor is our ignorance: there is much that we do not know. To start with, God will always remain beyond our ken; we never have our understanding of God "taped," sorted, or settled. Then, we remain

3. Adams, *Habermas and Theology*.
4. Burbules, *Dialogue in Teaching*, 42.

a mystery to ourselves, despite rare moments of insight, often granted to us by others who shock us by their observations of who we are and what we are like. As for other people, no matter how well we think we know them, they too escape our grasp; they have depths that we cannot reach. If we think of the church, she seems to be full of surprises for us, some welcome, others quite unwelcome. If we were not open to surprise, we would be closed to grace. Among the conditions which facilitate effective communication might be noted a recognition that no one has a monopoly on the truth, a presumption that those with whom we differ are acting in good faith, caution in ascribing motives to others for their adoption of particular arguments, and a willingness to put the best possible construction on differing positions, together with acceptance that one's own viewpoint might be mistaken.

What might dialogue—between parties who disagree about truth claims or about values—achieve? Dialogue could lead to some combination of benefits drawn from the following possibilities: agreement on substantive issues, more effective joint action and collaboration, agreement about procedures for dealing with neuralgic issues, reduced number of areas of disagreement about issues or increased number of areas of agreement. Or it might open the door to better mutual understanding and appreciation; it might resolve some misunderstandings or improve relationships between participants. Other potential gains might include a raised level of involvement in decision-making processes, a more internally cohesive community, and better witness externally. Educators might prompt students to ask: Can we approach others seeking to appreciate their position and passion, their experience and perspective, their pain and fear, their commitments and their way of reading threats to these commitments?

Teachers and educational leaders everywhere, if they are to be effective, should go beyond mere competence; they need honesty, humility, humanity, and hope. To sustain these for the long haul, they require conviction (with regard to their fundamental principles), courage (in how they put these into practice in face of difficulties, opposition, and disappointments), and compassion (for those on the receiving end of their work). The tone of voice to be adopted should be one that is confident, clear, open, humble, respectful, invitational, imaginative, constructive, and collaborative. When these elements are present, features of teaching for worthwhile learning that become evident include compassion for learners, rather than a need to exercise control over them; admiring contemplation of what is being studied, instead of efficient manipulation of it; and a stance of interdependence with students, fellow teachers, and the wider community, in place of treating either the classroom or the topic under investigation as personal possessions.

PART FIVE | CONNECTING TRADITION TO CULTURE

# COMMUNICATION MEDIA AND FAITH EDUCATION

More than a generation ago the cultural theorist and religious thinker Walter Ong (1912–2003) pointed out how changes in the media of communication used in a society alter the balance within what he called the "sensorium," the relative attention given to seeing, hearing, touching, tasting, and speaking in our engagement with the world around us.[5] Changes in the communication media employed by people in general and by teachers and learners in particular affect not only our language but our perceptions and our thinking, our modes of reasoning and valuing. It seems timely at this point in our cultural development, when waves of digital innovation in communication technologies wash over us with increasing rapidity, for Christian educators to reflect on how our interaction with communication media might affect our understanding of the task of communicating Christian faith.

Because of my low level of expertise in this field, I will rely heavily for this part of the chapter on my reading of some writers who have greatly enhanced our understanding of how communications media affect our engagement with reality. Apart from drawing upon Ong, I will also refer to the writer who first alerted me (in the 1980s) to the influence of television in framing the way we interpret the world, Neil Postman, before making use of the lenses provided by three other specialists in media and communication: Sven Birkerts, Luciano Floridi, and Peter Horsfield.[6]

Although my intention is not to concentrate on the media being used—or that might be used—in Christian education, nor is it to demonstrate a desire to be up to date or culturally "savvy" as to the potential of new communications technologies, I believe it is important to acknowledge, albeit only too briefly and inadequately, their bearing on any attempt to communicate or to witness to Christian faith in church or in educational settings (at any level). Wise educators should remain alert to the bearing of culture and its communication media on the outlooks and mindsets, the dispositions and expectations, the capacities and blind spots of teachers and students. The messages that are conveyed, the language that is used, the relationships that are fostered, the modes of presence that are established, and the kinds of learning that are facilitated in education cannot help but be deeply implicated in and pervasively influenced by the broader communication context.

---

5. Ong, *Presence of the Word*.
6. Postman, *Amusing Ourselves to Death*.

The rapid development of new and increasingly more sophisticated communication technologies has an impact on our understanding of knowledge (its sources, nature, structure, reliability, and interconnectedness or coherence), of text and of learning. It also modifies how we think about personal identity, self-expression, social conventions, community, authority, and our perception of moral norms. In doing so, the ways we read and respond to the world are shifting. Changes occur in our experience of time and space, our sense of presence—who is present to us and how; changes are also experienced in our views on of what is possible, what is plausible and what is permitted. Our awareness and appreciation of stability, of continuity, of achieving depth through long-term engagement with and commitment to others, with texts and the world around us may become interrupted and inhibited.

Religious faith is inevitably influenced by the cumulative effect of all these unforeseen consequences of technological change, along with alterations in our thinking, our habits, our imagination, desires, our priorities and the people we are in touch with. Affecting us in tandem, new technologies "modify our reflexes and expectations."[7] Technology changes the storyline of society in several ways: it significantly adds to the sheer number of stories to which we have access; it loosens our connection to traditional reference points for the stories we inherit; it modifies how we encounter stories, for example, beyond face-to-face encounters and listening to elders, to sources and agencies with which we do not enjoy a direct and ongoing relationship or holistic reinforcement experiences. Nearly twenty years ago an observer of cultural trends could comment: "Children used to grow up in a home where parents told most of the stories. Today television tells most of the stories to most of the people most of the time."[8] Despite the continuing cultural dominance of television, it is likely that this judgment has been rendered outdated, given the proliferation of new communications media now being deployed by children and young adults who live in a hypermedia environment where there is a blend of "text, still image, moving image, and sound, all arranged through a series of controlling icons."[9]

Walter Ong has argued that Socrates's complaints at the end of the *Phaedrus* about writing—that it diminishes memory, lacks interaction, disseminates at random, and disembodies speakers and hearers—are similar to late twentieth-century worries about computers as well as fifteenth-century

---

7. Birkerts, *Gutenberg Elegies*, xiii.
8. Warren, *Communications and Cultural Analysis*, 41, citing George Gerbner.
9. Purves, *Web of Text*, 112.

concerns about printing.[10] This complaint has been well described by John Durham Peters in his history of communication *Speaking into the Air*: "Writing parodies live presence; it is inhuman, lacks interiority, destroys authentic dialogue, is impersonal, and cannot acknowledge the individuality of its interlocutors; and it is promiscuous in distribution."[11] Not only, as Ong observes, might we apply this to computers; it has been lamented also with regard to many other technological innovations in communication.

Two major insights from Ong deserve mention here: first, his account of the "sensorium"; second, his analysis of key characteristics of media. In *The Presence of the Word* he describes the sensorium as the complete set of our bodily senses working together as an operational complex, explaining that the way we use our senses and the relative weight we attribute to each of them has a different configuration according to the culture in which we find ourselves. "Cultures vary greatly in their exploitation of the various senses and in the way they relate their conceptual apparatus to the various senses.... [A given culture] brings [a person] to organize his sensorium by attending to some types of perception more than others, by making an issue of certain ones while relatively neglecting other ones."[12] This is not to deny the fact that our senses provide both opportunities for, as well as constraints on, cultural developments; the influence between culture and senses is reciprocal. Our world is simultaneously both personal, as constructed by us, and objective, given to us. "The sensorial organization specific to any given time and culture may bring us to overspecialize in certain features of actuality and to neglect others."[13]

Following on from this, Ong draws attention to three characteristics of media. He shows how any particular medium used in communication addresses and activates one or more of the different physical senses of sight, sound, hearing, touch, and taste, affecting social perception as well as bodily engagement. Then, he links different media with particular associated ways of managing information, including its storage, retrieval, and dissemination, with attendant effects on how cultures develop and deploy systems of meaning. Finally, he shows how the use of different media frames the pattern of relationships and authority in a culture.

It is often the case that, for most of the time, we remain unaware of the ways that our use of media of communication influences our perceptions and behavior. In this respect, I found very helpful the work of Neil Postman,

10. Ong, *Orality and Literacy*, 79–81.
11. J. Peters, *Speaking into the Air*, 47.
12. Ong, *Presence of the Word*, 3, 6.
13. Ong, *Presence of the Word*, 175.

an expert on communication and culture, when I came across it thirty years ago. Postman pointed out that

> Each medium . . . makes possible a unique mode of discourse by providing a new orientation for thought, for expression, for sensibility. . . . Whether we are experiencing the world through the lens of speech or the printed word or the television camera, our media-metaphors classify the world for us, sequence it, frame it enlarge it, reduce it, color it, argue a case for what the world is like.[14]

In the cultural mindset fostered by television, Postman lamented the trivialization that pervades our information environment. He quotes a television editor's assumptions about a news show "that bite-sized is best, that complexity must be avoided, that nuances are dispensable, that qualifications impede the simple message, that visual stimulation is a substitute for thought, and that verbal precision is an anachronism."[15] In addition to being concerned about the deleterious effects on education and on the political health of democracies of the cultural mindset changes brought about by television, he noted that "questions about the psychic, political and social effects of information are as applicable to the computer as to television."[16] His argument was that cognitive habits, social relations, and value priorities are inevitably modified by the ideology-laden baggage that accompanies technological change.

Sven Birkerts enhances our appreciation of the nature of the changes brought about by the emergence of new communications media in two ways: first, by offering a balance sheet of gains and losses; second, by drawing attention to the new communal experience made possible through such media, a form of life he calls "electronic tribalism."[17] Birkerts mentions four principal gains for individuals from electronic postmodernity:

> an increased awareness of the "big picture," a global perspective that admits the extraordinary complexity of interrelations; an expanded neural capacity, an ability to accommodate a broad range of stimuli simultaneously; a relativistic comprehension of situations that promotes the erosion of old biases and often expresses itself as tolerance; a matter-of-fact and unencumbered

---

14. Postman, *Amusing Ourselves to Death*, 10.
15. Postman, *Amusing Ourselves to Death*, 107–8.
16. Postman, *Amusing Ourselves to Death*, 166.
17. Birkerts, *Gutenberg Elegies*, 27.

sort of readiness, a willingness to try new situations and arrangements.[18]

For educators these features deserve to be considered assets that support learning, rather than liabilities that impede it, even if they tend to erode fixed certainties and confidence in the reliability of traditions. These gains, however, for Birkerts, should be weighed against some accompanying losses, among which he includes:

> a fragmented sense of time and a loss of the so-called duration experience, that depth phenomenon we associate with reverie; a reduced attention span and a general impatience with sustained inquiry; a shattered faith in institutions and in the explanatory narratives that formerly gave shape to subjective experience; a divorce from the past, from a vital sense of history as a cumulative or organic process.[19]

It is interesting to note a rather different inflection of Birkert's loss column when assessing the consequences of widespread use of new communications media. Sherry Turkle laments the way that, in the various dimensions of their lives, people find ways around conversation, tempted by the possibilities of a text or an email in which they do not have to look, listen, or reveal themselves.[20] Her argument is that we are becoming addicted to connection over conversation, and this fact is stopping us from engaging in real debate, sharing our real opinions and reacting to our family, friends, partners, and colleagues in a way that either encourages necessary conflict or diffuses it. According to her, we are shying away from the real politics of the public square and heading for a subdued, online version of ourselves, allowing digital devices to dictate our daily life. Her thesis is that, in the bid for instant and permanent connectivity that is fueled by new digitized communication, real presence—along with deep and engaging conversations that require time—is put in jeopardy. Such connectivity, rather than serious and deep communication, is what Birkerts refers to as being enveloped in "hive life," a form of electronic tribalism, one that is being built out of multiple components:[21] "telephone, fax, computer-screen networks, e-mail, interactive television,"[22] to which we could add texting, Skype, and smartphone applications.

18. Birkerts, *Gutenberg Elegies*, 27.
19. Birkerts, *Gutenberg Elegies*, 27.
20. Turkle, *Reclaiming Conversation*.
21. Birkerts, *Gutenberg Elegies*, 228.
22. Birkerts, *Gutenberg Elegies*, 224.

The specialist in the philosophy and ethics of information Luciano Floridi refers to four revolutions brought about by Copernicus, Darwin, Freud, and Turing. Each of the first three of these revolutions displaces some aspect of our understanding of our place in the world and our own nature. As he says, with respect to the first three of these revolutions, "We are not immobile, at the center of [a] universe" that revolves around us, "we are not unnaturally separate and diverse from the rest of the animal kingdom, and we are far from being Cartesian minds entirely transparent to ourselves."[23] The fourth revolution, as described by Floridi, one inaugurated by Alan Turing in the 1940s, "displaced us from our privileged and unique position in the realm of logical reasoning, information processing, and smart behavior."[24] Our own creations, computers and related information and communications technologies, alerted us to our situation as "mutually connected and embedded in an informational environment (the infosphere), which we share with other informational agents, both natural and artificial, that also process information logically and autonomously."[25]

Key elements in this infosphere include (among others) "cloud computing, . . . smartphone apps, tablets and touch screens, GPS," as well as "identity theft, online courses, [and] social media" . . . all of which have become "environmental, anthropological, social, and interpretative forces," forces which cumulatively work together in such a way as to modify, pervasively, profoundly, and relentlessly, "how we relate to each other . . . and how we interpret the world."[26] The infosphere evidently includes, for Floridi, not only the technological tools and their properties, but also the agents who use them and the interactions and relations they make possible. Our whole environment now has to be understood as one that is inescapably interactional, governed by informational processes. In a striking comment, Floridi observes that "we grew up with cars, buildings, furniture, clothes, and all sorts of gadgets and technologies that were non-interactive, irresponsive, and incapable of communicating, learning, or memorizing," but this is no longer the case.[27] Increasingly and inexorably everything around us seems to be interactive and mutually responsive, so that, in terms of information, even if not in terms of emotional bonding, we are totally connected. According to Floridi, information and communication technologies (ICTs) have affected our understanding of what it is to be real; where once it was

23. Floridi, *Fourth Revolution*, 90.
24. Floridi, *Fourth Revolution*, 93.
25. Floridi, *Fourth Revolution*, 94.
26. Floridi, *Fourth Revolution*, vi.
27. Floridi, *Fourth Revolution*, 48.

thought that to be real was to be unchangeable (therefore only God has true being); then that to be real was to be capable of being perceived by the senses; through the impact of ICTs, to be real is to be something with which one can interact, even if that is transient and virtual, rather than real in the concrete sense intended when perceptibility was the yardstick.[28]

Christians are not immune from changes in the information and communication environment. They are inescapably influenced by what surrounds them both in what they think is plausible and how they express what is dear to them. Peter Horsfield links different interpretations and emphases within Christianity, and hence its diversity, to different responses by Christian groups to the communication possibilities made available by various media.

> Some Christian groups have been open to particular media practices but closed to others. Some have utilized similar media to others, but used them differently or ordered them in different hierarchies of value. Some have approached media from a purely utilitarian mindset, using whatever's available on the basis of its usefulness and effectiveness. Others have been selective in the media they use because of a given medium's different cultural associations. Some have seen technological forms of mediation as a priority; others have given higher priority to bodily, interpersonal forms of mediation.[29]

Christian educators must face the challenge of evaluating and working out the implications for their mission of the various features of our communication environment that have been noted in this section, whichever term one finds most helpful—hypermedia, the infosphere, the hive, connectivity, or informational matrix. They need to be alert to how communication media are shaping our environment in its multiple dimensions—cognitive, economic, political, social, cultural, moral, and even physical. A few comments on the bearing of such developments on education seem pertinent.

First, it must be acknowledged that "no communication arrangement can guarantee to make accessible the truths of Christian faith."[30] Such access, is subject to and requires both the gift of grace and the free response of the one who receives it.

Second, technology can do much but still remains in service to the underlying and enduring inner capacities or gifts of humanity, including imagination. This point is illustrated in the following brief anecdote. "When

---

28. Floridi, *Fourth Revolution*, 53.
29. Horsfield, *From Jesus to Internet*, 286.
30. Scharer and Hilberath, *Practice of Communicative Theology*, 21.

I grew up, I could not imagine a world without Kodak. Neither could the managers of Kodak. As a result of this assumption, Kodak has become history."[31] Even as humanity becomes increasingly dependent on technology, the technology still depends on our inner capacities and qualities, such as sensitivity, listening, intelligence, conscience, empathy, and judgment. Without these, connectivity will never lead to community or become mutual attunement.

Third, in order to move beyond mere connectivity, there is the need to nurture the willingness to engage in deeper listening. Many years ago Postman claimed that one of the benefits that education should give us is a built-in crap detector, the ability to tell when some person or group was trying to deceive or manipulate us.[32] Can we now hope that one of the benefits that education will give us is a better hearing aid? There are signs in our culture of greater openness about and willingness to share experiences, feelings, and a greater acknowledgment of our need for recognition, acceptance, and affirmation.

Fourth, with pluralism, postmodernity, and a widespread erosion of confidence in claims to certainty about metanarratives, perhaps education will begin to do justice to the diversity of ways of knowing, focusing not only cognitive, rational, and conceptual knowledge, but also aesthetic, symbolic/gestural, embodied, kinesthetic, and spiritual knowledge.

Fifth, in acknowledging much greater access to and democratization of knowledge—with multiple sources of information—Christian educational institutions should welcome and adjust to the ensuing distributed nature of authority. Centralization and concentration of authority, with associated pressures toward conformity and compliance, even though marked features of the church in recent centuries, do not fit well with the Christian mission to make mature, responsible, and committed disciples.

Sixth, if in the past a strong emphasis in Christian education has been to pass on a body of content (Scripture, doctrine, moral precepts), and if, in more recent times students have been encouraged to interrogate their own experience, in the light of current cultural developments in our communication environment, it is now necessary to give priority to equipping students to interpret and critique the culture, its assumptions and values, the habits it promotes, attentive to what it privileges and what it neglects, aware of how it frames our sense of identity, relationships, belonging, and expectations.

---

31. Byrnes, Review.
32. Postman and Weingartner, *Teaching as Subversive Activity*.

PART FIVE | CONNECTING TRADITION TO CULTURE

# INCULTURATION, MEDIATION, AND COMMUNICATION

Integral to being human is participation in a culture. Many people inhabit several cultures at the same time, although these do not all have the same degree of purchase on their lives. As was noted in part 2, the cultures one lives among affect a person's awareness and imagination, hopes and fears, expectations of others and assumptions about life. Cultural environments are permeated by messages mediated via many different modes of communication beyond immediate face-to-face contact, for example, television and the global internet, advertising and music, magazines and movies, video games and mobile phones, along with the whole range of what Floridi has named the infosphere, each of which exerts a subtle influence on how people think and value. Christian educators must be conscious of, informed about, and sensitive to the impact of culture on themselves and those they hope to address. The many types of activity that a Christian educator might be involved in, including proclamation and witness, worship and service, nurture and liberation, constantly have to be adjusted: as the surrounding culture changes, these activities are inevitably understood and expressed differently in a new mixture and set of priorities.

Some aspects of a culture will be hospitable to religious faith; some aspects will be hostile; while still other aspects will be indifferent. Christian educators need discernment—to avoid blanket acceptance or blind rejection of culture of the people with whom they are working. If Christians run away from the surrounding culture, so as not to be contaminated by it, they risk slipping into a ghetto, abdicate their responsibility to influence the world for the better, and fail the people God wants them to touch; their purity becomes irrelevant to the world. On the other hand, if they throw themselves into the world, they might soon find they have accepted too much of it on its own terms, and without realizing it they could become assimilated and swallowed up by it and unable to bring to it the distinctive salt and light of faith. The challenge is to learn how to swim in a culture without drowning in it. In order to be relevant, they need to be rooted in culture and local needs. But, to be adequately Christian, they also need to be able to transcend culture. They have to be both at home, familiar with and hospitable to a culture, but also, to some degree, also a stranger, unsettled and disturbing in it. They are called to be *in* the world, to prompt it lovingly towards God, yet not *of* the world, fully accepting it as it is.

In bridging the gap between faith and a particular culture, Christian educators need to emphasize both the "foreignness" of Christian faith—its supernatural character—and its connection to, its continuity with, and its befriending and enhancing of daily life—its natural aspects. They should avoid watering down the challenge and "foreignness" of faith and the gospel by domesticating the call to conversion of life and holiness. Yet they should also avoid causing unnecessary barriers for those on the path to faith by lacking imagination and creativity in their presentation of the Christian story. Thus, in one sense Christian educators today face the same challenge of holding in balance both closeness to and distance from the culture(s) surrounding them as the one with which all their predecessors had to deal. Yet, they also need to reflect carefully on the rapidly changing context brought about by Floridi's fourth revolution and its as-yet-unclear implications for our sense of identity, relationships, belonging, our thinking, valuing, and imagining, our memory, hopes, and constraints. Being immersed in a culture always entails being subject to unconscious codes that are difficult to discern, being complicit in hidden conflicts that can easily remain outside our consciousness, and being prompted to be creative with the resources available to us.[33]

The challenge entailed in connecting faith to culture is sometimes referred to as inculturation—the task of showing how the gospel relates to a particular time, place and cultural setting. This is a two-way process. Just as the gospel casts new light on each human situation, in turn that situation can bring different dimensions of the gospel into salience. Throughout history, each generation has had to read, receive and respond to the gospel in ways made possible by, but also in ways that are restricted by, the patterns of perception and behavior associated with life in the world. The gospel always has to take root, to touch down in flesh-and-blood people, in very particular circumstances. Inevitably, in doing so, it changes color, depending on what is already lighting up the lives of the people and what is darkening them

In an encounter with Christian faith, the culture will find itself challenged and be pressed to see itself in a new light. At the same time, when Christians encounter another culture, they will find their faith challenged, and they will find it necessary to reinterpret this faith and see it differently. Modifications in self-understanding are likely to be necessary on both sides as bridges are built between the heritage of Christian faith and the value systems, symbols, and cultures of learners. Incarnating the faith in a particular context will entail engagement by Christians with the language, perceptions, priorities, preoccupations, and practices of the people therein. Such engagement facilitates the reception and appropriation of Christian faith in terms understandable to the receiving culture. In turn however, all cultures need to be evangelized, brought into the light of the cross.

33. Gallagher, "University and Culture," 161.

The process of inculturation calls for two processes to take place in reciprocal interaction. There needs to be an intelligent "reading" of a culture, conducted in such a way that one's reading is minimally dominated by the thought forms of that culture (otherwise one's thinking will merely be a reflection of what is already there in the culture). This calls for a degree of standing back, of distancing, from that culture, in order to approach it freed from its presuppositions, insofar as this is possible. "The world's outlook evaluates and understands by equating the person with possessions, positions, achievements, actions, linguistic or religious or cultural groups."[34] There also needs to be an immersion into the outlook of Jesus. Integral to this challenge of holding together both processes—interpreting the culture and induction into a Christian perspective—there needs to a recognition that both worlds, that of our contemporary culture and the world of Jesus, do not appear before us transparently, nakedly, obviously, or simply in some unfiltered manner; they come to us via multiple mediations. The complex role of communication technologies in mediating to us our culture has already been apparent in part 2 of this chapter. The person and teaching of Jesus is accessible to us also only via multiple mediations: through Scripture, preaching, sacramental practice, ecclesial life, the witness of countless people of God, prayer, service, and conscience—all the elements that comprise a living tradition.

Christian educators, whether teaching in schools and colleges or contributing to church activities, must be conscious of, informed about and sensitive to the impact of culture on themselves and those they hope to address. The many types of activity that a Christian educator might be involved in, including proclamation and witness, worship and service, nurture and liberation, constantly have to be adjusted: as the surrounding culture changes, these activities are inevitably understood and expressed differently in a new mixture and set of priorities. St. Paul describes in 1 Cor 9:20–22 his flexible approach in adapting to different audiences and types of people. In the specific context of Catholic religious education, inculturation will require a combination of imagination, empathy, boldness, and fidelity if it is to be effective making links between the questions, language, thought forms, and concerns of the students' surrounding culture(s) and the living tradition of the church. Imagination will help in developing new expressions of faith; empathy will assist in getting close to the reality experienced by students; boldness will reinforce the communicative power of what is afforded by imagination; and fidelity will ensure that the teacher remains steeped in the church's teaching and way of life.

34. Mattam, "Inculturated Evangelization & Conversion," 229.

## CONCLUSION

I have been reflecting on the centrality of communication in our lives and the influence of new media of communication in our culture. Let me make a more explicit connection now with my understanding of education. Education is about the capacities of human nature: energy, emotions, intelligence, memory, will, conscience, imagination, and wonder—and how these are developed, oriented, ordered, and integrated. Christian education does all this in the light of Christ. Education can be an encounter and a journey in which many gifts and capacities are made possible. The following list, while long, remains incomplete. Education can enable people to think clearly, to analyze ideas, to weigh up the soundness and significance of claims, to express oneself convincingly, to interpret evidence, and to take into account different points of view. Through their example and with their guidance, teachers can help students learn how to listen sensitively, to read intelligently, to judge carefully, to appreciate the insights, gifts, and works of others, and to relate compassionately and cooperatively. To this treasury of gifts one might add further possibilities: learning to know oneself, to give oneself to commitments and to others, to love wisely and to develop confidence and competence in ongoing learning, together with the discipline and reinforced desire to find truth, beauty, and goodness, and the capacities to build a good life.

My own experience as a teacher, of children, young people, and adults is that students surprise us by their singularity. They learn something different than what we teach them. They break through our expectations (positive and negative). We experience them as a foreign country. They make demands on us that force us to be more attentive to their otherness, rather than taking them for granted. Although we want them to be like us in some aspect of knowledge or skill, they cannot be a copy; they are—like us—originals. Our courses are intended for the general student, but we face real individuals. The material is new for them; through them, it becomes new for us. Their worlds are (at least slightly) changed in their encounter with us; our world is also changed when we respond to who they are. This is a view of the relationship between teachers and students that would have been recognized by St. Augustine centuries ago. In his manual for catechists, he wrote: "So potent is the feeling of sympathy, that when they are moved as we speak and we as they learn, we abide each with the other; and thus they, as it were, speak in us what they hear, while we, in a manner, learn in them what we teach."[35] It is a view that is been echoed and expressed creatively a generation ago by Parker Palmer:

> The teacher who knows the subject well, must introduce it to students in the way one would introduce a friend. The students must know why the teacher values the subject, how the subject has transformed the teacher's life. By the same token, the teacher must value the students as potential friends, be vulnerable to the ways students may transform the teacher's relationship with the subject as well as be transformed. If I am invited into a valued friendship between two people, I will not enter in unless I feel that I am valued as well.[36]

The qualities that education both depends upon in its teachers and seeks to develop in students are illustrated by two comments that bring out, respectively, the impact of personal communication, and the need for a careful and intelligent reading of culture. The first comment comes from a young schoolteacher: "I remember my English teacher because . . . he inspired me to be better, to take risks, to ask awkward questions and to feel as if I mattered."[37] The second comment is made by a professor who is an experienced teacher-educator: "The authority of professors as scholars in their disciplines lies in their mastery of the discipline's discourse, but their authority as teachers lies in their skill at the boundaries between the disciplines and the many worlds from which their students come."[38] The former emphasizes the positive influence that effective personal communication by a teacher can exert on students; the latter stresses the need for teachers to build bridges between students and the various cultures that surround them. That bridging role—between individuals and culture—has always been central to education; as a priority today, it must now include a confident engagement with and a critical interrogation of the influence of new media of communication. Without this, it is only too likely that students will find themselves kidnapped, rather than liberated, by their culture. Without the qualities that are integral to effective personal communication, it is quite possible that differences between people will lead to unnecessary conflict between them and that the capacity for learning of students will be impaired.

---

35. Augustine, *On Catechizing the Uninstructed*, 31.
36. Palmer, *To Know as We are Known*, 104.
37. Nicholson-Ward, "Questions That Only Children," 9.
38. Kenneth Bruffee, quoted by Levisohn et al., "How to Do," 104–5.

# 23

# Being a Citizen in the Church

"You are no longer strangers and aliens, but you are citizens with the saints and also members of the household of God" (Eph 2:19). This means that we belong, that we have a part to play, and that we have rights in the church. However, the belonging that is part of citizenship (in the church and more broadly) must be distinguished from *groupthink* or tribalism. These distortions of belonging turn boundaries into barriers; they focus more on being against than being for; they slip into idolatry with regard to our positions, confusing signposts with destinations. It is when people are caught up in a crowd of the righteous that they sometimes find themselves crucifying outsiders.

There is another danger, and here I refer to the danger of the church being unbalanced—having a big head but too small a body—as explored in a new book by François Urvoy, *La tête sans corps*. A Call to Action (ACTA) is a group of Catholics in the UK—clergy, religious, and laypeople—committed to open, respectful, serious, mature, and honest dialogue within the church. ACTA seeks a better balance in the ethos and practice of communication and dialogue between members of the body of Christ. My hope for A Call to Action is that it works towards a church that, in striving to live out the gospel of Jesus Christ, is humble, inclusive, compassionate and committed to the dignity and equality of all its members. ACTA provides support for mutually responsive dialogue in which laity, bishops, clergy, and religious can share together their faith experience and their concerns for the church. A mature church is impossible if, instead of a climate of free and open discussion, there is a climate of fear and lack of consultation; if, instead of communication including all members of the church and respecting the voices, experiences, and insights of all, there is limited and unilateral communication from church leaders who assume they already possess the fullness of truth and that they adequately represent and speak for the people of God.

There are seven steps in the journey of this chapter. First, a comment on the phrase "not sheep," when applied to the laity. Second, I share some of the assumptions I am making. Third, key features of citizenship are unpacked. Fourth, I will say something about the problem of obedience, but perhaps with an unexpected emphasis. Fifth, I will claim that the climate for ecclesial citizenship has not been healthy, offering some examples. Sixth, as an extension of part 5, an imbalance between several types of ministry will receive attention. Seventh, rather fancifully, a comparison between the history wars and controversy in the church is made. I hope that these reflections stimulate readers in their own thinking about what is entailed by being citizens of the church.

## NOT SHEEP

"The Church is essentially an unequal society, that is, a society comprising two categories of persons, the pastors and the flock, those who occupy a rank in the different degrees of the hierarchy and multitude of the faithful. So distinct are these categories that with the pastoral body only rests the necessary right and authority for promoting the end of society and directing all its members towards that end; the one duty of the multitude is to allow themselves to be led and, like a docile flock, to follow the Pastors." That was Pope Pius X, writing in 1906.[1] Here the laity were to pay, pray, and obey. The 1983 *Code of Canon Law* says: What is proper to the laity excludes them from participation in the governance of the church. The ordained are to exercise power, while the laity may cooperate only in the exercise of power in the church.[2] Pope John Paul II made it clear that "opposition to the teaching of the Church's pastors cannot be seen as a legitimate expression either of Christian freedom or of the diversity of the Spirit's gifts."[3] Pope Benedict XVI reiterated to the church in China in 2007: "The principles of independence and autonomy, self-management and democratic administration of the Church are incompatible with Catholic doctrine."[4]

Let me paint for you a scenario; if necessary, please, temporarily suspend your disbelief about this scenario, just to enter, at least briefly, into

---

1. Pius X, *Vehementer Nos*, §8.
2. Canon Law Society, *Code of Canon Law*, canons 129, 274.
3. John Paul II, *Splendor of Truth*, §113.
4. Benedict XVI, "Letter," §7.

the situation. I would be fascinated if our bishops were asked the following question and then tried to address it:

*What is one meant to do if one believes that a good deal of what is said by the bishops and other institutional leaders of the church is not only misguided, inappropriate, and unwise, but also that it obscures the effective communication of the gospel, is damaging to the common good, indeed is even sinful in some of its assumptions and implications?*

In posing this question, I am assuming that such a person should pray seriously, asking for God's guidance, in all humility, and be aware that they may be wrong in their judgment; I am also taking it for granted that they should ensure that they are properly informed about the teaching and tradition of the church, and this should include reading authoritative texts. And I take it for granted that such a person should pray earnestly for the deeper conversion and enlightenment by the Holy Spirit of the church leaders she or he is questioning or criticizing. However, after that, then what? Is it always right to wait for better times? To keep silent? To leave the status quo as it is? To assume it is not for me to try to change things? If we are sheep, the answer is: it is not our business to question or correct our shepherds who know better than us. If we are ecclesial citizens, something more robust is called for.

The theologian Tom O'Loughlin, who spoke to us at the first ACTA gathering in London last October, gives a good example of what is expected of sheep in an article published a few months ago.

> Some couple of months ago, a new Parish Priest arrived in a north London parish and said, quite naturally, that he wanted to get to know all the organizations and groups in the parish. A woman, let's call her Gladys, had been running a book-reading group in the community, which varied between six and twelve people. They selected, in turn, a book that an individual had found useful, then, having read it, they shared their reactions. The model is a common one in reading groups across our society. Gladys invited the new Parish Priest to come to the group when the book for discussion was Victor Frankl's *Man's Search for Meaning*. At once he objected that this was not a suitable book for a Catholic reading group, and asked to suggest another, recommended Richard Rohr's *Falling Upwards*. Both these decisions were accepted. At the next meeting he prescribed another book, and when it was pointed out that it was now not his turn to pick the book, he replied that if they wished to call themselves a "Catholic" reading group, then only he, as a priest appointed by the bishop, could decide what books were suitable. Gladys,

rather embarrassed as she had initially invited him, went to see him to ask why he felt it was necessary to intervene like this, and was told that "the church is not a democracy" and arguing was setting her at odds with the Pope. Most of the members have now stopped attending the group and Gladys herself no longer thinks it a viable way of finding discussion partners for issues of concern to her.[5]

I remember a very similar experience myself. When the charismatic movement hit the UK in the second half of the 1970s, a group of us in my parish wanted to set up a prayer group. We were summoned by the parish priest and met in the lounge of his presbytery. He told us, in no uncertain terms, that we could indeed set up a prayer group but only on condition that we agreed to hold our gathering either in the church or in the lounge in his presbytery. As far as I remember, that group never took off after that.

Paul Lakeland makes an interesting comment about sheep: "The pattern of shepherd/sheep, while it is metaphorically appropriate to the description of the relationship between Christ and his church, is destructive of the daily life of the community of faith. Shared responsibility and accountability are the characteristics that need to replace this patriarchal and patronizing relationship."[6]

## SOME ASSUMPTIONS

Let me spell out some of my assumptions. First, as I understand it, discipleship entails a complex interaction between imitation and originality, docility and creativity. Just as Christ saves me in a unique way (in relation to my unique combination of needs, strengths, sins, gifts, blind spots, and situation), so my response must also be unique/particular and with my own input providing some element of originality—making something of what I have been given, doing something special with my inheritance. ACTA is necessary at the moment, though I hope one day it won't be necessary, because the present climate in the church in recent years has stifled the original aspect of discipleship, overemphasizing docility and inhibiting true ownership and appropriation, initiative, and responsible citizenship within the church—through a false understanding of how authority should work.

Second, I am assuming that healthy ecclesial citizenship depends on learning from the experience of trying to live gospel, and also on ownership, participation, trust, space to try things out and make mistakes

---

5. O'Loughlin, "Credibility of Catholic Church," 147.
6. Lakeland, *Liberation of the Laity*, 271.

(unpunished), and learn from these; such citizenship also needs a sense of partnership and interdependence.

Third, I assume that healthy citizenship in the church will produce not only map readers—readers of what has been handed on and learned in and from the past—but also mapmakers, people who are able to work at the frontiers of knowledge, in new contexts, creatively facing new questions. To be a mapmaker one has to spend some time "off the map" or beyond the current map, as well as being habituated to the use and interpretation of maps.

Fourth, another assumption is that we cannot be a leaven in and for the world without having a voice in the church. And that one of the places we should learn to ask good questions of the world is in the safety of being able to ask good questions of the church. Effective citizenship in the world can be boosted and reinforced by the experience of effective citizenship in the church; but a stunted role as an ecclesial citizen is likely to contribute to a restricted contribution as a citizen in the secular world.

Fifth, I agree with Paul Lakeland that "we should test the health of the ecclesial community in ways analogous to those we use to examine the health of the body politic. A healthy church will possess lively mediating structures, a strong public forum of ideas, and a clear conduit between those in positions of leadership and the members of the community. This conduit must be a two-way street."[7]

## CITIZENSHIP: FEATURES AND CONDITIONS

Good citizenship depends on citizens possessing a range of personal qualities. They need an informed awareness of public affairs (we might call this political literacy). They need a moral compass which helps them to take a principled and consistent view of what is right and wrong among the practical options available. They need to be committed to community and the common good (being willing to accept burdens and opportunities, responsibilities and rights), wanting to make a positive difference in the lives of others. In order to participate effectively, they must be able to collaborate with others and be part of a team, including being able to respond constructively to those who have different perspectives and beliefs. All this applies as much in the church as in society.

Good citizenship also depends on certain conditions being present in society. There should be mechanisms in place which allow for one's voice to be heard and taken into account and where one can call others to account.

7. Lakeland, *Liberation of the Laity*, 215.

There should be flourishing intermediate bodies, acting as buffer zones between the smallest and most intimate groupings such as the family, and the institutional weight of either the state or the international church. These intermediate bodies (for example, parishes in the church, or voluntary associations in secular society) can provide spaces for dialogue, argument, and exchange of experiences and perceptions between people (in the church or in society) with diverse roles and responsibilities, so that there can be mutual learning.

## THE PROBLEM OF OBEDIENCE

One of the problems with our church is that its leaders, obviously with quite a few honorable exceptions among individuals, as a general pattern of their behavior, seem to have no proper understanding of obedience or any serious appreciation of authority. The meaning of obedience is deep listening, taking seriously what you learn through that listening, and adjusting your behavior in response to that listening. Listening to what? Listening patiently and respectfully to the concerns, experiences, insights, questions, perplexities, hopes and fears of the people of God. As for authority, this is something given, by the people if and when they authorize others to act in their name; it is not something imposed on these people, from above, and without their consent.

In secular society these days, governments of all political leanings in our country find it necessary to check how close or far they are from people's experiences and perceptions. They set up fora, groups for sounding out views and responses to what has been offered in current policies. How often are we, as citizens of the church, asked by our leaders what we have learned about faith from our living with it, about our perceptions of our faith needs, and about what helps and hinders us as disciples? But this might make them vulnerable to criticism. Now, as Donald Cozzens reminds us, "One of the marks of a mature person is the capacity for self-criticism. It follows that a mature institution would be capable of self-criticism. [But] the Catholic Church abhors self-criticism as something that would weaken its credibility and moral authority."[8]

This failure to understand obedience, this failure to appreciate the nature of authority, flies in the face of what most of us have to learn in the course of normal life, in bringing up families, in teaching others, in working in organizations, in seeking to get the best from others in a team. Thus, it

---

8. Cozzens, *Notes from the Underground*, 203.

might be claimed that one problem with the church is that there is far too much disobedience, especially at the highest levels of leadership.

As for the misunderstanding of authority, this contributes to its abuse in three different ways (abuses, of course, shared by leaders in many walks of life, not just in the church). The main mistake is that of confusing compliance for commitment. These two are very different and the conditions that make for compliance are in many ways quite antithetical to the conditions that elicit commitment. Connected to this is the mistake of confusing disagreement with disloyalty, and thus wanting, wherever possible, to silence disagreement. Closely connected to this as a mistake is giving in to the temptation to micromanage what should properly be decided by people close to the action (in order to maintain control over them, lest through imagination, initiative, and by thinking for themselves, they act in ways that do not conform to the party line). When a pattern emerges of more authority being claimed than is accepted, and an atmosphere of evasion and unreality pervades ecclesial relations and communication—you pretend to teach us; we pretend to follow; but we won't kick up a fuss—eventually this undermines the church as a credible community. One cannot lead effectively if at the same time one fosters an unhealthy climate for communication. This is what ACTA is pressing for, as I understand it: a healthy climate for communication: mutual, respectful, serious, open, honest, engaged, and courageous conversations between laity, clergy, bishops, and religious. Why? In aid of more mature discipleship on all sides—and in order to promote more responsible participation in carrying the gospel forward.

## UNHEALTHY CLIMATE FOR ECCLESIAL CITIZENSHIP

The secular priest Donald Cozzens, in a searingly honest series of reflections on a church he both loves and has great concerns about, laments "the church's woefully underdeveloped, act-focused, medieval theology of human sexuality . . . the unmet spiritual needs of Catholics; the church's restrictive, subordinating attitude towards women; the absence of real financial transparency; and the shocking sexual abuse scandals and the arrogant episcopal cover-ups that made a terrible reality all the worse."[9] To these we might add the damaging implications of the language used by quite a number of church leaders about those who are homosexual.

The proper relationship between structure and life—where structure should serve and enable life—has been reversed. This is often as true for

---

9. Cozzens, *Notes from the Underground*, 90.

the church as it seems to be for schools, universities, businesses, and many public services, like hospitals. The Sabbath, Scripture tells us, is made for man, not man for the Sabbath. Yet, as Lakeland reminds us,

> At no time in history has the institution behaved more like a corporate giant than it does today, with head offices in Rome and branches throughout the world, staffed by managers called bishops.... [We have had] a pattern of episcopal appointments that has stressed loyalty to the head office over capacity to lead the local church.[10]

Sadly, it seems to me, a very unhealthy climate for ecclesial citizenship has arisen. Centralized control has led to a situation where too many in the hierarchy and even more so in the Curia in Rome are insufficiently honest, open, humble, listening, inclusive, or pastoral in outlook. Where this is true it obscures the gospel, it damages the credibility of the church, and it contributes to the desperate dysfunctionality of the church. Where this is true, it means the church is deaf to the work and voice of God in the world, and this leads to a stifling of creativity, sponsorship of inauthenticity, a stunting of the emergence of responsible discipleship; it has led to the nurture of careerism, priority given to secrecy, and this leaves the way open for abuse of power and dehumanizing manipulation. Such a modus operandi is gravely unethical and seriously disobedient, both to the injunctions of the gospel and to the voice of God as reflected in God's people. A pervasive divine-right construal of authority relies on a faulty understanding of the relationship between divine action and human cooperation, and it leads to a disregard for subsidiarity, excessive centralization, and the prevention of open discussion—treating any emphasis on the need for human consent as inevitably opposed to the discovery of divine truth.

I have for a long time proposed three questions as being very helpful in all kinds of work situations and in organizational relationships. For example, between teachers and students, between more senior staff and more junior ones, between people at one level in an organization and those at another level. It would be worthwhile if these three questions were posed in the context of the church too. First, what am I doing that you do find helpful? If I do not know the answer to that, I might stop doing the very thing that you find helpful. Second, what am I doing that you don't find helpful? If I decide I must still carry on with that, at the very least I owe you an explanation of my reasons for not stopping doing what you don't find helpful. Third, what am I not doing that you would find helpful? Although I cannot guarantee to take on all your suggestions, again I owe you an explanation

---

10. Lakeland, *Liberation of the Laity*, 240.

of why I can accommodate some but not others. To take on board these questions is not to give away authority; it is to exercise it in a way that helps it to be more legitimate.

In contrast, an authority that assumes that it already has the fullness of truth, that it knows all the answers, that is unwilling to face questions, that is not willing to learn from its mistakes, from those on the receiving end of its decisions, from the people it seeks to serve, from perspectives beyond the pale as well as those from within the ranks, from the dissatisfied as well as those who are happy as things are—such an authority is arrogant, blind, deaf—and self-defeating. Such an authority places unnecessary obstacles in the path of the people of God, obstacles to spiritual maturity, responsible discipleship, the development of a robust conscience, effective participation in the life and work of the church, and a flexible and creative response in addressing the needs of the world.

As citizens of the church wanting a more healthy ecclesial community, at the moment we have a situation where access to the Eucharist is treated as less important than preservation of clerical celibacy. And it is one in which the mission of the church is subordinate to its structure, instead of the other way round. This structure currently obscures the fact that laypeople are the vanguard of the church's mission. Compliance with the party line seems more essential for eligibility for leadership than pastoral experience, spiritual wisdom, or capacity to galvanize others into action. No wonder you won't often meet such leaders at the doctor's surgery, sitting next to you on the bus, in the line at the local supermarket checkout, for, outside of special contexts when they are on a pedestal, and usually beyond contradiction, there is not much chance of coming across church leaders where most people are to be found. Obviously there are honorable exceptions among our church leaders to this, for which we are, of course, very grateful.

Let me mention one feature of the church that militates against the development of mature ecclesial citizenship. One sentence stood out for me in an issue of *The Tablet* last year (in 2012). With "More Irish priests silenced by Vatican" in bold, it was stated: "In most cases, the CDF has acted on complaints by anonymous individuals."[11] If this is true, given that we are referring here to comments made by these priests in their talks or writings, not to actions they are accused of taking against individuals, this is a flagrant injustice and, as such, a deeply immoral practice. The default position of those in leadership positions, on receipt of such anonymous complaints, should be threefold. First, the complaints should be immediately destroyed, either by burning or in the shredder. Second, the recipient should pray for the soul

---

11. *Tablet*, "News Briefing."

of the sender, that they may find peace in their disturbed state. Third, such leaders should periodically issue public advice making clear that they do not welcome anonymous complaints and cannot act upon them, and that senders should have very grave reasons indeed if they have not first made every reasonable effort to persuade the person (who is accused of some error) of the nature and significance of that error and, after they have tried this and failed, at least have the decency to alert the person that a complaint will be sent, to whom, and ensuring that the complaint itself is copied to the person accused. This is what is required in order to create the conditions for healthy and honest communication within the church, without which a learning and loving community cannot be built.

## TYPES OF MINISTRY

There are several different types of ministry, for example, there is prophetic ministry, pastoral ministry, protective ministry, and educational ministry. All four of these are needed in the church. The exercise of each one calls for a different style or voice of authority. These four kinds of ministry are exercised by parents. One minute we have to speak out about what is right and what is wrong—by word, by example, and sometimes by using sanctions—our children are not naturally saintly all the time! We have a duty to teach them to think of others; to share; to say sorry, thank you, and please; to make sacrifices; to wait their turn; and so on. This is the prophetic ministry in a minor key; as you can see, it merges into the educational. At another moment, we have to pick up the pieces, mend wounds, heal hurts, make things better, put on plasters, offer medicine; we must accept and forgive—whoever was to blame for the pain. Our helping predominates when we are in pastoral mode. At a third moment, we must work to keep our children safe, without crushing their initiative, imagination, or self-confidence. We must explain why some actions, some places, some situations, perhaps some people, and certainly some kinds of behavior are dangerous. This is a protective ministry. And, often in unexpected ways, we find ourselves being teachers with our children, helping them to learn about bodies, food, animals, nature, other people, and the world around us. In these ways, parents exercise prophetic, pastoral, protective, and educational ministries in the domestic church that is the home; and on a smaller scale than the bigger church.

Unfortunately, in that bigger church, we have experienced for quite some time an unduly narrow exercise of authority and an unbalanced emphasis among these four types of ministry. While I acknowledge that there *is* a legitimate role for all four (prophetic, pastoral, protective, and educational) ministries, it seems to me that we much too often experience the first and the third, that is, the prophetic and the protective, and much less frequently experience the second and the fourth, that is, the pastoral and the educational emphasis. In the prophetic role of the church we hear what is counter to the church's teaching and must be resisted and rejected—and perhaps voted against at the next election or lobbied for in letters to our Member of Parliament. And, for our protection, we note the steps that are taken to prevent the deposit of faith from being contaminated by false interpretations, ensuring the isolation of the simple faithful from misleading theologians and others who might introduce them to errors, in what Cozzens calls "sentinel duty."[12]

## HISTORY WARS AND THE CHURCH

I recently read an article by Richard Evans called "Myth-Busting" in *The Guardian*. It was about recent struggles over the role of history in the school curriculum. As I read this article, I constantly found resonances with struggles in the church. Allow me some license in this fanciful application of mine. I will take three sentences from Evans, and after each one I will briefly reflect on how it might relate to the church and my topic today. You might call these brief comments "history wars applied to the church."

First, "If we want to help young people to develop a sense of citizenship, they have to be able and willing to think for themselves." So, too, if we want to help people, young and not so young, to develop a sense of citizenship in God's kingdom, they have to be able and willing to think for themselves. Insisting that maverick theologians must be censored and silenced in order to prevent the simple faithful from being disturbed—and giving so much credence to the self-appointed Catholic thought police (i.e., the inveterate heresy hunters)—is not the way to equip ecclesial citizens who can think for themselves.

Second, "National identity isn't something that can be manufactured or imposed on a people by a government. It has to emerge organically, by popular consent." Ecclesial identity isn't something that can be manufactured or imposed on a people by the hierarchy or Curia. It has to emerge organically, by drawing upon the experience, insights, and contributions of the people of God.

Third, "Do we want a narrow, partisan, isolationist national identity where foreigners and immigrants are regarded with hostility or suspicion,

---

12. Cozzens, *Notes from the Underground*, 175.

other countries treated as inferior, and triumphalist historical myths are drummed into our children?" Do we want a narrow, partisan, isolationist ecclesial identity where people of other faiths or other Christian denominations or unbelievers are regarded with hostility or suspicion or as inferior and a whitewashed and simplified version of the muddy, erratic, and complex history of the church is drummed into our children and adults?

* * *

Of course, some of this is painful, painful for me to say about a community I have lived, loved, and been committed to all my life; and it is uncomfortable for some people to hear. But pain and frustration, even if overstated, should not be simply suppressed as if they had no right to exist. They need to be brought into the open, reflected on, refuted where necessary, and responded to appropriately.

# BIBLIOGRAPHY

Abelard, Peter. *Sic et Non: A Critical Edition*. Edited by Blanche Boyer and Richard McKeon. Chicago: University of Chicago Press, 1996.
Adams, Nicholas. *Habermas and Theology*. Cambridge: Cambridge University Press, 2006.
Alford, Helen J., and Michael J. Naughton. *Managing as If Faith Mattered: Christian Social Principles in the Modern Organization*. Catholic Social Tradition. Notre Dame, IN: University of Notre Dame Press, 2001.
Anderson, Chris. *Teaching as Believing: Faith in the University*. Studies in Religion and Higher Education. Waco: Baylor University Press, 2004.
Anglican-Roman Catholic International Commission. *Walking Together on the Way: Learning to Be the Church—Local, Regional, Universal; An Agreed Statement of the Third Anglican-Roman Catholic International Commission (ARCIC III)*. London: SPCK, 2018.
Anthony, Cara. "Newman's Idea of a University: A Resource for Identity and Inclusion." *Journal of Catholic Higher Education* 31 (2012) 23–37.
Anthony, Michael J. "Pneumatology and Christian Education." In *A Theology for Christian Education*, by James R. Estep Jr. et al., 147–73. Nashville: B&H Academic, 2008.
Applebee, Arthur N. *Curriculum as Conversation: Transforming Traditions of Teaching and Learning*. Chicago: University of Chicago Press, 1996.
Aquino, Frederick D. *Communities of Informed Judgment: Newman's Illative Sense and Accounts of Rationality*. Washington, DC: Catholic University of America Press, 2004.
Aristotle. *Art of Rhetoric*. Translated by J. H. Freese. LCL. Cambridge, MA: Harvard University Press, 1976.
———. *Art of Rhetoric*. Translated by Hugh Lawson-Tancred. Penguin Classics. London: Penguin, 1991.
———. *Ethics*. Translated by J. A. K. Thomson. Penguin Classics. London: Penguin, 1979.
Arthur, James. *The Ebbing Tide: Policy and Principles of Catholic Education*. Leominster, UK: Gracewing, 1995.
Association of Benedictine Colleges and Universities. "Education Within the Benedictine Wisdom Tradition." University of Mary, Aug. 27, 2007. https://www.umary.edu/sites/default/files/2021-09/Benedictine-Wisdom-Tradition.pdf.
Aucante, Vincent. *Le discernement selon Edith Stein*. Paris: Parole et Silence, 2003.

Augustine. *On Catechizing the Uninstructed*. Translated by E. Phillips Barker. London: Methuen, 1912.

———. *On Christian Teaching*. Translated by R. P. H Green. Oxford World's Classics. Oxford: Oxford University Press, 1997.

Baehr, Jason. *The Inquiring Mind: On Intellectual Virtues and Virtue Epistemology*. Oxford: Oxford University Press, 2011.

Barcan, Ruth. "I Shouldn't Really Be Here." *Times Higher Education* (Jan. 9, 2014) 37–39.

Bass, Dorothy C. "Foreword." In *Educating People of Faith: Exploring the History of Jewish and Christian Communities*, edited by John Van Engen, ix–xiii. Grand Rapids: Eerdmans, 2004.

Bauberot, Jean. *Laïcité 1905–2005: Entre passion et raison*. Paris: Seuil, 2004.

Begley, Ronald B., and Joseph W. Koterski, eds. *Medieval Education*. Fordham Series in Medieval Studies. New York: Fordham University Press, 2005.

Bell, Luke. *Staying Tender*. Brooklyn: Angelico, 2020.

Benedict XVI. "Letter of the Holy Father." Vatican, May 27, 2007. https://www.vatican.va/content/benedict-xvi/en/letters/2007/documents/hf_ben-xvi_let_20070527_china.html.

Benne, Robert. *Quality With Soul: How Six Premier Colleges and Universities Keep Faith with Their Religious Traditions*. Grand Rapids: Eerdmans, 2001.

Bernard of Clairvaux. *On Grace & Free Choice*. Translated by Daniel O'Donovan. Cistercian Fathers 19. Kalamazoo, MI: Cistercian, 1988.

Birkerts, Sven. *The Gutenberg Elegies: The Fate of Reading in an Electronic Age*. New York: Faber and Faber, 2006.

Birzer, Bradley J. *Sanctifying the World: The Augustinian Life and Mind of Christopher Dawson*. Front Royal, VA: Christendom, 2007.

Bishops Conference. "The National Vocations Framework: Helping People Discover Discipleship." Family of Sites, July 2019. https://familyofsites.bishopsconference.org.uk/wp-content/uploads/sites/8/2019/07/national-vocations-framework.pdf.

Blackburn, Simon. Review of *Dishonest to God: On Keeping Religion out of Politics*, by Mary Warnock. *Times Higher Education* (Nov. 4, 2010) 56.

Blair, Anthony L. *Church and Academy in Harmony: Models of Collaboration for the Twenty-First Century*. Eugene, OR: Pickwick, 2010.

Blanchette, Oliva. *Maurice Blondel: A Philosophical Life*. Ressourcement: Retrieval and Renewal in Catholic Thought. Grand Rapids: Eerdmans, 2010.

Bliss, Frederick M. *Understanding Reception: A Backdrop to Its Ecumenical Use*. Marquette Studies in Theology 1. Milwaukee: Marquettte University Press, 1994.

Blondel, Maurice. *L'action*. Paris: Presses Universitaires de France, 1973.

———. *Carnets intimes*. 2 vols. Paris: Cerf, 1961, 1966.

———. *L'être et les êtres*. Paris: Presses Universitaires de France, 1935.

———. *Exigences philosophiques du christianisme*. Paris: Presses Universitaires de France, 1950.

———. "Histoire et dogme." In *Les premiers écrits de Maurice Blondel*, 149–228. Paris: Presses Universitaires de France, 1956.

———. *"Letter on Apologetics" and "History and Dogma."* Translated by Alexander Dru and Illtyd Trethowan. London: Harvill, 1964.

———. *La philosophie et l'esprit chrétien*. 2 vols. Paris: Presses Universitaires de France, 1946.

Blondel, Maurice, and Lucien Laberthonnière. *Correspondance philosophique*. Edited by Claude Tresmontant. Paris: Seuil, 1961.

Blondel, Maurice, and Johannès Wehrlé. *Correspondance*. Edited by Henri de Lubac. 2 vols. Paris: Aubier Montaigne, 1969.

Bonaventure. *On the Reduction of the Arts to Theology*. Translated by Zachary Hayes. New York: St. Bonaventure, 1996.

Borghesi, Massimo. *The Mind of Pope Francis: Jorge Mario Bergoglio's Intellectual Journey*. Collegeville, MN: Liturgical, 2018.

Borysov, Eduard. *Triadosis: Union with the Triune God; Interpretations of the Participationist Dimensions of Paul's Soteriology*. Eugene, OR: Pickwick, 2019.

Bouwens, Jan. "Recontextualizing Catholic School Identity: Five Criteria." In *Teaching and Tradition: On Their Dynamic Interaction*, edited by Jos Moons et al., 150–70. Studies in Catholic Theology 12. Leiden: Brill, 2023.

Breitenstein, Mirko. "The Success of Discipline: The Reception of Hugh of St. Victor's *De institutione novitiorum* Within the 13th and 14th Century." In *Rules and Observance: Devising Forms of Communal Life (Vita regularis: Ordnungen und Deutungen religiosen Lebens im Mittelalter)*, edited by Mirko Breitenstein et al., 183–222. Abhandlung 60. Berlin: Lit, 2014.

Brennan, John. *The Christian Management of Catholic Schools*. Northampton, UK: Becket, 1994.

Brien, S., and J. Hack. "Charism: Promise and Possibility—Part II." *RelEd* 59 (2011) 4–16.

Brown, Delwin. *Boundaries of Our Habitations: Tradition and Theological Construction*. SUNY Series in Religious Studies. New York: State University of New York Press, 1994.

Bruno-Jofré, Rosa, and Jon Igelmo Zaldivar. *Ivan Illich Fifty Years Later: Situating "Deschooling Society" in His Intellectual and Personal Journey*. Toronto: University of Toronto Press, 2022.

———. "Monsignor Ivan Illich's Critique of the Institutional Church, 1960–1966." *JEH* 67 (2016) 568–86. https://doi.org/10.1017/s0022046915003383.

Buchman, Margret, and Robert E. Floden. *Detachment and Concern: Conversations in the Philosophy of Teaching and Teacher Education*. Advances in Contemporary Educational Thought. London: Cassell, 1993.

Bunting, Madeleine. *Willing Slaves: How the Overwork Culture Is Ruling Our Lives*. London: HarperCollins, 2004.

Burbules, Nicholas C. *Dialogue in Teaching: Theory and Practice*. Advances in Contemporary Educational Thought. New York: Teachers College Press, 1993.

Burt, Noel Forlini. "'I Have Called You Friends': Toward a Pedagogy of Friendship in the Classroom." *Journal of Spiritual Formation & Soul Care* 14 (2021) 72–85.

Byrnes, Sholto. Review of *Can Singapore Survive?*, by Kishore Mahbubani. *Times Literary Supplement* 18 (2015) 30.

Callan, Eamonn. *Creating Citizens: Political Education and Liberal Democracy*. Oxford Political Theory. Oxford: Oxford University Press, 1997.

Candler, Peter M., Jr. *Theology, Rhetoric, Manuduction, or Reading Scripture Together on the Path to God*. Radical Traditions. New York: T&T Clark, 2006.

Canon Law Society of Great Britain and Ireland. *The Code of Canon Law*. London: Collins, 1983.

Carmody, Brendan. "Towards a Contemporary Catholic Philosophy of Education." *International Studies in Catholic Education* 3 (2011) 106–19.

Carrón, Julián. *Disarming Beauty: Essays on Faith, Truth, and Freedom. Catholic Ideas for a Secular World*. Notre Dame, IN: University of Notre Dame Press, 2017.

Cary, Philip. *Outward Signs: The Powerlessness of External Things in Augustine's Thought*. Oxford: Oxford University Press, 2008.

Casey, Michael. *Sacred Reading: The Ancient Art of Lectio Divina*. Liguori, MO: Liguori, 1995.

Casson, Ann E. *Fragmented Catholicity and Social Cohesion: Faith Schools in a Plural Society*. Religion, Education and Values 3. Bern: Lang, 2013.

*Catechism of the Catholic Church*. London: Chapman, 1994.

Cavallo, Guglielmo, and Roger Chartier. *A History of Reading in the West*. Translated by Lydia G. Cochrane. Studies in Print Culture and the History of the Book. Cambridge, MA: Polity, 2003.

Cayley, David. *Ivan Illich: An Intellectual Journey*. University Park: Pennsylvania State University Press, 2021.

———. *The Rivers North of the Future: The Testament of Ivan Illich*. Toronto: House of Anansi, 2005.

Cencini, Amadeo. *Éduquer, former, accompagner*. Translated by Maria Zurowska. Paris: Beatitudes, 2005.

Champion, Michael W. *Dorotheus of Gaza and Ascetic Education*. Oxford Early Christian Studies. Oxford: Oxford University Press, 2022.

Chesterton, Gilbert Keith. *The Victorian Age in Literature*. New York: Holt and Co., 1913.

Chittister, Joan. *Between the Dark and the Daylight: Embracing the Contradictions of Life*. New York: Image, 2015.

Claerbaut, David. *Faith and Learning on the Edge: A Bold New Look at Religion in Higher Education*. Grand Rapids: Zondervan, 2004.

Collins, Peter M. "Philosophy in Blessed John Paul II's Catholic University." *Logos: A Journal of Catholic Thought and Culture* 16 (2013) 114–25.

Congregation for Catholic Education (of Seminaries and Educational Institutions). "Educating Together in Catholic Schools: A Shared Mission Between Consecrated Persons and the Lay Faithful." Vatican, Sept. 8, 2007. https://www.vatican.va/roman_curia/congregations/ccatheduc/documents/rc_con_ccatheduc_doc_20070908_educare-insieme_en.html.

———. *The Religious Dimension of Education in a Catholic School: Guidelines for Reflection and Renewal*. London: Catholic Truth Society, 1988.

———. *Vademecum: Global Compact on Education*. Rome: Congregatio de Institutione Catholica (de Studiorum Institutis), 2021. https://drive.google.com/file/d/1mbumGU5BOOFXz-MgAKRBjrgnVlo1dd6A/view.

Congregation for Clergy. *General Directory for Catechesis*. London: Catholic Truth Society, 1997.

Conroy, James, ed. *Catholic Education Inside Out, Outside In*. Dublin: Veritas, 1999.

Conyers, A. J. *The Listening Heart: Vocation and the Crisis of Modern Culture*. Dallas: Spence, 2006.

Cooling, Trevor. *Doing God in Education*. London: Theos, 2010.

Coolman, Boyd Taylor. *Knowing God by Experience: The Spiritual Senses in the Theology of William of Auxerre*. Washington, DC: Catholic University of America Press, 2004.

———. *The Theology of Hugh of St. Victor: An Interpretation*. Cambridge: Cambridge University Press, 2010.

Coq, Guy. *La laïcité: Principe universel*. Paris: Felin, 2005.

———. "Quels sont les enjeux et les conditions d'un engagement dans l'éducation aujourd'hui?" In *Pour l'éducation et pour l'école: Des catholiques s'engagent*, edited by Claude Dagens, 37–49. Paris: Jacob, 2007.

Courtenay, William J. *Rituals for the Dead: Religion and Community in the Medieval University of Paris*. Conway Lectures in Medieval Studies. Notre Dame, IN: University of Notre Dame Press, 2019.

Cozzens, Donald. *Notes from the Underground: The Spiritual Journal of a Secular Priest*. Maryknoll, NY: Orbis, 2013.

Crawford, Marina, and Graham Rossiter. *Missionaries to a Teenage Culture: Religious Education in a Time of Rapid Change*. Strathfield, Aus.: Christian Brothers, 1988.

———. *Reasons for Living: School Education and Young People's Search for Meaning, Identity and Spirituality; A Handbook*. Camberwell, Aus.: Australian Council for Educational Research, 2006. https://asmre.org/rfl/ReasonsForLivingContentsIntroSomeEndorsementsForewordComplete.pdf.

Crosby, John F. *The Personalism of John Henry Newman*. Washington, DC: Catholic University of America Press, 2014.

Csepregi, Gabor. *In Vivo: A Phenomenology of Life-Defining Moments*. Montreal: McGill-Queens University Press, 2019.

Cully, Iris V., and Kendig Brubaker Cully, eds. *Harper's Encyclopedia of Religious Education*. San Francisco: Harper & Row, 1990.

Cunningham, Lawrence S. "Romano Guardini as Sapiential Theologian." In *Romano Guardini: Proclaiming the Sacred in a Modern World*, edited by Robert Anthony Krieg, 61–72. Chicago: Liturgy Training, 1995.

Davignon, Phil. *Practicing Christians, Practical Atheists: How Cultural Liturgies and Everyday Social Practices Shape the Christian Life*. Eugene, OR: Cascade, 2023.

Dawson, Christopher. *The Crisis of Western Education*. London: Sheed and Ward, 1961.

Dianzon, Bernadita. "October 23: Luke 12:39–48." In *Gospel Power 2024*, by Daughters of St. Paul. Liverpool: Pauline, 2023.

Dockery, David S. *Renewing Minds: Serving Church and Society Through Christian Higher Education*. Nashville: B&H, 2007.

Dockery, David S., and Gregory Alan Thornbury. *Shaping a Christian Worldview: The Foundation of Christian Higher Education*. Nashville: B&H, 2002.

D'Orsa, Jim, and Teresa D'Orsa. *Explorers, Guides & Meaning-Makers: Mission Theology for Catholic Educators*. Mission and Education. Mulgrave, Aus.: Garratt, 2010.

Douglass, R. Bruce, and David Hollenbach, eds. *Catholicism and Liberalism: Contributions to American Public Policy*. Cambridge Studies in Religion and American Public Life. Cambridge: Cambridge University Press, 1994.

Downey, Deane E. D., and Stanley E. Porter, eds. *Christian Worldview and the Academic Disciplines: Crossing the Academy*. McMaster General Studies. Eugene, OR: Pickwick, 2009.

Duffy, Eamon. "Who Leads the People?" *Priests & People*, Nov. 2001. https://priestsandpeople.co.uk/cgi-bin/archive_db.cgi?priestsppl-00069.

Dulles, Avery. *Evangelization for the Third Millennium*. New York: Paulist, 2009.

———. *Models of the Church*. Dublin: Gill and Macmillan, 1976.

Dwyer, James G. *Religious Schools v. Children's Rights*. Ithaca, NY: Cornell University Press, 1998.

Egan, Gerard. *Working the Shadow Side: A Guide to Positive Behind-the-Scenes Management*. San Francisco: Jossey-Bass, 1994.

Elder, E. Rozanne. "Formation for Wisdom, Not Education for Knowledge." In *Religious Education in Pre-Modern Europe*, edited by Ilinca Tanaseanu-Döbler and Marvin Döbler, 183–211. Numen 140. Leiden: Brill, 2012.

Elshtain, J. B. "What Have We Learned?" In *Higher Learning and Catholic Traditions*, edited by Robert E. Sullivan, 131–47. Erasmus Institute. Notre Dame, IN: University of Notre Dame Press, 2001.

Estep, James Riley, Jr. "What Makes Education Christian?" In *A Theology for Christian Education*, by James R. Estep Jr. et al., 25–43. Nashville: B&H Academic, 2008.

Evans, Donald. *Spirituality and Human Nature*. SUNY Series in Religious Studies. New York: State University of New York Press, 1993.

———. *Struggle and Fulfillment: The Inner Dynamics of Religion and Morality*. London: Collins, 1980.

Evans, G. R. *Getting It Wrong: The Mediaeval Epistemology of Error*. Studien und Texte zur Geistesgeschichte des Mittelalters 63. Leiden: Brill, 1998.

Evans, Richard J. "Myth-Busting." *Guardian*, July 13, 2013.

Even-Ezra, Ayelet. *Ecstasy in the Classroom: Trance, Self, and the Academic Profession in Medieval Paris*. Fordham Series in Medieval Studies. New York: Fordham University Press, 2019.

Falque, Emmanuel. "Le geste et la parole chez Hugues de Saint-Victor: L'institution des novice." *Revue des sciences philosophiques et théologique* 95 (2011) 383–412.

Farey, Caroline, et al., eds. *The Pedagogy of God: Its Centrality in Catechesis and Catechist Formation*. Steubenville, OH: Emmaus, 2011.

Feinberg, Walter. *For Goodness Sake: Religious Schools and Education for Democratic Citizenry*. New York: Routledge, 2006.

Fergusson, Maggie. "The Listening Cardinal." *Tablet* (Oct. 19, 2024) 4–6.

Fforde, Matthew. "La crise de l'Occident, le postmodernisme et les universités catholiques." In "Sécularisme & universités catholiques," special issue, *Annales de l'ICES* 3 (2013) 21–130.

Finucane, Daniel J. *Sensus Fidelium: The Use of a Concept in the Post–Vatican II Era*. San Francisco: International Scholars, 1996.

Flamand, Jacques. *L'idée de mediation chez M. Blondel*. Leuven: Nauwelaerts, 1969.

Floridi, Luciano. *The Fourth Revolution: How the Infosphere Is Reshaping Human Reality*. Oxford: Oxford University Press, 2014.

Foray, Philippe. *La laïcité scolaire: Autonomie individuelle et apprentissage du monde commun*. Exploration 140. Bern: Lang, 2008.

Francis. *Evangelii Gaudium: The Joy of the Gospel; Apostolic Exhortation on the Proclamation of the Gospel in Today's World*. London: Catholic Truth Society, 2013.

———. *Fratelli Tutti: On Fraternity and Social Friendship*. Encyclical Letter. London: Catholic Truth Society, 2020.

———. *Walking Together: The Way of Synodality*. Maryknoll, NY: Orbis, 2023.

Franchi, Leonardo, and Robert Davis. "Catholic Education and the Idea of Curriculum." *Journal of Catholic Education* 23 (2021) 104–19.
Fraser, James W. *Between Church and State: Religion & Public Education in a Multicultural America*. Basingstoke: Macmillan, 1999.
Freire, Paulo. *Pedagogy of Freedom: Ethics, Democracy, and Civic Courage*. Translated by Patrick Clarke. Critical Perspectives. Lanham, MD: Rowman & Littlefield, 1998.
———. *Pedagogy of the Oppressed*. Harmondsworth: Penguin, 1972.
Gadamer, Hans-Georg. *Truth and Method*. Translated by William-Glen Doepel. Edited by John Cumming and Garrett Barden. London: Sheed and Ward, 1975.
Gallagher, Michael Paul. "University and Culture: Towards a Retrieval of Humanism." *Gregorianum* 85 (2004) 149–71. https://www.jstor.org/stable/23581232.
Gardner, Howard. *Frames of Mind*. London: Fontana, 1993.
———. *Intelligence Reframed: Multiple Intelligences for the 21st Century*. New York: Basic Books, 2000.
———. *The Unschooled Mind: How Children Think & How Schools Should Teach*. London: Fontana, 1993.
Garver, Eugene. *Aristotle's Rhetoric: An Art of Character*. Chicago: University of Chicago Press, 1994.
Gascoigne, Robert. *The Public Forum & Christian Ethics*. New Studies in Christian Ethics 19. Cambridge: Cambridge University Press, 2001.
Georgedes, Kimberly. "Religion, Education, and the Role of Government in Medieval Universities: Lessons Learned or Lost?" *Forum on Public Policy* 2 (2006) 73–96.
Gibran, Kahlil. *The Prophet*. London: Heinemann, 1984.
Gil, Alberto, and Guido Gili. "Transmission or 'Creative Fidelity'? The Institutional Communicator's Role in the Church today." *Church, Communication and Culture* 5 (2020) 320–38.
Gillis, Chester. "Welcoming the Religiously Other to a Catholic University." *Integritas* [Boston College] 1 (2013) 1–18.
Gilson, Étienne. "The Eminence of Teaching." In *A Gilson Reader: Selections from the Writing of Étienne Gilson*, edited by Anton C. Pegis, 298–311. New York: Doubleday, 1957.
Giussani, Luigi. *The Risk of Education: Discovering Our Ultimate Destiny*. New York: Crossroad, 1995.
Glenn, Charles L. *The Ambiguous Embrace: Government and Faith-Based Schools and Social Agencies*. New Forum. Princeton, NJ: Princeton University Press, 2000.
Goethe, Johann Wolfgang von. *Goethe's "Faust": Part One*. Translated by Randall Jarrell. New York: Farrar, Straus & Giroux, 1976.
Golde, Chris M. "Preparing Stewards of the Discipline." In *Envisioning the Future of Doctoral Education: Preparing Stewards of the Discipline*, edited by Chris M. Golde and George E. Walker, 3–20. Carnegie Essays on the Doctorate. San Francisco: Jossey-Bass, 2006.
Grace, Gerald. *Catholic Schools: Mission, Markets, and Morality*. London: Routledge, 2002.
Gracia, Jorge J. E. *Old Wine in New Skins: The Role of Tradition in Communication, Knowledge, and Group Identity*. Aquinas Lecture. Milwaukee: Marquette University Press, 2003.
Graiver, Inbar. *Asceticism of the Mind: Forms of Attention and Self-Transformation in Late Antique Monasticism*. Toronto: Pontifical Institute of Medieval Studies, 2021.

Green, Elizabeth. "Distinctively Christian Pedagogy." In *Re-Imagining Christian Education for the 21st Century*, edited by Andrew B. Morris, 213–23. Chelmsford, UK: James, 2013.

Gregorian, Vartan. "Higher Education in an Age of Specialized Knowledge." In *Orthodoxy and Western Culture: A Collection of Essays Honoring Jaroslav Pelikan on His Eightieth Birthday*, edited by Valerie Hotchkiss and Patrick Henry, 139–64. Crestwood, NY: St. Vladimir's Seminary Press, 2005.

Gregory, Brad S. *The Unintended Reformation: How a Religious Revolution Secularized Society*. Cambridge, MA: Belknap, 2012.

Grey, Carmody, and Oliver Dürr. "On Changing the Subject: 'Secularity', 'Religion', and the Idea of the Human." *Religions* 14 (2023) 466 (1–18). https://doi.org/10.3390/rel14040466.

Griffiths, Paul. "Reading as a Spiritual Discipline." In *The Scope of Our Art: The Vocation of the Theological Teacher Paperback*, edited by L. Gregory Jones and Stephanie Paulsell, 32–47. Grand Rapids: Eerdmans, 2002.

———. *Religious Reading: The Place of Reading in the Practice of Religion*. New York: Oxford University Press, 1999.

Groome, Tom. *Educating for Life: A Spiritual Vision for Every Teacher and Parent*. Allen, TX: Thomas More, 1998.

Grossman, Edith. *Why Translation Matters*. Why X Matters. New Haven, CT: Yale University Press, 2010.

Guardini, Romano. *The End of the Modern World*. Wilmington, DE: Intercollegiate Studies Institute, 1998.

———. *Living the Drama of Faith: What Faith Is and Where It Leads You*. Manchester, NH: Sophia Institute, 1998.

———. *The Spirit of the Liturgy*. Translated by Ada Lane. New York: Crossroad, 1998.

———. *La vision catholique du monde*. Translated by Vincent Billot and Caroline Blanchet-Tilkin. Roma: Chora, 2019.

Gushurst-Moore, André. *Glory in All Things: Saint Benedict & Catholic Education Today*. Brooklyn: Angelico, 2020.

Halík, Tomáš. *Night of the Confessor: Christian Faith in an Age of Uncertainty*. Translated by Gerald Turner. New York: Image, 2012.

———. *Patience with God: The Story of Zacchaeus Continuing In Us*. Translated by Gerald Turner. New York: Doubleday, 2009.

———. "The Way, the Truth and the Life." *Tablet* (Feb. 11, 2023) 8–9.

Halverson, James L. "Restored Through Learning: Hugh of Saint Victor's Vision for Higher Education." *Christian Scholar's Review* 41 (2011) 35–58.

Hamilton, Michael S., and James A. Mathisen. "Faith and Learning at Wheaton." In *Models for Christian Higher Education: Strategies for Success in the Twenty-First Century*, edited by Richard T. Hughes and William B. Adrian, 261–83. Grand Rapids: Eerdmans, 1997.

Harkins, Franklin T. *Reading and the Work of Restoration: History and Scripture in the Theology of Hugh of St. Victor*. Edited by Joseph Goering and Giulio Silano. Mediaeval Law and Theology 2. Studies and Texts 167. Toronto: Pontifical Institute of Medieval Studies, 2009.

Harmon, Steve. *Towards Baptist Catholicity: Essays on Tradition and the Baptist Vision*. Studies in Baptist History and Thought. Carlisle, UK: Paternoster, 2006.

Harris, Robert A. *The Integration of Faith and Learning: A Worldview Approach.* Eugene, OR: Cascade, 2004.

Harrison, Verna. *God's Many-Splendored Image: Theological Anthropology for Christian Formation.* Grand Rapids: Baker Academic, 2010.

Haughey, John C. *Where Is Knowing Going? The Horizons of the Knowing Subject.* Washington, DC: Georgetown University Press, 2009.

Hayes, Michael A., and Liam Gearon, eds. *Contemporary Catholic Education.* Leominster, UK: Gracewing, 2002.

Herdt, Jennifer A. *Putting on Virtue: The Legacy of the Splendid Vices.* Chicago: University of Chicago Press, 2008.

Herrick, Vanessa, and Ivan Mann. *Jesus Wept: Reflections on Vulnerability in Leadership.* London: Darton, Longman & Todd, 1998.

Heywood, David. *Divine Revelation and Human Learning: A Christian Theory of Knowledge.* Explorations in Practical, Pastoral and Empirical Theology. Aldershot, UK: Ashgate, 2004.

———. *Kingdom Learning: Experiential and Reflective Approaches to Christian Formation.* London: SCM, 2017.

Hicks, Douglas A. *Religion and the Workplace: Pluralism, Spirituality, Leadership.* Cambridge: Cambridge University Press, 2003.

Higginson, Richard. *Transforming Leadership: A Christian Approach to Management; Based on the London Lectures in Contemporary Christianity.* London: SPCK, 1996.

Hildebrand, Dietrich von. *The Heart: An Analysis of Human and Divine Affectivity.* Edited by John Henry Crosby. South Bend, IN: St. Augustine's, 2007.

Himes, Michael. "Communicating the Faith." In *Handing On the Faith: The Church's Mission and Challenge*, edited by Robert P. Imbelli, 109–29. Church in the 21st Century. New York: Herder & Herder, 2006.

Hogan, Pádraig. *The Custody and Courtship of Experience: Western Education in Philosophical Perspective.* Maynooth Bicentenary. Dublin: Columba, 1995.

———. *The New Significance of Learning: Imagination's Heartwork.* Abingdon: Routledge, 2010.

Hoinacki, Lee. "The Trajectory of Ivan Illich." *Bulletin of Science, Technology & Society* 23 (2003) 382–89. https://doi.org/10.1177/0270467603259776.

Horsfield, Peter. *From Jesus to the Internet: A History of Christianity and Media.* Chichester: Wiley-Blackwell, 2015.

Horujy, Sergey S. *Practices of the Self and Spiritual Practices: Michel Foucault and the Eastern Christian Discourse.* Edited by Kristina Stoeckl. Translated by Boris Jakim. Grand Rapids: Eerdmans, 2015.

Hügel, Friedrich von. *Essays and Addresses on the Philosophy of Religion.* London: Dent, 1921.

———. *Essays and Addresses on the Philosophy of Religion.* 2nd ser. London: Dent, 1926.

———. *Eternal Life: A Study of Its Implications.* Edinburgh: T&T Clark, 1913.

———. *Letters from Baron Friedrich von Hügel to a Niece.* Edited by Gwendolen Greene. London: Dent, 1928.

———. *The Mystical Element of Religion.* 2 vols. London: Dent, 1908.

———. *"The Reality of God" and "Religion & Agnosticism": Being the Literary Remains of Baron Friedrich von Hügel.* Edited by Edmund Gardner. London: Dent, 1931.

———. *Selected Letters, 1896–1924.* London: Dent, 1927.

Hügel, Fredrich von, and Norman Kemp Smith. *The Letters of Baron Friedrich von Hügel and Professor Norman Kemp Smith*. Edited by Lawrence F. Barmann. New York: Fordham University Press, 1981.

Hugh of Saint Victor. "De institutione novitiorum." In *L'oeuvre de Hugues de Saint-Victor*, edited by Hugh Feiss and Patrice Sicard, 1:18–99. Turnhout, Belg.: Brepols, 1997.

———. *The Didascalicon: A Medieval Guide to the Arts*. Edited and translated by Jerome Taylor. Records of Western Civilization. New York: Columbia University Press, 1991.

———. *Hugh of Saint Victor on the Sacraments of the Christian Faith (De Sacramentis)*. Translated by Roy J. Deferrari. Eugene: OR: Wipf & Stock, 2007.

———. *Selected Spiritual Writings*. Translated by a Religious of CSMV. Eugene, OR: Wipf & Stock, 1962.

———. *Soliloquy on the Earnest Money of the Soul*. Translated by Kevin Herbert. Milwaukee: Marquette University Press, 1956.

Hughes, Kyle R. *Teaching for Spiritual Formation: A Patristic Approach to Christian Education in a Convulsed Age*. Eugene, OR: Cascade, 2022.

Hugonis de Sancto Victore. *Didascalicon de Studio Legendi: A Critical Text*. Edited by Charles Henry Buttimer. Washington, DC: Catholic University of America Press, 1939.

Hull, John. "Christian Theology and Educational Theory: Can There Be Connections?" *British Journal of Educational Studies* 24 (1976) 127–43.

Hunt, Thomas C., et al., eds. *Catholic School Leadership: An Invitation to Lead*. London: Falmer, 2000.

Hunter, James Davison. *To Change the World: The Irony, Tragedy, and Possibility of Christianity in the Late Modern World*. New York: Oxford University Press, 2010.

Ibarra, Luz M. *Maritain, Religion, and Education: A Theocentric Humanism Approach*. American University Studies 326. New York: Lang, 2013.

Illich, Ivan. "The Educational Enterprise in the Light of the Gospel." David Tinapple, Nov. 13, 1988. Lecture manuscript. Edited by Lee Hoinacki. https://www.davidtinapple.com/illich/1988_Educational.html.

———. *In the Mirror of the Past: Lectures and Addresses 1978–1990*. New York: Boyars, 1992.

———. *In the Vineyard of the Text: A Commentary to Hugh's "Didascalicon."* Chicago: University of Chicago Press, 1993.

———. "Lima Discourse: A Paper Read to the World Council of Christian Education Conference in Lima, Peru, on 18th July 1971." *Learning for Living* 13 (1974) 85–89. https://doi.org/10.1080/00239707408557026.

———. *Medical Nemesis: The Expropriation of Health*. London: Calder & Boyars, 1975.

———. *"The Powerless Church" and Other Selected Writings, 1955–1985*. Assembled by Valentina Borremans and Sajay Samuel. Ivan Illich: 21st-Century Perspectives. University Park: Pennsylvania State University Press, 2018.

International Theological Commission. "Synodality in the Life and Mission of the Church." Vatican, Mar. 2, 2018. https://www.vatican.va/roman_curia/congregations/cfaith/cti_documents/rc_cti_20180302_sinodalita_en.html.

Irving, Justin A., and Mark L. Strauss. *Leadership in Christian Perspective: Biblical Foundations and Contemporary Practices for Servant Leaders*. Grand Rapids: Baker Academic, 2019.

Irving-Stonebraker, Sarah. *Priests of History: Stewarding the Past in an Ahistoric Age.* Nashville: Zondervan Academic, 2024.
Jacobsen, Douglas, and Rhonda Hustedt Jacobsen, eds. *Scholarship & Christian Faith: Enlarging the Conversation.* New York: Oxford University Press, 2004.
Jaeger, C. Stephen. *The Envy of Angels: Cathedral Schools and Social Ideals in Medieval Europe, 950–1200.* Middle Ages. Philadelphia: University of Pennsylvania Press, 1994.
Jensen, Stephen. "Faith Integration and the Irreducible Metaphors of Disciplinary Discourse." *Christian Scholars Review* 39 (2009) 37–55.
John Paul II. *Catechesi Tradendae/On Catechesis in Our Time.* London: Catholic Truth Society, 1979.
———. *On Catholic Universities:* Ex Corde Ecclesiae. Apostolic Constitution. Washington, DC: United States Catholic Conference, 1996.
———. *The Splendor of Truth:* Veritatis Splendor; *Regarding Certain Fundamental Questions of the Church's Moral Teaching.* Encyclical Letter. Washington, DC: United States Conference of Catholic Bishops, 1993.
Joseph, Ellis A. "Philosophical Foundations of the Catholic College and University Curriculum." In *Handbook of Research in Catholic Higher Education*, edited by Thomas C. Hunt et al., 137–54. Greenwich, CT: Information Age, 2003.
Kampowski, Stephan. *Embracing Our Finitude: Exercises in Christian Anthropology Between Dependence and Gratitude.* Eugene, OR: Cascade, 2018.
Kanpol, Barry, and May Poplin. *Christianity and the Secular Border Control: The Loss of Judeo-Christian Knowledge.* Critical Education and Ethics 9. New York: Lang, 2017.
Kapic, Kelly. Review of *God's Provision, Humanity's Need: The Gift of Our Dependence*, by Christa McKirkland. *Studies in Christian Ethics* 36 (2023) 954–57.
Kay, William K., and Leslie J. Francis, eds. *Distance Learning.* Vol. 4 of *Religion in Education.* Leominster, UK: Gracewing, 2003.
Keator, Mary. *Lectio Divina as Contemplative Pedagogy: Re-Appropriating Monastic Practice for the Humanities.* Routledge Research in Education. London: Routledge, 2019.
Keenan, James F. "Proposing Cardinal Virtues." *TS* 56 (1995) 709–29.
Kegan, Robert. *In Over Our Heads: The Mental Demands of Modern Life.* Cambridge, MA: Harvard University Press, 1994.
Kelly, James J. *Baron Friedrich von Hügel's Philosophy of Religion.* BETL. Leuven: Leuven University Press, 1983.
Kivy, Peter. *The Performance of Reading: An Essay in the Philosophy of Literature.* New Directions in Aesthetics. Oxford: Blackwell, 2006.
Klassen, Norman, and Jens Zimmermann. *The Passionate Intellect: Incarnational Humanism and the Future of University Education.* Grand Rapids: Baker Academic, 2006.
Kreiner, Jamie. *The Wandering Mind: What Medieval Monks Tell Us About Distraction.* New York: Liveright, 2023.
Krieg, Robert A. *Romano Guardini: A Precursor of Vatican II.* Notre Dame, IN: University of Notre Dame Press, 1997.
———, ed. *Romano Guardini: Proclaiming the Sacred in a Modern World.* Chicago: Liturgy Training, 1995.

Lacey, Michael J. "Prologue: The Problem of Authority and Limits." In *The Crisis of Authority in Catholic Modernity*, edited by Michael J. Lacey and Francis Oakley, 1–27. New York: Oxford University Press, 2011.

Lafforgue, Laurent. "La recherché fondamentale a-t-elle un sens?" *Comm* 38 (2013) 27–41.

Lakeland, Paul. *The Liberation of the Laity: In Search of an Accountable Church*. New York: Continuum, 2003.

Lavelle, Louis. *The Dilemma of Narcissus*. Translated by William Gairdner. New York: Larson, 1993.

Lawler, M. G., and T. A. Salzman. "Virtue Ethics: Natural and Christian." *TS* 74 (2013) 442–73.

Leclercq, Jean. *The Love of Learning and the Desire for God: A Study of Monastic Culture*. Translated by Catharine Misrahi. London: SPCK, 1978.

Lee-Barker, Jane. *God's World. No String Puppets: Providence in the Writings of Romano Guardini*. Eugene, OR: Pickwick, 2022.

Leonard, Richard. "A Season of Joy." *Tablet* (Mar. 4, 2023) 10–11.

Levinson, Meira. *The Demands of Liberal Education*. Oxford: Oxford University Press, 1999.

Levisohn, Jon A., et al. "How to Do Philosophy of Religious Education?" *RelEd* 100 (2005) 90–106. https://doi.org/10.1080/00344080590904725.

Leyerle, Blake. "Monastic Formation and Christian Practice: Food in the Desert." In *Educating People of Faith: Exploring the History of Jewish and Christian Communities*, edited by John Van Engen, 85–112. Grand Rapids: Eerdmans, 2004.

Lichtmann, Maria. *The Teacher's Way: Teaching and the Contemplative Life*. New York: Paulist, 2005.

Linnig, Waltraud. "The Pedagogy of God: Source and Model for the Pedagogy of the Faith." In *The Pedagogy of God: Its Centrality in Catechesis and Catechist Formation*, edited by Caroline Farey et al., 151–62. Steubenville, OH: Emmaus, 2011.

Litfin, Duane. *Conceiving the Christian College*. Grand Rapids: Eerdmans, 2004.

Loader, David. *The Inner Principal: Student Outcomes and the Reform of Education*. London: Falmer, 1997.

Lonergan, Bernard J. *Insight: A Study of Human Understanding*. London: Darton, Longman & Todd, 1958.

———. *Method in Theology*. London: Darton, Longman & Todd, 1972.

Long, Micol, et al., eds. *Horizontal Learning in the High Middle Ages: Peer-to-Peer Knowledge Transfer in Religious Communities*. Knowledge Communities 7. Amsterdam: Amsterdam University Press, 2019.

Lose, D. J. "How Do We Make Space for Students to Seek Truth? Teaching with Conviction." In *Teaching Reflectively in Theological Contexts: Promises and Contradictions*, edited by Mary E. Hess and Stephen D. Brookfield, 19–31. Malabar, FL: Krieger, 2008.

Losinger, Anton. *Relative Autonomy: The Key to Understanding Vatican II*. Frankfurt am Main: Lang, 1997.

Loughlin, Michael. *Ethics, Management and Mythology: Rational Decision Making for Health Service Professionals*. Abingdon, UK: Radcliffe Medical, 2002.

Lubac, Henri de. *Paradoxes of Faith*. San Francisco: Ignatius, 1987.

BIBLIOGRAPHY

Lucas, Hanna J. *Sensing the Sacred: Recovering a Mystagogical Vision of Knowledge and Salvation*. Veritas. Eugene, OR: Cascade, 2023.

MacInnis, John. "Theological Education as Formation for Ministry." In *Theological Literacy for the Twenty-First Century*, edited by Rodney L. Petersen with Nancy M. Rourke, 382–91. Grand Rapids: Eerdmans, 2002.

MacIntyre, Alasdair. *After Virtue*. London: Duckworth, 1985.

———. "Catholic Universities: Dangers, Hopes, Choices." In *Higher Learning and Catholic Traditions*, edited by Robert E. Sullivan, 1–21. Erasmus Institute. Notre Dame, IN: University of Notre Dame Press, 2001.

———. *Rational Dependent Animals*. London: Duckworth, 1999.

———. *Three Versions of Moral Enquiry*. London: Duckworth, 1990.

———. *Whose Justice? Which Rationality?* London: Duckworth, 1988.

Marcel, Gabriel. *A Gabriel Marcel Reader*. Edited by Brenda Sweetman. South Bend, IN: St. Augustine's, 2011.

Maritain, Jacques. *Education at the Crossroads*. New Haven, CT: Yale University Press, 1943.

Martin, Janet Roland. *Education Reconfigured: Culture, Encounter, and Change*. London: Routledge, 2011.

Martin, Mike W. *Meaningful Work: Rethinking Professional Ethics*. Practical and Professional Ethics. New York: Oxford University Press, 2000.

Marty, Martin E., with Jonathan Moore. *Education, Religion and the Common Good: Advancing a Distinctly American Conversation About Religion's Role in Our Shared Life*. San Francisco: Jossey-Bass, 2000.

Mascall, E. L. *The Openness of Being: Natural Theology Today*. London: Darton, Longman & Todd, 1971.

Maspero, Giulio. *After the Pandemic, After Modernity: The Relational Revolution*. South Bend, IN: St. Augustine's, 2022.

Masson, Catherine. "L'université catholique de Lille: Quelle catholicité?" In "Sécularisme & universités catholiques," special issue, *Annales de l'ICES* 3 (2013) 131–51.

Mattam, Joseph. "Inculturated Evangelization & Conversion." *TD* 50 (2003) 229–35.

McDonough, Graham P. *Beyond Obedience and Abandonment: Toward a Theory of Dissent in Catholic Education*. Montreal: McGill-Queen's University Press, 2012.

McGilchrist, Iain. *The Master and His Emissary: The Divided Brain and the Making of the Western World*. New Haven, CT: Yale University Press, 2009.

McGrath, John A. *Baron Friedrich von Hügel and the Debate on Historical Christianity*. San Francisco: Mellen Research University Press, 1993.

McGregor, Peter. J. "Resources for a Theological Anthropology of the Heart." In *Theological Anthropology at the Beginning of the Third Millennium*, edited by Kevin Wagner et al., 228–53. Theology at the Beginning of the Third Millennium. Eugene, OR: Pickwick, 2022.

McKinney, Stephen J., and John Sullivan, eds. *Education in a Catholic Perspective*. Aldershot, UK: Ashgate, 2013.

———. "Exploring Practical Implications." In *Education in a Catholic Perspective*, edited by Stephen J. McKinney and John Sullivan, 209–25. Aldershot, UK: Ashgate, 2013.

McLaughlin, Terence, et al., eds. *The Contemporary Catholic School: Context, Identity and Diversity*. London: Falmer, 1996.

McLaughlin, Terence H. "Values, Coherence and the School." *Cambridge Journal of Education* 24 (1994) 453–70.

McLuhan, Marshall. *The Medium and the Light: Reflections on Religion and Media*. Edited by Eric McLuhan and Jacek Szklarek. Eugene, OR: Wipf & Stock, 2010.

———. *Understanding Media: The Extensions of Man*. London: Ark, 1987.

Medley, Mark S. "Stewards, Interrogators, and Inventors: Toward a Practice of Tradition." *ProEccl* 18 (2009) 69–92.

Melina, Livio. *The Epiphany of Love: Toward a Theological Understanding of Christian Action*. Retrieval & Renewal in Catholic Thought. Grand Rapids: Eerdmans, 2010.

Mendlewicz, Miquel Seguró. *On Vulnerability: A Philosophical Anthropology*. Translated by Silvia Ardevol. Lanham, MD: Lexington, 2024.

Milis, Ludo J. R. *Angelic Monks and Earthly Men: Monasticism and Its Meaning to Medieval Society*. Woodbridge, UK: Boydell, 1992.

Millare, Roland. "The Hermeneutic of Continuity and Discontinuity Between Romano Guardini and Joseph Ratzinger: The Primacy of Logos." *NV* 18 (2020) 521–63. https://doi.org/10.1353/nov.2020.0034.

———. "The Primacy of Logos over Ethos: The Influence of Romano Guardini on Post-Conciliar Theology." *HeyJ* 57 (6) (2016) 974–83. https://doi.org/10.1111/heyj.12029.

Miller, J. A. "On the Way to Divine Providence: From the Abyss of Time to the Throne of Eternity." *TS* 84 (2023) 657–78.

Miller, Colin. "Ivan Illich, Catholic Theologian (Part I)." *ProEccl* 26 (2017) 81–110. https:// doi.org/10.1177/106385121702600109.

Miller, Michael R., ed. *Doing More With Life: Connecting Christian Higher Education to a Call to Service*. Studies in Religion and Higher Education. Waco: Baylor University Press, 2007.

Möhler, Johann Adam. *Unity in the Church, or, the Principle of Catholicism: Presented in the Spirit of the Church Fathers of the First Three Centuries*. Translated by Peter C. Erb. Washington, DC: Catholic University of America Press, 1996.

Moog, François. *À quoi sert l'école catholique*. Paris: Bayard, 2012.

Mougniotte, Alain. *Maritain et l'éducation*. Paris: Bosco, 1997.

Nagel, Thomas. *Equality and Impartiality*. New York: Oxford University Press, 1991.

Newman, John Henry. *The Development of Christian Doctrine*. London: Sheed and Ward, 1960.

———. *An Essay in Aid of a Grammar of Assent*. Notre Dame, IN: University of Notre Dame Press, 1979.

———. *The Idea of a University*. London: Longmans, Green & Co., 1912.

———. "Letter to the Duke of Norfolk." In *Difficulties of Anglicans*, 179–378. London: Pickering, 1876.

———. *Parochial and Plain Sermons*. 2 vols. London: Rivingtons, 1868.

———. *University Sermons*. London: SPCK, 1970.

Nicholson-Ward, Lauren. "The Questions That Only Children Have the Ability to Ask, Deserved to Be Heard." *Tablet* (Nov. 28, 2015) 9–10.

Norris, Louis William. *Polarity: A Philosophy of Tensions Among Values*. Chicago: Regnery, 1956.

Norton, David L. *Imagination, Understanding, and the Virtue of Liberality*. Lanham, MD: Rowman & Littlefield, 1996.

Nussbaum, Martha C. *Not For Profit: Why Democracy Needs the Humanities*. Public Square. Princeton, NJ: Princeton University Press, 2010.

O'Loughlin, Tom. "The Credibility of the Catholic Church as Public Actor." *New Blackfriars* 94 (2013) 129–47. https://doi.org/10.1111/nbfr.12011.

Ong, Walter J. *Orality and Literacy: The Technologizing of the Word*. London: Routledge, 1982.

———. *The Presence of the Word*. New Haven, CT: Yale University Press, 1967.

Orji, Cyril. *The Catholic University and the Search for Truth*. Winona, MN: Anselm Academic, 2013.

Orphanopoulos, C. M. "Reframing Vulnerability Through an Embodied Theological Lens: Towards Ethical Engagement in a Globalized Context." *Religions* 15 (2024) 766 (1–20). https://doi.org/10.3390/rel15070766.

Ostler, Nicholas. *Ad Infinitum: A Biography of Latin*. London: Harper, 2007.

Palmer, Parker J. *To Know as We Are Known: Education as a Spiritual Journey*. San Francisco: Harper & Row, 1983.

Pattison, Stephen. *The Faith of the Managers: When Management Becomes Religion*. London: Cassell, 1997.

Paul VI. "*Gaudium et Spes*: On the Church in the Modern World." Vatican, Dec. 7, 1965. https://www.vatican.va/archive/hist_councils/ii_vatican_council/documents/vat-ii_const_19651207_gaudium-et-spes_en.html.

Pelias, Ronald J. *A Methodology of the Heart: Evoking Academic and Daily Life*. Walnut Creek, CA: AltaMira, 2004.

Pena-Ruiz, Henri. *Dieu et Marianne: Philosophie de la laïcité*. Paris: Presses Universitaires de France, 1999.

Peters, Greg. *The Monkhood of all Believers: The Monastic Foundation of Christian Spirituality*. Grand Rapids: Baker Academic, 2018.

Peters, John Durham. *Speaking into the Air: A History of the Idea of Communication*. Chicago: University of Chicago Press, 1999.

Pike, Mark. "From Beliefs to Skills: The Secularization of Literacy and the Moral Development of Citizens." *Journal of Beliefs & Values* 27 (2006) 281–89.

———. "The Bible and the Reader's Response." *Journal of Education & Christian Belief* 7 (2003) 37–51.

Pius X. *Vehementer Nos*. Rome: Libreria Editrice Vaticana, 1906.

———. "*Vehementer Nos*: On the French Law of Separation." Vatican, Feb. 11, 1906. https://www.vatican.va/content/pius-x/en/encyclicals/documents/hf_p-x_enc_11021906_vehementer-nos.html.

Poirel, Dominique. "The Spirituality and Theology of Beauty in Hugh of St. Victor." In *From Knowledge to Beatitude: St. Victor, Twelfth-Century Scholars, and Beyond; Essays in Honor of Grover A. Zinn, Jr.*, edited by E. Ann Matter and Lesley Smith, 247–80. Notre Dame, IN: University of Notre Dame Press, 2013.

Pontifical Council for Justice and Peace. *Compendium of the Social Doctrine of the Church*. Rome: Libreria Editrice Vaticana, 2004.

Pontifical Council for Promoting New Evangelization. *Directory for Catechesis*. London: Catholic Truth Society, 2020.

Poplin, Mary. "The Radical Call to Service: The Five Tasks." In *Gladly Learn, Gladly Teach: Living Out One's Calling in the Twenty-First-Century Academy*, edited by John Marson Dunaway, 146–71. Macon: Mercer University Press, 2005.

Porwoll, Robert John. "Parisian Pedagogies: The Educational Debate Between Peter Abelard, Hugh of St. Victor, Peter Lombard, and John of Salisbury." PhD diss., University of Chicago, 2019.

Postman, Neil. *Amusing Ourselves to Death*. London: Methuen, 1987.

———. *The End of Education*. New York: Vintage, 1996.

Postman, Neil, and Charles Weingartner. *Teaching as a Subversive Activity*. London: Penguin, 1971.

Poulat, Emile. *Notre laïcité publique: "La France est une république laïque" (Constitutions de 1946 et 1958)*. Paris: Berg International, 2003.

Powers, Patrick. "Catholic Education and Formation in the Arts and Sciences: Listening to Josef Pieper and Hugh of Saint Victor." In *Leisure and Labor: Essays on the Liberal Arts in Catholic Higher Education*, edited by Anthony P. Coleman, 79–90. Lanham, MD: Rowman & Littlefield, 2020.

Purves, Alan C. *The Web of Text and the Web of God: An Essay on the Third Information Transformation*. New York: Guilford, 1998.

Radner, Ephraim. *A Time to Keep: Theology, Mortality, and the Shape of a Human Life*. Waco: Baylor University Press, 2016.

Ratzinger, Josef. "Chapter 1" [no further title]. In *Commentary on the Documents of Vatican II*, edited by Herbert Vorgrimler, 5:115–63. New York: Herder and Herder, 1967.

———. *On the Pastoral Care of the Divorced and Remarried*. Rome: Libreria Editrice Vaticana, 1998.

Rengger, Nicholas. "The Idea of Politics in a Christian University." In *The Idea of a Christian University: Essays on Theology and Higher Education*, edited by Jeff Astley et al., 234–45. Milton Keynes: Paternoster, 2004.

Ricard, Jean-Pierre. "Ouverture du colloque." In "Sécularisme & universités catholiques," special issue, *Annales de l'ICES* 3 (2013) 93–96.

Ricoeur, Paul. *On Translation*. Translated by Eileen Brennan. Thinking in Action. London: Routledge, 2006.

Roberts, Robert C., and W. Jay Wood. *Intellectual Virtues: An Essay in Regulative Epistemology*. Oxford: Clarendon, 2007.

Rohr, Richard, with Joseph Martos. *Why Be Catholic? Understanding Our Experience and Tradition*. Cincinnati: St. Anthony Messenger, 1989.

Rolheiser, Ronald. *Domestic Monastery*. London: Darton, Longman & Todd, 2019.

Rorem, Paul. *Hugh of Saint Victor*. Great Medieval Thinkers. Oxford: Oxford University Press, 2009.

Rosenblatt, Louise M. *The Reader, the Text, the Poem: The Transactional Theory of the Literary Work*. Carbondale: Southern Illinois University Press, 1978.

Rosser, Gervase. *The Art of Solidarity in the Middle Ages: Guilds in England 1250–1550*. Oxford: Oxford University Press, 2015.

Rossiter, Graham. "Religious Education: Where to from Here? Reflections on the Trajectory of Australian Catholic School Religious Education 1965–2017." In *Christian Faith, Formation and Education*, edited by Ros Stuart-Buttle and John Shortt, 181–96. London: Palgrave Macmillan, 2018.

———. "What Sort of School Religious Education Is Needed? And Why Is It So Important Today?" In *Does Religious Education Matter?*, edited by Mary Shanahan, 25–36. London: Routledge, 2017.

Rowland, Tracey. *Beyond Kant and Nietzsche: The Munich Defence of Christian Humanism*. Edited by Francesca Aran Murphy and Balázs M. Mezei. Illuminating Modernity. London: T&T Clark, 2021.

Rule, Philip C. *Coleridge and Newman: The Centrality of Conscience*. Studies in Religion and Literature 8. New York: Fordham University Press, 2004.

Rus, Éric de. *L'art d'éduquer selon Edith Stein: Anthropologie, éducation, vie spirituelle*. Cahier d'études steiniennes 1. Paris: Cerf, 2008.

———. *Intériorité de la personne et education chez Edith Stein: La nuit surveillée*. Paris: Cerf, 2006.

Rush, Ormond. *The Eyes of Faith: The Sense of the Faithful and the Church's Reception of Revelation*. Washington, DC: Catholic University of America Press, 2009.

———. *The Reception of Doctrine: An Appropriation of Hans Robert Jauss' Reception Aesthetics and Literary Hermeneutics*. Rome: Editrice Pontificia Universita Gregoriana, 1997.

Saint-Jean, Raymond. *L'apologétique philosophique: Blondel 1893–1913*. Paris: Desclée de Brouwer, 1966.

Salzmann, Andrew. "The Soul's Reformation and the Arts in Hugh of St. Victor: A Book Written Twice Without." In *Handbook to Medieval Christian Humanism: Essays on Principal Thinkers*, edited by John P. Bequette, 142–67. Companions to the Christian Tradition 69. Leiden: Brill, 2016.

Sarisky, Darren, ed. *Theologies of Retrieval: An Exploration and Appraisal*. London: T&T Clark, 2019.

Scharer, Matthias, and Bernd Jochen Hilberath. *The Practice of Communicative Theology: An Introduction to a New Theological Culture*. New York: Crossroad, 2008.

Schner, George. *Education for Ministry: Reform and Renewal In Theological Education*. Kansas City: Sheed & Ward, 1993.

Schwartz, Daniel L. *Paideia and Cult: Christian Initiation in Theodore of Mopsuestia*. Cambridge, MA: Harvard University Press, 2013.

Schwehn, Mark. "Lutheran Higher Education in the Twenty-First Century." In *The Future of Religious Colleges: The Proceedings of the Harvard Conference on the Future of Religious Colleges, October 6–7, 2000*, edited by Paul J. Dovre, 208–23. Grand Rapids: Eerdmans, 2002.

Scruton, Roger. *The Face of God*. Gifford Lectures. London: Continuum, 2012.

Searle, Joshua T. *Theology After Christendom: Forming Prophets for a Post-Christian World*. Eugene, OR: Cascade, 2018.

Sergiovanni, Thomas J. *Leadership*. Edited by Kate Myers and John MacBeath. What's in It for Schools? London: RoutledgeFalmer, 2001.

Silf, Margaret. *Landscapes of Prayer: Finding God in Your World and Your Life*. Oxford: Lion Hudson, 2011.

Simon, Caroline, et al. *Mentoring for Mission: Nurturing New Faculty at Church-Related Colleges*. Grand Rapids: Eerdmans, 2003.

Sire, James W. *Naming the Elephant: Worldview as a Concept*. Downers Grove, IL: IVP Academic, 2004.

Smith, David I. "The Poet, the Child and the Blackbird: Aesthetic Reading and Spiritual Development." *International Journal of Children's Spirituality* 9 (2004) 143–54.

Snijders, Tjamke. "Communal Learning and Communal Identities in Medieval Studies." In *Horizontal Learning in the High Middle Ages: Peer-to-Peer Knowledge Transfer in Religious Communities*, edited by Micol Long et al., 17–46. Knowledge Communities 7. Amsterdam: Amsterdam University Press, 2019.

Sommerfeldt, John. *Bernard of Clairvaux: On the Life of the Mind*. New York: Newman, 2004.

Soukup, Paul A. *A Media Ecology of Theology: Communicating Faith Throughout the Christian Tradition*. Waco: Baylor University Press, 2022.

Springer, William C. *This Is My Body: An Existential Analysis of the Living Body*. Lanham, MD: University of America Press, 2009.

Stanford, Peter. "The Exile Returns." *Tablet* (Nov. 21, 2019) 9.

Starratt, Robert J. *The Drama of Leadership*. London: Falmer, 1993.

Steck, Christopher. Review of *The Dramatic Encounter of Divine and Human Freedom in the Theology of Hans Urs von Balthasar*, by Thomas G. Dalzell. *HeyJ* 48 (2007) 157–58. https://doi.org/10.1111/j.1468-2265.2007.00308_33.x.

Steckel, Sita. "Concluding Observations." "Communal Learning and Communal Identities in Medieval Studies." In *Horizontal Learning in the High Middle Ages: Peer-to-Peer Knowledge Transfer in Religious Communities*, edited by Micol Long et al., 235–56. Knowledge Communities 7. Amsterdam: Amsterdam University Press, 2019.

Sternberg, Robert. *Thinking Styles*. Cambridge: Cambridge University Press, 1997.

Stiltner, Brian. *Religion and the Common Good: Catholic Contributions to Building Community in a Liberal Society*. Lanham, MD: Rowman & Littlefield, 2000.

Stock, Brian. *Augustine the Reader: Meditation, Self-Knowledge, and the Ethics of Interpretation*. Cambridge, MA: Harvard University Press, 1996.

Sullivan, John. "Blondel and a Living Tradition for Catholic Education." *Catholic Education: A Journal of Inquiry and Practice* 1 (1997) 67–76.

———. "Blondel and the Cost of Commitment." *Downside Review* 104 (1986) 1–9.

———. *Catholic Education: Distinctive and Inclusive*. Dordrecht: Kluwer/Springer, 2001.

———. *Catholic Schools in Contention: Competing Metaphors and Leadership Implications*. Dublin: Veritas, 2000.

———. "Catholics, Culture and the Renewal of Christian Humanism." *Religions* 12 (2021) 325. https://doi.org/10.3390/rel12050325.

———. *The Christian Academic in Higher Education: The Consecration of Learning*. London: Palgrave Macmillan, 2018.

———. "Church and World." In *Education in a Catholic Perspective*, edited by Stephen J. McKinney and John Sullivan, 155–72. Aldershot, UK: Ashgate, 2013.

———, ed. *Communicating Faith*. Washington, DC: Catholic University of America Press, 2011.

———. "Communication, Media, and Inculturation." *Educa—International Catholic Journal of Education* 2 (2016) 9–28.

———. "Connection Without Control: Theology and the University Curriculum." In *Learning the Language of Faith*, edited by John Sullivan, 183–99. Chelmsford, UK: James, 2010.

———. "The Dynamics of Ownership." *Journal of Education & Christian Belief* 9 (2005) 21–33.

———. "Education and Evangelization." In *Learning the Language of Faith*, edited by John Sullivan, 32–46. Chelmsford, UK: James, 2010.

———. "Education and Religious Faith as a Dance." In *Communicating Faith*, edited by John Sullivan, 344–58. Washington, DC: Catholic University of America Press, 2011.

———. "Faith Schools: A Culture Within a Culture in a Changing World." In *International Handbook of the Religious, Moral and Spiritual Dimensions of Education: Part One*, edited by Marian de Souza et al., 937–47. International Handbooks of Religion and Education 1. Dordrecht: Springer, 2006.

———. "From Formation to the Frontiers." *Journal of Education & Christian Belief* 7 (2003) 7–21.

———. "From Formation to the Frontiers: The Dialectic of Christian Education." In *Communicating Faith*, edited by John Sullivan, 3–15. Washington, DC: Catholic University of America Press, 2011.

———. "Friendship and Spiritual Learning: Seedbed for Synodality." *Religions* 14 (2023) 592. https://doi.org/10.3390/rel14050592.

———. "Hugh of St. Victor: Medieval Wisdom for Modern Educators." *Downside Review* 139 (2021) 165–82.

———. "Individual and Institution." In *Education in a Catholic Perspective*, edited by Stephen J. McKinney and John Sullivan, 139–54. Aldershot, UK: Ashgate, 2013.

———. "Keeping Company." *New Theologian* 13 (2003) 25–28.

———. "Leadership and Management." In *Contemporary Catholic Schools*, edited by Michael A. Hayes and Liam Gearon, 91–106. Leominster, UK: Gracewing, 2002.

———. *Lights for the Path*. Dublin: Veritas, 2022.

———. "Living Logos." *Networking* 3 (2002) 28–31.

———. "Matter for Heaven: Blondel, Christ and Creation." *BETL* 64 (1988) 60–83.

———. "Philosophy of Catholic Education." In *Exploring Religious Education: Catholic Religious Education in an Intercultural Europe*, edited by Patricia Kieran and Anne Hession, 27–34. Dublin: Veritas, 2008.

———. "Responsibility, Vocation and Critique." In *The Idea of a Christian University: Essays on Theology and Higher Education*, edited by Jeff Astley et al., 263–78. Milton Keynes: Paternoster, 2004.

———. "The Skills Based Model of School Leadership." In *Distance Learning*, edited by William K. Kay and Leslie J. Francis, 199–232. Vol. 4 of *Religion in Education*. Leominster, UK: Gracewing, 2003.

———. "St Augustine, Maurice Blondel and Christian Education." In *Education in a Catholic Perspective*, edited by Stephen J. McKinney and John Sullivan, 31–48. Aldershot, UK: Ashgate, 2013.

———. "Teaching as Contemplative." In *Teacher Education in Challenging Times: Lessons for Professionalism, Partnership and Practice*, edited by Philip M. Bamber and Jane C. Moore, 44–57. Routledge Research in Teacher Education. London: Routledge, 2017.

———. "Text and Context: Mediating the Mission in Catholic Schools." In *Communicating Faith*, edited by John Sullivan, 101–16. Washington, DC: Catholic University of America Press, 2011.

———. "Towards a Curriculum for Life." *Journal of Religious Education and Theology* 1 (2021) 18–31.

———. "Transcending the Technocratic Mentality Through the Humanities." *Religions* 12 (2021) 676. https://doi.org/10.3390/rel12090676.

———. "The University." In *The Oxford Handbook of John Henry Newman*, edited by Frederick D. Aquino and Benjamin J. King, 538–56. Oxford Handbooks. Oxford: Oxford University Press, 2018.

———. "University, Christian Faith and the Church." In *The Idea of a Christian University: Essays on Theology and Higher Education*, edited by Jeff Astley et al., 14–34. Milton Keynes: Paternoster, 2004.

———. "Vocation and Profession in Teacher Education." In *The Foundation of Hope: Turning Dreams into Reality*, edited by R. John Elford, 152–69. Liverpool: Liverpool Hope University Press, 2003.

———. "Vulnerability in Teaching and Learning." In *The Christian Academic in Higher Education: The Consecration of Learning*, 281–302. London: Palgrave Macmillan, 2018.

———. "Wrestling with Managerialism." In *Commitment to Diversity: Catholics and Education in a Changing World*, edited by Mary Eaton et al., 240–59. London: Cassell, 2000.

Sullivan, John, et al. "The Story of an Educational Innovation: The MA in Catholic School Leadership at St. Mary's University College, Twickenham, 1997–2013; Principles, Pedagogy and Research Studies." *International Studies in Catholic Education* 7 (2015) 28–45.

Sultmann, Bill, and Denis McLaughlin. *The Spirit of Leadership*. Johannesburg: Catholic Institute of Education, 2000.

Summit, Jennifer, and Blakey Vermeule. *Action Versus Contemplation: Why an Ancient Debate Still Matters*. Chicago: University of Chicago Press, 2018.

Taylor, Charles. *A Secular Age*. Cambridge, MA: Belknap, 2007.

*Tablet*. "Defence of Communion Ban Reissued." *Tablet* (Mar. 12, 2011) 29.

———. "News Briefing from Britain and Ireland." *Tablet* (Apr. 21, 2012) 31.

Theobald, Christoph. *Vous avez dit vocation?* Théologie. Paris: Bayard, 2010.

Thiel, John E. *Senses of Tradition: Continuity and Development in Catholic Faith*. New York: Oxford University Press, 2000.

Thiessen, Elmer John. *The Ethics of Evangelism: A Philosophical Defense of Proselytizing and Persuasion*. Milton Keynes: Paternoster, 2011.

———. *In Defence of Religious Schools and Colleges*. Montreal: McGill-Queen's University Press, 2001.

Tilley, Terrence W. *Inventing Catholic Tradition*. Maryknoll, NY: Orbis, 2000.

Tóth, Beáta. *The Heart Has Its Reasons: Towards a Theological Anthropology of the Heart*. Cambridge, UK: Clarke & Co., 2016.

Treston, Kevin. *Creative Christian Leadership: Skills for More Effective Ministry*. Mystic, CT: Twenty-Third, 1995.

Trowbridge, Kevin S. "A Christian Perspective on Communication and Media." In *Faith and Learning: A Handbook for Christian Higher Education*, edited by David S. Dockery, 323–44. Nashville: B&H Academic, 2012.

Turkle, Sherry. *Reclaiming Conversation: The Power of Talk in a Digital Age*. New York: Penguin, 2015.

Urvoy, François. *La tête sans corps: Pour la vie du laïc dans sa plénitude*. Paris: Harmattan, 2013.

Van Brummelen, Harro. *Steppingstones to Curriculum: A Biblical Path*. Seattle: Alta Vista College Press, 1994.

Van Engen, John, ed. *Educating People of Faith: Exploring the History of Jewish and Christian Communities*. Grand Rapids: Eerdmans, 2004.

Van 't Spijker, Ineke. *Fictions of the Inner Life: Religious Literature and Formation of the Self in the Eleventh and Twelfth Centuries*. Turnhout, Belg.: Brepols, 2004.

Vitz, Evelyn Birge. "Liturgy as Education in the Middle Ages." In *Medieval Education*, edited by Ronald B. Begley and Joseph W. Koterski, 20–34. Fordham Series in Medieval Studies. New York: Fordham University Press, 2005.

Volf, Miroslav. *After Our Likeness: The Church as the Image of the Trinity*. Sacra Doctrina: Christian Theology for a Postmodern Age. Grand Rapids: Eerdmans, 1998.

———. *Work in the Spirit: Toward a Theology of Work*. New York: Oxford University Press, 1991.

Voulgaraki-Pissina, Evi. "Theology, Witness, and Spirituality in a Post-Secularized Historical Context." *Religions* 14 (2023) 179 (1–17). https://doi.org/10.3390/rel14020179.

Wacquet, Françoise. *Latin; or, The Empire of a Sign*. Translated by John Howe. London: Verso, 2001.

Waller, Joanna. "Gained in Translation." *Tablet* (June 11, 2011) 4–5.

Warren, Michael. *Communications and Cultural Analysis: A Religious View*. Westport, CT: Bergin and Harvey, 1992.

Webb, Stephen H. *The Divine Voice: Christian Proclamation and the Theology of Sound*. Grand Rapids: Brazos, 2004.

Webb-Mitchell, Brett P. *Christly Gestures: Learning to Be Members of the Body of Christ*. Grand Rapids: Eerdmans, 2003.

Weddell, Sherry A. *Forming Intentional Disciples: The Path to Knowing and Following Jesus*. Huntington, IN: Our Sunday Visitor, 2012.

Wei, Ian P. *Intellectual Culture in Medieval Paris: Theologians and the University, c. 1100–1330*. Cambridge: Cambridge University Press, 2012.

Wenger, Etienne. *Communities of Practice: Learning, Meaning, and Identity*. Learning in Doing: Social, Cognitive and Computational Perspectives. Cambridge: Cambridge University Press, 1998.

Westphal, Merold. *Whose Community? Which Interpretation? Philosophical Hermeneutics for the Church*. Edited by James K. A. Smith. Church and Postmodern Culture. Grand Rapids: Baker Academic, 2009.

Wheatley, Margaret. *Leadership and the New Science: Discovering Order in a Chaotic World*. Oakland: Berrett-Koehler, 1992.

Willey, Petroc. "The Pedagogue and the Teacher." In *The Pedagogy of God: Its Centrality in Catechesis and Catechist Formation*, edited by Caroline Farey et al., 29–50. Steubenville, OH: Emmaus, 2011.

———. "The Pedagogy of God: An Aim and Process." In *The Pedagogy of God: Its Centrality in Catechesis and Catechist Formation*, edited by Caroline Farey et al., 51–79. Steubenville, OH: Emmaus, 2011.

Williams, Brian A. "To Wonder, Learn, and Love: Christian Humanism in the Modern University." *Word & World*, May 22, 2019. https://ifesworld.org/en/journal/to-wonder-learn-and-love-brian-a-williams/?switch_language=en.

Williams, David M. *Receiving the Bible in Faith: Historical and Theological Exegesis*. Washington, DC: Catholic University of America Press, 2004.

Wittgenstein, Ludwig. *Tractatus Logico-Philosophicus*. Translated by D. F. Pears and B. F. McGuinness. International Library of Philosophy and Scientific Method. London: Routledge & Kegan Paul, 1961.

Wolfe, Judith. Review of *The Face of God*, by Roger Scruton. *Tablet* (May 19, 2012) 19.

Zimmermann, Jens. *Incarnational Humanism: A Philosophy of Culture for the Church in the World*. Strategic Initiatives in Evangelical Theology. Downers Grove, IL: IVP Academic, 2012.

———, ed. *Re-Envisioning Christian Humanism: Education and the Restoration of Humanity*. Oxford: Oxford University Press, 2017.

Zuck, Roy B. *Spirit-Filled Teaching: The Power of the Holy Spirit in Your Ministry*. Edited by Charles R. Swindoll. Resources for Successful Leaders. Nashville: Nelson, 1998.

# Index

affective formation, 145, 156, 158–59, 162, 164
agency, xvii, 163–4, 167, 175, 177, 1967, 260–65, 268–69, 271–76, 279
Anderson, Chris, 245, 256
Applebee, Arthur, 192–93
Aquinas, Thomas, 75, 240, 265, 316
Aquino, Frederick, 109
Aristotle, 118–20, 130
arts, the, 28, 32–33, 37
asceticism, 36, 63, 155, 160, 298
  ascetic training, 145, 148, 156, 158–59, 164
Augustine, 30, 170, 177, 213, 240, 249–50, 343

Benedict XVI, Pope, 292, 320, 346
Benedictines, 20–21, 24, 30
Bernard of Clairvaux, 21, 29, 239–40, 251, 279, 315
Birkerts, Sven, 332–33, 335–36
Blair, Anthony, 7, 11–12
Blondel, Maurice, 249–57, 188, 207, 212, 317
body, the, 22, 24, 28, 36, 38–39, 43, 60–61, 127–28, 153, 157, 160, 183, 185, 193, 199, 206, 251, 254, 295
Bonaventure, 30, 124, 291
Bunting, Madeleine, 96–97

capacitation, 145, 161
  capacities, 5, 21, 32, 37, 44, 84, 137, 145, 182, 191, 200, 217, 235, 248, 252–54, 270, 275, 328, 332, 338–39, 343
Carmody, Brendan, 310–12, 314
Carrón, Julian, 173 263–64
Casson, Ann, 265–66
Catholic education, 48–49, 56, 58, 75, 86–87, 166, 261, 266, 275, 284, 312–13, 315–24, 370
Catholic universities, 3, 67, 69–70, 72–74, 198, 200, 205
Cencini, Amadeo, 235–36
Christian anthropology, 10, 145, 182
  educators, xiv–xv, 1, 20, 24–25, 83–84, 148, 157, 193, 196, 222, 225, 227, 229–30, 236, 239–40, 255, 281, 283–84, 332, 338, 340–42
  formation, 20, 23–24, 218–26, 228
  literacy, 221
  scholarship, xix
church, xvi, xvii, 10, 13, 15, 19–21, 25, 37–38, 49–54, 56–57, 59, 63–65, 72, 74, 77, 87–88, 92–94, 110, 115–18, 130, 132–34, 136–37, 139–40, 166, 168, 198, 200–203, 215–24, 227, 238, 240–41, 260–61, 264–69, 272–78, 281, 283–84, 287–88, 290–94, 296, 299–304, 306–11, 313–14, 318–20, 326–27, 331–32, 339, 342, 345–56
  church and academy, 2, 5, 12, 17–18
  learning church, 52, 133

1

INDEX

*(church continiued)*
  church school leadership, 80, 84, 92–93
  church schools and colleges, 95, 99–100, 108–10
citizen, 163, 268, 349
  citizenship, 15, 36, 89–90, 154, 300, 345–46, 348–49, 353–53, 355
classroom, 14, 40, 70, 88, 117, 121, 137, 142–45, 151, 154, 162, 166, 168, 171, 200, 245, 256, 322, 331
clericalism, 52
collaboration, 17, 19, 41, 78, 109, 139, 143, 331
communication, 9, 29, 34, 77, 98, 100, 119, 121, 127–29, 166, 168, 171, 176, 213, 250, 254, 284–85, 291, 308, 321, 327–40, 342, 344–45, 351, 354
community, xiii, 7, 13–14, 21–23, 25, 29, 31, 36, 38–41, 43, 54–55, 77, 81, 84–88, 90, 102, 106–9, 111–13, 119, 139–40, 201, 219, 227, 232, 234, 237–38, 241–42, 245–48, 250, 262, 269, 287, 290, 295, 297, 304, 307–8, 312, 331, 333, 339, 347–49, 351, 353–54, 356
  community life, 151, 153, 158
contemplative, 28, 46, 149, 208, 252–53
Cozzens, Donald, 350–51, 355
creativity, xv, 42, 56, 75, 88, 104, 117, 165, 167–68, 177, 210, 241, 261, 275–56, 279, 306, 319, 321, 341, 352
critical questioning, 13, 88, 107, 199, 312
  critical retrieval, 2, 144, 148–50, 265, 284, 310
Csepregi, Gabor, 222–23
culture, xix, 16, 24–25, 36, 58–59, 67, 74, 90, 99–100, 114–15, 149, 156, 168, 203, 207, 216, 221–22, 225, 232, 241, 275, 281–90, 292–5, 297–303, 309, 327–28, 334–35, 339–42, 344

curriculum, 9–10, 13, 31, 37, 43–44, 55–56, 68, 70, 83–87, 100, 103, 107, 112, 116, 129, 135, 143, 166, 192, 195–96, 199–200, 202, 205–6, 210, 214, 209, 226–27, 230, 249, 262, 302, 305–6, 355
  curriculum for life, 217, 220, 222, 225–27

Davignon, Phil, 289
Davis, Robert, 168
decisions, xv, xix, 4, 8, 14, 17, 112, 119, 121, 129, 132–33, 135, 156, 185, 217, 220, 222–23, 227, 232, 241, 274, 298, 312, 353
*De institutione novitiorum*, 30, 38
dependence, 74, 153, 180, 186–87, 201, 213, 278, 304–6
  dependency, 167, 178–79, 295, 302
development, xiv, xviii, 1, 3, 10, 14, 19, 21–22, 27–28, 32, 41, 46, 55, 57–60, 62, 64, 67, 83–84, 86–89, 93–94, 100, 107, 109, 133, 135–36, 147, 150–51, 154, 159–60, 197–200, 221, 239, 253, 256, 260–61, 271, 274, 279, 295, 315, 324, 332, 353
dialogue, 11, 18, 25, 73–74, 87, 91–95, 144, 205, 213, 218, 221, 229, 268–69, 281, 288–89, 293, 309, 311, 329–31, 345, 350
  with the past, 150
Dianzon, Bernadita, xv
*Didascalicon*, 28, 30–8, 251
discernment, xviii, 38, 74–75, 88, 98, 110, 139, 150, 159, 161, 231–32, 234–38, 242, 283–84, 296, 309, 323, 328, 340
discipline, xiii, xix, 12, 21–22, 28, 30–31, 33, 36, 38–39, 43, 46–47, 51, 54, 61, 64–65, 95, 147, 149–50, 153, 160, 204–6, 210, 235, 244, 246, 249, 251–52, 261–63, 271, 343
distance, xvi, 88, 99, 106, 113, 120, 131, 149, 151, 167, 189–90, 230, 256, 294, 300–301, 341
  underdistancing, 106

overdistancing, 106
distinctiveness, 56–59, 66, 70, 80, 90–93, 135
domination, 5, 13–16, 297
Dorotheus of Gaza, 152, 160–62
Duffy, Eamon, 77, 239, 315
Dulles, Avery, 115
Dürr, Oliver, 290
ecclesial citizenship, 346, 348, 352–53
educating faith, 199, 202
education and religious faith, 2, 5, 9, 13
 as spiritual endeavour, xx
educator in faith, 195
Egan, Gerard, 100–101, 114–15
Even-Ezra, Avelet, 157
Evans, Donald, 186–87
Evans, Gillian, 34
Evans, Richard, 355
*Ex Corde Ecclesiae*, 3, 205
example, 23, 28, 31, 36, 38–39, 41, 43, 45, 78, 127, 135, 143, 153, 171, 200, 213, 219, 224, 273, 308, 343, 347, 354
eyes, 22, 44, 112, 138, 161, 171, 204, 219, 250, 261

Falque, Emmanuel, 38
Feinberg, Walter, 4
fidelity, xv, xviii, 1, 3, 7–8, 56, 75, 117, 199, 251, 308, 320, 324, 342
firmness, 3, 67–75
Floridi, Luciano, 332, 337–38, 340
formation, 1, 8–9, 18, 20–25, 28, 30–31, 38, 42, 44–45, 55, 59, 84–86, 88, 92, 139, 145, 150, 156, 158–62, 164, 196, 204, 215–28, 235, 243, 261, 264, 267, 279, 290–91, 295, 301–2, 317
Franchi, Leonardo, 168
Francis, Pope, 226, 299
freedom, 8–9, 16–17, 21–24, 66, 68, 72, 104, 125, 160, 165–66, 168, 172, 177, 181, 184, 190, 205, 210, 230, 232, 234–35, 241, 249, 254–55, 263–65, 268, 276, 279, 295, 298–301, 303–4, 306–8, 317, 325, 329, 346

Freire, Paulo, 263
friendship, 146, 170, 184, 222, 302, 308–9, 344
friction, 62–64

Gadamer, Hans-Georg, 192, 271, 322
Gardner, Howard, 126, 214, 226, 
gentleness, 145, 166, 171–72, 194, 291
Gibran, Kahlil, 280
Gil, Alberto, 168
Gili, Guido, 168
Goethe, Johann, xvii
Golde, Chris, xiii
gospel, xv, xvii, 2, 10, 18–19, 52, 68, 78–79, 81, 87, 90, 92, 115, 117, 133, 135, 140, 166, 189, 194–95, 199, 215, 218–19, 224, 228, 239, 281–85, 289, 303–4, 307–8, 315, 319–20, 327–28, 341, 345, 347–48, 351–52
Graiver, Inbar, 155, 160
Gracia, Jorge, xviii
Grey, Carmody, 290
Griffiths, Paul, 155, 247
Groome, Thomas, 227
Grossman, Edith, 324
Guardini, Romano, 182–83, 284, 286, 291–300, 309

*habitus*, 13, 22, 148, 154, 156–58, 207
Halík, Tomáš, 278–79
Harrison, Nonna, 177, 211
Hauerwas, Stanley, 17
heads/headship, 88, 93, 111, 118, 120–21, 126–29
Heywood, David, 219, 221.
Himes, Michael, 311, 325
historical perspective, 13, 149, 255, 299–301
history wars, 346, 355
Hogan, Padraig, 261, 269–73, 276
Holy Spirit, 46, 49, 56–57, 83, 92, 140, 186, 195, 228–29, 238–39, 252, 281, 294–96, 307–9, 314–15, 319, 326, 347

## INDEX

hope, 5, 7, 68, 77, 118, 128, 156, 159, 168, 181, 186, 194, 207, 230, 278, 309, 311, 323, 331
Horsfield, Peter, 332, 338
Hügel, Friedrich von, 2, 59–66, 103, 107, 110, 248
Hugh of St Victor, 2, 28–41, 43–47, 153, 251, 301, 317
Hughes, Kyle, 152, 160
Hull, John, 11
human mind, the, 61, 194, 265

Illich, Ivan, 34–35, 284, 286, 291, 298–309
image of God, 31, 33, 40, 44, 83, 145, 167, 176–77, 181, 194, 200, 233, 236, 239, 315
imitation, 23, 28, 36, 38–41, 43, 150, 153, 224, 264, 276–77, 348
improvisation, xvi, 1, 88
inclusiveness, 7, 55, 58–59, 66, 90, 95, 108, 213, 319
inculturation, xix, 117, 282–84, 319, 327–28, 341–42
infosphere, 337–38, 340
integration, xx, 12–13, 27, 85, 87, 133, 139, 169, 193, 196, 199–210, 212–14, 233, 236, 275, 311, 314
interconnectedness, xx, 67, 84, 88, 157, 207, 209, 226, 333

Jacobsen, Douglas and Rhonda, 13, 156, 207–9
Jaeger, Stephen, 22, 127, 153, 157
Jensen, Robert, 204–5
John Paul II, Pope, 3, 37, 67, 71, 202, 205, 236, 292, 346

Keator, Mary, 46, 154–55, 159
Kegan, Robert, 104–5, 225–26
knowledge, *passim*
  premodern approaches, 25, 29–30, 32–34, 36, 38, 40, 44, 46, 156, 161, 164, 250, 252–54
  self-knowledge, 43, 46, 85, 140, 145, 148, 154, 156, 158, 164, 169, 173–74, 176, 190–91, 201, 210, 233, 236–37
Krieg, Robert, 292

*laïcité*, 15
Lakeland, Paul, 348–49, 352
language, 2, 43, 49, 60, 62, 68, 97, 118, 143, 159, 171, 177, 195, 203, 225, 262, 264, 282, 284, 290, 293, 310, 318–21, 324–25, 329–30, 332, 341–42, 351
  Latin, 291, 310, 318–21
Lavelle, Louis, 263
leadership, xiv, 18, 68, 76–77, 81, 97, 100, 102, 110, 115–16, 123, 131–34, 226, 288
  of faith-based schools, 78, 80, 82–94, 123, 135
  Christian, 77–78, 83, 124, 349, 353
  ethical, 111, 113, 121–2
  spiritual, 30, 85, 87
  ideas-based, 78, 81, 125–26
learning, xvi, 2, 9–12, 16–23, 27–34, 40–46, 49, 54–55, 67, 72, 75, 79, 82–83, 87, 95, 104, 107–9, 117, 125, 127–28, 137–46, 149–54, 156–59, 163, 172, 175–77, 179, 185, 188–90, 192–93, 195–97, 203, 205, 207–10, 212–18, 251–53, 257–58, 261–64, 268–71, 274–77, 305–7, 312–13, 331–33, 336–37, 343–44
  Christian learning, xx, 45, 83–84, 125, 161, 207, 216–23, 227–28, 230, 241–42, 248–50, 309, 323, 348, 350, 354
  learning Church, 52, 133
Leclercq, Jean, 36, 250–51
*lectio divina*, 21, 46, 155, 159
Lee-Barker, Jane, 291, 296
Leo XIII, Pope, 75
Leyerle, Blake, 23
Lichtmann, Maria, 46, 170
Limitation, 172, 177–78, 221, 242, 308
Little, Sara, 10–11
liturgy, 11, 20–21, 23–25, 85, 217, 219, 238, 275, 291, 293–95, 297,

# INDEX

299, 302, 304, 309, 314, 318–20, 324
living logo, 124, 129–31
living logos, 78, 84, 123–31
*logos*, 127, 176, 297, 321–22
Lonergan, Bernard, 213, 310–11, 313–14, 316
love, 3, 21, 44, 72, 83, 124, 130, 144, 154, 167, 176, 179, 181–82, 184, 191, 193–94, 207, 219, 222, 230, 237, 240–41, 246, 249, 251–54, 280, 290, 294, 296–98, 304, 316, 321, 323–24, 343
Lucas, Hanna, 155, 161

MacIntyre, Alasdair, 179, 203, 271
McDonough, Graham, 261, 266–69, 272–73
McGilchrist, Iain, 207, 225
management, 76–77, 83, 86–87, 93, 97, 102, 104, 112–14, 116, 121, 126, 129, 131, 226, 288, 346
Maritain, Jacques, 265, 276, 300, 317
Martin, Jane Roland, 273–74
Martin, Mike, 106
media, 37, 43, 132, 194, 284, 288, 291, 298, 309, 327–28, 330, 332–38, 343–44
medieval, 22, 24, 26–30, 32, 34–36, 39, 41–43, 153, 157, 244, 249–52, 255, 300, 351
  Christianity, 2, 300
  monasticism, 2
*memoria*/memory, 5, 21, 23–24, 28, 35, 36–37, 43, 46, 82, 163, 177, 182, 193–94, 200, 202, 217–18, 246, 250–51, 255, 333, 341, 343
mind of Christ, 218
ministry, 29, 84, 87, 90, 116, 124, 133, 136, 138, 173, 215, 221, 226–27, 229, 291, 302, 346, 354
mission, xiv, xvi, 10, 12, 53, 56–57, 70, 72, 77, 79, 89–90, 95–100, 102–3, 105–7, 110, 113–16, 118, 120–22, 128, 131, 133, 135, 138–40, 210, 219, 232, 281, 287, 303–3, 307, 309, 312, 317, 324, 338–39, 353

models, 12, 27, 39–40, 54, 137, 208, 222–24, 232, 277, 305–6
  of church, 115
modernity, xiii, 155, 162, 302, 306–9
monks, 21–23, 26, 29, 39
moral persuasiveness, 121–22

nature, human, 5, 22, 24, 33–34, 37, 41, 44–46, 62, 72–73, 94, 104, 145, 148, 159–61, 177, 179, 187, 191, 193, 200–201, 217, 220, 224, 233, 253, 261, 290, 298, 311, 313, 317, 343,
  and grace, 31, 33, 46, 60, 66, 85, 160, 178–79, 191, 207, 225, 237, 240, 279, 296, 311
Newman, John Henry, 41, 57, 170–71, 181–82, 196, 201–2, 205–6, 274, 317
Norris, Louis, 72–73

obedience, xv, xviii, 21–22, 88, 104, 152, 246–47, 276, 279, 308, 346, 350
O'Loughlin, Tom, 347
Ong, Walter, 332–34
open-mindedness, 74, 163
openness, 3, 21, 31, 42, 56–57, 59, 61, 64, 68, 70–75, 117, 120, 144, 154, 159, 166, 171–72, 179, 186–88, 190–91, 194, 206, 236, 242, 246, 281, 300, 309, 319–20, 330, 339
originality, 8, 39, 276–78, 348
Orji, Cyril, 74–75
ownership, 8, 70, 96–98, 120, 124, 175, 261–62, 274–77, 306, 312, 329, 348
  demographics, 99
  dynamics, 98-100
  proprietary, 78, 96, 102–3, 109–10
  professional, 78, 96, 102–7, 109–10
  participative, 78, 96, 102, 107–10

Palmer, Parker, 170, 344
particularity, xvi–xvii, 8, 66
pastoral, 20, 95, 133, 174, 176, 218, 220, 226, 229–30, 284, 286

5

# INDEX

pedagogy of God, 238–39, 313–15
peer/horizontal learning, 28, 39–41
Pelikan, Jaroslav, 21
perichoretic pedagogy, 145, 166, 169
personal rendition, 196, 261, 279
personhood, 39, 70, 145, 165–66, 169, 173, 181, 202, 235, 317
Pike, Mark, 245
pilgrim, 145, 148–49, 155, 163, 250, 252, 292
polarities, 72–73, 145, 167
Postman, Neil, 48–49, 332, 334–535 339
practical atheism, 289
presence, divine, 11, 43, 50, 61, 84, 133, 144, 154, 186, 193, 215, 224, 238, 240, 276, 316
   leaders' and teachers', 127, 130–31, 145, 165–66, 169–71, 173–75, 219, 290, 330, 332
   physical, 40, 336
   professional, xvi, xix, 18, 27, 80, 85, 87–9, 93, 95, 98–99, 106–7, 135, 137, 139, 144–45, 165–66, 169, 174, 200, 235, 243, 271, 283, 306, 324
project managers, 145, 148–49, 155, 163
prophetic, 19, 86, 117, 284, 289, 292, 299, 301, 303, 308, 354–55
prototype of the Gospel, 218–19
providence, 293, 296–97, 309
purposes, educational, 9–10, 87, 90, 121, 128, 229, 245, 252, 257, 312–13
   formational, 21, 23, 159, 164, 217–18
   of leadership, 76, 80–83, 86, 98, 104, 116, 126, 136
Radcliffe, Timothy, 281
Radner, Ephraim, 224
Rahner, Karl, 292, 311, 325
reading, xvi, 1, 15, 23–4, 28–29, 34–36, 44–45, 88, 95, 117, 128–30, 142, 150–51, 187, 196, 219, 222, 234, 243–59, 289, 293–94, 201–2, 304, 313, 331–32, 342, 344, 347

religious readers, 246–47
religion and education, 5, 10
religious education, 135, 199, 202, 216, 230, 265, 267, 342
renunciation of power, 160, 295, 302, 304, 307–9
restoration, 28, 31, 35, 37, 43–44, 251
revelation, 6, 10, 12, 14, 43, 53, 152, 182, 199, 208, 239, 263, 275–76, 294, 297–98, 302, 311, 314, 325
rhetoric, 32–33, 78, 111, 113, 116, 118–21, 129–30, 321
Ricoeur, Paul, 268, 323–24
ritual activity, 151
Rossiter, Graham, 216
Rowland, Tracey, 298
Rush, Ormond, 244, 325–26

saints, 20, 36, 38–40, 217–18, 277, 320, 345
Scripture, 24, 31, 37, 43–45, 85, 130, 144, 182, 202–3, 208, 220, 230, 234, 238, 253–54, 281, 311, 313–14, 320, 339, 342, 352
scrutiny, 33–34, 113, 116, 152, 162, 237, 246, 252, 262
secularization, 69, 90, 286–87, 290, 297
self-knowledge, 43, 46, 85, 140, 145, 148, 154, 156, 158, 164, 169, 173–74, 176, 190–91, 201, 210, 233, 236–37
self-reflection, 177, 211–12
Sergiovanni, Thomas, 81, 123, 125–26
service, xv, 11–12, 18, 21, 41, 55, 86–87, 89, 95, 106–8, 124, 136, 140, 165–66, 180, 208, 215, 229, 233, 269, 276, 283, 340, 342
shadows, 78, 100, 111, 116, 122
   shadow side, 34, 96, 100–102, 113–15, 215, 326
signs of the times, 117, 125, 281, 289
spiritual senses, 252–54
St Paul, xiv, 218, 342
stakeholders, 84, 100–101, 112, 120
Starratt, Robert, 131
steward, xiii–xv, xx, 76, 196, 281

## INDEX

Stonebraker, Sarah Irving, xiii
succession planning, 78, 132–36, 138, 140
synthesis of faith, life and culture, 3, 58–59, 64–66

teachers, 1–2, 9–10, 27, 29, 33, 36, 38, 40, 42–44, 55, 69–70, 86, 89, 91, 93–94, 103–4, 106–7, 112–13, 116–17, 121, 126–28, 137–38, 143–45, 149, 152–53, 157, 159, 161–62, 165–75, 173–74, 187, 189, 193, 195–96, 200, 205, 216, 221, 238, 243, 245, 260–68, 270, 273–78, 280, 313–14, 316, 322, 324–25, 331–32, 343–44, 352, 354
teaching, 2, 9–10, 13–14, 18, 21, 27–28, 38, 54–55, 69, 83, 90–91, 103–4, 112, 117, 119, 130, 142–43, 145, 173–74, 200–201, 213, 216–17, 219–20, 227, 229–30, 252, 258, 263–65, 267–76, 282, 284, 307, 311, 313, 321–22, 325, 331, 342
technocratic mentality, 295
technology, 6, 42, 93, 97, 148, 154, 242, 286, 297, 299–300, 333, 338–39
text, 24, 36, 57, 117, 128, 151, 167, 196, 244–47, 255–58, 262, 284, 300, 310, 320–24, 333
theology and education, 10–11
*theosis*, 239, 315
Thiel, John, xviii–xix
Thiessen, Elmer, 14–16
tradition(s), xiii–xx, 1–5, 7–8, 20, 25, 37, 45, 49–57, 67–8, 70–72, 74–75, 81, 85, 87–88, 90–92, 95, 103–4, 107, 109, 114, 116–17, 130, 144, 148–52, 160, 164, 166–68, 170, 192, 195–96, 198, 204, 208, 216, 220–22, 224, 227, 246, 248, 255–56, 260–62, 264, 266–67, 269–76, 279, 281–84, 287, 290, 292–93, 300, 302, 304, 307, 309, 311, 313, 316, 319–20, 322–26, 328, 342, 347

translation, 284, 310, 318–26
Trowbridge, Kevin, 328
truth, 3, 5, 8, 12, 15–16, 19, 22, 31–32, 34, 39, 42–44, 50–51, 54–57, 65–66, 67, 71–72, 75, 78, 125, 129, 148, 153–56, 160–61, 165–66, 171, 174, 202–3, 205, 218–19, 222, 230, 246, 248–49, 252, 277, 292, 295, 309, 320–21, 328–31, 353
  God's truth, 46, 92, 218, 264, 294, 352
understanding cf overstanding, 243–59
universality, xvii, 8, 65, 245, 319
university, 15, 18, 27–28, 38, 41–42, 67–69, 72, 147, 151, 164, 195–96, 201–3, 205, 210–14, 216, 234, 243–45, 256

values, 4, 7, 10, 12, 17, 29, 41, 48, 55, 61, 67, 71–73, 77–78, 93–94, 98–99, 106, 108, 111–13, 115–17, 119, 121, 129, 131, 142, 148, 156, 158, 163, 166–67, 183–84, 194, 201, 207, 210, 223, 233, 235, 245, 266, 274, 283, 288–90, 297, 304, 317, 331, 339
Vatican II, 65, 292–93, 310, 318
Victorines, 30
virtues, 27, 29, 46, 73–4, 99, 124, 130, 136, 145, 150, 153–54, 158–59, 163, 172, 177, 194, 253–54, 277, 284, 289, 328, 330
Vitz, Evelyn, 24–25
vocation, 20, 34, 85, 87–88, 135, 167, 173, 196, 212, 215, 221–22, 229–38, 241–42, 309, 312, 317, 324
Volf, Miroslav, 104
vulnerability, 14, 86, 120, 125, 137, 145–6, 167, 176–81, 185, 188–91, 221, 235-6

Waller, Joanna, 321
Westphal, Merold, 322, 324
Willey, Petroc, 238, 314
William of Auxerre, 252-54,

INDEX

work, subjective dimension, 96-98, 104–105, 107, 114, 128, 143, 154, 173, 207, 314
workers, 30, 45, 97, 104–105
worldview, 4, 6, 8, 15–16, 24, 29, 31, 44–45, 47–48, 57, 69, 71, 85, 91–93, 102, 143, 148, 157–58, 198, 200, 209, 227, 287, 291–97, 299, 309

www.ingramcontent.com/pod-product-compliance
Lightning Source LLC
Chambersburg PA
CBHW071229290426
44108CB00013B/1348